NEW A

OLD W[...]

PHILOSOPHY

NEW AND OLD WORLD PHILOSOPHY

Introductory Readings

Vincent Luizzi
Southwest Texas State University

Audrey McKinney
Southwest Texas State University

Prentice
Hall

Upper Saddle River, New Jersey 07458

Library of Congress Cataloging-in-Publication Data

New and old world philosophy: introductory readings / [edited by] VINCENT LUIZZI, AUDREY MCKINNEY.
    p. cm.
   Includes bibliographical references.
   ISBN 0-13-015768-6
   1. Philosophy—Introductions. I. Luizzi, Vincent. II. McKinney, Audrey.

BD21.N39 2001
100—dc21   00-055791

VP, Editorial Director: *Charlyce Jones Owen*
Acquisitions Editor: *Ross Miller*
Assistant Editor: *Katie Janssen*
Editorial/production supervision: *Edie Riker*
Prepress and Manufacturing Buyer: *Sherry Lewis*
Marketing Coordinator: *Don Allmon*
Cover Director: *Jayne Conte*
Cover design: *Bruce Kenselaar*
Cover Art: *Birmingham Central Library, U.K.*

This book was set in 10/12 Stone Serif by East End Publishing Services, Inc., and was printed and bound by RR Donnelley & Sons Company. The cover was printed by Phoenix Color Corp.

© 2001 by Prentice-Hall, Inc.
A Division of Pearson Education
Upper Saddle River, New Jersey 07458

Printed in the United States of America

10 9 8 7 6 5 4 3 2 1

ISBN   0-13-015768-6

Prentice-Hall International (UK) Limited, *London*
Prentice-Hall of Australia Pty. Limited, *Sydney*
Prentice-Hall Canada Inc., *Toronto*
Prentice-Hall Hispanoamericana, S.A., *Mexico*
Prentice-Hall of India Private Limited, *New Delhi*
Prentice-Hall of Japan, Inc., *Tokyo*
Pearson Education Asia Pte. Ltd., *Singapore*
Editora Prentice-Hall do Brasil, Ltda., *Rio de Janeiro*

To Two American Thinkers

Elnora Luizzi (1910–   )

Jane McKinney (1922–1989)

CONTENTS

PREFACE   xxi

ACKNOWLEDGMENTS   xxiii

PHILOSOPHY   1

Introduction   1

AMERICAN PRAGMATISM

Charles Sanders Peirce   4
*Philosophy Can Learn from the Experimental Sciences
and the Sciences Can Learn from Philosophy*

William James   7
Base the Choice of a Theory on its Practical Consequences

John Dewey   10
Philosophy, Education, and Social Problems Are Interconnected

Jane Addams   12
*The Developmental Approach of Pragmatism Can Fruitfully
Guide Our Understanding of Justice and Technology*

THE HOW OF PHILOSOPHY

Socrates   14
*Admit Ignorance, Cross-Examine People, and Dismiss
their False Claims*

René Descartes   18
Seek Certainty with a Method of Doubt

Benjamin Franklin   21
Morality Is a Part of Rationality

Jorge Valadez   22
Engage in Liberated Dialogue to End Oppression

Stephen L. Carter   26
Recognize the Rhetoric of Silencing

Henry David Thoreau   28
Writing Helps Us to Think Critically

THE WHY OF PHILOSOPHY

Lucretius   30
Philosophy Frees Us from Superstition

Boethius   31
*Philosophy Transforms the Deceived and Drowsy Person
Into One Who Is Knowledgeable and Spiritually Strong*

Ludwig Wittgenstein   33
Philosophy Clarifies Our Thoughts

Bertrand Russell   35
Philosophy Opens Our Minds

Ayn Rand   **36**
Only Philosophy Can Answer Three Basic Questions
that Trouble All of Us

THE WHO OF PHILOSOPHY

Raymond Corbey   **39**
Apes Might Well Be Self-Conscious, Free Agents,
and More Like Humans than We Think

AND AN ESSAY BY ONE MORE THINKER IN AMERICA

George Santayana   **42**
"Three American Philosophers"

REALITY   45

Introduction   **45**

AMERICAN PRAGMATISM

Charles Sanders Peirce   **49**
Reality Is What the Community of Thinkers Agrees Upon

William James   **52**
Reality Is What Truths Have to Take Account of

John Dewey   **54**
Science Doesn't Have the Last or Only Word on What Is Real

Jane Addams   **56**
The Art of Children Offers New Ways of Seeing the World
Because Children Are Better in Tune with Nature

MORE ON REALITY

Plato   **58**
Reality Is a Realm of Essences

René Descartes   65
Reality Consists of Mental and Physical Substances,
and the Two Substances Are Connected in Us

Morris Berman   66
Non-Human Animals Are Not Mindless Machines

Donna Haraway   68
We Are All Cyborgs

Raymond Moody and Carol Zaleski   70
Do Near Death Experiences Confirm the Existence
of the Immaterial Soul?

Benjamin Whorf   75
The Language of the Hopi Provides a Metaphysics
Without Space and Time

Nelson Goodman   78
There Are Many Ways the World Is

Charles Hartshorne   81
Philosophers and Metaphysicians Can Contribute to Science

Oliver Wendell Holmes   83
Truth Is the System of My Intellectual Limitations

AND AN ESSAY BY ONE MORE THINKER IN AMERICA

Josiah Royce   85
"Doubting and Working"

KNOWLEDGE   91

Introduction   91

AMERICAN PRAGMATISM

Charles Sanders Peirce   93
Acting Is the End Point of Doubting, Thinking, and Believing

William James   **95**
Consciousness Is a Stream Always Moving On

John Dewey   **97**
Knowledge Is an Instrument for Enhancing Human Satisfaction

Jane Addams   **100**
The Value of Knowledge Is in Its Use

RATIONALISM

René Descartes   **102**
The Source of Knowledge Is the Mind

EMPIRICISM

John Locke   **104**
The Source of Knowledge Is the Senses

David Hume   **105**
The Source of Knowledge Is the Senses

KANTIANISM

Immanuel Kant   **107**
The Source of Knowledge Is the Mind and the Senses

MORE ON KNOWLEDGE

David Hume   **109**
*Animals Don't Reason But Do Learn from Experience
and Custom and Are Guided by Instinct*

Elizabeth Fee   **113**
To Know Is to Be Connected with What Is Known

Patricia Hill Collins   **117**
*An Afrocentric/Feminist Standpoint Challenges the Tradition
of Positivism*

Ralph Waldo Emerson   **120**
The Mind Structures Sensory Input

Willard Van Orman Quine   122
Knowledge Involves Justified True Belief with Some Qualifications

Adrienne Rich   125
Students Must Claim an Education

AND AN ESSAY BY ONE MORE THINKER IN AMERICA

George Santayana   126
"Public Opinion"

MORALITY 131

Introduction   131

AMERICAN PRAGMATISM

Charles Sanders Peirce   134
Look to Science for Advice on Moral Development

William James   136
*Take a Scientific Approach to Ethics to Maximize
Human Satisfaction*

John Dewey   138
Abandon Dogmatic Theories of Morality

Jane Addams   141
The Moral Equation Is Action Plus Its Social Significance

ETHICAL EGOISM

Ayn Rand   143
Act to Further Self Interest

EXISTENTIALISM

Hazel Barnes   146
We Are Free to Create Our Own Values

CHRISTIAN ETHICS

Anne Bradstreet   148
Good Christians Don't Have Much Self-Love

UTILITARIANISM

Jeremy Bentham   151
Create the Greatest Good for the Greatest Number

John Stuart Mill   153
Happiness Is the Ultimate End of Human Conduct

KANTIAN ETHICS

Immanuel Kant   156
*Honor Rationality by Following
Universalizable Rules*

Robert Kane   161
*Begin a Search for Absolute Values with Kantian
Openness and Tolerance*

MORAL DEVELOPMENT

Lawrence Kohlberg   166
Kantianism Is the Highest Stage of Moral Development

Carol Gilligan   168
Women Approach Morality with an Eye to Caring for Others

MORAL RELATIONSHIPS

Adrienne Rich   171
Lying Is Self-Destructive and Interferes with Loving Relationships

ETHICAL RELATIVISM

Ruth Benedict   173
Ethical Correctness Is a Function of One's Culture

ETHICAL SKEPTICISM

David Hume   176
Ethical Correctness Is a Function of One's Feelings

ETHICAL NIHILISM

Ivan Turgenev   177
There Are No Moral Truths

ENVIRONMENTAL ETHICS

Aldo Leopold   179
The Moral Community Includes the Land and Natural Processes

Ed McGaa (Eagle Man)   181
Native American Values Promote Living in Harmony with Nature

ANIMAL ORIGINS

Frans De Waal   187
Animals Behave in Moral Ways

AND AN ESSAY BY ONE MORE THINKER IN AMERICA

George Herbert Mead   189
"Fragments on Ethics"

RELIGION 193

Introduction   193

AMERICAN PRAGMATISM

Charles Sanders Peirce   197
*Love and Instinct Rather than Argument Guide Us
in Deciding Whether God Exists*

William James   199
*It Is Not Irrational to Believe Religious Teachings
Which are Unproved*

John Dewey   203
*Redefining God as a Union of the Ideal and the Actual
Helps to Secure Useful Values*

Jane Addams   205
*Religious Teachings Should Serve as Guides
for Human Betterment*

ARGUMENTS FOR THE EXISTENCE OF GOD

William Paley   207
We Can Infer God's Existence from Evidence of Design in Nature

Charles Darwin   210
The Human Eye Is the Result of Natural Evolution

Clarence Darrow   212
*Arguments that Attempt to Prove God's Existence
from Design and Purpose are Flawed*

Saint Thomas Aquinas   214
There Is a First Cause of the Universe: God

Stephen W. Hawking   215
The Universe Began with a Big Bang

Jonathan Edwards   219
The World Is Coming to an End

C. S. Lewis   220
Miracles Do Occur and Are Evidence of God's Existence

David Hume   222
There Are No Reliable Reports of Miracles

ARGUMENTS AGAINST THE EXISTENCE OF GOD

Mark Twain   223
*We Cannot Square the Usual Idea of God with All
of the Evil in the World*

Josiah Royce   226
The Evil of Suffering Is Necessary

Lucretius   229
  Religion Has Caused People to Do Great Evil

Sigmund Freud   230
  Religion Is Humanity's Neurosis

REASON, FAITH, GOD, AND NATURE

Tertullian   233
  Faith Is One Thing and Reason Another

Søren Kierkegaard   235
  Faith Makes Certain what Reason Finds Uncertain or Absurd

Immanuel Kant   237
  I Deny Knowledge (Not Reason) to Make Room for Faith

Blaise Pascal   239
  Wager!

Albert Einstein   240
  *Be Truly Religious by Abandoning Belief in a Personal God
  and Appreciating the Rational Order of the Universe*

Charles Hartshorne   242
  God Is Social; God Is Personal

Jeffrey Masson and Susan McCarthy   244
  *Non-Human Animals Perhaps Perform Rituals for their Dead
  and Worship*

N. Scott Momaday   247
  *The Native American Has a Personal Relationship
  with Nature*

AND AN ESSAY BY ONE MORE THINKER IN AMERICA

Chauncey Wright   250
  "Letter to Mr. F.E. Abbot"

ART 6 253

Introduction   253

AMERICAN PRAGMATISM

Charles Sanders Peirce   256
*Raphael Has a Feminine Mind and Michelangelo
a Masculine Mind*

William James   258
Artists Capture Experiences which Give Life Meaning

John Dewey   260
Art Should Connect to Human Experience

Jane Addams   262
Art Enlivens Our Thinking

MORE ON ART

Plato   263
*Keep Artists Out of Society, Since they Lead us Away
from Reality and Upset the Psychic Harmony of the Soul*

ALLAN BLOOM   266
*Plato Helps Us to Understand How Rock Music Interferes
with Liberal Education*

Aristotle   269
*Plato Is Wrong—Art Gives Us Knowledge and Provides
a Valuable Outlet for Our Emotions*

George Santayana   271
Art Is Liberating

Lucy Lippard   273
*Women Should Express their Bodily and Intellectual
Experiences to Create a Women's Art*

Walt Whitman   277
America Is Poetry

Leslie Marmon Silko   280
Aesthetics Cannot Be Separated from Metaphysics

Gloria Anzaldúa   282
Art and Ritual Cannot Be Separated in Tribal Cultures

Andy Warhol   285
Art Is Junk

AND AN ESSAY BY ONE MORE THINKER IN AMERICA

W.E.B. Du Bois   287
"The Art and Art Galleries of Modern Europe"

SOCIETY 7 291

Introduction   291

AMERICAN PRAGMATISM

Charles Sanders Peirce   295
Logic Requires Us to Be Concerned with the Whole Community

William James   297
End War, Establish Peace, but Preserve the Manly Virtues

John Dewey   300
Experiment with Forms of Government

Jane Addams   302
A Separation of the Haves from the Have-Nots Preserves Social Ills

CONTRACT THEORY OF GOVERNMENT

Thomas Hobbes   305
We Should Agree to Establish Government to Secure Peace

Jean-Jacques Rousseau   308
We Should Agree to Pool Our Individual Wills with the General Will

David Hume   311
  History Shows the Implausibility of a Social Contract

John Rawls   313
  *Consider What Principles People Would Agree to
  in an Initial Position*

Thomas Jefferson   315
  Each Generation Makes Its Own Government

CONSERVATIVE THEORY OF GOVERNMENT

Edmund Burke   317
  The State Is a Contract of a Very Special Sort

LIBERAL THEORY OF GOVERNMENT

John Stuart Mill   320
  *Government Should Not Interfere with Self-Government
  Unless there Is Harm to Other People*

MARXIST THEORY

Karl Marx and Friedrich Engels   322
  Workers of the World Unite!

Edward Bellamy   325
  Here Is How a Marxist Society Works

ANARCHIST THEORY

Robert Paul Wolff   328
  Create a Society with No Government

AGGRESSION, WAR, AND PEACE

Sigmund Freud   329
  War Is Not Inevitable

Black Elk   332
  Smoke the Peace Pipe to Bring Good Among People

Robert Nozick   335
Some Governmental Constraints on Aggressive Behavior
Are Justifiable

THE INDIVIDUAL AND SOCIETY

Stephen L. Carter   338
The Exercise of Free Choice Is Properly Constrained by Morality

Xiaorong Li   340
The Asian Conception of Society Does Not Negate Human Rights

Martin Luther King, Jr.   342
Challenge Unjust Laws through Nonviolent Acts
of Civil Disobedience

Malcolm X   345
Use Violence in the Fight against Injustice But Only in Self-Defense

Ayn Rand   349
To Change the World, Speak!

Audre Lorde   353
Oppressed People Should Seize all Opportunities
to Better Themselves

George Herbert Mead   356
The Mind and the Self Are Products of Society

C.I. Lewis   358
Individuals Profit from Society, and Society Profits from Individuals

Henry David Thoreau   360
We May Have Bigger Houses But Have We Advanced
from Our Savage Condition?

Frederick Douglass   362
The Right to Vote Belongs to All People

AND AN ESSAY BY ONE MORE THINKER IN AMERICA

Emma Goldman   363
"Woman Suffrage"

PREFACE

It has always struck us as odd that most introductory philosophy texts offer little if anything to acquaint students with pragmatism or to convey the fact that this distinctively American philosophy is a major contribution to world philosophy. Equally troubling is the failure to present the diversity of thinking in America. Our response was the development of *New and Old World Philosophy* that shows how the divergent voices of American thought have drawn upon, extended, and challenged the Western European philosophical tradition. Selections from American pragmatists C.S. Peirce, William James, John Dewey, and Jane Addams begin each chapter and are followed by writings of both "Old World" philosophers like Plato, Descartes, Kant, and Rousseau and "New World" thinkers like Anzaldúa, Du Bois, Santayana, and Warhol.

To enrich and broaden the philosophical discussion, we incorporated selections from a variety of disciplinary perspectives, including anthropology, primatology, cultural history, and literature. We made special efforts to include short passages from primary sources and concise commentary to encourage readers to join the dialogue and develop as critical thinkers as they read about the nature of philosophy, reality, knowledge, morality, art, religion, and society. We conclude the chapters, each containing a mix of New and Old World voices, with an essay by one more prominent thinker in America.

We thank Thomas Alexander, Abraham Edel, Peter Hare, Larry Hickman, and Jorge Valadez for support and ideas for developing our project. Patricia Shields deserves special thanks for encouraging us to include selections by Addams alongside those by Peirce, James, and Dewey. We are also grateful to Clinton Hopper for assistance with the bio-lines for each author and to Beverly Pairett for the preparation of the manuscript. Finally, we would like to thank our students whose responses to a host of philosophical works guided us in selecting the readings for this text.

Vincent Luizzi
Audrey McKinney
Austin, Texas

ACKNOWLEDGMENTS

CHAPTER ONE

CHARLES S. PEIRCE: From "What Pragmatism Is" by Charles S. Peirce. In *The Monist*, vol. 14 (April 1905).

From the Johns Hopkins University Circulars (Nov. 1882). Reprinted by permission of the publisher from *The Collected Papers of Charles Sanders Peirce, Volume 1* edited by Charles Hartshorne and Paul Weiss, Cambridge, MA: The Belknap Press of Harvard University Press, Copyright © 1931, 1959 by the President and Fellows of Harvard College.

WILLIAM JAMES: From *Pragmatism* by William James. First published by Penguin Putnam in 1907.

JOHN DEWEY: Reprinted with permission of Scribner, a Division of Simon & Schuster from *Democracy and Education* by John Dewey. Copyright © by Macmillan, 1916, renewed 1944 by John Dewey.

JANE ADDAMS: Reprinted with permission of Scribner, a Division of Simon & Schuster from *Twenty Years at Hull House* by Jane Addams. Copyright © 1910 by Macmillan Publishing Company, renewed 1938 by James W. Linn.

SOCRATES: From *The Last Days of Socrates by Plato*, translated by Hugh Tredennick (Penguin Classics 1954, Second revised edition, 1969) copyright © Hugh Tredennick, 1954, 1959, 1969. Reproduced by permission of Penguin Books Ltd.

RENÉ DESCARTES: From *Discourse on Method* by René Descartes, translated by Laurence L. LaFleur (1956). Reprinted by permission of Prentice Hall, Upper Saddle River, NJ.

BENJAMIN FRANKLIN: From "Plan for Future Conduct" by Benjamin Franklin. In *Autobiography and Other Writings*. Edited by L. Jesse Lemisch. (New York: New American Library, 1961).

JORGE VALADEZ: From "The Metaphysics of Oppression" by Jorge Valadez in *The University in Your Life*. (Dubuque: Brown & Benchmark/Times Mirror, 1996). Copyright © 1996 by Jorge Valadez. Reprinted by permission of the author.

STEPHEN L. CARTER: From *Civility* by Stephen L. Carter. (New York: Basic Books, 1998).

HENRY DAVID THOREAU: From *Henry D. Thoreau: Early Essays and Miscellanies*, edited by Joseph Moldenhauer and Edwin Moser. (Princeton: Princeton University Press, 1975). Reprinted by permission of Princeton University Press.

LUCRETIUS: From *On the Nature of the Universe* by Lucretius, translated by R.E. Latham (Penguin Classics, 1951) copyright © Ronald Latham, 1951. Reprinted with permission.

BOETHIUS: From *The Consolation of Philosophy* by Boethius. Translated by W.V. Cooper. J.M. Dent, London, 1902.

LUDWIG WITTGENSTEIN: From *Tractatus Logico-Philosophicus*, translated by D.F. Pears and B.F. McGuinness. (New York: The Humanities Press, 1961). Reprinted with permission of ITPS Ltd.

BERTRAND RUSSELL: Reprinted from *The Problems of Philosophy* by Bertrand Russell (1912) by permission of Oxford University Press.

AYN RAND: Reprinted with the permission of Scribner, a Division of Simon & Schuster from *Philosophy: Who Needs It* by Ayn Rand. Copyright © 1982 by Leonard Peikoff, Paul Gitlin, and Eugene Winick, Executors, Estate of Ayn Rand.

RAYMOND CORBEY: From "Ambiguous Apes" by Raymond Corbey, in *The Great Ape Project: Equality Beyond Humanity*, edited by P. Cavalieri and Peter Singer. (New York: St. Martin's Griffin, 1993.) Copyright © 1993 by Raymond Corbey. Reprinted by permission of the author.

GEORGE SANTAYANA: From *The Birth of Reason and Other Essays* by George Santayana. Edited by Daniel Corey. Copyright (c) 1968 Columbia University Press. Reprinted by permission of the publisher.

CHAPTER TWO

CHARLES S. PEIRCE: From "Critical Review of Berkeley's Idealism" by Charles S. Peirce. *North American Review*, vol. 93, 1871.

From "The Fixation of Belief" by Charles S. Peirce. *Popular Science Monthly*, 1877.

From "Some Consequences of Four Incapacities" by Charles S. Peirce. *Journal of Speculative Philosophy*, 1868.

WILLIAM JAMES: From *Pragmatism* by William James. First published in 1907.

From *Pragmatism* by William James. First published in 1907.

JOHN DEWEY: From *Reconstruction in Philosophy*, by John Dewey. Copyright © 1920 by Henry Holt & Company, New York.

From *Essays in Experimental Logic* by John Dewey. Copyright © 1916 by the University of Chicago Press.

JANE ADDAMS: Reprinted with the permission of Scribner, a Division of Simon & Schuster from *The Second Twenty Years at Hull House* by Jane Addams. Copyright © 1930 by Macmillan Publishing Company, renewed 1958 by John A. Brittain.

PLATO: From *The Republic*. In *The Dialogues of Plato*. Translated by Benjamin Jowett. New Random House, 1937.

From *The Phaedo*. In *The Dialogues of Plato*. Translated by Benjamin Jowett. New Random House, 1937.

RENÉ DESCARTES: From *Meditations on First Philosophy* by René Descartes. In the jointly bound edition of *Discourse on Method and Meditations*. Translated by Donald A. Cress. Copyright © 1998 by Hackett Publishing Company, Inc. Reprinted with the permission of Hackett Publishing Company, Inc. All rights reserved.

MORRIS BERMAN: From *Coming to Our Senses* by Morris Berman. (New York: Bantam Books, 1998). Copyright Morris Berman.

DONNA HARAWAY: From "A Cyborg Manifesto: Science, Technology, and Socialist-Feminism in the Late Twentieth Century" by Donna Haraway, in *Simians, Cyborgs and Women: The Reinvention of Nature* (New York: Routledge, 1991).

RAYMOND MOODY: From *Life After Life* by Raymond Moody, copyright © 1975. Used by permission of MBB, Taos, New Mexico.

CAROL ZALESKI: From *Otherworldly Journeys: Accounts of Near-Death Experience in Medieval and Modern Times* by Carol Zaleski, copyright © 1988 by Oxford University Press, Inc. Used by permission of Oxford University Press, Inc.

BENJAMIN WHORF: From *Language, Thought, and Reality: Selected Writings of Benjamin Whorf*, edited by John M. Carrol, copyright © 1956 by The MIT Press. Reprinted with permission of The MIT Press.

NELSON GOODMAN: From *Ways of Worldmaking* by Nelson Goodman. Copyright © 1978 by Hackett Publishing Company, Inc. Reprinted by permission of Hackett Publishing Company, Inc. All rights reserved.

CHARLES HARTSHORNE: From "Metaphysics Contributes to Ornithology" by Charles Hartshorne, in *Theoria to Theory*, vol 13 (1979). Copyright by OPA (Overseas Publishers Association) NV. Reprinted with permission of Gordon and Breach Publishers.

OLIVER WENDALL HOLMES: From "Natural Law" by Oliver Wendall Holmes, in *The Harvard Law Review*, vol. 32 (1918). Copyright © 1918 by the Harvard Law Review Association. Reprinted with permission of the Harvard Law Review.

JOSIAH ROYCE: From "Doubting and Working" by Josiah Royce, in *Fugitive Essays*. Copyright © 1925 by Harvard University Press.

CHAPTER THREE

CHARLES S. PEIRCE: From "The Fixation of Belief" by Charles S. Peirce. *Popular Science Monthly*, vol. 12, 1877.

CHAPTER FOUR

CHARLES S. PEIRCE: From "The Scientific Attitude and Fallibilism" by Charles S. Peirce. In *The Philosophy of Peirce: Selected Writings*. Edited by Justus Buchler. Kegan Paul, Trench, Trubner & Co., Ltd., London, 1940.

From "Two Notes" by Charles S. Peirce. In *The Philosophy of Peirce: Selected Writings*. Edited by Justus Buchler. Kegan Paul, Trench, Trubner & Co., Ltd., London, 1940.

WILLIAM JAMES: From "The Moral Philosopher and the Moral Life" by William James. *International Journal of Ethics* April, 1891.

JOHN DEWEY: From *Ethics* by John Dewey and James H. Tufts. Henry Holt & Company, 1907, revised edition, 1932.

JANE ADDAMS: From *Democracy and Social Ethics* by Jane Addams, copyright © 1907 by Macmillan. Reprinted by permission of John Brittain.

AYN RAND: From *The Virtue of Selfishness: a New Concept of Egoism* by Ayn Rand. (New York: Signet Books, 1970).

From *The Fountainhead* by Ayn Rand. New York: Penguin Books USA Inc. Copyright © 1943 The Bobbs-Merrill Company. Copyright renewed 1971 by Ayn Rand.

HAZEL BARNES: From *An Existentialist Ethics* by Hazel Barnes. (New York: Alfred A. Knopf, 1969). Copyright © 1969 by Hazel Barnes. Reprinted by permission fo the author.

ANNE BRADSTREET: From "Meditations Divine and Moral" by Anne Bradstreet, in *American Women Philosophers: 1650-1930*, edited by Terese Boos Dykeman. © 1993. Reprinted by permission of The Edwin Mellen Press.

JEREMY BENTHAM: From *Introduction to the Principles of Morals and Legislation* by Jeremy Bentham. First published in 1789.

JOHN STUART MILL: From *Utilitarianism* by John Stuart Mill. Longman's, Green, Reader, and Dyer, 1871.

IMMANUEL KANT: From *Grounding for a Metaphysic of Morals* by Immanuel Kant. Translated by James W. Ellington. Copyright © by Hackett Publishing Company, Inc. Reprinted by permission of Hackett Publishing Company, Inc. All rights reserved.

ROBERT KANE: From *Through the Moral Maze* by Robert Kane. Copyright © 1994 by Paragon Press. Reprinted with permission of Paragon Press.

LAWRENCE KOHLBERG: From "Education for Justice: A Modern Statement of the Platonic View" by Lawrence Kohlberg. Reprinted by permission of the publisher from *Moral Education*, edited by Nancy F. and Theodore Sizer, Cambridge, MA: Harvard University Press, Copyright © 1970 by the President and Fellows of Harvard College.

CAROL GILLIGAN: From *In a Different Voice* by Carol Gilligan, Cambridge, MA: Harvard University Press, Copyright © 1982, 1993 by Carol Gilligan. Reprinted by permission of the publisher.

ADRIENNE RICH: Excerpts from "Women and Honor: Some Notes on Lying," from *On Lies, Secrets, and Silence: Selected Prose 1966–1978* by Adrienne Rich. Copyright © 1979 by W.W. Norton & Company, Inc. Used with permission of the author and W.W. Norton & Company, Inc.

RUTH BENEDICT: From "Anthropology and the Abnormal" by Ruth Benedict. *Journal of General Psychology*, vol 10 (1934). Copyright © 1934 by Clark University Press.

DAVID HUME: Reprinted from *A Treatise of Human Nature* by David Hume. Edited by L.A. Selby-Bigge, revised by P.H. Nidditch (2nd edition 1978) by permission of Oxford University Press.

IVAN TURGENEV: From *Fathers and Sons* by Ivan Turgenev. Translated by Constance Garnett, (New York: Random House, 1917).

ALDO LEOPOLD: From *A Sand County Almanac: And Sketches from Here and There* by Aldo Leopold. (New York: Oxford University Press, 1949, renewed 1977).

ED MCGAA: From *Mother Earth Spirituality* by Ed McGaa, pp. 203–209. Copyright © 1990 by Ed McGaa. Reprinted by permission of HarperCollins Publishers, Inc.

FRANS DE WAAL: From *Good Natured: The Origins of Right and Wrong in Humans and Other Animals* by Frans de Waal, Cambridge, MA: Harvard University Press, copyright © 1996 by Frans B.M. de Waal. Reprinted by permission of the publisher.

GEORGE MEAD: From "Fragments on Ethics" by George Mead. In *Mind, Self, and Society*. Edited by Charles W. Morris. Copyright © 1962 by Charles W. Morris. Reprinted with permission of University of Chicago Press.

CHAPTER FIVE

CHARLES S. PEIRCE: From "The Concept of God" by Charles S. Peirce. In *The Philosophy of Peirce: Selected Writings*, edited by Justus Buchler. Kegan Paul, Trench, Trubner & Co., Ltd., London, 1940.

WILLIAM JAMES: From "The Will to Believe," an address to the Philosophical Clubs of Yale and Brown Universities. Published in *The New World*. June, 1896.

JOHN DEWEY: From *A Common Faith* by John Dewey, copyright © 1934. Reprinted by permission of Yale University Press.

JANE ADDAMS: From *The Spirit of Youth and the City Streets*, copyright © 1910. Reprinted by permission of John Brittain.

WILLIAM PALEY: From *Natural Theology* by William Paley. First published in 1800.

CHARLES DARWIN: From *The Origin of Species: By Means of Natural Selection or the Preservation of Favoured Races in the Struggle for Life* by Charles Darwin. Reprinted with the permission of Simon & Schuster. Copyright © 1962 by the Crowell-Collier Publishing Company.

CLARENCE DARROW: From *The Story of My Life* by Clarence Darrow. (New York: Charles Scribner's Sons, 1960).

ST. THOMAS AQUINAS: From *Summa Theologica*, St. Thomas Aquinas. Translated by Laurence Shapcote. Benziger, 1911.

STEPHEN W. HAWKING: From *A Brief History of Time* by Stephen W. Hawking, copyright © 1988 by Stephen W. Hawking. Interior illustrations copyright ©

by Ron Miller. Used by permission of Bantam Books, a Division of Random House, Inc.

JONATHAN EDWARDS: From *The Philosophy of Jonathan Edwards From His Private Notebooks.* Edited by Harvey G. Townsend. Copyright © 1955 University of Oregon Monographs.

C.S. LEWIS: From *Miracles* by C.S. Lewis copyright © C.S. Lewis Pte. Ltd 1947, 1960. Extract reprinted by permission.

DAVID HUME: From *An Inquiry Concerning Human Understanding* by David Hume. First published in 1748.

MARK TWAIN: From *Letter from the Earth* by Mark Twain, pp. 59–63. Edited by Bernard Devoto. Copyright 1938, 1944, 1946, 1959, 1962 by The Mark Twain Company. Copyright renewed. Reprinted by permission of HarperCollins Publishers, Inc.

JOSIAH ROYCE: From *Studies in Good and Evil* by Josiah Royce. D. Appleton & Company, 1898.

LUCRETIUS: From Lucretius, *On the Nature of the Universe*, translated by R.E. Latham (Penguin Classics, 1951) copyright © Ronald Latham, 1951. Reprinted with permission.

SIGMUND FREUD: From *New Introductory Lectures on Psycho-Analysis* by Sigmund Freud, translated by James Strachey. Copyright © 1964, 1965 by James Strachey. Used by permission of W.W. Norton & Company, Inc.

TERTULLIAN: From *Early Latin Theology* (Library of Christian Classics) by S.L. Greenslade. Used by permission of Westminster John Knox Press.

SØREN KIERKEGAARD: From *Concluding Unscientific Postscript to the Philosophical Fragments* by Søren Kierkegaard, translated by D. F. Swenson, Lillian M. Swenson and Walter Lowrie. Copyright © 1946 by Princeton University Press. Reprinted with permission.

IMMANUEL KANT: From *Critique of Pure Reason* by Immanuel Kant. Translated by Norman Kemp Smith. Macmillan Co., Ltd., 1929.

BLAISE PASCAL: From *Pensées* by Blaise Pascal. In *The Philosophy of the 16th and 17th Centuries,* edited by Richard H. Popkin (p. 222). Reprinted with the permission of The Free Press, a Division of Simon & Schuster, Inc.

ALBERT EINSTEIN: From *Out of My Later Years.* New York: Thames and Hudson, 1950.

CHARLES HARTSHORNE: From *The Divine Relativity* by Charles Hartshorne. Copyright © 1948 by Yale University Press. Reprinted with permission of Yale University Press.

JEFFREY MASSON AND SUSAN MCCARTHY: From *When Elephants Weep* by Jeffrey Masson and Susan McCarthy, copyright © 1995 by Jeffrey Masson and Susan McCarthy. Used by permission of Dell Publishing, a Division of Random House, Inc.

N. SCOTT MOMADAY: "Native American Attitudes to the Environment" by N. Scott Momaday from *Seeing with a Native Eye* by Walter Holden Capps. Copyright © 1976 by Walter Holden Capps. Reprinted by permission of HarperCollins Publishers, Inc.

CHAUNCEY WRIGHT: From *Letters* by Chauncey Wright. Edited by James Bradley Thayer. Cambridge, 1878.

CHAPTER SIX

CHARLES S. PEIRCE: From *Writings of Charles S. Peirce: A Chronological Edition*, vol. 1. Max Fisch, general editor. Copyright © 1982, by Indiana University Press. Reprinted with permission of Indiana University Press.

WILLIAM JAMES: From *Talks to Teachers on Psychology: And to Students on Some of Life's Ideals,* by William James. Henry Holt & Company, 1907.

From *Talks to Teachers on Psychology: And to Students on Some of Life's Ideals*, by William James. Henry Holt & Company, 1907.

JOHN DEWEY: From *Art as Experience* by John Dewey, copyright 1934 by John Dewey, renewed 1973 by The John Dewey Foundation. Used by permission of G. P. Putnam's Sons, a Division of Penguin Putnam Inc.

JANE ADDAMS: Reprinted with permission of Scribner, a Division of Simon & Schuster from *Twenty Years at Hull House* by Jane Addams. Copyright © 1910 by Macmillan Publishing Company, renewed 1938 by James W. Linn.

PLATO: Reprinted by permission of the publishers and the Loeb Classical Library from *Plato: the Republic, Volume V*, Cambridge, MA: Harvard University Press, 1930.

ALLAN BLOOM: From *The Closing of the American Mind.* (New York: Simon & Schuster, Inc., 1987). Copyright © 1987 by Allan Bloom.

ARISTOTLE: From *De Poetica* by Aristotle. Translated by Ingram Bywater, in *Introduction to Aristotle*, edited by Richard McKeon. (New York: The Modern Library, 1947.)

GEORGE SANTAYANA: From George Santayana, *The Life of Reason.* Copyright © 1953 by The MIT Press. Reprinted by permission of The MIT Press.

LUCY LIPPARD: From "Six" by Lucy Lippard. Copyright by Lucy Lippard. Reprinted by permission of the author.

WALT WHITMAN: From "Leaves of Grass" by Walt Whitman. In *Walt Whitman: Poetry and Prose*. The Library of America, 1982.

LESLIE MARMON SILKO: From "Interior and Exterior Landscapes: The Pueblo Migration Stories." *Antaeus*, no. 57 (Autumn 1986).

GLORIA ANZALDÚA: From *Borderlands/La Frontera: The New Mestiza.* Copyright © 1987 by Gloria Anzaldúa. Reprinted with permission.

ANDY WARHOL: Excerpts from *The Philosophy of Andy Warhol (From A to B and Back Again)*, copyright © 1975 by Andy Warhol, reprinted with permission of Harcourt, Inc.

W.E.B. DU BOIS: Reprinted from *Against Racism: Unpublished Essays, Papers, Addresses, 1887–1961* by W.E.B. Du Bois, Edited by Herbert Aptheker (Amherst: University of Massachusetts Press, 1985), copyright © 1985 by The University of Massachusetts Press.

CHAPTER SEVEN

CHARLES S. PEIRCE: From *Writings of Charles S. Peirce: A Chronological Edition*, vol. 2. Max Fisch, general editor. Copyright © 1982, by Indiana University Press. Reprinted with permission of Indiana University Press.

From "On the Doctrine of Chances, with Later Reflections" by Charles S. Peirce. In *The Philosophy of Peirce: Selected Writings*. Edited by Justus Buchler. Kegan Paul, Trench, Trubner & Co., Ltd., London, 1940.

WILLIAM JAMES: From "The Moral Equivalent of War" by William James, a speech given at Stanford University, 1906.

JOHN DEWEY: From *The Public and Its Problems* by John Dewey. Copyright © 1954, reprinted 1991 by Ohio University Press/Swallow Press. Reprinted with the permission of Ohio University Press/Swallow Press, Athens, Ohio.

JANE ADDAMS: From *Twenty Years at Hull House* by Jane Addams. Reprinted with permission of Scribner, a Division of Simon & Schuster. Copyright © 1910 by Macmillan Publishing Company, renewed 1938 by James W. Linn.

THOMAS HOBBES: From *Leviathan* by Thomas Hobbes. First published in 1651.

JEAN-JACQUES ROUSSEAU: From *A Discourse on the Origin of Inequality* in *The Social Contract and The Discourses* by Jean Jacques Rousseau, translated by G.D.H. Cole. (New York: Alfred A. Knopf, 1993.)

From *The Social Contract* in *The Social Contract and The Discourses* by Jean Jacques Rousseau, translated by G.D.H. Cole. (New York: Alfred A. Knopf, 1993.)

DAVID HUME: From *An Enquiry Concerning the Principles of Morals*. First published in 1777.

From "Of the Original Contract" by David Hume. First published in the 1777 edition of *Essays, Moral and Political*.

JOHN RAWLS: From *A Theory of Justice* by John Rawls, Cambridge, MA: The Belknap Press of Harvard University Press, Copyright © 1971 by the President and Fellows of Harvard College. Reprinted by permission of the publisher.

THOMAS JEFFERSON: *The Wisdom of Thomas Jefferson*, selected and edited by Edward Boykin. (Garden City: Garden City Publishing Co., Inc., 1941).

EDMUND BURKE: From *Reflections on the Revolution in France* by Edmund Burke. Edited by J.G.A. Pocock. Copyright © 1984 by Hackett Publishing Company, Inc. Reprinted by permission of Hackett Publishing Company, Inc. All rights reserved.

JOHN STUART MILL: From *On Liberty* by John Stuart Mill. London, 1859.

KARL MARX: From "Economic and Philosophical Manuscripts," by Karl Marx. Translated by David McClellan. In *Selected Writings: Karl Marx*, edited by David McClellan, copyright © 1977 by Oxford University Press, Inc.

KARL MARX AND FRIEDRICH ENGELS: From *The Communist Manifesto*, by Karl Marx and Friedrich Engels, translated by Samuel Moore. First published in 1848.

EDWARD BELLAMY: From *Looking Backward* by Edward Bellamy. First published in 1897.

ROBERT PAUL WOLFF: From *In Defense of Anarchism* by Robert Paul Wolff. (Los Angeles, CA: University of California Press, 1998.) Used by permission of the author.

SIGMUND FREUD: From *The Collected Papers, Volume 1* by Sigmund Freud. Authorized translation under the supervision of Joan Riviere. Published by Basic Books, Inc., by arrangement with the Hogarth Press, Ltd. and the Institute of

Psychoanalysis, London. Reprinted by permission of Basic Books, a member of Perseus Books, L.L.C.

BLACK ELK: From *Black Elk Speaks*, as told through John G. Niehardt, with introduction by Vine Deloria, Jr. Copyright © 1972 University of Nebraska Press. Reprinted by permission of University of Nebraska Press.

ROBERT NOZICK: From *Anarchy, State and Utopia* by Robert Nozick. Copyright © 1974 by Basic Books, Inc. Reprinted by permission of Basic Books, a member of Perseus Books, L.L.C.

STEPHEN L. CARTER: From *Civility* by Stephen L. Carter. (New York: Basic Books, 1998.)

XIAORONG LI: From "Asian Values and the Universality of Human Rights" by Xiaorong Li. *Philosophy and Public Policy*, vol. 16. Spring 1996. Reprinted by permission of Institute for Philosophy & Public Policy, University of Maryland, College Park, MD.

MARTIN LUTHER KING, JR.: From "Letter from Birmingham City Jail" by Martin Luther King, Jr. Originally published in *Liberation* (June 1963). Copyright 1963 by Martin Luther King, Jr., copyright renewed 1991 by Coretta Scott King. Reprinted by arrangement with The Heirs to the Estate of Martin Luther King, Jr., c/o Writers House, Inc. as agent for the proprietor.

MALCOLM X: From *By Any Means Necessary* by Malcolm X. Edited by George Breitman. Copyright © 1970, 1972 by Betty Shabazz and Pathfinder Press. Reprinted by permission.

From *The Autobiography of Malcolm X*, by Malcolm X and Alex Haley. Copyright ©1964 by Malcolm X and Alex Haley. ©1965 by Alex Haley and Betty Shabazz. Reprinted by permission of Random House, Inc.

AYN RAND: Reprinted with the permission of Scribner, a Division of Simon & Schuster from *Philosophy: Who Needs It* by Ayn Rand. Copyright © 1982 by Leonard Peikoff, Paul Gitlin, and Eugene Winick, Executors, Estate of Ayn Rand.

AUDRE LORDE: Reprinted with permission from *Sister Outsider* by Audre Lorde. Published by Crossing Press, Freedom, CA.

GEORGE HERBERT MEAD: From *Mind, Self, and Society* by George Herbert Mead. Edited by Charles W. Morris. Copyright © 1962 by Charles W. Morris. Reprinted with permission of University of Chicago Press.

C.I. LEWIS: From "The Individual and the Social Order" by C.I. Lewis. In *Collected Papers of Clarence Irving Lewis*, edited by John D. Goheen and John L. Mothershead, Jr. Copyright © 1970 Stanford University Press. Reprinted with the permission of Stanford University Press.

HENRY DAVID THOREAU: From *Walden; or Life in the Woods* by Henry David Thoreau. First published in 1854 by Ticknor and Fields.

FREDERICK DOUGLASS: From "An Appeal to Congress for Impartial Suffrage" by Frederick Douglass. *Atlantic Monthly*, vol 19. January 1867.

EMMA GOLDMAN: From "Woman Suffrage" by Emma Goldman, in *Anarchism and Other Essays*. Mother Earth Publishing Association and A.C. Fifield, 1911.

ILLUSTRATIONS

Cover: *Typus orbis Terrarum* in G. Mercator's *Atlas Minor,* J. Hondius, 1610. Reproduced, with the permission of the Birmingham Central Library, U.K., from that library's copy of this atlas.

p. xxxiv: Charles Sanders Peirce from the Harvard Class Album of 1859. Houghton Library of Harvard College Library. William James from Houghton Library of Harvard College Library. John Dewey in The John Dewey Papers, Bentley Historical Library, University of Michigan, and reproduced with that library's permission. Jane Addams from the image in Jane Addams's *Twenty Years at Hull-House,* New York: The Macmillan Co., 1910.

p. 25: *The Philosopher's Stone. Theatrum Chemicum Britannicum, 1652.* By permission of the British Library.

p. 46: Illustration of the cosmos by William Blake in his *Milton,* 1804. From the image of it in A. Roob's *Alchemy and Mysticism,* Koln, Germany: Taschen, 1997, p. 119.

p. 63: Reprinted, by permission, from *Indian Rock Art of the Southwest,* by Polly Schaafsma. Figure 76: Detail of Anthropomorphs on San Juan River at Butler Wash. Photograph by Curtis Schaafsma. Copyright © 1980 by the School of American Research, Santa Fe.

p. 90: *Can the Pupil Know More?* F. Goya. Etching no. 37, *Los Caprichos.* Prado Museum.

p. 112: *Please Help Me. My Brain Is Burning.* Painting by Julie Speed, 1994.

p. 130: Woodcut illustration of Adam and Eve (*Genesis 3)* from the *Coverdale Bible* (RBC Folio BS 145 1535). Annandale Rare Book and Manuscript Library, University of Pennsylvania.

p. 186: *The Two-tailed Monkey.* Painting by Julie Speed, 1997.

p. 194: *Witches Apprehended, Examined and Executed.* London, 1613. Reproduced by permission of The Huntington, San Marino, California.

p. 218: Page from *The New England Primer.* Late seventeenth century. Courtesy of the Library of Congress.

p. 254: *Bird.* Painting by gorilla, Koko. Courtesy of The Gorilla Foundation. Photo by Ronald H. Cohn.

p. 278: *Tribute to American Jazz.* Collage with artists' construction paper. Alan M. Cano. 1991.

p. 292: Wood engraving. Johann Froschauer. *c.* 1505. Reproduction of the image of it in F.J. Pohl's *Amerigo Vespucci, Pilot Major* by permission of Columbia University Press.

p. 303: *Nationalities Map No. 3.* By the Residents of Hull House in *Hull-House Maps and Papers,* New York: Arno Press and *The New York Times,* 1970.

Charles Sanders Peirce

William James

John Dewey

Jane Addams

American Pragmatists

PHILOSOPHY

INTRODUCTION

The enticing notion of a fresh start or a new beginning applies to many aspects of this book. For one thing, it is your gateway to the study of philosophy and serves to acquaint you with what philosophers have thought and to introduce you to the art of philosophical thinking. For another thing, it features how thinkers in America have enriched philosophy as they contributed new ideas from a new world and places special emphasis on the philosophy of pragmatism. This new way of seeing things stands as America's distinctive contribution to world philosophy. And, as we shall see, however much the American pragmatists were paving the way for casting philosophy in a new role, they were, in an important sense, pressing on with the script which guides all philosophers: the quest to make sense of ourselves in our world.

Pragmatism continues to develop as a philosophy, but perhaps the best way of capturing its essence is to highlight throughout this book the contributions of three of its earliest and most prominent exponents: Charles Sanders Peirce, William James, and John Dewey. Peirce and James were founding members of a philosophy club, "The Metaphysical Club," which met in Cambridge, Massachusetts during the 1870s and which is credited with giving birth to pragmatism. Dewey developed the thinking of these earliest pragmatists and is especially known for the social dimension he contributed to pragmatism.

To this triumvirate of philosophers we add the social reformer, Jane Addams. Addams's leadership in social reform can be looked at as applied pragmatism or pragmatism in action. Her work at Hull-House, a settlement house that assisted immigrants' adjustment to America, embodies the pragmatists' call to unite theory and value with action as much as it typifies the experimental approach of pragmatism. Addams documents conversations she had with Dewey and relates how his thinking influenced her. Further, Addams is very much concerned with her identity as an American and ingeniously weaves this concern into her thinking about society and her experiments at Hull-House. Ultimately, we acquire a deeper understanding of pragmatism as we consider it from the perspective of this American woman who made her primary contribution not in philosophy but in progressive social reform.

Historians of philosophy have dubbed the days of these thinkers the "Golden Age of American Pragmatism" which spanned roughly the last quarter of the nineteenth century through the first quarter of the twentieth century. As Peirce, James, Dewey, and Addams suggest how we should rethink philosophy, they give us insights into what philosophy has been and thus prepare us for our study of the philosophers of the Old World.

Let us return for a moment to the general nature of philosophy—making sense of ourselves in our world. When we believe we have made this sense, we would say that we have figured something out, and that we have done so by thinking about it. So essentially, philosophy is a field in which thinking is primary, and the Greek word, *philosophia*, from which our word derives, bears out the primacy of thought; it means a love of thinking. Insofar as we are philosophers, we are thinkers or rational beings striving to make sense of ourselves in our world. As we move from one philosopher to another in this chapter, we see how, over and over, each addresses some facet of the thinking which is so essentially tied to philosophy.

Some of the authors we have selected emphasize philosophical method or how we should direct our thinking. We find appeals to search for something which is absolutely certain (Descartes), to weed out error and false opinion (Socrates), and to look to the practical implications of various ideas for our lives (the pragmatists). Other philosophers highlight the value or purpose of thinking and point to how philosophy assists us with clarifying our ideas (Wittgenstein), expanding our sense of what is possible in human experience (Russell), and becoming educated (Dewey).

In turning to the how and the why of philosophy to understand better the nature of philosophy, we find that many times there is no absolute separation. Descartes, the philosopher who emphasizes that we take a skeptical approach to what people claim to be knowledge (the how of philosophy) also had a goal in mind of discovering what really is true (the why of philosophy).

One matter rarely addressed is the who of philosophy—who is able to philosophize? William Corbey notes that apes have powers traditionally thought to be exclusively human. But can apes philosophize? The chapter ends with an essay by the prominent American thinker, George Santayana. He discusses two of the pragmatists, James and Dewey, and evaluates his own work as a product of an American philosopher.

CHARLES SANDERS PEIRCE

Philosophy Can Learn from the Experimental Sciences and the Sciences Can Learn from Philosophy

Charles Sanders Peirce (1839–1914) was an American philosopher, mathematician, and physicist who is credited as the founder of the American school of pragmatism.

Charles Sanders Peirce was impressed by the experimental sciences. He tells us how he was similarly impressed by the thinking of the eighteenth-century European philosophers Kant, Berkeley, and Spinoza because of the experimental themes in their philosophies. Peirce considered what significance an experimental approach has for philosophy. Scientists experiment to discover how various entities, events, and phenomena affect our lives. They experiment to determine whether smoking causes lung cancer, to determine the conditions under which cyclones form, or to ascertain the effect of zero gravity on an astronaut. Drawing on this approach as a model for philosophy, Peirce would have us think of any concept in this way—we should consider what it practically means for our lives. As we consider these practical consequences, we think in terms which connect human knowledge and human purpose or what we know with why we want to know it. Thus, we may want to know more about the formation of cyclones so that we can take measures in advance to protect ourselves when they arrive. In the first passage, Peirce identifies this experimental approach in philosophy as pragmatism.

We learn in the second passage how philosophy can in turn advise the sciences. People may specialize in one science or another with each one having a method peculiar to it. But there are general principles of correct thinking which guide people in any area of specialization and which lie at the foundation of each area. These principles assist us in pressing forward effectively with our inquiries in any of these specialized areas as well as assisting us with seeing how a piece is part of a larger puzzle. The study of these principles is logic, which is traditionally considered one of the four main divisions of philosophy along with the study of reality, ethics, and knowledge. Peirce sees logic as the cornerstone of a liberal education and the main thing that university students should be striving to master. So philosophy can improve by becoming more experimental like the sciences, but all of the sciences, indeed any area of intellectual endeavor, can benefit from logic.

That laboratory life did not prevent the writer (who here and in what follows simply exemplifies the experimentalist type) from becoming interested in methods of thinking; and when he came to read metaphysics, although much of it seemed to him loosely reasoned and determined by accidental prepossessions, yet in the writings of some philosophers, especially Kant, Berkeley, and Spinoza, he sometimes came upon strains of thought that recalled the ways of thinking of the laboratory, so that he felt he might trust to them; all of which has been true of other laboratory men.

Endeavoring, as a man of that type naturally would, to formulate what he so approved, he framed the theory that a *conception,* that is, the rational purport of a word or other expression, lies exclusively in its conceivable bearing upon the conduct of life; so that, since obviously nothing that might not result from experiment can have any direct bearing upon conduct if one can define accurately all the conceivable experimental phenomena which the affirmation or denial of a concept could imply, one will have therein a complete definition of the concept, and *there is absolutely nothing more in it.* For this doctrine he invented the name *pragmatism.* Some of his friends wished him to call it *practicism* or *practicalism* (perhaps on the ground that *praktikos* is better Greek than *pragmatikos).* But for one who had learned philosophy out of Kant, as the writer, along with nineteen out of every twenty experimentalists who have turned to philosophy, had done, and who still thought in Kantian terms most readily, *praktisch* and *pragmatisch* were as far apart as the two poles, the former belong in a region of thought where no mind of the experimentalist type can ever make sure of solid ground under his feet, the latter expressing relation to some definite human purpose. Now quite the most striking feature of the new theory was its recognition of an inseparable connection between rational cognition and rational purpose; and that consideration it was which determined the preference for the name *pragmatism.*

From Charles S. Peirce, "What Pragmatism Is," *The Monist,* vol. 14 (April 1905).

When new paths have to be struck out, a spinal cord is not enough; a brain is needed, and that brain an organ of mind, and that mind perfected by a liberal education. And a liberal education—so far as its relation to the understanding goes—means *logic.* That is indispensable to it, and no other one thing is. . . .

In order to adapt to his own science the method of another with which he is less familiar, and to properly modify it so as to suit it to its new use, an acquaintance with the principles upon which it depends will be of the greatest benefit. For that sort of work a man needs to be more than a specialist; he needs such a general training of his mind and such knowledge as shall show him how to make his powers most effective in a new direction. That knowledge is logic.

In short, if my view is the true one, a young man wants a physical education and an aesthetic education, an education in the ways of the world and a moral education, and with all these logic has nothing in particular to do; but so far as he wants an intellectual education, it is precisely logic that he wants; and whether it be in one lecture-room or another, his ultimate purpose is to improve his logical power and his knowledge of methods. To this great end a young man's attention ought to be directed when he first comes to the university; he ought to keep it steadily in view during the whole period of his studies; and finally, he will do well to review his whole work in the light which an education in logic throws upon it.

From the *Johns Hopkins University Circulars* (Nov. 1882).

WILLIAM JAMES

Base the Choice of a Theory on its Practical Consequences

William James (1842–1910) was an American pragmatist philosopher and psychologist.

William James begins his famous work, Pragmatism, *with a charming story about people who are watching the activities of a man and a squirrel and who have different theories to interpret them. James offers the pragmatic method in philosophy as a means of settling the spat as well as longstanding metaphysical debates in philosophy: select one theory over another based on a consideration of the practical consequences for us of each theory. In effect James endorses Peirce's advice that we interpret things by considering their consequences for us, but directly links it to selecting one theory over another. Elsewhere James augments his advice of selecting a theory based on its practical consequences as he advises, more specifically, that we consider the theory's simplicity, cogency, explanatory power, and consistency with other theories. In so advising, James, like other pragmatists, rejects the notion of absolute truth. According to James, truth is what works and is in the making. Some intellectual historians claim that thinkers like James are using the Darwinian theory of evolution as a model for thinking about knowledge and truth; knowledge and truth, the analogues of organisms, are evolving entities rather than fixed or given entities.*

Some years ago, being with a camping party in the mountains, I returned from a solitary ramble to find every one engaged in a ferocious metaphysical dispute. The corpus of the dispute was a squirrel—a live squirrel supposed to be clinging to one side of a tree-trunk; while over against the tree's opposite side a human being was imagined to stand. This human witness tries to get sight of the squirrel by moving rapidly round the tree, but no matter how fast he goes, the squirrel moves as fast in the opposite direction, and always keeps the tree between himself and the man, so that never a glimpse of him is caught. The resultant metaphysical problem now is this: *Does the man go round the squirrel or not?* He goes round the tree, sure enough, and the squirrel is on the tree; but does he go round the squirrel? In the unlimited leisure of the wilderness, discussion had been worn threadbare. Everyone had taken sides, and was obstinate; and the numbers on both sides were even. Each side, when I appeared therefore appealed to me to make it a majority. Mindful of the scholastic adage that whenever you meet a contradiction you must make a distinction, I immediately sought and found one, as follows: "Which party is right," I said, "depends on what you practically mean by 'going round' the squirrel. If you mean passing from the north of him to the east, then to the south, then to the west, and then to the north of him again, obviously the man does go round him, for he occupies these successive positions. But if on the contrary you mean being first in front of him, then on the right of him, then behind him, then on his left, and finally in front again, it is quite as obvious that the man fails to go round him, for by the compensating movements the squirrel makes, he keeps his belly turned towards the man all the time, and his back turned away. Make the distinction, and there is no occasion for any farther dispute. You are both right and both wrong according as you conceive the verb 'to go round' in one practical fashion or the other."

Although one or two of the hotter disputants called my speech a shuffling evasion, saying they wanted no quibbling or scholastic hair-splitting, but meant just plain honest English 'round,' the majority seemed to think that the distinction had assuaged the dispute.

I tell this trivial anecdote because it is a peculiarly simple example of what I wish now to speak of as the pragmatic method. The pragmatic method is primarily a method of settling metaphysical disputes that otherwise might be interminable. Is the world one or many?—fated or free?—material or spiritual?—here are notions either of which may or may not hold good of the world; and disputes over such notions are unending. The pragmatic method in such cases is to try to interpret each notion by tracing its respective practical consequences. What difference would it practically make to any one if this notion rather than that notion were true? If no practical difference whatever can be traced, then the alternatives mean practically the same thing, and all dispute is idle. Whenever a dispute is serious, we ought to be able to show some practical difference that must follow from one side or the other's being right.

A glance at the history of the idea will show you still better what pragmatism means. The term is derived from the same Greek word πρᾶγμα, meaning action, from which our words 'practice' and 'practical' come. It was first introduced into philosophy by Mr. Charles Peirce in 1878. In an article entitled "How to Make our Ideas Clear," in the "Popular Science Monthly" for January of that year Mr. Peirce, after pointing out that our beliefs are really rules for action, said that, to develop a thought's meaning, we need only determine what conduct it is fitted to produce: that conduct is for us its sole significance. And the tangible fact at the root of all our thought-distinctions, however subtle, is that there is no one of them so fine as to consist in anything but a possible difference of practice. To attain perfect clearness in our thoughts of an object, then, we need only consider what conceivable effects of a practical kind the object may involve—what sensations we are to expect from it, and what reactions we must prepare. Our conception of these effects, whether immediate or remote, is then for us the whole of our conception of the object, so far as that conception has positive significance at all.

From William James, *Pragmatism*.

John Dewey

Philosophy, Education, and Social Problems Are Interconnected

John Dewey (1859–1952) was an American pragmatist philosopher, social critic and educator.

For John Dewey, like Peirce and James, the practical consequences of theories are important components of how we conceive the business of philosophy. Dewey builds on this notion and crafts a conception of philosophy which essentially links it with education and the origin and resolution of social issues. While Peirce saw logic as the field of philosophy which was basic for liberal education and progress in science, Dewey defines philosophy itself as a general theory of education. He brings out how we first need to recognize that social problems prompt philosophizing. We can think of many instances today just in the realm of medicine where people differ on the social issues of abortion, euthanasia, and health care. As we strive to resolve these matters, we raise and try to answer questions which have a clear philosophical import. Is there a right to abortion, euthanasia, or health care? Is a fetus a human being? What is a human being? Is there ever a time when life is not worth living? What is a worthwhile life? Is there a level of health to which all people are entitled? What is a right? We ask these questions to guide us in the resolution of these social issues. By answering the questions, we expect to learn how best to resolve the issues; we expect to educate ourselves about their solutions. So, as we keep in mind the origin and purpose of philosophizing, we see clearly its essential connection not just with education but also with how philosophy can make a difference in our lives and how it has practical consequences for our lives.

The fact that philosophic problems arise because of widespread and widely felt difficulties in social practice is disguised because philosophers become a specialized class which uses a technical language, unlike the vocabulary in which the direct difficulties are stated. But where a system becomes influential, its connection with a conflict of interests calling for some program of social adjustment may always be discovered. At this point, the intimate connection between philosophy and education appears. In fact, education offers a vantage ground from which to penetrate to the human, as distinct from the technical, significance of philosophic discussions. The student of philosophy "in itself" is always in danger of taking it as so much nimble or severe intellectual exercise—as something said by philosophers and concerning them alone. But when philosophic issues are approached from the side of the kind of mental disposition to which they correspond, the life-situations which they formulate can never be far from view. If a theory makes no difference in educational endeavor, it must be artificial. The educational point of view enables one to envisage the philosophic problems where they arise and thrive, where they are at home, and where acceptance or rejection makes a difference in practice.

If we are willing to conceive education as the process of forming fundamental dispositions, intellectual and emotional, toward nature and fellow men, philosophy may even be defined *as the general theory of education.* Unless a philosophy is to remain symbolic—or verbal—or a sentimental indulgence for a few, or else mere arbitrary dogma, its auditing of past experience and its program of values must take effect in conduct. Public agitation, propaganda, legislative and administrative action are effective in producing the change of disposition which a philosophy indicates as desirable, but only in the degree in which they are educative—that is to say, in the degree in which they modify mental and moral attitudes. And at the best, such methods are compromised by the fact they are used with those whose habits are already largely set, while education of youth has a fairer and freer field of operation. On the other side, the business of schooling tends to become a routine empirical affair unless its aims and methods are animated by such a broad and sympathetic survey of its place in contemporary life as it is the business of philosophy to provide.

The reconstruction of philosophy, of education, and of social ideals and methods thus go hand in hand. If there is especial need of educational reconstruction at the present time, if this need makes urgent a reconsideration of the basic ideas of traditional philosophic systems, it is because of the thoroughgoing change in social life accompanying the advance of science, the industrial revolution, and the development of democracy. Such practical changes cannot take place without demanding an educational re-formation to meet them, and without leading men to ask what ideas and ideals are implicit in these social changes, and what revisions they require of the ideas and ideals which are inherited from older and unlike cultures.

From: John Dewey, *Democracy and Education.*

Jane Addams

The Developmental Approach of Pragmatism Can Fruitfully Guide Our Understanding of Justice and Technology

Jane Addams (1860–1935) was an American social reformer and recipient of the Nobel Peace Prize.

A common theme in the thinking of the pragmatists is that human accomplishment results from an ongoing building on, and sometimes transformation of, past experience. Things we have of significance we created in this developmental process. Jane Addams invokes this way of thinking as she talks first about justice, which she dubs her "premature pragmatism," and then about technology.

I do not wish to take callow writing too seriously, but I reproduce from an oratorical contest the following bit of premature pragmatism, doubtless due much more to temperament than to perception, because I am still ready to subscribe to it, although the grandiloquent style is, I hope, a thing of the past: "Those who believe that Justice is but a poetical longing within us, the enthusiast who thinks it will come in the form of a millennium, those who see it established by the strong-arm of a hero, are not those who have comprehended the vast truths of life. The actual justice must come by trained intelligence, by broadened sympathies toward the individual man or woman who crosses our path; one item added to another is the only method by which to build up a conception lofty enough to be of use in the world.". . .

Could we not interest the young people working in the neighboring factories, in these older forms of industry, so that, through their own parents and grandparents, they would find a dramatic representation of the inherited resources of their daily occupation. If these young people could actually see that the complicated machinery of the factory had been evolved from simple tools, they might at least make a beginning towards that education which Dr. Dewey defines as "a continuing reconstruction of experience." They might also lay a foundation for reverence of the past which Goethe declares to be the basis of all sound progress.

My exciting walk on Polk Street was followed by many talks with Dr. Dewey and with one of the teachers in his school who was a resident at Hull-House. Within a month a room was fitted up to which we might invite those of our neighbors who were possessed of old crafts and who were eager to use them. We found in the immediate neighborhood, at least four varieties of these most primitive methods of spinning and three distinct variations of the same spindle in connection with wheels. It was possible to put these seven into historic sequence and order and to connect the whole with the present method of factory spinning. The same thing was done for weaving, and on every Saturday evening a little exhibit was made of these various forms of labor in the textile industry. Within one room a Syrian woman, a Greek, an Italian, a Russian, and an Irishwoman enabled even the most casual observer to see that there is no break in orderly evolution if we look at history from the industrial standpoint; that industry develops similarly and peacefully year by year among the workers of each nation, heedless of differences in language, religion, and political experiences.

From Jane Addams, *Twenty Years at Hull-House.*

SOCRATES

Admit Ignorance, Cross-Examine People, and Dismiss their False Claims

Socrates (c. 470–399 B.C.E.) was an Athenian philosopher who championed the role of reason in the search for truth.

If one person comes to mind as standing for philosophy, that person is probably Socrates. And if that person is not Socrates, it is probably Plato who was Socrates's student. We have no writings of Socrates, but he does appear as a participant in almost all of the dialogue which Plato wrote. In one of these dialogues, The Apology, *Socrates reveals his approach to learning which had earned him the title of the wisest of men. Socrates is puzzled when he hears that an oracle, a spokesperson for an ancient Greek god, dubbed him the wisest. He sets out to discover the meaning of this claim which he finds so curious, given that he is so willing to admit his ignorance and there seem to be so many people who know so much. He goes to the politicians, the writers, and the craftsmen, but finds, upon questioning them, that, however much they may claim to have knowledge, they in fact do not. Socrates tells of how young people enjoy witnessing his cross-examinations and even want to imitate him. Consider whether you find Socrates worth imitating in this respect. Certainly the good philosopher and critical thinker wants to be able to see through people's puffery and to be able to identify and dismiss their false claims, but is there something else? Let us consider Socrates first and then turn to the approaches of other philosophers.*

You know Chaerephon, of course. He was a friend of mine from boyhood, and a good democrat who played his part with the rest of you in the recent expulsion and restoration. And you know what he was like, how enthusiastic he was over anything that he had once undertaken. Well, one day he actually went to Delphi and asked this question of the god—as I said before, gentlemen, please do not interrupt—he asked whether there was anyone wiser than myself. The priestess replied that there was no one. As Chaerephon is dead, the evidence for my statement will be supplied by his brother, who is here in court.

Please consider my object in telling you this. I want to explain to you how the attack upon my reputation first started. When I heard about the oracle's answer, I said to myself, What does the god mean? Why does he not use plain language? I am only too conscious that I have no claim to wisdom, great or small. So what can he mean by asserting that I am the wisest man in the world? He cannot be telling a lie; that would not be right for him.

After puzzling about it for some time, I set myself at last with considerable reluctance to check the truth of it in the following way. I went to interview a man with a high reputation for wisdom, because I felt that here if anywhere I should succeed in disproving the oracle and pointing out to my divine authority, You said that I was the wisest of men, but here is a man who is wiser than I am.

Well, I gave a thorough examination to this person—I need not mention his name, but it was one of our politicians that I was studying when I had this experience—and in conversation with him I formed the impression that although in many people's opinion, and especially in his own, he appeared to be wise, in fact he was not. Then when I began to try to show him that he only thought he was wise and was not really so, my efforts were resented both by him and by many of the other people present. However, I reflected as I walked away, Well, I am certainly wiser than this man. It is only too likely that neither of us has any knowledge to boast of, but he thinks that he knows something which he does not know, whereas I am quite conscious of my ignorance. At any rate it seems that I am wiser than he is to this small extent, that I do not think that I know what I do not know.

After this I went on to interview a man with an even greater reputation for wisdom, and I formed the same impression again, and here too I incurred the resentment of the man himself and a number of others.

From that time on I interviewed one person after another. I realized with distress and alarm that I was making myself unpopular, but I felt compelled to put my religious duty first. Since I was trying to find out the meaning of the oracle, I was bound to interview everyone who had a reputation for knowledge. And by god, gentlemen, for I must be frank with you, my honest impression was this. It seemed to me, as I pursued my investigation at the god's command, that the people with the greatest reputations were almost entirely deficient, while others who were supposed to be their inferiors were much better qualified in practical intelligence.

I want you to think of my adventures as a sort of pilgrimage undertaken to establish the truth of the oracle once for all. After I had finished with the politicians I turned to the poets, dramatic, lyric, and all the rest, in the belief that here I should expose myself as a comparative ignoramus. I used to pick up what I thought were some of their most perfect works and question them closely about the meaning of what they had written, in the hope of incidentally enlarging my own knowledge. Well, gentlemen, I hesitate to tell you the truth, but it must be told. It is hardly an exaggeration to say that any of the bystanders could have explained those poems better than their actual authors. So I soon made up my mind about the poets too. I decided that it was not wisdom that enabled them to write their poetry, but a kind of instinct or inspiration, such as you find in seers and prophets who, deliver all their sublime messages without knowing in the least what they mean. It seemed clear to me that the poets were in much the same case, and I also observed that the very fact that they were poets made them think that they had a perfect understanding of all other subjects, of which they were totally ignorant. So I left that line of inquiry too with the same sense of advantage that I had felt in the case of the politicians.

Last of all I turned to the skilled craftsmen. I knew quite well that I had practically no technical qualifications myself, and I was sure that I should find them full of impressive knowledge. In this I was not disappointed. They understood things which I did not, and to that extent they were wiser than I was. But gentlemen, these professional experts seemed to share the same failing which I had noticed in the poets. I mean that on the strength of their technical proficiency they claimed a perfect understanding of every other subject, however important, and I felt that this error more than outweighed their positive wisdom. So I made myself spokesman for the oracle, and asked myself whether I would rather be as I was—neither wise with their wisdom nor stupid with their stupidity—or possess both qualities as they did. I replied through myself to the oracle that it was best for me to be as I was.

The effect of these investigations of mine, gentlemen, has been to arouse against me a great deal of hostility, and hostility of a particularly bitter and persistent kind, which has resulted in various malicious suggestions, including the description of me as a professor of wisdom. This is due to the fact that whenever I succeed in disproving another person's claim to wisdom in a given subject, the bystanders assume that I know everything about that subject myself. But the truth of the matter, gentlemen, is pretty certainly this, that real wisdom is the property of God, and this oracle is his way of telling us that human wisdom has little or no value. It seems to me that he is not referring literally to Socrates, but has merely taken my name as an example, as if he would say to us, The wisest of you men is he who has realized, like Socrates, that in respect of wisdom he is really worthless.

That is why I still go about seeking and searching in obedience to the divine command, if I think that anyone is wise, whether citizen or stranger, and when I think that any person is not wise, I try to help the cause of God by proving that he is not. This occupation has kept me too busy to do much either in politics or in my own affairs. In fact, my service to God has reduced me to extreme poverty.

There is another reason for my being unpopular. A number of young men with wealthy fathers and plenty of leisure have deliberately attached themselves to me because they enjoy hearing other people cross-questioned. These often take me as their model, and go on to try to question other persons. Whereupon, I suppose, they find an unlimited number of people who think that they know something, but really know little or nothing. Consequently their victims become annoyed, not with themselves but with me, and they complain that there is a pestilential busybody called Socrates who fills young people's heads with wrong ideas. If you ask them what he does, and what he teaches that has this effect, they have no answer, not knowing what to say. But as they do not want to admit their confusion, they fall back on the stock charges against any philosopher, that he teaches his pupils about things in the heavens and below the earth, and to disbelieve in gods, and to make the weaker argument defeat the stronger. They would be very loath, I fancy, to admit the truth—which is that they are being convicted of pretending to knowledge when they are entirely ignorant. So, jealous, I suppose, for their own reputation, and also energetic and numerically strong, and provided with a plausible and carefully worked-out case against me, these people have been dinning into your ears for a long time past their violent denunciations of myself.

From Plato, *Apology*. Translated by Hugh Tredemick.

RENÉ DESCARTES

Seek Certainty with a Method of Doubt

René Descartes (1596–1650) is a French philosopher and mathematician cited as the "father of modern philosophy."

We saw how Socrates looked critically at the ideas of other people and dismissed claims to knowledge when he found them faulty. René Descartes subjects his own ideas to a critical examination of this sort, but he subjects his ideas to the strongest of tests if he is to accept them. In his first rule of his famous rules of method, Descartes, in effect, resolves to reject any idea of which he has even the slightest doubt of its truth. His test is that of the clarity and the distinctness of his idea. While Descartes is geared toward dismissing falsehood as Socrates was, his method is so defined by his skeptical approach that commentators refer to it as Descartes's doubting method. But, since Descartes is doubting or being skeptical as a means or method for discovering the truth, we might call him a methodological skeptic. As he subjects each idea to his test of clarity and distinctness, he finds that each fails but one, "I think, therefore I am." He figured that, even if he was considering or thinking about false ideas, he at least could be sure that he, who was doing the thinking, existed. So, Descartes's method has led him to what he was seeking, something which passed his test of clarity and distinctness, something which is certain. This finding is sometimes called Descartes' "Cogito" which is shorthand for its expression in Latin, Cogito ergo sum. *Descartes may have found with his* Cogito *a point of certainty from which he could press on with his inquiries. But he recognized that his method for rational inquiry needed to be located within a moral context and added a moral code with four maxims to his four rules of method.*

THE PRINCIPAL RULES OF THE METHOD

The first rule was never to accept anything as true unless I recognized it to be evidently such: that is, carefully to avoid precipitation and prejudgment, and to include nothing in my conclusions unless it presented itself so clearly and distinctly to my mind that there was no occasion to doubt it.

The second was to divide each of the difficulties which I encountered into as many parts as possible, and as might be required for an easier solution.

Third was to think in an orderly fashion, beginning with the things which were simplest and easiest to understand, and gradually and by degrees reaching toward more complex knowledge, even treating as though ordered materials which were not necessarily so.

The last was always to make enumerations so complete, and reviews so general, that I would be certain that nothing was omitted. . . .

I had noticed for a long time that in practice it is sometimes necessary to follow opinions which we know to be very uncertain, just as though they were indubitable, as I stated before; but inasmuch as I desired to devote myself wholly to the search for truth, I thought I should take a course precisely contrary, and reject as absolutely false anything of which I could have the least doubt, in order to see whether anything would be left after this procedure which could be called wholly certain. Thus, as our senses deceive us at times, I was ready to suppose that nothing was at all the way our senses represented them to be. As there are men who make mistakes in reasoning even on the simplest topics in geometry, I judged that I was as liable to error as any other, and rejected as false all the reasoning which I had previously accepted as valid demonstration. Finally, as the same precepts which we have when awake may come to us when asleep without their being true, I decided to suppose that nothing that had ever entered my mind was more real than the illusions of my dreams. But I soon noticed that while I thus wished to think everything false, it was necessarily true that I who thought so was something. Since this truth, *I think, therefore I am*, was so firm and assured that all the most extravagant suppositions of the sceptics were unable to shake it, I judged that I could safely accept it as the first principle of the philosophy I was seeking.

I then examined closely what I was, and saw that I could imagine that I had no body, and that there was no world nor any place that I occupied, but that I could not imagine for a moment that I did not exist. On the contrary, from the very fact that I doubted the truth of other things, it followed very evidently and very certainly that I existed; therefore I concluded that I was a substance whose whole essence or nature was only to think, and which, to exist, has no need of space nor of any material thing. Thus it follows that this ego, this soul, by which I am what I am, is entirely distinct from the body and is easier to know than the latter, and that even if the body were not, the soul would not cease to be all that it now is. . . .

Now just as it is not enough, before beginning to rebuild the house where one lives, to pull it down, to make provisions for materials and architects, or to take a try at architecture for oneself, and also to have carefully worked out the floorplan; one must provide for something else in addition, namely where one can be conveniently sheltered while working on the other building, so too, in order not to remain irresolute in my actions while reason requires me to be so in my judgments, and in order not to cease living during that time as happily as possible, I formulated a provisional code of morals, which consisted of but three or four maxims, that I want to share with you.

The first was to obey the laws and the customs of my country, firmly holding on to the religion in which, by God's grace, I was instructed from childhood, and governing myself in all other things according to the most moderate opinions and those furthest from excess that were commonly accepted in practice by the most sensible of those people with whom I would have to live. . . .

My second maxim was to be as firm and resolute in my actions as I could be, and to follow with no less constancy the most doubtful opinions, once I have decided on them, than if they were very certain. In this I would imitate travelers who, finding themselves lost in a forest, ought not wander this way and that, or, what is worse, remain in one place, but ought always walk as straight a line as they can in one direction and not change course for feeble reasons, even if at the outset it was perhaps only chance that made them choose it; for by this means, if they are not going where they wish, they will finally arrive at least somewhere where they probably will be better off than in the middle of a forest. . . .

My third maxim was always to try to conquer myself rather than fortune, to change my desires rather than the order of the world; and generally to become accustomed to believing that there is nothing that is utterly within our power, except for our thoughts, so that, after having done our best regarding things external to us, everything that fails to bring us success, from our point of view, is absolutely impossible. And this principle alone seemed sufficient to stop me from desiring anything in the future that I would not acquire, and thus seemed sufficient to make me contented.

Finally, to conclude this code of morals, I thought it advisable to review the various occupations that men take up in this life, so as to try to choose the best one; and, not wanting to say anything about the occupations of others, I believed I could not do better than to continue in the occupation I was in at that time, namely cultivating my reason all my life and advancing, as best as I could, in the knowledge of truth, following the method I had prescribed to myself. I had met with such intense satisfaction, since the time I had begun to make use of this method, that I did not believe one could receive sweeter or more innocent satisfaction in this life; and, discovering every day by its means some truths that seemed important to me and commonly ignored by other men, I had a satisfaction that so filled my mind that nothing else was of any consequence to me.

From René Descartes's *Discourse on Method*, translated by Laurence L. LaFleur.

BENJAMIN FRANKLIN

Morality Is a Part of Rationality

Benjamin Franklin (1702-1790) was an American statesman, scientist, and moralist.

We have already seen some philosophers grappling with the connection between morality and rationality. Recall how Peirce claimed that such things as morality, aesthetics, and the ways of the world have little to do with the study of logic. And we just saw how Descartes turned to a moral code to assist him as he pressed on with his rational inquiries. Benjamin Franklin sets out four rules which he claims are guidelines for "living in all respects like a rational creature." In so doing, he locates his commitment to truth as no less a feature of rationality than his commitment to sincerity, industry, patience, and speaking only good of other people.

Those who write of the art of poetry teach us that if we would write what may be worth the reading, we ought always, before we begin, to form a regular plan and design of our piece: otherwise, we shall be in danger of incongruity. I am apt to think it is the same as to life. I have never fixed a regular design in life; by which means it has been a confused variety of different scenes. I am now entering upon a new one: let me, therefore, make some resolutions, and form some scheme of action, that, henceforth, I may live in all respects like a rational creature.

1. It is necessary for me to be extremely frugal for some time, till I have paid what I owe.
2. To endeavour to speak truth in every instance; to give nobody expectations that are not likely to be answered, but aim at sincerity in every word and action—the most amiable excellence in a rational being.
3. To apply myself industriously to whatever business I take in hand, and not divert my mind from my business by any foolish project of growing suddenly rich; for industry and patience are the surest means of plenty.
4. I resolve to speak ill of no man whatever, not even in a matter of truth; but rather by some means excuse the faults I hear charged upon others, and upon proper occasions speak all the good I know of every body.

From Benjamin Franklin, "Plan for Future Conduct."

JORGE VALADEZ
Engage in Liberated Dialogue to End Oppression

Jorge Valadez (1951–   ) is an American philosopher who specializes in metaphysics and political philosophy.

Contemporary philosopher Jorge Valadez places an interesting spin on the significance for philosophy which Socrates and Plato attach to dialogue. Valadez sees dialogue as essential for philosophizing but is concerned that cultural oppression may inhibit genuine dialogue. After suggesting with a vivid example that such oppression exists, Valadez articulates conditions for a liberated dialogue. This liberated dialogue, he believes, will allow us to learn from other cultures as we respect them, their people, and how they think about reality. Where Socrates's interaction with other people led to the dismissal of their claims to knowledge, Valadez seems to pave the way for dialogue being the key to appreciating the views of other people.

Consuelo had been living at a frantic pace for months. She was deeply involved in an organization of mothers who were demanding that the Guatemalan government account for their sons and daughters who had disappeared. Many of the mothers believed that their sons or daughters had probably already been killed by the government security forces, but they continued to hope that perhaps they might be alive and jailed with other political prisoners. The crimes of their loved ones consisted of their having protested and opposed the policies of the militarily controlled government. In Guatemala the degree of poverty and human suffering is staggering and many of the people from the poor and disfranchised class had finally decided that it was necessary to speak up against the government, even if it meant placing themselves and others close to them in danger.

Consuelo knew all of this, and she also knew that the bloated bodies of some of the disappeared were sometimes found floating in a river or buried in shallow graves. But despite it all she felt that it was preferable for her to know what had happened to her twenty year old son. Even the knowledge that he was dead was better than this insufferable uncertainty that weighed down her waking hours and haunted her dreams. At least the body could then receive a proper burial.

Early on in her life Consuelo had learned about responsibility and about hardship, and the latter she had come to accept as an inevitable aspect of her existence. She was the eldest child, and by age twelve she had assumed the duties of an adult. She had married while still an adolescent. Later, in her tenth year of marriage her husband left to seek work in the U.S. Whether he actually ever made it across the border she never knew, since she had not heard from him since. Through the years, she had convinced herself that it was best to think of him only as part of those joyful scenes that she stored in her memory like precious secret jewels.

Nothing in her life, however, had prepared her for what occurred that warm Sunday evening when the four armed men broke into her house. The organization of mothers which she headed had been particularly vocal during the last few months and the government wanted to set an example. While two of the men held her, the others grabbed her six year old child. One of them took out a pointed pair of pliers and in a savagely methodical motion pulled out the fingernail from one of the horrified child's fingers. The image of her son's contorted face and the sound of his uncontrolled screams pierced and bored into her brain. The child kicked and twisted his whole body in a crazed effort to get free, but the butchers had had practice. One of them put his knee on the boy's chest and pinned him against the floor while holding down the other small flailing arm. His partner then completed the gruesome task.

The event just described actually occurred, and incidents of this degree of brutality are not rare in Guatemala and other Central American countries. In recent years the United States has provided tens of millions of dollars in military aid to the Guatemalan government. Even though that government has an elected civilian president, the real power is in the hands of the military, for the most powerful appointed officials in the government are military officers. Death squads and special security forces play a crucial role in the maintenance of power by the military. In Guatemala approximately 2 percent of the population own about 75 percent of the country's land and resources. It is a country where great inequalities of wealth exist between the privileged few and the mostly poor Indian population. About 73 percent of all children under the age of five are malnourished and, for every 1,000 births, 270 will die before reaching the age of five. The national illiteracy rate is 65 percent. Government violence has been responsible for more than 100,000 deaths in the last 30 years. . . .

Just as the philosophical point of view has deepened our understanding of oppression, can it now offer us some insights that can serve as a starting point for resolving the problem of oppression in the Third World and in Latin America? Even though philosophical reflection by itself will certainly not resolve this problem, philosophy can nevertheless help us to formulate a useful approach to dealing with this issue. The approach which I want to propose can be called the multi-cultural perspective. According to this perspective, an adequate understanding of reality is one which emerges as the result of an open liberated dialogue between the participants of different cultural traditions. One of the first goals of this dialogue would be for the participants to understand and appreciate the perspectives from which the others perceive reality. The articulation and negotiation of their different needs and concerns would then be based on this prior understanding. None of the perspectives would have an initial or *a priori* privileged status nor would there be an initial hierarchical differentiation between perspectives or between the elements of the perspectives.

It is important to note that there would be certain normative principles implicit in the adoption of this multi-cultural perspective. The liberated dialogue would in essence be free from ideological distortions; its participants would have an equal access to information (and would have developed the critical understanding necessary for evaluating that information); and there would be a lack of hierarchical controls in the information, etc. The practical and political implications of these principles are profound and wide-ranging. Consider the second of the conditions just mentioned. If the participants in the dialogue are to have an equal access to as well as a critical understanding of any information that may be relevant for the negotiation of a case at hand, then this implies at least an approximate parity in the educational preparation of the participants, as well as an elimination of economic restrictions that would impose arbitrary limitations on the use of available information. Furthermore, a critical understanding of this information presupposes an absence of sexist, racist, classist, and other ideological factors that may distort its meaning and interpretation.

The satisfaction of these conditions for liberated dialogue implies the elimination of substantial differences in the economic and educational status of the participants. In the multi-cultural perspective the connection between the socioeconomic position of the participants of a political community and their capacity to participate meaningfully in the decision-making process of that community is emphasized. This perspective thus avoids the naive viewpoint of classical liberal political theory that severs the connection between political and economic power and the capacity to equally exercise one's civil rights in a real political setting.

Finally, I want to clarify the multi-cultural perspective by saying what it is not. It is not a relativistic or perspectival approach according to which all cultural perspectives are "equally valid." It is entirely possible that the participants in the open liberated dialogue may determine that certain cultural practices are oppressive or unethical (traditional views of women are a case in point). Thus we do not naively idealize or romanticize other cultures. This perspective does not tell us ahead of time which practices of what culture are oppressive or not. Instead, what it does is to give us a methodology by which the identification of such practices is to be achieved. Also, the multi-cultural perspective is not a Marxist perspective, because, although it recognizes the important role of economic factors in oppression, it leaves it as an open question whether it is in the best interests of the members of a community (either local, national, or international) to adopt a capitalist, socialist, communist, or mixed economic system. It is certainly logically possible that one or another of these systems may be more effective and desirable to different communities at different points in time.

It is unlikely that we will be able to deal adequately with the issues of poverty and oppression in the Third World until we recognize the philosophical assumptions which shape the way in which we understand these issues. In our dealings with the Third World and in our own domestic policies we should have the moral courage to strive for economic and social justice, for this is the ethically correct thing to do. But in addition to this compelling moral reason, we have strong practical reasons to do so. We can no longer afford not to. We must reevaluate the philosophy of egoism and ontocentrism which is so central to our conceptual orientations. And, most importantly, we must realize that refusing to deal with oppression involves an alienation from our own humanity and compassion. The struggle with the problem of oppression is not to be taken lightly, for ultimately the battle is to reclaim our own souls.

From Jorge Valadez, "The Metaphysics of Oppression."

The Philosopher's Stone. 1652. The philosopher's stone was considered to be a substance with powers ranging from transformation to regeneration and redemption. Alchemists thought it could transform base metals into gold.

STEPHEN L. CARTER

Recognize the Rhetoric of Silencing

Stephen L. Carter (1954–   ) is an American legal scholar, author, and social critic.

Stephen L. Carter explores the techniques by which discourses are "bounded" and dialogue is stifled and distorted. Positions are labelled in such a derogatory way that they are effectively put outside the realm of debate. The risk of bounding discourse is great: those ideas that are dismissed as not worthy of discussion might, indeed, turn out to be true. It is no accident that those in power attempt to rule as unworthy of debate any ideas contrary to their own interests. But Carter believes there must be some ideas that are "undebatable," that serve as a bedrock, if nations are to be formed and endure.

> *Civility assumes that we will disagree; it requires us not to mask our differences but to resolve them respectfully.*

Sadly, we are losing the skill for respectful debate. . . everybody tries to find ways to put their own cherished positions beyond debate. . . .

We employ, all of us, a rhetoric of silencing, trying to deter opposition, perhaps so that we will not have to spend energy refuting it. A few decades ago, the vocabulary of silencing featured "un-American," which became a catchall for many forms of liberal dissent from the moderately conservative post-World War II consensus, as well as a part of the name of an often malevolent committee of the House of Representatives. More recently, we saw the left briefly accede to the idea that anybody troubled by affirmative action was a racist, and the right, for a while, to the idea that nobody but those memorably dismissed as "feminazis" cared about sexual harrasment in the workplace. Fortunately, most of this labeling turns out to be a passing fad. But even today, in a bit of a paradox, the more certain we are of our rightness, the less interested we seem to be in debate.

Pick any divisive issue: gay rights, for example, where the nation has recently fought pitched rhetorical battles over everything from marriage to military service. The strongest advocates of gay rights are sure that those who disagree with them are necessarily homophobic—gay-hating—and the strongest opponents are sure that those who disagree with them are necessarily ungodly. In both cases, the certainty that one side is right makes the other side not worth debating, for who can hold a conversation with such monstrous evil?

One of the cleverest moves is to define the debate in a way that excludes some ideas from consideration before the argument even begins. The technique involves designing a universe of "bounded discourse"—an arena in which some ideas can be debated and others cannot. The bounds always sound reasonable, whether they are or not. In the middle years of this century, any position that smacked even vaguely of communism was prohibited (sometimes legally prohibited) in public debate. More recently, in what should be an academic embarrassment, liberal theorists have spent much effort in creating rules for public dialogue that leave well outside the universe of discourse points of view with which liberalism is uncomfortable–religious argument, for one.

The purpose and effect of bounding discourse is to make some ideas not so much undebatable as inexpressible. In one sense, this is important to the proper functioning of democracy, because conversation, like every other human activity, can help define a people when it proceeds from common norms. Besides, one cannot build a nation in which everything is on the table for discussion: such a nation would stand for nothing, resting on no enduring principles, and could scarcely funtion because of the chaos created by an inability to predict what might change tomorrow. So, in America, we take off the table a commitment to equal opportunity, respect for private property, universal adult suffrage, and many aspects of individual liberty. We cherish them sufficiently that we put them in the Constitution. All these precepts, of course, are freely debatable, but if there were any serious prospect of their repeal, we would scarcely *be* America.

The difficulty, however, is that the effort to bound discourse limits our horizons: the ideas we freeze out can never come dominant. Historically, every group that has found itself, for a time, in power, has tried to take off the table ideas that were contrary to its own interests. So the antebellum Congress refused to discuss an end to slavery, the early industrial capitalists insisted that unions were un-American, and most American churches until fairly recently, treated any question of enhancing the role of women in the church as a joke. This is the point, and it is also the risk: the rules of discourse are always made by those who hold power, and the ideas they rule out of bounds will almost certainly be the ones they dislike.

From Stephen L. Carter, *Civility*.

HENRY DAVID THOREAU
Writing Helps Us to Think Critically

Henry David Thoreau (1817–1862) was an American transcendental philosopher and essayist.

Henry David Thoreau observes that daily writing can assist with detecting falsehood and bringing clarity to our ideas both of which we have seen philosophers identify as part of, or objectives of, philosophy.

JANUARY 17, 1835

Of keeping a private journal or record of our thoughts, feelings, studies, and daily experience, containing abstracts of books, and the opinions we formed of them on first reading them.

As those pieces which the painter sketches for his own amusement in his leisure hours, are often superior to his most elaborate productions, so it is that ideas often suggest themselves to us spontaneously, as it were, far surpassing in beauty those which arise in the mind upon applying ourselves to any particular subject. Hence, could a machine be invented which would instantaneously arrange on paper each idea as it occurs to us, without any exertion on our part, how extremely useful would it be considered. The relation between this and the practice of keeping a journal is obvious. But yet, the preservation of our scattered thoughts is to be considered an object but of minor importance.

Every one can think, but comparatively few can write, can express their thoughts. Indeed, how often do we hear one complain of his inability to express what he feels! How many have occasion to make the following remark, "I am sensible that I understand this perfectly, but am not able to find words to convey my idea to others."

But if each one would employ a certain portion of each day in looking back upon the time which has passed, and in writing down his thoughts and feelings, in reckoning up his daily gains, that he may be able to detect whatever false coins have crept into his coffers, and, as it were, in settling accounts with his mind, not only would his daily experience be greatly increased, since his feelings and ideas would thus be more clearly defined, but he would be ready to turn over a new leaf, having carefully perused the preceding one, and would not continue to glance carelessly over the same page, without being able to distinguish it from a new one.

Most of us are apt to neglect the study of our own characters, thoughts, and feelings, and for the purpose of forming our own minds, look to others, who should merely be considered as different editions of the same great work. To be sure, it would be well for us to examine the various copies, that we might detect any errors, but yet, it would be foolish for one to borrow a work which he possessed himself, but had not perused.

In fine, if we endeavoured more to improve ourselves by reflection, by making a business of thinking, and giving our thoughts form and expression, we should be led to "read not to contradict and confute, nor to believe and take for granted, nor to find talk and discourse, but to weigh and consider."

From *Henry D. Thoreau Early Essays and Miscellanies,* edited by Joseph Moldenhauer and Edwin Moser.

LUCRETIUS

Philosophy Frees Us from Superstition

Lucretius (c. 99–55 B.C.E.) was a Roman metaphysical poet.

Lucretius sees superstition as crippling to the human spirit. He credits Socrates, whom he refers to as "a man of Greece" in the following passage, for being the first person to assist us with breaking from superstition. Lucretius speaks of Socrates's mind prevailing and crushing superstition. So for humans to prosper, they must, like Socrates, employ and be guided by reason instead of ignorance and superstition.

When human life lay grovelling in all men's sight, crushed to the earth under the dead weight of superstition whose grim features loured menacingly upon mortals from the four quarters of the sky, a man of Greece was first to raise mortal eyes in defiance, first to stand erect and brave the challenge. Fables of the gods did not crush him, nor the lightning flash and the growling menace of the sky. Rather, they quickened his manhood, so that he, first of all men, longed to smash the constraining locks of nature's doors. The vital vigour of his mind prevailed. He ventured far out beyond the flaming ramparts of the world and voyaged in mind throughout infinity. Returning victorious, he proclaimed to us what can be and what cannot: how a limit is fixed to the power of everything and an immovable frontier post. Therefore superstition in its turn lies crushed beneath his feet, and we by his triumph are lifted level with the skies.

From Lucretius, *On the Nature of the Universe*, translated by Ronald Latham.

BOETHIUS

Philosophy Transforms the Deceived and Drowsy Person Into One Who Is Knowledgeable and Spiritually Strong

Boethius (c. 480–524 B.C.E.) was a Roman philosopher and legislator.

Boethius personifies philosophy and depicts her coming to him at a time of unhappiness. Philosophy diagnoses his problem as one of having fallen from the ways and teachings of philosophy and knuckling under to deception. Philosophy strives to assist Boethius by bringing him back to her and to insure that his soul remains strong even in the face of challenges to wisdom by shameless people.

"**B**ut now," said she, "is the time for the physician's art, rather than for complaining." Then fixing her eyes wholly on me, she said, "Are you the man who was nourished upon the milk of my learning, brought up with my food until you had won your way to the power of a manly soul? Surely I had given you such weapons as would keep you safe, and your strength unconquered; if you had not thrown them away. Do you know me? Why do you keep silence? Are you dumb from shame or from dull amazement? I would it were from shame, but I see that amazement has overwhelmed you."

When she saw that I was not only silent, but utterly tongue-tied and dumb, she put her hand gently upon my breast, and said, "There is no danger: he is suffering from drowsiness, that disease which attacks so many minds which have been deceived. He has forgotten himself for a moment and will quickly remember, as soon as he recognises me. That he may do so, let me brush away from his eyes the darkening cloud of thoughts of matters perishable." So saying, she gathered her robe into a fold and dried my swimming eyes. . . .

In such a manner were the clouds of grief scattered. Then I drew breath again and engaged my mind in taking knowledge of my physician's countenance. So when I turned my eyes towards her and fixed my gaze upon her, I recognised my nurse, Philosophy, in whose chambers I had spent my life from earliest manhood. And I asked her, "Wherefore have you, mistress of all virtues, come down from heaven above to visit my lonely place of banishment? Is it that you, as well as I,

31

may be harried, the victim of false charges?" "Should I," said she, "desert you, my nursling?"

Should I not share and bear my part of the burden which has been laid upon you from spite against my name? Surely Philosophy never allowed herself to let the innocent go upon their journey unbefriended. Think you I would fear calumnies? That I would be terrified as though they were a new misfortune? Think you that this is the first time that wisdom has been harassed by dangers among men of shameless ways? In ancient days before the time of my child, Plato, have we not as well as nowadays fought many a mighty battle against the recklessness of folly? And though Plato did survive, did not his master, Socrates, win his victory of an unjust death, with me present at his side? . . .

Naught else brought them to ruin but that, being built up in my ways, they appeared at variance with the desires of unscrupulous men. So it is no matter for your wonder if, in this sea of life, we are tossed about by storms from all sides; for to oppose evil men is the chief aim we set before ourselves. Though the band of such men is great in numbers, yet is it to be contemned: for it is guided by no leader, but is hurried along at random only by error running riot everywhere. If this band when warring against us presses too strongly upon us, our leader, Reason, gathers her forces into her citadel, while the enemy are busied in plundering useless baggage. As they seize the most worthless things, we laugh at them from above, untroubled by the whole band of mad marauders, and we are defended by that rampart to which riotous folly may not hope to attain.

From Boethius, *The Consolation of Philosophy*. Translated by W. V. Cooper.

Ludwig Wittgenstein
Philosophy Clarifies Our Thoughts

Ludwig Wittgenstein (1889–1951) was an Austrian-born philosopher and logician.

Descartes employed his test of clarity and distinctness in order to find truth. Ludwig Wittgenstein is also guided by clarity in his conception of philosophy, but clarity itself is the goal and value of philosophy. Philosophy has no subject matter of its own, and, if we want to identify a philosophical method, we could do no more than be silent, since science says all that can be said and philosophy has nothing to do with science. But as philosophy brings clarity to what is said, it draws boundaries and identifies what cannot be thought or said. Put differently, as philosophy clarifies our thoughts, it assists in identifying the domain of science.

4.1   Propositions represent the existence and non-existence of states of affairs.

4.11   The totality of true propositions is the whole of natural science (or the whole corpus of the natural sciences).

4.111   Philosophy is not one of the natural sciences.(The word 'philosophy' must mean something whose place is above or below the natural sciences, not beside them.)

4.112   Philosophy aims at the logical clarification of thoughts.

        Philosophy is not a body of doctrine but an activity.

        A philosophical work consists essentially of elucidations.

        Philosophy does not result in philosophical propositions, but rather in the clarification of propositions.

        Without philosophy thoughts are, as it were, cloudy and indistinct: its task is to make them clear and to give them sharp boundaries. . . .

6.53   The correct method in philosophy would really be the following: to say nothing except what can be said, i.e. propositions of natural science— i.e. something that has nothing to do with philosophy—and then, whenever someone else wanted to say something metaphysical, to demonstrate to him that he had failed to give a meaning to certain signs in his propositions. Although it would not be satisfying to the other person—he would not have the feeling that we were teaching him philosophy—this method would be the only strictly correct one.

6.54   My propositions serve as elucidations in the following way: anyone who understands me eventually recognizes them as nonsensical, when he has used them—as steps—to climb up beyond them. (He must, so to speak, throw away the ladder after he has climbed up it.)

He must transcend these propositions, and then he will see the world aright.

What we cannot speak about we must pass over in silence.

From Ludwig Wittgenstein, *Tractatus Logico-Philosophicus*, translated by D.F. Pears and B.F. McGuinness.

BERTRAND RUSSELL
Philosophy Opens Our Minds

Bertrand Russell (1872–1970), a recipient of the Nobel Prize for Literature, was a British philosopher, mathematician and antiwar activist.

Bertrand Russell would agree with Wittgenstein that philosophy brings clarity to our thoughts. But he is in fundamental disagreement about what this push for clarity holds for the thinking potential of the human. While Wittgenstein sees the clarification setting boundaries to thought, Russell points out that the critical analysis and clarification that philosophy brings to questions which we commonly ask serves to open our minds to what is possible in the universe.

Is there any knowledge in the world which is so certain that no reasonable man could doubt it? This question, which at first sight might not seem difficult, is really one of the most difficult that can be asked. When we have realized the obstacles in the way of a straightforward and confident answer, we shall be well launched on the study of philosophy—for philosophy is merely the attempt to answer such ultimate questions, not carelessly and dogmatically, as we do in ordinary life and even in the sciences, but critically, after exploring all that makes such questions puzzling, and after realizing all the vagueness and confusion that underlie our ordinary ideas. . . .

Philosophy is to be studied, not for the sake of any definite answers to its questions, since no definite answers can, as a rule, be known to be true, but rather for the sake of the questions themselves; because these questions enlarge our conception of what is possible, enrich our intellectual imagination and diminish the dogmatic assurance which closes the mind against speculation; but above all because, through the greatness of the universe which philosophy contemplates, the mind also is rendered great, and becomes capable of that union with the universe which constitutes its highest good.

From Bertrand Russell, *The Problems of Philosophy*.

AYN RAND

Only Philosophy Can Answer Three Basic Questions that Trouble All of Us

Ayn Rand (1905–1982), a Russian-born emigré to the United States, was a novelist, essayist, and philosopher.

Ayn Rand claims that all of us as humans are concerned with basic questions about who we are, how we know it, and what we should do. And people often adopt inadequate answers to these questions which are no less troubling. It makes sense to study philosophy, since it is the only field which undertakes a proper investigation of the questions which most concern us. In telling more about how philosophy assists us with answering these questions, Rand identifies major areas of philosophical inquiry including metaphysics, epistemology, ethics, politics, and aesthetics.

Since I am a fiction writer, let us start with a short short story. Suppose that you are an astronaut whose spaceship gets out of control and crashes on an unknown planet. When you regain consciousness and find that you are not hurt badly, the first three questions in your mind would be: Where am I? How can I discover it? What should I do?

You see unfamiliar vegetation outside, and there is air to breathe; the sunlight seems paler than you remember it and colder. You turn to look at the sky, but stop. You are struck by a sudden feeling: if you don't look, you won't have to know that you are, perhaps, too far from the earth and no return is possible; so long as you don't know it, you are free to believe what you wish—and you experience a foggy, pleasant, but somehow guilty, kind of hope.

You turn to your instruments: they may be damaged, you don't know how seriously. But you stop, struck by a sudden fear: how can you trust these instruments? How can you be sure that they won't mislead you? How can you know whether they will work in a different world? You turn away from the instruments.

Now you begin to wonder why you have no desire to do anything. It seems so much safer just to wait for something to turn up somehow; it is better, you tell yourself, not to rock the spaceship. Far in the distance, you see some sort of living creatures approaching; you don't know whether they are human, but they walk on two feet. They, you decide, will tell you what to do.

You are never heard from again.

This is fantasy, you say? You would not act like that and no astronaut ever would? Perhaps not. But this is the way most men live their lives, here, on earth.

Most men spend their days struggling to evade three questions, the answers to which underlie man's every thought, feeling and action, whether he is consciously aware of it or not: Where am I? How do I know it? What should I do?

By the time they are old enough to understand these questions, men believe that they know the answers. Where am I? Say, in New York City. How do I know it? It's self-evident. What should I do? Here, they are not too sure—but the usual answer is: whatever everybody does. The only trouble seems to be that they are not very active, not very confident, not very happy—and they experience, at times, a causeless fear and an undefined guilt, which they cannot explain or get rid of.

They have never discovered the fact that the trouble comes from the three unanswered questions—and that there is only one science that can answer them: *philosophy.*

Philosophy studies the fundamental nature of existence, of man, and of man's relationship to existence. As against the special sciences, which deal only with particular aspects, philosophy deals with those aspects of the universe which pertain to everything that exists. In the realm of cognition, the special sciences are the trees, but philosophy is the soil which makes the forest possible.

Philosophy would not tell you, for instance, whether you are in New York City or in Zanzibar (though it would give you the means to find out). But here is what it *would* tell you: Are you in a universe which is ruled by natural laws and, therefore, is stable, firm, absolute—and knowable? Or are you in an incomprehensible chaos, a realm of inexplicable miracles, an unpredictable, unknowable flux, which your mind is impotent to grasp? Are the things you see around you real—or are they only an illusion? Do they exist independent of any observer—or are they created by the observer? Are they the object or the subject of man's consciousness? Are they *what they are*—or can they be changed by a mere act of your consciousness, such as a wish?

The nature of your actions—and of your ambition—will be different, according to which set of answers you come to accept. These answers are the province of *metaphysics*—the study of existence as such or, in Aristotle's words, of "being qua being"—the basic branch of philosophy.

No matter what conclusions you reach, you will be confronted by the necessity to answer another, *corollary* question: How do I know it? Since man is not omniscient or infallible, you have to discover what you can claim as knowledge and how to *prove* the validity of your conclusions. Does man acquire knowledge by a process of reason—or by sudden revelation from a supernatural power? Is reason a faculty that identifies and integrates the material provided by man's senses—or is it fed by innate ideas, implanted in man's mind before he was born? Is reason competent to perceive reality—or does man possess some other cognitive faculty which is superior to reason? Can man achieve certainty—or is he doomed to perpetual doubt?

The extent of your self-confidence—and of your success—will be different, according to which set of answers you accept. These answers are the province of *epistemology*, the theory of knowledge, which studies man's means of cognition.

These two branches are the theoretical foundation of philosophy. The third branch—*ethics*—may be regarded as its technology. Ethics does not apply to everything that exists, only to man, but it applies to every aspect of man's life: his character, his actions, his values, his relationship to all of existence. Ethics, or morality, defines a code of values to guide man's choices and actions—the choices and actions that determine the course of his life.

Just as the astronaut in my story did not know what he should do, because he refused to know where he was and how to discover it, so you cannot know what you should do until you know the nature of the universe you deal with, the nature of your means of cognition—and your own nature. Before you come to ethics, you must answer the questions posed by metaphysics and epistemology: Is man a rational being, able to deal with reality—or is he a helplessly blind misfit, a chip buffeted by the universal flux? Are achievement and enjoyment possible to man on earth—or is he doomed to failure and disaster? Depending on the answers, you can proceed to consider the questions posed by ethics: What is good or evil for man—and why? Should man's primary concern be a quest for joy—or an escape from suffering? Should man hold self-fulfillment—or self-destruction—as the goal of his life? Should man pursue his values—or should he place the interests of others above *his* own? Should man seek happiness or self-sacrifice?

I do not have to point out the different consequences of these two sets of answers. You can see them everywhere within you and around you.

The answers given by ethics determine how man should treat other men, and this determines the fourth branch of philosophy: politics, which defines the principles of a proper social system. As an example of philosophy's function, political philosophy will not tell you how much rationed gas you should be given and on which day of the week—it will tell you whether the government has the right to impose any rationing on anything.

The fifth and last branch of philosophy is *esthetics*, the study of art, which is based on metaphysics, epistemology and ethics. Art deals with the needs—the refueling—of man's consciousness.

Now some of you might say, as many people do: "Aw, I never think in such abstract terms—I want to deal with concrete, particular, real-life problems—what do I need philosophy for?" My answer is: In order to be able to deal with concrete, particular, real-life problems— i.e., in order to be able to live on earth.

From Ayn Rand, "Philosophy Who Needs It."

RAYMOND CORBEY

Apes Might Well Be Self-Conscious, Free Agents, and More Like Humans than We Think

Raymond Corbey (1954–) is a philosopher and anthropologist in the Netherlands.

Raymond Corbey notes how a number of philosophers have drawn a sharp distinction between humans and lower animals as well as between humans and non-human primates. The distinction usually rests on the claim that humans alone can reason, be aware of themselves, and act freely; any nonhuman nature is simply driven by instinct. Corbey calls for a re-evaluation of the matter in the light of new evidence and flaws evident in earlier investigations.

More often than not, animals in general, and nonhuman primates in particular, have been stereotyped as low, brutish beings, and excluded from the community of beings worthy of moral respect in the same degree as humans. An important historical background to this attitude was the conviction that there is an absolute, rather than relative, distinction between humans and animals, one of an essential nature, not of gradual differences, to be found in the human mind. In the foregoing, we have been assuming that this is an incorrect view, and that therefore animals deserve more respect as knowing and feeling subjects. But is that really so? The presupposition that there are only gradual differences between humans and animals may seem plausible at first sight, perhaps even self-evident, but it is in fact contested and controversial, especially among philosophers.

While in the English-speaking world most philosophers would subscribe—or would at least be inclined to do so—to the idea of perhaps large, but ultimately gradual differences between humans and animals, most philosophers from the European continent would not underwrite the continuity of beasts and humans. A considerable number of continental philosophers operate in the wake of Aristotle or Descartes rather than that of Locke or Hume. They engage in Kantian criticism rather than evolutionary epistemology, in phenomenology or hermeneutics rather than naturalistic philosophy of mind. As different as these continental philosophical outlooks may be, they do have one thing in common: they all, in one way or another, draw a strict boundary line between animals and humans, and assume the gap between both is un-bridgeably wide.

They do so because, in the process of analysing according to their specific methods, they encounter a characteristic which in their eyes is uniquely human—reason, mind, rationality, intentionality, self-con-sciousness, or whatever term they use for it. They all see no possibility of fully accounting for this characteristic in terms of gradual differences or continuity with characteristics found in animals, the central nervous system, organic processes in general, or indeed anything three-dimen-sional and physical. In their eyes, the human, rational, self-conscious mind is a qualitatively different, irreducible phenomenon that gives to the entity which possesses it a very special place in nature compared to those who do not.

One typical and influential advocate of this point of view was the phenomenologist Max Scherer, who during the 1920s—like his German colleagues Martin Heidegger and Helmuth Plessner—tried to make sense of the first experiments on the cognitive abilities of chimpanzees, conducted by the German biologist Wolfgang Köhler. Scheler argued that although chimpanzees are intelligent, their behaviour and percep-tions are still determined directly and fully by their instinctive impulses and needs. Therefore, they are not 'open to the world'—*weltoffen*. They have not entered that dimension of existence in which it is possible to know the (things of the) world as such—cut loose from meanings lent by instincts, such as being edible, being dangerous or providing shelter and, concurrently, in the same movement of mind, to know oneself as such. Conscious apes, Scheler holds, are not present to themselves in the way self-conscious humans are, and their behaviour comes about in a mechanical way rather than by free choice.

Philosophical positions of this type are defended by many, with sophisticated and elaborate arguments. It is too easy simply to discard such interpretations of animal subjectivity as an ideology justifying our exploitation of animals. Addressing and refuting the arguments is a bet-ter strategy. Scheler's argument that apes do not know the things of the world as such, for instance, is, among other things, based on the as-sumption that they are not able to transfer or translate information from one sensory modality (e.g. auditory) to another (e.g. tactile or vi-sual), or to integrate information available in several sensory modalities into an awareness of one underlying thing in the world to which all these different data pertain. Recent research, however, has shown that apes are very well able to make such transfers, which refutes at least this line of argument. As to its moral side, even if philosophical positions such as Max Scheler's turn out to be right, it does not follow automati-cally that humans deserve more respect because they are rational and self-conscious.

Most of traditional philosophy has not reflected upon real ani-mals, but upon malignant stereotypes which turned the animals into brutish monsters. Therefore it is necessary to rethink our conceptions of animals, especially apes, philosophically and morally, in the light of new empirical knowledge now available showing that apes are more similar to us than we have ever realised and would ever have dared to realise. Apes may well turn out to be human in terms of several traditional components of that concept, such as the possession of self-consciousness and a free will.

From Raymond Corbey, "Ambiguous Apes."

GEORGE SANTAYANA

"Three American Philosophers"

George Santayana (1863–1952), born in Spain and raised in America, was a
metaphysician and aesthetician.

George Santayana writes of his own career as an American philosopher as he compares himself to James and Dewey.

The Article in the November issue of *Humana* on "Spirito e Orientamento della Filosofia in America," excellent on its general theme, prompts me to add something concerning the special characters, backgrounds, and doctrines of the three persons considered.

It is only John Dewey who genuinely represents the mind of the vast mass of native, sanguine, enterprising Americans. He alone has formed a philosophic sect and become a dominant academic influence. He inherits the Puritan conscience, grown duly practical, democratic, and positivistic; and he accepts industrial society and scientific technique as the field where true philosophy may be cultivated and tested.

Dewey is a native of Vermont, the most rural and retired of the New England States, where philosophy was represented in his youth mainly by popular preachers; but his critical mind at once rejected all that seemed myth or dogma, and adopted the general outlook of Hegel, whom he still praises for his breadth of view. This initial attachment is important because it explains how society and history may be regarded as composing the reality ultimately to be appealed to in philosophy; the physical world and the individual mind may then be dismissed as conventional and specious units, what Hegel called abstractions. For Hegel, society and history composed the "Phenomenology of Spirit"; but Spirit is not mentioned by Dewey, and the panorama of the world remains the ever varying subject matter of knowledge, a panorama floating and growing in its own medium.

In middle life, Dewey passed to Chicago where he founded his school of pragmatic or instrumental logic; the atmosphere could not have been more radically practical and realistic. But the value of pure disinterested speculation was duly acknowledged, because out of its apparently most useless flights important practical results may follow unexpectedly, as from the relativity of Einstein or the splitting of the atom.

Later, passing to New York, Dewey became a leader also in humanitarian and political movements, even far away from America, in

China or in the Russia of Trotsky. From the centre of capitalist and imperialistic America he seemed to diffuse a contrary purely humanitarian influence; yet with a special qualification. Luxury and inequality were indeed to be deprecated: on the other hand, ignorance and poverty were to be extirpated all the world over. To remain simple peasants from generation to generation was not to be allowed. The whole world must be raised to American standards.

I think we may fairly say that in Dewey, devotion to the distinctly modern and American subject matter of social experience has caused him to ignore two prior realities which the existence of that experience presupposes. One reality is the material world in which this experience arises and by which its development is controlled. The other reality is the transcendental spirit by which that whole dramatic process is witnessed, reconsidered, and judged. His system therefore may be called a social moralism, without cosmology and without psychological analysis.

In William James, on the contrary, who jointly with Dewey was the apostle of pragmatism, psychological analysis was the high court of appeal. His breeding and background were those of a man of the world and largely European, his education irregular, and his interests manifold. At first he wished to be a painter, then studied medicine, finally from medicine, or as a part of it, turned to psychiatry and psychology. In general philosophy he resisted the systematic Germans and followed the British empiricists, then represented by J. S. Mill. But there was another interest, contrary to a dry empiricism, which inwardly preoccupied him. His father was one of those independent American sages, in the style of Emerson and the Transcendentalists of New England, who possessed inarticulate profound insights and browsed on the mystic wisdom of all ages and countries. The son too had an irresistible intuition of spiritual freedom and, his wife being a Swedenborgian, was especially drawn to the study of psychical revelations. Ultimately he wrote his *Varieties of Religious Experience*—by far his most influential book—in which he showed his strong inclination to credit supernormal influences and the immortality of the soul. All this, however, was a somewhat troubled hope which he conscientiously tested by all available evidence; and his most trusted authorities were often French, Renouvier and later Bergson; thus the textbook in psychology which we had under him in 1883, at Harvard, was Taine's *De l'Intelligence*. It was only much later that he produced the sensational theories by which he is known, at least by hearsay, all the world over: his *Pragmatism*, in which the reality of truth seemed to be denied, and his article entitled "Does Consciousness Exist?" where he answered this question in the negative.

In that article James takes an important, if not the final, step in the phenomenalistic analysis of experience. If we reject matter with Berkeley and spirit with Hume, we have only data or phenomena with which to compose the universe. But the immense extent and dark detail of nature, as science conceives them, are not data for human beings; if we are to credit science, as pragmatism should, we must therefore admit that the world is composed of phenomena that are self-existent; and those that fall within the magnetic field of our action will form our minds, while the rest, equally selfexistent, will compose the rest of the universe. Things and ideas, on this view, are of the same stuff, but belong to different sequences or movements in nature. This system has been worked out later by Bertrand Russell and the school of "Logical Realists" or "Logical Analysts," and if it were found tenable would give William James a high place among modern philosophers.

As for me, it is only by accident that I am numbered among American philosophers. I cannot be classed otherwise, since I write in English and studied and taught for many years at Harvard College. My mother's older children by her first marriage were Americans on their father's side; and that fact caused my father to take me to Boston to be educated. But in feeling and in legal allegiance I have always remained a Spaniard. My first philosophical enthusiasm was for Catholic theology; I admired, and still admire, that magnificent construction and the spiritual discipline it can inspire; but I soon learned to admire also Hellenistic and Indian wisdom. All religions and moralities seem to me forms of paganism; only that in ages of ripe experience or of decadence they become penitential and subjective. When a student my *vade mecum* was Lucretius; and of modern philosophers I never intimately accepted any except Spinoza, and in a measure Schopenhauer, if we may take "Will" to be a metaphorical substitute for the automatism of nature, as when he says that the Will to Live of a possible child causes young people to fall in love. I cannot understand what satisfaction a philosopher can find in artifices, or in deceiving himself and others. I therefore like to call myself a materialist; but I leave the study and also the worship of matter to others, and my later writings have been devoted to discovering the natural categories of my spontaneous thought, and restating my opinions in those honest terms. It is essentially a literary labour, a form of art; and I do not attempt to drive other people to think as I do. Let them be their own poets.

From George Santayana, "Three American Philosophers."

REALITY

INTRODUCTION

What could be more obvious than our inhabiting a world teeming with things—tables, chairs, televisions, automobiles, pets, and other people? Even as I try to imagine that the world around me doesn't exist, I might receive a telephone call from a friend or bump up against a table leg. What then are philosophers up to when they pose metaphysical questions about the nature of existence?

Philosophers from the time of the early Greeks on have been attentive to the distinction between appearance and reality: the moon looks to be the size of a quarter, a stick that appears straight seems to bend when it is placed in water, a pool of water appears to be on the road ahead only to disappear as the observer draws closer. Once one acknowledges that what really exists—the objective realm—does not always correspond to appearances—the subjective realm—one gives a foothold to questions about the nature of being. If things aren't always as they appear, then what *really* does exist?

Deeply intertwined with the question of the nature of reality is the question of what route we should take to discover reality. The Greek philosopher Plato so distrusted the evidence of the senses that he completely rejected any reliance on sense experience in his quest to discover ultimate reality. Plato argues for a transcendent conception of reality and believes

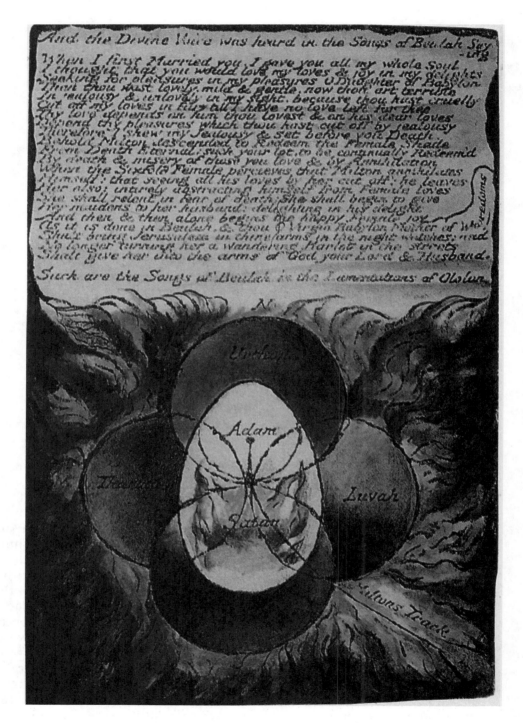

Illustration of the cosmos by William Blake in his *Milton*, 1804. The basic forces of mind, body, passion, and imagination surround a cosmic egg or realm of chaos and deception created by Satan and Adam.

that it is eternal essences, called Forms, that are the true existents. The flesh and blood horse that I think I see is but a mere appearance: what really exists is the essence of the horse, a non-physical substance which exists forever, never changing, knowable only through direct intellectual apprehension.

While Plato's view of reality might seem farfetched to those who, like John Dewey, take as a starting point the common sense view of the physical world, an integral part of the common sense view—modern science—can itself lead to some thorny problems concerning the nature of being. Common sense tells us that three-dimensional physical objects exist: we see them; we touch them. But doesn't science "tell us" that these three-dimensional physical objects are nothing but collections of molecules in motion (and that the molecules themselves are made up of even smaller units)? So, do the three-dimensional physical objects really exist after all, or are they "mere appearances" of a reality that we can't perceive directly?

One way to avoid such puzzles is to follow the line taken by philosophers called *idealists* who deny that there is any reality beyond the realm of appearance. In the words of the eighteenth-century idealist, George Berkeley, *esse est percipi*—to be is to be perceived. According to these thinkers, physical objects do not really exist independently of our experience of them; physical objects are collections of sense experiences. So, the "reality" of a table, for an idealist, is nothing but the range of experiences perceivers have of the table!

If you think that the idealists have gone "too far" when they reduce all of reality to appearance, you might find more congenial the view of *common sense realism*, espoused by the English philosopher G. E. Moore and by Ludwig Wittgenstein in his later work. The idea that physical objects and persons have objective existence is, according to Wittgenstein, part of the "bedrock" of our lives and is so firmly embedded in our way of looking at the world that we cannot intelligibly reject their existence. But is a commitment to "common sense" nothing more than a reliance on a well-accepted, traditional way of looking at the world? Might there not be other "world views," taken by other groups of people, which have a very different notion of the commonsensical? See, for example, the selection from Benjamin Lee Whorf, where he suggests that the Hopi Indians had no concepts for space and time, certainly two "bedrock" notions in "our" way of looking at the world. And, once we accept the idea that there can be more than one way of conceptualizing "reality," is there any sense to be made of thinking that just one of those ways of looking at reality is the correct way?

And, even if we remain steadfast to our familiar view of the world, questions will still remain. Our worldview would have us rely on our sensory experiences to find out what exists in the world; to paraphrase Samuel Johnson, if I stub my toe on a rock, the rock exists. But are there things that exist that cannot be captured by sense experience? Does God exist? Since God is not a physical object, we can't in any literal sense see or touch God. What kinds of evidence or argument are needed to establish the existence of entities like God that lie outside the range of sensory experience?

Questions of these sort concern not only objects and beings external to yourself, but they concern your very nature as well. It is obvious from the perspective of common sense that you have a body. (Just call to mind last time you over-exercised or over-indulged in food or drink: your body, doubtless, made itself felt.) But are you just a body; are you "nothing but" a complex, highly sophisticated physical organism? Is there some part of your self that cannot be reduced to your physical being? Do you have a soul that is not itself physical? If there are souls, who has them? *Mind-body dualists* believe that a person's consciousness and core self is "housed" in the mind or soul and believe that the soul is a nonphysical substance. You will find two quite different arguments for dualism in the selections from Descartes and Moody. Opposed to the dualists are the *mind-body materialists* who believe consciousness and the core self are all ultimately to be explained in physical terms. The selection from Carol Zaleski should give you a taste of how a materialist would try to grapple with some of the arguments of the dualist. The selection from Morris Berman reveals the moral importance of determining what beings have souls and what is at stake if we believe that nonhuman animals do not have souls.

CHARLES SANDERS PEIRCE
Reality Is What the Community of Thinkers Agrees Upon

Charles Sanders Peirce is convinced that science provides the best method for arriving at the truth. Other methods, including the methods of tenacity and authority (and the related a priori *method) impede inquiry. In Peirce's view, there will be a time when all of the evidence is in and the community of thinkers can form an opinion, the final opinion, which is reality. Until then, we can still think about what is real in terms of what we continue to affirm as true.*

This conception of reality is so familiar that it is unnecessary to dwell upon it; but the other, or realist conception, if less familiar, is even more natural and obvious. All human thought and opinion contains an arbitrary, accidental element, dependent on the limitations in circumstances, power, and bent of the individual; an element of error, in short. But human opinion universally tends in the long run to a definite form, which is the truth. Let any human being have enough information and exert enough thought upon any question, and the result will be that he will arrive at a certain definite conclusion, which is the same that any other mind will reach under sufficiently favorable circumstances. Suppose two men, one deaf, the other blind. One hears a man declare he means to kill another, hears the report of the pistol, and hears the victim cry; the other sees the murder done. Their sensations are affected in the highest degree with their individual peculiarities. The first information that their sensations will give them, their first inferences, will be more nearly alike, but still different; the one having, for example, the idea of a man shouting, the other of a man with a threatening aspect; but their final conclusions, the thought the remotest from sense, will be identical and free from the one-sidedness of their idiosyncrasies. There is, then, to every question a true answer, a final conclusion, to which the opinion of every man is constantly gravitating. He may for a time recede from it, but give him more experience and time for consideration, and he will finally approach it. The individual may not live to reach the truth; there is a residuum of error in every individual's opinions. No matter; it remains that there is a definite opinion to which the mind of man is, on the whole and in the long run, tending. On many questions the final agreement is already reached, on all it will be reached if time enough is given. The arbitrary will or other individual peculiarities of a sufficiently large number of minds may postpone the general agreement in that opinion indefinitely; but it cannot affect what the character of that opinion shall be when it is reached. This final opinion, then, is independent, not indeed of thought in general, but of all that is arbitrary and individual in thought; is quite independent of how you, or I, or any number of men think.

Everything, therefore, which will be thought to exist in the final opinion is real, and nothing else.

From C. S. Peirce, "Critical Review of Berkeley's Idealism."

To satisfy our doubts, therefore, it is necessary that a method should be found by which our beliefs may be determined by nothing human, but by some external permanency—by something upon which our thinking has no effect. Some mystics imagine that they have such a method in a private inspiration from on high. But that is only a form of the method of tenacity, in which the conception of truth as something public is not yet developed. Our external permanency would not be external, in our sense, if it was restricted in its influence to one individual. It must be something which affects, or might affect, every man. And, though these affections are necessarily as various as are individual conditions, yet the method must be such that the ultimate conclusion of every man shall be the same. Such is the method of science. Its fundamental hypothesis, restated in more familiar language, is this: There are Real things, whose characters are entirely independent of our opinions about them; those Reals affect our senses according to regular laws, and, though our sensations are as different as are our relations to the objects, yet, by taking advantage of the laws of perception, we can ascertain by reasoning how things really and truly are; and any man, if he have sufficient experience and he reason enough about it, will be led to the one True conclusion. The new conception here involved is that of Reality.

From C. S. Peirce, "The Fixation of Belief."

And what do we mean by the real? It is a conception which we must first have had when we discovered that there was an unreal, an illusion; that is, when we first corrected ourselves. Now the distinction for which alone this fact logically called, was between an *ens* relative to private inward determinations, to the negations belonging to idiosyncrasy, and an *ens* such as would stand in the long run. The real, then, is that which, sooner or later, information and reasoning would finally result in, and which is therefore independent of the vagaries of me and you. Thus, the very origin of the conception of reality shows that this conception essentially involves the notion of a community, without definite limits, and capable of a definite increase of knowledge. And so those two series of cognitions—the real and the unreal—consist of those which, at a time sufficiently future, the community will always continue to re-affirm; and of those which, under the same conditions, will ever after be denied.

From C. S. Peirce, "Some Consequences of Four Incapacities."

WILLIAM JAMES
Reality Is What Truths Have to Take Account of

William James develops his idea that reality is what truths must take account of by identifying three parts of reality—our sensations, their relations, and previous truths. Vital to understanding such a conception of reality is his pragmatic conception of truth as being what we can validate, corroborate, and assimilate and as having a cash-in value for our experience.

"*R*eality" is in general what truths have to take account of; and the *first* part of reality from this point of view is the flux of our sensations. Sensations are forced upon us, coming we know not whence. Over their nature, order and quantity we have as good as no control. . . . *They* are neither true nor false; they simply *are.* It is only what we say about them, only the names we give them, our theories of their source and nature and remote relations, that may be true or not.

The *second* part of reality, as something that our beliefs must also obediently take account of is the *relations* that obtain between our sensations or between their copies in our minds. This part falls into two subparts: 1) the relations that are mutable and accidental, as those of date and place; and 2) those that are fixed and essential because they are grounded on the inner natures of their terms. Both sorts of relation are matters of immediate perception. Both are 'facts.' But it is the latter kind of fact that forms the more important subpart of reality for our theories of knowledge. Inner relations namely are 'eternal,' are perceived whenever their sensible terms are compared; and of them our thought—mathematical and logical thought so-called—must eternally take account.

The *third* part of reality, additional to these perceptions (though largely based upon them), is the *previous truths* of which every new inquiry takes account. This third part is a much less obdurately resisting factor: it often ends by giving way. In speaking of these three portions of reality as at all times controlling our belief's formation, I am only reminding you of what we heard in our last hour.

From William James, *Pragmatism.*

Pragmatism, on the other hand, asks its usual question. "Grant an idea or belief to be true," it says, "what concrete difference will its being true make in any one's actual life? How will the truth be realized? What experiences will be different from those which would obtain if the belief were false? What, in short, is the truth's cash-value in experiential terms?"

The moment pragmatism asks this question, it sees the answer: *True ideas are those that we can assimilate, validate, corroborate and verify. False ideas are those that we can not.* That is the practical difference it makes to us to have true ideas; that, therefore, is the meaning of truth, for it is all that truth is known-as.

This thesis is what I have to defend. The truth of an idea is not a stagnant property inherent in it. Truth happens to an idea. It *becomes* true, is *made* true by events. Its verity *is* in fact an event, a process: the process namely of its verifying itself, its veri-*fication*. Its validity is the process of its valid-*ation*.

But what do the words verification and validation themselves pragmatically mean? They again signify certain practical consequences of the verified and validated idea. It is hard to find any one phrase that characterizes these consequences better than the ordinary agreement-formula—just such consequences being what we have in mind whenever we say that our ideas 'agree' with reality. They lead us, namely, through the acts and other ideas which they instigate, into or up to, or towards, other parts of experience with which we feel all the while—such feeling being among our potentialities—that the original ideas remain in agreement. The connexions and transitions come to us from point to point as being progressive, harmonious, satisfactory. This function of agreeable leading is what we mean by an idea's verification. Such an account is vague and it sounds at first quite trivial, but it has results which it will take the rest of my hour to explain.

From William James, *Pragmatism.*

JOHN DEWEY

Science Doesn't Have the Last or Only Word on What Is Real

According to John Dewey, philosophy has been of great disservice to the human race when it depicts reality as a higher realm which is independent of human experience. He advises that philosophy can learn something from science which thoroughly integrates its claims about what is real with experimentation in the world of human experience. Still, we cannot conceive the scientist as the only person who makes claims about the real. As we explore the possibilities of science for daily life, we get not only a fuller sense of what is real but also confirm in a deeper way the findings of the scientist.

The division of the world into two kinds of Being, one superior, accessible only to reason and ideal in nature, the other inferior, material, changeable, empirical, accessible to sense-observation, turns inevitably into the idea that knowledge is contemplative in nature. It assumes a contrast between theory and practice which was all to the disadvantage of the latter. But in the actual course of the development of science, a tremendous change has come about. When the practice of knowledge ceased to be dialectical and became experimental, knowing became preoccupied with changes and the test of knowledge became the ability to bring about certain changes. Knowing, for the experimental sciences, means a certain kind of intelligently conducted doing; it ceases to be contemplative and becomes in a true sense practical. Now this implies that philosophy, unless it is to undergo a complete break with the authorized spirit of science, must also alter its nature. It must assume a practical nature; it must become operative and experimental.

From John Dewey, *Reconstruction in Philosophy*.

And assuredly any philosophy which takes science to be not an *account* of the world (which it is), but a literal and exhaustive apprehension of it in its full reality, a philosophy which therefore has no place for poetry or possibilities, still needs a theory of experience. . . .

There is then a great difference between the entities of science and the things of daily life. . . .

The "real" or "true" objects of science are those which best fulfil the demands of secure and fertile inference. To arrive at them is such a difficult operation, there are so many specious candidates clamoring for the office, that it is no wonder that when the objects suitable for inference are constituted, they tend to impose themselves as *the* real objects, in comparison with which the things of ordinary life are but impressions made upon us (according to much modern thought), or defective samples of Being—according to much of ancient thought. . . .

The entities of science are not only *from* the scientist; they are also for him. They express, that is, not only the outcome of reflective inquiries, but express them in the particular form in which they can enter most directly and efficiently into subsequent inquiries. The fact that they are sustained within the universe of inquiry accounts for their remoteness from the things of daily life. . . .

But lest the man of science, the man of dominantly reflective habits, be puffed up with his own conceits, he must bear in mind that practical application—that is, experiment—is a condition of his own calling, that it is indispensable to the institution of knowledge or truth. Consequently, in order that he keep his own balance, it is needed that his findings be everywhere applied. The more their application is confined within his own special calling, the less meaning do the conceptions possess, and the more exposed they are to error. The widest possible range of application is the means of the deepest verification. As long as the specialist hugs his own results they are vague in meaning and unsafe in content. That individuals in every branch of human endeavor should be experimentalists engaged in testing the findings of the theorist is the sole final guaranty for the sanity of the theorist.

From John Dewey, *Essays in Experimental Logic.*

JANE ADDAMS

The Art of Children Offers New Ways of Seeing the World Because Children Are Better in Tune with Nature

Jane Addams recounts her experiences with children in art classes at Hull-House. She credits them with wonderful imaginations and an ability to invigorate the world as they show it from their fresh perspectives. Addams employs Dewey's insight, that it is natural for children to create imaginative worlds and dwell in them sometimes for weeks, to justify the many opportunities which Hull-House provides children for artistic expression. But she presses beyond the notion that these worlds are strictly imaginative as she quotes from the diary of one of her teachers at Hull-House.

Because the modern industrial city is so new, we are as yet ignorant of its ultimate reactions upon human life, and we know little of the impressions and even of the scars which this new type of living makes upon that most highly sensitized material, the body and mind of the young at the moment they are most acutely alive to their surroundings. We only know that young people, with their new-born instincts, whether walking in crowded streets or in the open fields, continually test the achievements and shortcomings of the life about them by standards of romance—new to them but as old as the world.

Because the youth of Chicago have been brought together from all parts of the world into one cosmopolitan community, in sentimental moments certain lines of Swinburne seem so appropriate that we can almost imagine them chanting together:

We mix from many lands
We march from very far
The light we walk in
Darkens sun and moon and star.

We realize afresh that it is the business of youth to reaffirm the beauty and joy in the world that such spontaneity may become a source of new vitality, a wellspring of refreshment to a jaded city. It is easy to fail to utilize it, the artists are preoccupied trying to recapture it after the first bloom has escaped them and only occasionally do the educators demonstrate that each child lives not only in an actual environment visible to all, but in enchanted surroundings which may be reproduced by the child himself.

The early School of Education at the University of Chicago, founded by Dr. John Dewey, demonstrated that a child after an historic period had made itself at home in his imagination would wholeheartedly live in it for weeks at a time. He energetically dug, built, wove and cooked, sometimes according to his need in a primitive hut, at other times in a medieval castle surrounded by a moat. But because this fresh imaginative life with its instinct for play is in a sense the mission of art itself we have found at Hull-House that our educational efforts tend constantly toward a training for artistic expression; in a music school, a school of dramatics, classes in rhythm and dancing and the school of the plastic and graphic arts. . . .

One of the younger teachers considers it her chief business to discover and remove inhibitions, because she finds that joy is the most important factor in freeing the child's expression, she has apparently discovered with Count Keyserling, that an inhibited artist is of no use in the practical world. Norah Hamilton, the head of our little art school, says that if such artistic children have no early outlet for their gifts they may never find a real place in the world about them and their possible contribution will be lost. She further adds:

The children seem to find in their inner lives a world of color and beauty in which they are perfectly at home. They work with freedom and endless facility, with faith in their own way of seeing, and with faith in hands and material to carry out their vision. They give their best, and take it for granted that what they give is good. They are free from our inhibitions, use their full selves and make use also, perhaps, of an instinctive self. They give the reality as it comes to them but the reality is living and filled with the spirit of play, that "other seeing" that finds the play world as real as the material world "peopled with psychic beings kin to them," as were the hills and streams to the Greeks, the kings of all artists. To sum up the charm of the children's work, they give us a new world seen with new eyes. Perhaps, with the great primitives, they follow nature's very ways, are close to her rhythm; perhaps obey some law inherent in things as they are.

From Jane Addams, *The Second Twenty Years at Hull-House.*

PLATO

Reality Is a Realm of Essences

Plato (c. 430–350 B.C.E.), the Greek philosopher who was a student of Socrates and teacher of Aristotle, is one of the most influential thinkers in the Western tradition.

Plato's view of reality is an excellent example of the type of worldview which Dewey found faulty. Dewey was critical of any metaphysics which separated reality from human experience as Plato's does. Plato thinks of our world of sensory experience as being mere appearance. What is real is a realm of essences or forms or ideas. In effect these are concepts, like justice, truth, and beauty, which exist external to the mind. Our natural world is a reflection of these real essences. We are wise, for example, to the extent that we participate in the form of wisdom. Plato uses an allegory to convince people of this view of reality. He compares prisoners in a dark cave who have never seen the light of day to those of us who have never been in contact with the forms and think that reality is our world of sense experience. In another passage, we learn that it is only at death, when our souls leave our bodies and are no longer distracted by our bodies, that we can best perceive these ideas.

And now, I said, let me show in a figure how far our nature is enlightened or unenlightened:—Behold! human beings living in an underground den, which has a mouth open towards the light and reaching all along the den; here they have been from their childhood, and have their legs and necks chained so that they cannot move, and can only see before them, being prevented by the chains from turning round their heads. Above and behind them a fire is blazing at a distance, and between the fire and the prisoners there is a raised way; and you will see, if you look, a low wall built along the way, like the screen which marionette players have in front of them, over which they show the puppets.

I see.

And do you see, I said, men passing along the wall carrying all sorts of vessels, and statues and figures of animals made of wood and stone and various materials, which appear over the wall? Some of them are talking, others, silent.

You have shown me a strange image, and they are strange prisoners.

Like ourselves, I replied; and they see only their own shadows, or the shadows of one another, which the fire throws on the opposite wall of the cave?

True, he said; how could they see anything but the shadows if they were never allowed to move their heads?

And of the objects which are being carried in like manner they would only see the shadows?

Yes, he said.

And if they were able to converse with one another, would they not suppose that they were naming what was actually before them?

Very true.

And suppose further that the prison had an echo which came from the other side, would they not be sure to fancy when one of the passers-by spoke that the voice which they heard came from the passing shadow?

No question, he replied.

To them, I said, the truth would be literally nothing but the shadows of the images.

That is certain.

And now look again, and see what will naturally follow if the prisoners are released and disabused of their error. At first, when any of them is liberated and compelled suddenly to stand up and turn his neck round and walk and look towards the light, he will suffer sharp pains; the glare will distress him, and he will be unable to see the realities of which in his former state he had seen the shadows; and then conceive some one saying to him, that what he saw before was an illusion, but that now, when he is approaching nearer to being and his eye is turned towards more real existence, he has a clearer vision,—what will be his reply? And you may further imagine that his instructor is pointing to the objects as they pass and requiring him to name them,— will he not be perplexed? Will he not fancy that the shadows which he formerly saw are truer than the objects which are now shown to him?

Far truer.

And if he is compelled to look straight at the light, will he not have a pain in his eyes which will make him turn away to take refuge in the objects of vision which he can see, and which he will conceive to be in reality clearer than the things which are now being shown to him?

True, he said.

And suppose once more, that he is reluctantly dragged up a steep and rugged ascent, and held fast until he is forced into the presence of the sun himself, is he not likely to be pained and irritated? When he approaches the light his eyes will be dazzled, and he will not be able to see anything at all of what are now called realities.

Not all in a moment, he said.

He will require to grow accustomed to the sight of the upper world. And first he will see the shadows best, next the reflections of men and other objects in the water, and then the objects themselves; then he will gaze upon the light of the moon and the stars and the spangled heaven; and he will see the sky and the stars by night better than the sun or the light of the sun by day?

Certainly.

Last of all he will be able to see the sun, and not mere reflections of him in the water, but he will see him in his own proper place, and not in another; and he will contemplate him as he is.

Certainly.

He will then proceed to argue that this is he who gives the season and the years, and is the guardian of all that is in the visible world, and in a certain way the cause of all things which he and his fellows have been accustomed to behold?

Clearly, he said, he would first see the sun and then reason about him.

And when he remembered his old habitation, and the wisdom of the den and his fellow-prisoners, do you not suppose that he would felicitate himself on the change, and pity them?

Certainly, he would.

And if they were in the habit of conferring honours among themselves on those who were quickest to observe the passing shadows and to remark which of them went before, and which followed after, and which were together; and who were therefore best able to draw conclusions as to the future, do you think that he would care for such honours and glories, or envy the possessors of them? Would he not say with Homer,

'Better to be the poor servant of a poor master,' and to endure anything, rather than think as they do and live after their manner?

Yes, he said, I think that he would rather suffer anything than entertain these false notions and live in this miserable manner. Imagine once more, I said, such a one coming suddenly out of the sun to be replaced in his old situation; would he not be certain to have his eyes full of darkness?

To be sure, he said.

And if there were a contest, and he had to compete in measuring the shadows with the prisoners who had never moved out of the den, while his sight was still weak, and before his eyes had become steady (and the time which would be needed to acquire this new habit of sight might be very considerable), would he not be ridiculous? Men would say of him that up he went and down he came without his eyes; and that it was better not even to think of ascending; and if any one tried to loose another and lead him up to the light, let them only catch the offender, and they would put him to death.

No question, he said.

This entire allegory, I said, you may now append, dear Glaucon, to the previous argument; the prison-house is the world of sight, the light of the fire is the sun, and you will not misapprehend me if you interpret the journey upwards to be the ascent of the soul into the intellectual world according to my poor belief, which, at your desire, I have expressed—whether rightly or wrongly God knows. But, whether true or false, my opinion is that in the world of knowledge the idea of good appears last of all, and is seen only with an effort; and, when seen, is also inferred to be the universal author of all things beautiful and right, parent of light and of the lord of light in this visible world, and the immediate source of reason and truth in the intellectual; and that this is the power upon which he who would act rationally either in public or private life must have his eye fixed.

From Plato, *The Republic*.

And now, 0 my judges, I desire to prove to you that the real philosopher has reason to be of good cheer when he is about to die, and that after death he may hope to obtain the greatest good in the other world. And how this may be, Simmias and Cebes, I will endeavour to explain. For I deem that the true votary of philosophy is likely to be misunderstood by other men; they do not perceive that he is always pursuing death and dying; and if this be so, and he has had the desire of death all his life long, why when his time comes should he repine at that which he has been always pursuing and desiring?

Simmias said laughingly: Though not in a laughing humour, you have made me laugh, Socrates; for I cannot help thinking that the many when they hear your words will say how truly you have described philosophers, and our people at home will likewise say that the life which philosophers desire is in reality death, and that they have found them out to be deserving of the death which they desire.

And they are right, Simmias, in thinking so, with the exception of the words 'they have found them out'; for they have not found out either what is the nature of that death which the true philosopher deserves, or how he deserves or desires death. But enough of them:—let us discuss the matter among ourselves. Do we believe that there is such a thing as death?

To be sure, replied Simmias.

Is it not the separation of soul and body? And to be dead is the completion of this; when the soul exists in herself, and is released from the body and the body is released from the soul, what is this but death?

Just so, he replied.

There is another question, which will probably throw light on our present enquiry if you and I can agree about it:—Ought the philosopher to care about the pleasures—if they are to be called pleasures—of eating and drinking?

Certainly not, answered Simmias.

And what about the pleasures of love—should he care for them?

By no means.

And will he think much of the other ways of indulging the body, for example, the acquisition of costly raiment, or sandals, or other adornments of the body? Instead of caring about them, does he not rather despise anything more than nature needs? What do you say? I should say that the true philosopher would despise them.

Would you not say that he is entirely concerned with the soul and not with the body? He would like, as far as he can, to get away from the body and to turn to the soul.

Quite true.

In matters of this sort philosophers, above all other men, may be observed in every sort of way to dissever the soul from the communion of the body.

Very true.

Whereas, Simmias, the rest of the world are of opinion that to him who has no sense of pleasure and no part in bodily pleasure, life is not worth having; and that he who is indifferent about them is as good as dead.

That is also true.

What again shall we say of the actual acquirement of knowledge—is the body, if invited to share in the enquiry, a hinderer or a helper? I mean to say, have sight and hearing any truth in them? Are they not, as the poets are always telling us, inaccurate witnesses? and yet, if even they are inaccurate and indistinct, what is to be said of the other senses?—for you will allow that they are the best of them?

Certainly, he replied.

Then when does the soul attain truth—for in attempting to consider anything in company with the body she is obviously deceived.

True.

Then must not true existence be revealed to her in thought, if it, all?

Yes.

And thought is best when the mind is gathered into herself and none of these things trouble her—neither sounds nor sights nor pain nor any pleasure,—when she takes leave of the body, and has as little as possible to do with it, when she has no bodily sense or desire, but is aspiring after true being?

Certainly.

And in this the philosopher dishonours the body; his soul runs away from his body and desires to be alone and by herself?

That is true.

Well, but there is another thing, Simmias: Is there or is there not an absolute justice?

Assuredly there is.

And an absolute beauty and absolute good?

Of course.

But did you ever behold any of them with your eyes?

Certainly not.

Or did you ever reach them with any other bodily sense?—and I speak not of these alone, but of absolute greatness, and health, and strength, and of the essence or true nature of everything. Has the reality of them ever been perceived by you through the bodily organs? or rather, is not the nearest approach to the knowledge of their several natures made by him who so orders his intellectual vision as to have the most exact conception of the essence of each thing which he considers?

Native American rock art. Detail of Anthropomorphs on San Juan River at Butler Wash.

Certainly.

And he attains to the purest knowledge of them who goes to each with the mind alone, not introducing or intruding in the act of thought sight or any other sense together with reason, but with the very light of the mind in her own clearness searches into the very truth of each; he who has got rid, as far as he can, of eyes and ears and, so to speak, of the whole body, these being in his opinion distracting elements which when they infect the soul hinder her from acquiring truth and knowledge—who, if not he, is likely to attain to the knowledge of true being?

What you say has a wonderful truth in it, Socrates, replied Simmias.

From Plato, *Phaedo*, translated by B. Jowett.

RENÉ DESCARTES

Reality Consists of Mental and Physical Substances, and the Two Substances Are Connected in Us

René Descartes (1596–1650) is a French philosopher and mathematician cited as the "father of modern philosophy."

We saw in Chapter 1 how René Descartes's method of doubt led him to his cogito *and to a recognition of the connection between his thinking and his existence. Ultimately Descartes settles on the reality of two very different substances—mind, a thinking thing which has none of the properties of physical objects like length and depth, and body, which does have such properties. Descartes sees himself as being both mind and body and determines that these very different substances in fact connect in the human being.*

Lately I have become accustomed to withdrawing my mind from the senses, and I have carefully taken note of the fact that very few things are truly perceived regarding corporeal things, although a great many more things are known regarding the human mind, and still many more things regarding God. The upshot is that I now have no difficulty directing my thought away from things that can be imagined to things that can be grasped only by the understanding and are wholly separate from matter. In fact the idea I clearly have of the human mind—insofar as it is a thinking thing, not extended in length, breadth or depth, and having nothing else from the body—is far more distinct than the idea of any corporeal thing. . . .

By means of these sensations of pain, hunger, thirst and so on, nature also teaches not merely that I am present to my body in the way a sailor is present in a ship, but that I am most tightly joined and, so to speak, commingled with it, so much so that I and the body constitute one single thing. For if this were not the case, then I, who am only a thinking thing, would not sense pain when the body is injured; rather, I would perceive the wound by means of the pure intellect, just as a sailor perceives by sight whether anything in his ship is broken. And when the body is in need of food or drink, I should understand this explicitly, instead of having confused sensations of hunger and thirst. For clearly these sensations of thirst, hunger, pain, and so on are nothing but certain confused modes of thinking arising from the union and, as it were, the commingling of the mind with the body.

From René Descartes, *Meditations on First Philosophy*, translated by Donald A. Cress.

MORRIS BERMAN

Non-Human Animals Are Not Mindless Machines

Morris Berman (1944–   ) is a writer, cultural historian and social critic.

Morris Berman argues that Descartes's dualism, which positions mind and body as different substances, has led historically to the classification of non-human animals as mindless machines. Such a view ignores the ability of animals to experience pleasure and pain and opens the door to cruel experimentation on them.

Perhaps the central feature of the shift from a medieval to a modern or from a sacred to a secular one, was the rise of what has been called the mechanical philosophy, the idea that everything in the world, from atoms to galaxies, is composed of material particles and operates on the model of a machine. This change of outlook is, philosophically speaking, the most obvious characteristic of seventeenth-century thought. There is no reason why animals should have been exempted from this worldview, and in fact, they were especially vulnerable to it. According to that great mechanistic thinker, René Descartes, animals were nothing more than automata; they did not suffer pain any more than did a clock. From this time on, experimentation of live animals became widespread in western Europe. If animals were nothing more than clocks, their suffering could be dismissed as mere noise, and they were routinely nailed to boards for vivisection or for illustrating anatomical facts such as the circulation of the blood. The nineteenth century saw the rise of animal protection societies, partly in reaction to this. Apparently, the first antivivisection society in Europe was founded by the wife and daughter of the famous experimental biologist Claude Bernard, following their discovery that the good doctor had vivisected the family dog. Bernard regarded any discussion of animal suffering as totally unscientific, and therefore as being beneath any serious consideration; and despite the rise of animal protection societies, that attitude continues to be the dominant (or "official") mode of thought in the West. Peter Singer, who has documented the torture of animals carried out in the name of scientific progress, states that it is in the twentieth century that we probably inflict more pain on animals than at any other time in history—and this includes the period of the Roman Empire, when animals were routinely slaughtered in gladiatorial combats for popular entertainment. As Singer points out, millions upon millions of animals are routinely tortured every year in the United States and Europe within the framework of experiments that are motivated by nothing more than goalless curiosity—i.e., in experiments that haven't the remotest prospect of any medical or scientific benefits. Many more experiments are carried out for commercial purposes, such as the testing of cosmetics or food coloring agents. And both types of experiments are frequently barbaric, involving prolonged electric shocks, techniques for making animals crazy or depressed, starvation, poisoning, heating to death, and so on.

From Morris Berman, *Coming to Our Senses*.

DONNA HARAWAY
We Are All Cyborgs

Donna Haraway (1944–) is a scientist, philosopher of science, and cultural critic.

Donna Haraway calls into question not only Descartes's distinction between ensouled beings (humans) and brutes (non-human animals) but also the distinction between organisms and artifacts. She claims that we human beings engage in a distortive mythology by regarding ourselves as wholly distinct from the machine realm; we are all cyborgs—a combination of machine and organism.

A cyborg is a cybernetic organism, a hybrid of machine and organism, a creature of social reality as well as a creature of fiction. . . . Contemporary science fiction is full of cyborg-creatures simultaneously animal and machine, who populate worlds ambiguously natural and crafted. Modern medicine is also full of cyborgs, of couplings between organism and machine, each conceived as coded devices, in an intimacy and with a power that was not generated in the history of sexuality. . . . By the late twentieth century, our time, a mythic time, we are all chimeras, theorized and fabricated hybrids of machine and organism; in short, we are cyborgs. . . . The cyborg is a creature in a post-gender world; it has no truck with bisexuality, pre-oedipal symbiosis, unalienated labour, or other seductions to organic wholeness through a final appropriation of all the powers of the parts into a higher unity. In a sense, the cyborg has no origin story in the Western sense. . . . An origin story in the "Western" humanist sense depends on the myth of original unity, fullness, bliss and terror. . . . The cyborg is resolutely committed to partiality, irony, intimacy, and perversity. It is oppositional, utopian, and completely without innocence. . . .

By the late twentieth century in United States scientific culture, the boundary between human and animal is thoroughly breached. The last beachheads of uniqueness have been polluted if not turned into amusement parks—language, tool use, social behaviours, mental events, nothing really convincingly settles the separation of human and animal. And many people no longer feel the need for such a separation; indeed, many branches of feminist culture affirm the pleasure of connection of human and other living creatures. Movements for animal rights are not irrational denials of human uniqueness; they are a clear-sighted recognition of connection across the discredited breach of nature and culture. . . .

The second leaky distinction is between animal-human (organism) and machine. Pre-cybernetic machines could be haunted; there was always the spectre of the ghost in the machine. This dualism structured the dialogue between materialism and idealism that was settled by a dialectical progeny, called spirit or history, according to taste. But basically machines were not self-moving, self-designing, autonomous. They could not achieve man's dream, only mock it. They were not man, an author to himself, but only a caricature of that masculinist reproductive dream. To think they were otherwise was paranoid. Now we are not so sure. Late twentieth-century machines have made thoroughly ambiguous the difference between natural and artificial, mind and body, self-developing and externally designed, and many other distinctions that used to apply to organisms and machines. Our machines are disturbingly lively, and we ourselves are frighteningly inert. . . .

From one perspective, a cyborg world is about the final imposition of a grid of control on the planet, about the final abstraction embodied in a Star Wars apocalypse waged in the name of defence, about the final appropriation of women's bodies in a masculinist orgy of war. From another perspective, a cyborg world might be about lived social and bodily realities in which people are not afraid of their joint kinship with animals and machines, not afraid of permanently partial identities and contradictory standpoints. . . .

From Donna Haraway, "A Cyborg Manifesto: Science, Technology, and Socialist-Feminism in the Late Twentieth-Century."

Raymond Moody and Carol Zaleski

Do Near Death Experiences Confirm the Existence of the Immaterial Soul?

Raymond Moody (1944–) is an American physician and philosopher who has written extensively on near-death experiences.

Carol Zaleski (1950–) is an American religious scholar with a special interest in the nature of the afterlife.

Plato and Descartes both thought it made sense to think of the mind as an entity which is distinct from our bodies and physical substance. Do our minds continue to live and learn after our bodies die? Some people have turned to near-death experiences for confirmation of these teachings. In the first passage, Raymond Moody tells us about the typical account given by people who have had near-death experiences. In the second passage, Carol Zaleski evaluates the evidence.

From Moody's *Life After Life:*

Despite the wide variation in the circumstances surrounding close calls with death and in the types of persons undergoing them, it remains true that there is a striking similarity among the accounts of the experiences themselves. In fact, the similarities among various reports are so great that one can easily pick out about fifteen separate elements which recur again and again in the mass of narratives that I have collected. On the basis of these points of likeness, let me now construct a brief, theoretically "ideal" or "complete" experience which embodies all of the common elements, in the order in which it is typical for them to occur.

A man is dying and, as he reaches the point of greatest physical distress, he hears himself pronounced dead by his doctor. He begins to hear an uncomfortable noise, a loud ringing or buzzing, and at the same time feels himself moving very rapidly through a long dark tunnel. After this, he suddenly finds himself outside of his own physical body, but still in the immediate physical environment, and he sees his own body from a distance, as though he is a spectator. He watches the resuscitation attempt from this unusual vantage point and is in a state of emotional upheaval.

After a while, he collects himself and becomes more accustomed to his odd condition. He notices that he still has a "body," but one of a very different nature and with very different powers from the physical body he has left behind. Soon other things begin to happen. Others come to meet and to help him. He glimpses the spirits of relatives and friends who have already died, and a loving, warm spirit of a kind he has never encountered before—a being of light—appears before him. This being asks him a question, nonverbally, to make him evaluate his life and helps him along by showing him a panoramic, instantaneous playback of the major events of his life. At some point he finds himself approaching some sort of barrier or border, apparently representing the limit between earthly life and the next life. Yet, he finds that he must go back to the earth, that the time for his death has not yet come. At this point he resists, for by now he is taken up with his experiences in the afterlife and does not want to return. He is overwhelmed by intense feelings of joy, love, and peace. Despite his attitude, though, he somehow reunites with his physical body and lives.

Later he tries to tell others, but he has trouble doing so. In the first place, he can find no human words adequate to describe these unearthly episodes. He also finds that others scoff, so he stops telling other people. Still, the experience affects his life profoundly, especially his views about death and its relationship to life.

From Raymond Moody, *Life after Life.*

FROM ZALESKI'S *OTHERWORLD JOURNEYS:*

First, it will be helpful to review the main grounds on which the researchers argue for the validity of near-death experience. . . The researchers agree that the similarities of near-death reports are more striking than their differences and see this unanimity as a key to the validity of near-death experience. . . . Ring, arguing against the idea that near-death experience is dreamlike, comments that it is unlikely that "at the moment of (apparent) death everyone should dream fragments of a common dream." . . .What makes the apparent unanimity of near-death reports so impressive to the researchers is that it seems undisturbed by differences in cultural, medical, and demographic circumstances. . . . Near-death reports do not conform to individual or socially conditioned expectations. Osis and Haraldsson, among others, cite cases in which the content of the vision appears to conflict with the subject's professed desires, fears, or beliefs. . . . According to some investigators the presence of verified paranormal episodes is the best evidence for the extraordinary character of near-death experience. If a patient can accurately describe the events of his resuscitation, then his account of another world may be accurate too. In addition to veridical out-of-body reports, researchers point to the life review, with its time-defying simultaneity and rare precognitive flashes, and to the appearance of appropriate otherworld figures: the child who sees a dead uncle instead of the living parent he might like to imagine, or the patient who is surprised by the spirit of someone he did not know was dead. On the other hand, paranormal events are occasionally invoked as an argument against the out-of-body hypothesis. . . . Reports of lucidity and painlessness suggest to some interpreters that the subject was disengaged, at least partly, from his afflicted flesh. In addition, many investigators seem to believe, even if they do not say it explicitly, that near-death experience is evidence for a transcendent reality simply because it surpasses normal states of mind. Near-death reports convey an experience that is so profound, timeless, joyful, and revelatory as to seem self-endorsing; and some interpreters assume that for such a state of consciousness to occur there must be a special realm of existence that corresponds to it. . . . If the joyful and mystical insights of near-death experience can carry over into life, then that is a kind of evidence of its lasting validity. Thus, some investigators follow the time-honored principle of judging a revelation by moral and spiritual effects. This provides double reinforcement: as transforming effects witness to the soundness of the vision, so conviction that the vision was true helps to sustain the transformation.

Osis maintains that while the case for survival of death cannot be made on the basis of a single "crucial experiment," it is supported by the convergence of many different kinds of experimental evidence. . . . Similarly, some investigators consider the most telling argument for the extraordinary character of near-death experience to be the cumulative weight of the points made above and the inadequacy of any single "explanation" to account for all its features. Critics argue, on the other hand, that the combination of different kinds of evidence is no stronger than its weakest link. . . .

Unless Occam's razor has dulled, the responsible investigator will search diligently for natural explanations for unusual phenomena. If near-death visions can be explained as hallucinations, following standard etiology, then there is no need to resort to more exotic interpretations. On this both the near-death researchers and their critics agree; the question under debate is whether any adequate natural explanations exist. While the skeptics propose an abundance of physiological, pharmacological, and psychological solutions to the puzzle, the researchers resolutely defend the unexplained status of near-death experience; for every explanation, they offer a counterexplanation. . . .

Near-death visions are labeled hallucinatory on several grounds: (1) they occur under the influence of drugs, anesthetics, or stressful conditions that are known to trigger hallucination; (2) they display patterns of imagery similar to those found in hallucinations and dreams; (3) they fill psychological needs, mimic the symptoms of mental or emotional disorders, or reflect unconscious fantasies and drives.

It is undeniable that near-death experiences occur to patients under the influence of a wide range of medications, including tranquilizers, analgesics, anesthetics, insulin, steroids, psychoactive drugs, stimulants (such as adrenaline and amphetamine), and depressants (such as alcohol, barbiturates, and narcotics). Whether used for therapy, entertainment, or self-destruction, these drugs have the potential to bring on dissociative or visionary experience. . . .Yet . . . not all near-death subjects were under medication, and, in any case, the effects of different drugs vary endlessly. Since the critics, like the researchers, wish to find a comprehensive explanation for the recurrent features of near-death experience, they look to underlying physiological and psychological mechanisms as a source for visionary states.

If near-death reports cannot be explained by drugs alone, there is good reason to consider other toxic conditions that may have hallucinogenic effects. No matter how lucid the subject feels, if he is physically on the point of death, then he is bound to suffer from some kind of metabolic disturbance, whether it be fever, exhaustion, trauma, infection, liver poisoning, uremia, or blood gas imbalance. Any one of these conditions can be a potent source of delirium and delusion; but the critics most often cite oxygen deprivation—hypoxia or anoxia—as the cause of near-death experience. . . . Reduced supply of oxygen, which, according to Rodin, is the "final common pathway" of death, can in turn trigger seizure activity in the brain's limbic system, which includes the hippocampus, hypothalamus, amygdala, temporal lobe, and other structures associated with memory, mood, and emotion. Several neurologists and psychologists believe that limbic lobe agitation may be the physiological basis for near-death experience. . . . Given that most near-death subjects are not epileptic, however, partisans of the limbic lobe theory have had to look for some aspect of the physiology of dying that might be responsible for agitating limbic lobe neurons. . . . Cart suggests that the trigger may be endogenous aped peptides, such as endorphin and enkephalins, the morphinelike chemicals secreted by certain brain cells during extreme stress. Popularly known as the brain's natural painkillers, endorphin and their relatives bind to opiate receptors to block some of the worst effects of shock, infection, trauma, vigorous exercise, severe psychological distress, and other insults to the organism.

The endorphin explanation remains controversial nonetheless. To be on safer ground and to provide a more general and inclusive account of the source of near-death visions, some investigators turn instead to the hallucinogenic effects of sensory deprivation and social isolation. . . . Perhaps the dying patient, restricted to his bed, in a sterile monotonous environment, cut off from other people, is . . . like the polar explorer, mountain climber, desert wanderer, shipwrecked sailor, or long-distance trucker, whose mind compensates for loneliness and embellishes the blank landscape by supplying imaginary companions, consoling mirages, and diverting graphics.

Siegel derives his analysis of near-death experience from an elaborate theory of hallucination, based on the work of psychoneurologist

Heinrich Kluver, who developed a taxonomy of mescaline visions, and on his own previous studies of the subjective reports of marijuana users. He draws on analogy: "the remarkable similarity of imagery in life after death experiences and imagery in hallucinatory experiences invites inquiry about common mechanisms of action." Whether the trigger is sensory deprivation, drugs, toxic conditions, or severe psychological stress, Siegel claims that the hallucinatory pattern remains the same. By arguing from analogy rather than cause, he is able to make a more sweeping—and less testable—dismissal of the validity of near-death visions. . . .

Many critics look to psychology as the court of final appeal, the source of the most embracing and most effectively debunking verdict on near-death experience. . . . Although contemporary psychological treatments of this subject differ, all rest on the axiom that the mind will resort to any stratagem to push from view the prospect of its own annihilation; according to Freud, both logical paradox and ontological revulsion prevent us from facing the truth:

> Our own death is indeed unimaginable, and whenever we make the attempt to imagine it we can perceive that we really survive as spectators. Hence the psychoanalytic school could venture on the assertion that at bottom no one believes in his own death, or to put the same thing in another way, in the unconscious every one is convinced of his own immortality.

Clearly, we need to find a middle path between the extremes of dismissing near-death testimony as "nothing but" and embracing it as "proof." . . . Paradoxically, the researchers play into the debunkers' hands by assuming that the validity of near-death experience stands or falls on our ability to discriminate it from dream, hallucination, intoxication, or indoctrination; to link it with medical signs of death; and to corroborate its paranormal elements. In staking their claim on the unexplained status of near-death experience, the researchers put their material at the mercy of scientific progress; on these terms, if an explanation should be found, then near-death literature would lose its power to elicit a sense of wonder, or to hint at the possibility of freedom from ordinary, habitual modes of experience. There is an alternative to this religion of the gaps, however. It lies in the recognition that the "explained" phenomena of nature and human experience are no less hospitable to spiritual interpretation than the assortment of oddities that have thus far—but perhaps only temporarily—eluded science. Even if it is possible to account for every feature of near-death experience under every condition in which it occurs, the task of interpretation remains unfinished.

From Carol Zaleski, *Otherworld Journeys.*

BENJAMIN WHORF

The Language of the Hopi Provides a Metaphysics Without Space and Time

Benjamin Whorf (1897–1941) was an American linguist and cognitive scientist.

Benjamin Whorf studied the language of the Hopi natives of America. He found no counterpart to the conceptions of space and time which many people believe to be objectively real. For example, the Hopi have no counterparts in their language to temporal notions of past, present, and future. But their language does give them a way of accounting in a pragmatic way for all observable phenomena. So it does, Whorf brings out, contain a metaphysics, albeit one quite different from most familiar ones.

I find it gratuitous to assume that a Hopi who knows only the Hopi language and the cultural ideas of his own society has the same notions, often supposed to be intuitions, of time and space that we have, and that are generally assumed to be universal. In particular, he has no general notion or intuition of time as a smooth flowing continuum in which everything in the universe proceeds at an equal rate, out of a future, through a present, into a past; or, in which, to reverse the picture, the observer is being carried in the stream of duration continuously away from a past and into a future.

After long and careful study and analysis, the Hopi language is seen to contain no words, grammatical forms, constructions or expressions that refer directly to what we call "time," or to past, present, or future, or to enduring or lasting, or to motion as kinematic rather than dynamic (i.e. as a continuous translation in space and time rather than as an exhibition of dynamic effort in a certain process), or that even refer to space in such a way as to exclude that element of extension or existence that we call time, and so by implication leave a residue that could be referred to as time. Hence, the Hopi language contains no reference to "time," either explicit or implicit.

At the same time, the Hopi language is capable of accounting for and describing correctly, in a pragmatic or operational sense, all observable phenomena of the universe. Hence, I find it gratuitous to assume that Hopi thinking contains any such notion as the supposed intuitively felt flowing of time, or that the intuition of a Hopi gives him this as one of its data. Just as it is possible to have any number of geometries other than the Euclidean which give an equally perfect account of space configurations, so it is possible to have descriptions of the universe, all equally valid, that do not contain our familiar contrasts of time and space. The relativity viewpoint of modern physics is one such view, conceived in mathematical terms, and the Hopi Weltanschauung is another and quite different one, nonmathematical and linguistic.

Thus, the Hopi language and culture conceals a METAPHYSICS, such as our so-called naive view of space and time does, or as the relativity theory does; yet it is a different metaphysics from either. In order to describe the structure of the universe according to the Hopi, it is necessary to attempt—insofar as it is possible—to make explicit this metaphysics, properly describable only in the Hopi language, by means of an approximation expressed in our own language, somewhat inadequately it is true, yet by availing ourselves of such concepts as we have worked up into relative consonance with the system underlying the Hopi view of the universe.

In this Hopi view, time disappears and space is altered, so that it is no longer the homogeneous and instantaneous timeless space of our supposed intuition or of classical Newtonian mechanics. At the same time, new concepts and abstractions flow into the picture, taking up the task of describing the universe. . . .

The objective or manifested comprises all that is or has been accessible to the senses, the historical physical universe, in fact, with no attempt to distinguish between present and past, but excluding everything that we call future. The subjective or manifesting comprises all that we call future, BUT NOT MERELY THIS; it includes equally and indistinguishably all that we call mental—everything that appears or exists in the mind, or, as the Hopi would prefer to say, in the HEART, not only the heart of man, but the heart of animals, plants, and things, and behind and within all the forms and appearances of nature in the heart of nature, and by an implication and extension which has been felt by more than one anthropologist, yet would hardly ever be spoken of by a Hopi himself, so charged is the idea with religious and magical awesomeness, in the very heart of the Cosmos, itself. The subjective realm (subjective from our viewpoint, but intensely real and quivering with life, power, and potency to the Hopi) embraces not only our FUTURE, much of which the Hopi regards as more or less predestined in essence if not in exact form, but also all mentality, intellection, and emotion, the essence and typical form of which is the striving of purposeful desire, intelligent in character, toward manifestation—a manifestation which is much resisted and delayed, but in some form or other is inevitable. It is the realm of expectancy, of desire and purpose, of vitalizing life, of efficient causes, of thought thinking itself out from an inner realm (the Hopian HEART) into manifestation. It is in a dynamic state, yet not a state of motion—it is not advancing toward us out of a future, but ALREADY WITH us in vital and mental form, and its dynamism is at work in the field of eventuating or manifesting, that is, evolving without motion from the subjective by degrees to a result which is the objective. In translating into English, the Hopi will say that these entities in process of causation "will come" or that they—the Hopi—"will come to" them, but, in their own language, there are no verbs corresponding to our "come" and "go" that mean simple and abstract motion, our purely kinematic concept. The words in this case translated "come" refer to the process of eventuating without calling it motion—they are "eventuates to here" (*pew'i*) or "eventuates from it" (*angqo*) or "arrived" (*pitu*, pl. *oki*) which refers only to the terminal manifestation, the actual arrival at a given point, not to any motion preceding it.

From Benjamin Lee Whorf, "An American Indian Model of the Universe."

NELSON GOODMAN

There Are Many Ways the World Is

Nelson Goodman (1906–   ) is a contemporary American pragmatist and philosopher of science and language.

Nelson Goodman rejects the notion of a reality independent of and unknowable by us. Goodman offers frames of reference or ways of structuring reality as our only sensible means of talking about reality. In this sense there are many worlds. An artwork might provide us with a frame of reference as might science or religion. The frame of reference provided by science has no special claim as the most fundamental or best. Our task, rather than to identify the *correct version of reality, is to identify the many "right versions of it."*

In just what sense are there many worlds? What distinguishes genuine from spurious worlds? What are worlds made of? How are they made? What role do symbols play in the making? And how is worldmaking related to knowing? These questions must be faced even if full and final answers are far off. . . .

As intimated by William James's equivocal title *A Pluralistic Universe,* the issue between monism and pluralism tends to evaporate under analysis. If there is but one world, it embraces a multiplicity of contrasting aspects; if there are many worlds, the collection of them all is one. The one world may be taken as many, or the many worlds taken as one; whether one or many depends on the way of taking.

Consider, to begin with, the statements "The sun always moves" and "The sun never moves" which, though equally true, are at odds with each other. Shall we say, then, that they describe different worlds, and indeed that there are as many different worlds as there are such mutually exclusive truths? Rather, we are inclined to regard the two strings of words not as complete statements with truth-values of their own but as elliptical for some such statements as "Under frame of reference A, the sun always moves" and "Under frame of reference B, the sun never moves"—statements that may both be true of the same world.

Frames of reference, though, seem to belong less to what is described than to systems of description: and each of the two statements relates what is described to such a system. If I ask about the world, you can offer to tell me how it is under one or more frames of reference; but if I insist that you tell me how it is apart from all frames, what can you say? We are confined to ways of describing whatever is described. Our universe, so to speak, consists of these ways rather than of a world or of worlds.

The alternative descriptions of motion, all of them in much the same terms and routinely transformable into one another, provide only a minor and rather pallid example of diversity in accounts of the world. Much more striking is the vast variety of versions and visions in the several sciences, in the works of different painters and writers, and in our perceptions as informed by these, by circumstances, and by our own insights, interests, and past experiences. Even with all illusory or wrong or dubious versions dropped, the rest exhibit new dimensions of disparity. Here we have no neat set of frames of reference, no ready rules for transforming physics, biology, and psychology into one another, and no way at all of transforming any of these into Van Gogh's vision, or Van Gogh's into Canaletto's. Such of these versions as are depictions rather than descriptions have no truth-value in the literal sense, and cannot be combined by conjunction. The difference between juxtaposing and conjoining two statements has no evident analogue for two pictures or for a picture and a statement. The dramatically contrasting versions of the world can of course be relativized: each is right under a given system—for a given science, a given artist, or a given perceiver and situation. Here again we turn from describing or depicting 'the world' to talking of descriptions and depictions, but now without even the consolation of intertranslatability among or any evident organization of the several systems in question.

Yet doesn't a right version differ from a wrong one just in applying to the world, so that rightness itself depends upon and implies a world? We might better say that 'the world' depends upon rightness. We cannot test a version by comparing it with a world undescribed, undepicted, unperceived, but only by other means that I shall discuss later. While we may speak of determining what versions are right as 'learning about the world', 'the world' supposedly being that which all right versions describe, all we learn about the world is contained in right versions of it; and while the underlying world, bereft of these, need not be denied to those who love it, it is perhaps on the whole a world well lost. . . .

A reduction from one system to another can make a genuine contribution to understanding the interrelationships among world-versions; but reduction in any reasonably strict sense is rare, almost always partial, and seldom if ever unique. To demand full and sole reducibility to physics or any other one version is to forego nearly all other versions. The pluralists' acceptance of versions other than physics implies no relaxation of rigor but a recognition that standards different from yet no less exacting than those applied in science are appropriate for appraising what is conveyed in perceptual or pictorial or literary versions.

So long as contrasting right versions not all reducible to one are countenanced, unity is to be sought not in an ambivalent or neutral *something* beneath these versions, but in an overall organization embracing them.

From Nelson Goodman, *Ways of Worldmaking.*

CHARLES HARTSHORNE
Philosophers and Metaphysicians Can Contribute to Science

Charles Hartshorne (1897–   ) is an American process theologian and philosopher of religion.

Charles Hartshorne tells how philosophers have contributed to other fields including science and gives examples from antiquity to modern times. Perhaps his most interesting example is his account of his experience as both a philosopher and an ornithologist, someone who studies birds. He challenged a widely held metaphysical assumption that appreciation of music is unique to our species. Working with a different view that allows the possibility that "sub-human music is a reality," Hartshorne began asking questions about songbirds that were never asked before. Once he raised these questions, Hartshorne was able to proceed as a scientist and test the hypotheses his questions generated. Hartshorne was eventually able to establish his "aesthetic hypothesis," that one of the motivations for songbirds to sing is an innate ability to enjoy music.

Philosophers have often been something more than just philosophers. Many have been mathematicians, formal logicians, empirical scientists of note, or theologians; a few have contributed to all these forms of inquiry. Intellectual history also shows that purely metaphysical speculations have sometimes (not always!) had fortunate effects upon the development of empirical science. The Democritean atomic theory of the fifth century B.C., helpful in the rise of modern science, was a brilliant modification of the Parmenidean doctrine (sixth century B.C.) of *being* (or all reality) as one, indivisible, and unchangeable. Democritus and his teacher Leucippus regarded, not all reality, but each atom as indivisible and unchangeable in its internal being, yet able to occupy successively diverse locations in the "non-being" of space. This view, still apparent in the work of Newton in the seventeenth and Maxwell in the nineteenth centuries, was superseded only in the present century.

In my own intellectual work, metaphysics and a branch of empirical science have been the most persistent concerns. The metaphysics was widely different from that of Parmenides, and the branch of science was more narrowly specialized than physics, being a limited part of ethology, or the study of animal behavior. My limited part of this is the study of bird song, or, a little more generally, of the making by nonhuman animals of sounds having objectively some resemblance to those which in the human case are called musical. . . .

The basic theory, which I call "the aesthetic hypothesis," is that songbirds are motivated to sing, at least partly, by an innate capacity to enjoy the making and hearing of musical sounds. They sing a great deal and can hardly be constantly saying to themselves, as it were, "I must sing to warn off territorial intruders or attract and keep a mate," any more—rather less—than human beings make love simply to produce offspring. In both cases sensations or feelings (the former being, as I argued in my first book, a form of the latter) favor the action, make it self-rewarding or self-reinforcing. And this is what "aesthetic" basically means. Songbirds, in short, have a primitive form of musical sense. Evolutionary pressures favor its development in some species because its behavioral expressions make for reproductive success in those species. *A primitive aesthetic musical sense is in some species biologically useful.* Singing by those species is done so much and so well because it is enjoyed as such. In selecting for the behavior, evolution selects for the feeling that activates it.

In my opinion any success I have had in my venture into ornithology is one more example of how metaphysical principles can help empirical science. They do this by suggesting questions that only empirical tests can answer but that mere observation might not lead one to ask. No one had asked, "Can we measure singing skills, and have they any correlation with amounts of singing per year?" Indeed there had been only one or two efforts to measure these amounts. Other neglected questions were: "Why are parrots so little musical yet so skillful in imitation," "Why are imitative species in general somewhat less musically exquisite than many highly developed non-imitative singers?" . . .

My book thus contains empirical evidence bearing on many previously unasked questions. None of this might have happened had I accepted the widespread belief that aesthetic values are entirely peculiar to our species. I had come to see that cognitive, technological, moral, and religious values are most distinctive in *Homo sapiens* and that aesthetic principles apply to precognitive and pre-moral experiences as well as to cognitive and moral ones. An infant can be bored by monotony or thrilled by novelty before it can do much by way of thinking and long before it can have a sense of obligation. Subhuman music is a reality.

From Charles Hartshorne, "Metaphysics Contributes to Ornithology."

OLIVER WENDELL HOLMES
Truth Is the System of My Intellectual Limitations

Oliver Wendell Holmes (1809–1894) was an American legal scholar and essayist.

Oliver Wendell Holmes was a member of the Metaphysical Club which met in Cambridge, Massachusetts and was frequented by Peirce and James. In his short essay, "Natural Law," Holmes offers a glimpse of his view of reality and our place in it. We are part of a vastness which always will elude us, yet we can sensibly strive for goals important to us and which bring enjoyment to us. "Truth," according to Holmes, is "the system of my (intellectual) limitations" and all we really have are commitments we hold to because they are in some way congenial to us, probably because they remind us of something joyful we experienced in childhood.

Holmes brings this analysis of reality and truth around to his own field of study, the law. He rejects an idea with a long history in legal thinking that such things as natural laws exist. Natural law theorists claim there is a set of absolute truths we should use to guide us in building our legal systems. When America's founding fathers said, "We take these truths as self evident, that all men are created equal . . .," they were referring to principles of natural law. Holmes would want us to think of such principles not as really existing but as values close to our hearts.

It is not enough for the knight of romance that you agree that his lady is a very nice girl—if you do not admit that she is the best that God ever made or will make, you must fight. There is in all men a demand for the superlative, so much so that the poor devil who has no other way of reaching it attains it by getting drunk. It seems to me that this demand is at the bottom of the philosopher's effort to prove that truth is absolute and of the jurist's search for criteria of universal validity which he collects under the head of natural law. . . . [A]s I have suggested elsewhere, the truth may be defined as the system of my (intellectual) limitations. . . .

Certitude is not the test of certainty. We have been cock-sure of many things that were not so. If I may quote myself again, property, friendship, and truth have a common root in time. One can not be wrenched from the rocky crevices into which one has grown for many years without feeling that one is attacked in one's life. What we most love and revere generally is determined by early associations. I love granite rocks and barberry bushes, no doubt because with them were my earliest joys that reach back through the past eternity of my life. But while one's experience thus makes certain preferences dogmatic for oneself, recognition of how they came to be so leaves one able to see that others, poor souls, may be equally dogmatic about something else. And this again means scepticism. Not that one's belief or love does not remain. Not that we would not fight and die for it if important—we all, whether we know it or not, are fighting to make the kind of a world that we should like—but that we have learned to recognize that others will fight and die to make a different world, with equal sincerity or belief. Deep-seated preferences can not be argued about—you can not argue a man into liking a glass of beer—and therefore, when differences are sufficiently far reaching, we try to kill the other man rather than let him have his way. But that is perfectly consistent with admitting that, so far as appears, his grounds are just as good as ours.

The jurists who believe in natural law seem to me to be in that naive state of mind that accepts what has been familiar and accepted by them and their neighbors as something that must be accepted by all men everywhere. . . .

Now when we come to our attitude toward the universe I do not see any rational ground for demanding the superlative—for being dissatisfied unless we are assured that our truth is cosmic truth, if there is such a thing.

That the universe has in it more than we understand, that the private soldiers have not been told the plan of campaign, or even that there is one, rather than some vaster unthinkable to which every predicate is an impertinence, has no bearing upon our conduct. We still shall fight—all of us because we want to live, some, at least, because we want to realize our spontaneity and prove our powers, for the joy of it, and we may leave to the unknown the supposed final valuation of that which in any event has value to us. It is enough for us that the universe has produced us and has within it, as less than it, all that we believe and love. If we think of our existence not as that of a little god outside, but as that of a ganglion within, we have the infinite behind us. It gives us our only but our adequate significance. A grain of sand has the same, but what competent person supposes that he understands a grain of sand? That is as much beyond our grasp as man. If our imagination is strong enough to accept the vision of ourselves as parts inseverable from the rest, and to extend our final interest beyond the boundary of our skins, it justifies the sacrifice even of our lives for ends outside of ourselves. The motive, to be sure, is the common wants and ideals that we find in man. Philosophy does not furnish motives, but it shows men that they are not fools for doing what they already want to do. It opens to the forlorn hopes on which we throw ourselves away, the vista of the farthest stretch of human thought, the chords of a harmony that breathes from the unknown.

From Oliver Wendell Holmes, "Natural Law."

JOSIAH ROYCE
"Doubting and Working"

Josiah Royce (1855–1916) was an American idealist philosopher.

Josiah Royce devotes the first half of his essay, "Doubting and Working," to developing Holmes's claim that people live in very different worlds. Royce thinks we may well live in different worlds due to differences in ways we remember and sense—not to mention differences in how we view such complex things as the value of life and the world. Is this way of living–with all of us in our own worlds—a bad thing? The best case scenario is that our great thinkers are "finite minds full of fallacy and self-confidence" which leaves the rest of us, by implication, to be even worse off.

Royce proposes that we take a skeptical attitude toward all of our beliefs and accept only what we can establish rationally. We should do this because we recognize that simply sticking to beliefs which we find agreeable is selfish whereas working to find the truth will benefit all of humanity. These efforts will harmonize conflicting opinions and usher in complete toleration and unity. But the doubting process and the good that can come from it require a lot of work on the part of each of us.

There is a well known speculation of Dr. Holmes as to the number of people who really are concerned in a conversation between any two men. Each one of these men has a real and true character—is what he is. Each one of the men has a notion of the other's character, and probably thinks his notion a very fair one. And each one has a still more distinct and fixed idea as to his own character. Now, the words of each man are determined by what he himself really is, by what he thinks of himself, and by what he holds of the other. So that in fact six people, two real and four imaginary—to wit, the two real men, their ideas of themselves and their ideas of each other—take part in this simplest form of human society. How complicated then, must be the state of things when a whole group of people are concerned, each one speaking forth his own true nature, but affected in his words by what he supposes his own nature to be, and by the way in which he fancies his sayings will impress the ghostly images that are what he takes to be his real companions.

This speculation suggests a like one as to the number of partly imaginary worlds that form subjects of study and amusement for the myriads of human beings in the one actual world. It is commonplace that in some sense every man may be said to move in a world of his own. Yet the consequences of this commonplace are not always considered. Think of them a moment. Here is an ordinary person before us, taken as a type of humanity. His view of the world might be taken as an example, so it would seem, of the way in which the people of this planet know and appreciate the universe. Yet, no. Could you look in to his soul for a minute it is probable that you would find very much in his consciousness that would be strange to you and to other men. Think first of his senses themselves. Experience has shown that common men can go through the world for a very long time without suspecting or showing that they have some very important defect of the senses. Cross-eyed men, I have heard, sometimes by a painless process lose the sight of one eye, and yet go for years without finding out their defect until chance or necessity brings them under the skilled examination of an oculist. Late statistics make a basis for the claim that as many as one in every twenty-five male persons will be found to be color-blind. Yet only by careful tests are color-blind people to be distinguished from people with normal vision. It is probable that there are often somewhat similar defects in the sense of hearing which go unnoticed for a long time. Yet more, the researches of men like Helmholtz have proved that there are many optical illusions common to most or to all of us, which are unnoticed or unconsciously corrected our lives long, and which never could become known without skillful experiment. And if all this is true, how can we ever feel sure that in the field that lies beyond the reach of possible experiment, in the field of each man's own primary sensations themselves, there are not entirely mysterious sources of variety, so that the ultimate sensations of one person may be of their nature not comparable at all with the ultimate sensations of his neighbor? Thus, then, our normal man may be in fact a creature of entirely peculiar constitution; yet we may not know the fact. His world may be one that would be inconceivably strange to us. Yet we talk with him in common fashion day after day. But, leaving the field of conjecture and coming back to the point where it is possible to judge and compare, I say that we may very probably find upon examination that there are peculiarities in the mind of the person we are considering which may make the simplest operation of his thought such as we can neither imitate nor easily understand. Take, for example, his memory. There seem to be two somewhat different kinds of memories in the world. I suppose that there are all the gradations between the two extremes, but at the extremes the contrast is very marked. One kind of memory is that which is especially helped by images, which is in fact largely a reimaging in the mind of things past, so that they appear much as they actually seemed when they were presented to the outward senses, only fainter. The other is a memory moving less in distinct and vivid images than in faint and broken incomplete mind-symbols that come up one after another, as association or volition calls them into consciousness. How, for example, do you remember that seven multiplied by seven equals forty-nine? If you have the image-memory, you may picture well before you a bit of the multiplication table, as you once saw it, with figures of some definite color, on a ground of some definite color. Clearly stand out the images in your mind as soon as you think of the numbers. You simply read off the result. If you have the other kind of memory, probably there arises a confused and faint form of the figures, curiously mingled with a memory somewhat more well defined, of the sound of the names of these numbers. The imaging is so obscure that you doubtless are inclined to say that you know not how you do remember at all, but merely know that you remember. . . .

I have mentioned differences in men's views of the world as thus exemplified in the more elementary activities of mental life. What shall we say when we come to the more complicated structures of the human mind, to those vague forms of consciousness in which are expressed our sense of the value of life and of the world, and to our opinions? Who shall serve for our normal specimen man here? How vastly we differ in all these things. How hard it is for us to come to an understanding. How the delights of one man appear as the most hateful of things to another, and the ideals of one party seem inventions of the devil to their opponents. All this illustrates the fact that we live in worlds differing far more from one another than we commonly like to think. Our normal man would surely be hard to choose. . . .

The difference between Mr. Herbert Spencer and Cardinal Newman, or between Professor Huxley and Mr. Ruskin, or between Hegel and Heinrich Heine—shall we call it merely a difference in the interpretation of the recorded facts of experience? No; evidently there are here different kinds of experience concerned, actually different worlds, different orders of truth. These men cannot come to a good understanding, because they have qualitatively different minds, irreconcilably various mental visions. Each of two such individuals may be inclined to regard the other as perverse. Both are, in fact, shut up within the narrow bounds of a poor individual experience. They will never understand one another so long as they remain what they are—finite minds full of fallacy and self-confidence, and of a darkness that is broken only here and there by flashes of light.

If the world's leaders are thus such narrow men, what are we who follow? How poor and narrow and uncertain must our world-pictures be. . . .

What kind of truth may I hope to discover? In what spirit ought I to search for truth? Am I to hope for much success? Am I to bear myself as one to whom truth will certainly be revealed, if he but work for it? . . .

The first answer to this question seems an obvious one. We must begin our undertaking in a spirit of self-distrust. For our former confidence in our chance opinions we must substitute complete skepticism. We must doubt every belief that we possess until we have proved it. . . .

Now, what would be the abiding and satisfactory truth if we found it? Evidently, this truth would have one great characteristic. It would be of a nature to demand acceptance from all men. It would be the one faith opposed to the many opinions, and certain to conquer them. It would be the one reality that could wait for ages for a discoverer. So, at least, we suppose. That is our ideal of truth. What, then, is the practical aim in seeking for truth? Evidently, the practical aim is to harmonize the conflicting opinions of men, to substitute for the narrowness and instability of personal view the broadness of view that should characterize the free man. And so we come to the real core of the matter. You may not, you dare not, if it is your vocation, to think at all—you dare not accept a faith simply for the satisfaction it gives you. You dare not, I say, because as a thinker your true aim is not to please yourself, but to work for the harmonizing of the views of mankind, to do your part in a perfectly unselfish task. . . .

But I must conclude this imperfect study of a great subject. We began with the fact that every individual is a creature of peculiar constitution, with possibly indefinitely great idiosyncrasies of senses and feeling. We have been led from this to think of ideal truth as it would appear in the mind of one who was not bound by accidents of sense and emotion to a narrow range of conflicting opinions. To approach this perfect individual, I have said that we must begin our efforts with conscientious and thorough-going doubt of all that we find uncriticized and yet claiming authority in our minds. I have tried to justify this doubting by showing that it is not merely a privilege, but a duty, of any one who proposes to do the least bit of genuine thinking for the good of his fellow-creatures.

I have stated at length the argument according to which at least our religious persuasions, as the expressions of the highest needs of our minds, must be exempted from even provisional doubts. In answer to this argument, I have tried to show that in so far as one's own comfort is concerned, truth-seeking ought not to regard personal comfort at all, and that in so far as humanity is concerned, religious beliefs can be made in the highest sense useful only when they have stood the test of doubt and study. . . .As my discussion is purely general, I would not be understood as bringing the least material argument to bear against the particular convictions of anybody. If you have reasoned fairly and earnestly, have criticized conscientiously, and still retain your religious belief, you have no doubt a glorious possession, worth far more than it ever could have been worth to you if you had not reasoned about it. Perhaps you are still in error. Perhaps the highest truth is already within your grasp, and you have solved in your own person the puzzles of ages. If so, you are to be congratulated. Your treasure is worth more to you than all the wealth in the world would be. But remember, no man liveth to himself. Remember your duty to mankind. Remember that your personal satisfaction with your creed is nothing, your desire to bring all mankind to the truth everything. Never rest quiet with your belief, therefore, until every means has been taken by you to purify it from all taint of your own narrowmindedness. If any one of us has so purified his belief, he is, I am persuaded, the greatest genius that the world ever saw. If he has not, it is his duty in the service of humanity to be in so far skeptical. If he has attained the perfect belief, then he must never rest in his efforts to teach it to others. I should fear as a general thing to have power given me to ordain for other human beings what their lives should be. But I wish that just for this moment it were given me to summon every man to a calling that should remain his calling for life, and to which he should willingly devote himself. I should summon every one to a life of unswerving devotion to this one end—the making of human life broader, fuller, more harmonious, better possessed of abiding belief. As it is, I can only recommend that you be ceaselessly active for this great end. And as for the end itself, I know not if it will ever be attained in any great measure, but I know that if it ever is attained it will be by the self-sacrifice of countless millions, who, through their own failures, shall secure the success of those that come after them.

From Josiah Royce, "Doubting and Working."

Si sabrá mas el discipulo.

Can the Pupil Know More? Etching by F. Goya

3

KNOWLEDGE

INTRODUCTION

We all seek to gain knowledge about our world and our place in it. I might want to know the shortest route by car from Peoria to Chicago; you might want to know today's closing Dow Jones index. The philosopher, in the role of critical inquirer, wants to know about knowledge itself. Questions that philosophers ask about knowledge often fall under one of the following four categories: (a) What is the nature of knowledge? (b) What is the source of knowledge? (c) What is the scope of knowledge? and (d) What is the value of knowledge?

What must be true if we are said to have knowledge? Philosophers from Plato to the present have been vexed with the problem of corralling the concept of knowledge and with marking the difference (if such there be) between "mere" belief and true knowledge. Does knowledge require certainty, complete immunity from doubt, as René Descartes and others have believed? Or, should the enterprise of science—hypothesis testing and confirmation—provide our model for all knowledge? Is our knowledge ever completely secure, or should we regard all "truths about the world" to be liable to future revision in the face of new experience?

Where should we look for knowledge? Common sense suggests that we look to experience—the evidence of our senses—to gain knowledge. After all, don't I learn that Elsie the cow has been nibbling my geraniums by looking out the window and catching her in the act? Philosophers known as empiricists—John Locke, David Hume, as well as the pragmatists Peirce, Dewey, James, and Lewis—argue strenuously that common sense is correct on this point, but other philosophers called rationalists—Plato, Descartes, and Leibniz, for example—think common sense misleads us. The only true knowledge, they believe, requires a degree of certainty that sense experience cannot provide. After all, my eyes might be deceiving me when I believe I spy Elsie. To gain certainty—and thereby knowledge—the rationalists believe that I must reflect upon and understand concepts themselves, uncorrupted by experience. The only reliable source for knowledge, given the rationalist view, is the mind itself.

What is the scope of knowledge? Are there domains of inquiry that cannot yield knowledge, only opinion and speculation? What of claims to religious knowledge? Can the realm of the divine be directly known? Can mystical experiences, for example, provide avenues of knowledge not captured by science and ordinary sense experience? Can I have knowledge of aesthetic and moral values? Some philosophers, known as epistemological skeptics, have taken a very hard line and argued that we have no knowledge whatsoever! Other philosophers, like the empiricists mentioned earlier, argue that we can have knowledge but only if we confine ourselves to the realm of the senses: that which we cannot experience through our ordinary senses is beyond the realm of the knowable. On this view, science is the touchstone of knowledge.

What is the value of knowledge? Francis Bacon is credited with the slogan "knowledge is power," and indeed, knowledge is the ingredient which, when mixed with our abilities to reason and imagine, allows us to manipulate the world in which we live and bring our plans and projects to fruition. Our ability to learn from past experience is a crucial feature of our human lives that allows us to construct a future from the many possibilities open to us. However, feminist philosophers, among others, warn us not to view knowledge simply as a means to control the world around us: knowledge, rather than a route to the control of a reality distinct from ourselves, is an interactive communion with a world of which we are just a part.

CHARLES SANDERS PEIRCE
Acting Is the End Point of Doubting, Thinking, and Believing

Charles Sanders Peirce focuses on reason from a functional standpoint. He identifies the settlement of opinion as the sole object of inquiry. But reasoning cannot begin to perform its function of settling opinion, according to Peirce, unless we are in a state of doubt. Doubt triggers inquiry, since the state of doubt is an irritating one. Reasoning brings doubt to an end as we settle upon an acceptable belief. Peirce expresses the pragmatist vision of the connection between knowledge and action when he claims that belief is that upon which we are prepared to act.

We generally know when we wish to ask a question and when we wish to pronounce a judgment, for there is a dissimilarity between the sensation of doubting and that of believing.

But this is not all which distinguishes doubt from belief. There is a practical difference. Our beliefs guide our desires and shape our actions. The Assassins, or followers of the Old Man of the Mountain, used to rush into death at his least command, because they believed that obedience to him would insure everlasting felicity. Had they doubted this, they would not have acted as they did. So it is with every belief, according to its degree. The feeling of believing is a more or less sure indication of there being established in our nature some habit which will determine our actions. Doubt never has such an effect.

Nor must we overlook a third point of difference. Doubt is an uneasy and dissatisfied state from which we struggle to free ourselves and pass into the state of belief; while the latter is a calm and satisfactory state which we do not wish to avoid, or to change to a belief in anything else. On the contrary, we cling tenaciously, not merely to believing, but to believing just what we do believe.

Thus, both doubt and belief have positive effects upon us, though very different ones. Belief does not make us act at once, but puts us into such a condition that we shall behave in a certain way, when the occasion arises. Doubt has not the least effect of this sort, but stimulates us to action until it is destroyed. This reminds us of the irritation of a nerve and the reflex action produced thereby; while for the analogue of belief, in the nervous system, we must look to what are called nervous associations—for example, to that habit of the nerves in consequence of which the smell of a peach will make the mouth water.

The irritation of doubt causes a struggle to attain a state of belief. I shall term this struggle inquiry, though it must be admitted that this is sometimes not a very apt designation.

The irritation of doubt is the only immediate motive for the struggle to attain belief. It is certainly best for us that our beliefs should be such as may truly guide our actions so to satisfy our desires; and this reflection will make us reject any belief which does not seem to have been so formed as to insure this result. But it will only do so by creating a doubt in the place of that belief. With the doubt, therefore, the struggle begins, and with the cessation of doubt it ends. Hence, the sole object of inquiry is the settlement of opinion. We may fancy that this is not enough for us, and that we seek not merely an opinion, but a true opinion. But put this fancy to the test, and it proves groundless; for as soon as a firm belief is reached we are entirely satisfied, whether the belief be false or true. And it is clear that nothing out of the sphere of our knowledge can be our object, for nothing which does not affect the mind can be a motive for a mental effort. The most that can be maintained is that we seek for a belief that we shall *think* to be true. But we think each one of our beliefs to be true, and, indeed, it is mere tautology to say so.

That the settlement of opinion is the sole end of inquiry is a very important proposition. It sweeps away at once various vague and erroneous conceptions of proof. A few of these may be noticed here.

1. Some philosophers have imagined that to start an inquiry it was only necessary to utter or question or set it down on paper, and have even recommended us to begin our studies with questioning everything! But the mere putting of a proposition into the interrogative form does not stimulate the mind to any struggle after belief. There must be a real and living doubt, and without all this, discussion is idle.

2. It is a very common idea that a demonstration must rest on some ultimate and absolutely indubitable propositions. These, according to one school, are first principles of a general nature; according to another, are first sensations. But, in point of fact an inquiry, to have that completely satisfactory result called demonstration, has only to start with propositions perfectly free from all actual doubt. If the premises are not in fact doubted at all, they cannot be more satisfactory than they are.

3. Some people seem to love to argue a point after all the world is fully convinced of it. But no further advance can be made. When doubt ceases, mental action on the subject comes to an end; and, if it did go on, it would be without a purpose, except that of self-criticism.

From C. S. Peirce, "The Fixation of Belief."

WILLIAM JAMES
Consciousness Is a Stream Always Moving On

What is the nature of the ideas that are present to consciousness? Some philosophers talk about our ideas as entities, each one clearly demarcated from the rest; we can focus on an idea of an elephant, and then move on to one of the moon, and then to one of God. This conception of consciousness, which prevailed through the seventeenth and eighteenth centuries, is challenged by William James who urges us to think about consciousness as a stream of ideas.

I said a few minutes ago that the most general elements and workings of the mind are all that the teacher absolutely needs to be acquainted with for his purposes.

Now the *immediate* fact which psychology, the science of mind, has to study is also the most general fact. It is the fact that in each of us, when awake (and often when asleep), *some kind of consciousness is always going on.* There is a stream, a succession of states, or waves, or fields (or of whatever you please to call them), of knowledge, of feeling, of desire, of deliberation, etc., that constantly pass and repass, and that constitute our inner life. The existence of this stream is the primal fact, the nature and origin of it form the essential problem, of our science. So far as we class the states or fields of consciousness, write down their several natures, analyze their contents into elements, or trace their habits of succession, we are on the descriptive or analytic level. So far as we ask where they come from or why they are just what they are, we are on the explanatory level. . . .

The truth is that we really *do not know* the answers to the problems on the explanatory level, even though in some directions of inquiry there may be promising speculations to be found. For our present purposes I shall therefore dismiss them entirely, and turn to mere description. This state of things was what I had in mind when, a moment ago, I said there was no 'new psychology' worthy of the name.

We have thus fields of consciousness—that is the first general fact; and the second general fact is that the concrete fields are always complex. They contain sensations of our bodies and of the objects around us, memories of past experiences and thoughts of distant things, feelings of satisfaction and dissatisfaction, desires and aversions, and other emotional conditions, together with determinations of the will, in every variety of permutation and combination.

In most of our concrete states of consciousness all these different classes of ingredients are found simultaneously present to some degree, though the relative proportion they bear to one another is very shifting. One state will seem to be composed of hardly anything but sensations, another of hardly anything but memories, etc. But around the sensation, if one consider carefully, there will always be some fringe of thought or will, and around the memory some margin or penumbra of emotion or sensation.

In most of our fields of consciousness there is a core of sensation that is very pronounced. You, for example, now, although you are also thinking and feeling, are getting through your eyes sensations of my face and figure, and through your ears sensations of my voice. The sensations are the *centre* or *focus*, the thoughts and feelings the margin, of your actually present conscious field.

On the other hand, some object of thought, some distant image, may have become the focus of your mental attention even while I am speaking, your mind, in short, may have wandered from the lecture; and, in that case, the sensations of my face and voice, although not absolutely vanishing from your conscious field, may have taken up there a very faint and marginal place. . . .

Vague and hazy as such an account of our stream of consciousness may be, it is at least secure from positive error and free from admixture of conjecture or hypothesis. An influential school of psychology, seeking to avoid haziness of outline, has tried to make things appear more exact and scientific by making the analysis more sharp. The various fields of consciousness, according to this school, result from a definite number of perfectly definite elementary mental states, mechanically associated into a mosaic or chemically combined. According to some thinkers—Spencer, for example, or Taine—these resolve themselves at last into little elementary psychic particles or atoms of 'mind-stuff,' out of which all the more immediately known mental states are said to be built up. Locke introduced this theory in a somewhat vague form. Simple 'ideas' of sensation and reflection, as he called them, were for him the bricks of which our mental architecture is built up. If I ever have to refer to this theory again, I shall refer to it as the theory of 'ideas.' But I shall try to steer clear of it altogether. Whether it be true or false, it is at any rate only conjectural; and, for your practical purposes as teachers, the more unpretending conception of the stream of consciousness, with its total waves or fields incessantly changing, will amply suffice.

From William James, *Talks to Teachers*.

JOHN DEWEY

Knowledge Is an Instrument for Enhancing Human Satisfaction

John Dewey rejects traditional models of knowing on the grounds that they depict the knower as passive. Rationalists, many of whom think that there is innate knowledge or knowledge in the mind at birth, suggest that we need merely to acquaint ourselves with the contents of our minds in order to know. Empiricists, who insist that the senses are the source of knowledge, also position knowers as passive receivers of information; for Dewey, the empiricists see the senses as "gateways to knowledge." What is missing in these analyses, according to Dewey, is the significance of human action in knowing. We glean knowledge about our world as we interact with it, and we use that knowledge to guide and enrich our future interaction with the environment. We learn that the stove is hot and will burn us from touching it, and we thus use caution next time we are near the stove. Moreover, we should think of knowledge as an instrument for bringing satisfactions into human experience, hence Dewey's "instrumental" theory of knowledge.

What is experience and what is Reason, Mind? What is the scope of experience and what are its limits? How far is it a sure ground of belief and a safe guide of conduct? Can we trust it in science and in behavior? Or is it a quagmire as soon as we pass beyond a few low material interests? Is it so shaky, shifting, and shallow that instead of affording sure footing, safe paths to fertile fields, it misleads, betrays, and engulfs? Is a Reason outside experience and above it needed to supply assured principles to science and conduct?

We know the answers of traditional philosophy. They do not thoroughly agree among themselves, but they agree that experience never rises above the level of the particular, the contingent, and the probable. Only a power transcending in origin and content any and all conceivable experience can attain to universal, necessary and certain authority and direction. The empiricists themselves admitted the correctness of these assertions. They only said that since there is no faculty of Pure Reason in the possession of mankind, we must put up with what we have, experience, and make the most possible out of it. . . .

Two things have rendered possible a new conception of experience and a new conception of the relation of reason to experience, or, more accurately, of the place of reason in experience. The primary factor is the change that has taken place in the actual nature of experience, its contents and methods, as it is actually lived. The other is the development of a psychology based upon biology which makes possible a new scientific formulation of the nature of experience.

Let us begin with the technical side—the change in psychology. We are only just now commencing to appreciate how completely exploded is the psychology that dominated philosophy throughout the eighteenth and nineteenth centuries. According to this theory, mental life originated in sensations which are separately and passively received, and which are formed, through laws of retention and association, into a mosaic of images, perceptions, and conceptions. The senses were regarded as gateways or avenues of knowledge. Except in combining atomic sensations, the mind was wholly passive and acquiescent in knowing. . . .

The effect of the development of biology has been to reverse the picture. Wherever there is life, there is behavior, activity. In order that life may persist, this activity has to be both continuous and adapted to the environment. This adaptive adjustment, moreover, is not wholly passive; is not a mere matter of the moulding of the organism by the environment. Even a clam acts upon the environment and modifies it to some extent. It selects materials for food and for the shell that protects it. It does something to the environment as well as has something done to itself. . . .

The higher the form of life, the more important is the active reconstruction of the medium.

. . .civilized man goes to distant mountains and dams streams. He builds reservoirs, digs channels, and conducts the waters to what had been a desert. He searches the world to find plants and animals that will thrive. He takes native plants and by selection and cross-fertilization improves them. He introduces machinery to till the soil and care for the harvest. By such means he may succeed in making the wilderness blossom like the rose. . . .

Experience becomes an affair primarily of doing. The organism does not stand about, Micawberlike, waiting for something to turn up. It does not wait passive and inert for something to impress itself upon it from without. The organism acts in accordance with its own structure, simple or complex, upon its surroundings. As a consequence the changes produced in the environment react upon the organism and its activities.

. . .suppose a busy infant puts his finger in the fire; the doing is random, aimless, without intention or reflection. But something happens in consequence. The child undergoes heat, he suffers pain. The doing and undergoing, the reaching and the burn, are connected. One comes to suggest and mean the other. Then there is experience in a vital and significant sense.

Certain important implications for philosophy follow. In the first place, the interaction of organism and environment, resulting in some adaptation which secures utilization of the latter, is the primary fact, the basic category. Knowledge is relegated to a derived position, secondary in origin, even if its importance, when once it is established, is overshadowing. Knowledge is not something separate and self-sufficing, but is involved in the process by which life is sustained and evolved. The senses lose their place as gateways of knowing to take their rightful place as stimuli to action. To an animal an affection of the eye or ear is not an idle piece of information about something indifferently going on in the world. It is an invitation and inducement to act in a needed way. It is a clue in behavior, a directive factor in adaptation of life in its surroundings. It is urgent not cognitive in quality. The whole controversy between empiricism and rationalism as to the intellectual worth of sensations is rendered strangely obsolete. The discussion of sensations belongs under the head of immediate stimulus and response, not under the head of knowledge.

From John Dewey, *Reconstruction in Philosophy*.

The thesis of the essays is that thinking is instrumental to a control of the environment, a control effected through acts which would not be undertaken without the prior resolution of a complex situation into assured elements and an accompanying projection of possibilities—without, that is to say, thinking. . . .

In the logical version of pragmatism termed instrumentalism, action or practice does indeed play a fundamental role. But it concerns not the nature of consequences but the nature of knowing. To use a term which is now more fashionable (and surely to some extent in consequence of pragmatism) than it was earlier, instrumentalism means a behaviorist theory of thinking and knowing. It means that knowing is literally something which we do. . . .

From John Dewey, *Essays in Experimental Logic*.

JANE ADDAMS
The Value of Knowledge Is in Its Use

Jane Addams credits James and Dewey with getting us to think of knowledge in terms of its use, how it guides our conduct and bears on solutions to our problems. But this insight about knowledge itself is at the level of theory. Some group still needs to concern itself with the actual testing of human knowledge to determine its value. Addams sees settlement homes like her Hull-House, homes designed to assist immigrants with their transition to America, as institutions which can serve this purpose.

It is frequently stated that the most pressing problem of modern life is that of a reconstruction and a reorganization of the knowledge which we possess; that we are at last struggling to realize in terms of life all that has been discovered and absorbed, to make it over into healthy and direct expressions of free living. Dr. John Dewey, of the University of Chicago, has written: "Knowledge is no longer its own justification, the interest in it has at last transferred itself from accumulation and verification to its application to life." And he adds: "When a theory of knowledge forgets that its value rests in solving the problem out of which it has arisen, that of securing a method of action, knowledge begins to cumber the ground. It is a luxury, and becomes a social nuisance and disturber."

We may quote further from Professor James, of Harvard University, who recently said in an address before the Philosophical Union of the University of California: "Beliefs, in short, are really rules of action, and the whole function of thinking is but one step in the production of habits of action," or "the ultimate test for us of what a truth means is indeed the conduct it dictates or inspires."

Having thus the support of two philosophers, let us assume that the dominating interest in knowledge has become its use, the conditions under which, and ways in which it may be most effectively employed in human conduct; and that at last certain people have consciously formed themselves into groups for the express purpose of effective application. These groups which are called settlements have naturally sought the spots where the dearth of this applied knowledge was most obvious, the depressed quarters of great cities. They gravitate to these spots, not with the object of finding clinical material, not to found "sociological laboratories," not, indeed, with the analytical motive at all, but rather in a reaction from that motive, with a desire to use synthetically and directly whatever knowledge they, as a group, may possess, to test its validity and to discover the conditions under which this knowledge may be employed.

That, just as groups of men, for hundreds of years, have organized themselves into colleges, for the purpose of handing on and disseminating knowledge already accumulated, and as other groups have been organized into seminars and universities, for the purpose of research and the extension of the bounds of knowledge, so at last groups have been consciously formed for the purpose of the application of knowledge to life. This third attempt also would claim for itself the enthusiasm and advantage of collective living. It has come to be a group of people who share their methods, and who mean to make experience continuous beyond the individual. It may be urged that this function of application has always been undertaken by individuals and unconscious groups. This is doubtless true, just as much classic learning has always been disseminated outside of the colleges, and just as some of the most notable discoveries of pure science have been made outside of the universities. Still both these institutions do in the main accomplish the bulk of the disseminating, and the discovering; and it is upon the same basis that the third group may establish its value.

The ideal and developed settlement would attempt to test the value of human knowledge by action, and realization, quite as the complete and ideal university would concern itself with the discovery of knowledge in all branches. The settlement stands for application as opposed to research; for emotion as opposed to abstraction, for universal interest as opposed to specialization. This certainly claims too much, absurdly too much, for a settlement, in the light of its achievements, but perhaps not in the light of its possibilities.

This, then, will be my definition of the settlement: that it is an attempt to express the meaning of life in terms of life itself, in forms of activity. There is no doubt that the deed often reveals when the idea does not, just as art makes us understand and feel what might be incomprehensible and inexpressible in the form of an argument. And as the artist tests the success of his art when the recipient feels that he knew the thing before, but had not been able to express it, so the settlement, when it attempts to reveal and apply knowledge, deems its results practicable, when it has made knowledge available which before was abstract, when through use, it has made common that knowledge which was partial before, because it could only be apprehended by the intellect.

From Jane Addams, "A Function of the Social Settlement."

RENÉ DESCARTES
The Source of Knowledge Is the Mind

René Descartes (1596–1650) is a French philosopher and mathematician cited as the "father of modern philosophy."

René Descartes, examining a piece of wax, wondered which of his faculties informed him that it was wax–his senses, his imagination, or his mind? He reasons that his senses are not the source of his knowledge since the information they convey to him changes as the wax changes when it is held to a flame. And his imagination isn't the source because his imagination fails to inform him in advance of all the forms the wax might take. It must, then, says Descartes, be the mind which is the source of his knowledge of the wax. In identifying our rational faculties, rather than our senses, as the source of knowledge, Descartes commits himself to the view known as rationalism.

Let us now consider the commonest things, which are commonly believed to be the most distinctly known and the easiest of all to know namely, the bodies which we touch and see. I do not intend to speak of bodies in general, for general notions are usually somewhat more confused; let us rather consider one body in particular. Let us take, for example, this bit of wax which has just been taken from the hive. It has not yet completely lost the sweetness of the honey it contained; it still retains something of the odor of the flowers from which it was collected; its color, shape, and size are apparent; it is hard and cold; it can easily be touched; and, if you knock on it, it will give out some sound. Thus everything which can make a body distinctly known are found in this example.

But now while I am talking I bring it close to the fire. What remains of the taste evaporates; the odor vanishes; its color changes; its shape is lost; its size increases; it becomes liquid; it grows hot; one can hardly touch it; and although it is knocked upon, it will give out no sound. Does the same wax remain after this change? We must admit that it does; no one denies it, no one judges otherwise. What is it then in this bit of wax that we recognize with so much distinctness? Certainly it cannot be anything that I observed by means of the senses, since everything in the field of taste, smell, sight, touch, and hearing are changed, and since the same wax nevertheless remains.

The truth of the matter perhaps, as I now suspect, is that this wax was neither that sweetness of honey, nor that pleasant odor of flowers, nor that whiteness, nor that shape, nor that sound, but only a body which a little while ago appeared to my senses under these forms and which now makes itself felt under others. But what is it, to speak precisely, that I imagine when I conceive it in this fashion? Let us consider it attentively and, rejecting everything that does not belong to the wax, see what remains. Certainly nothing is left but something extended, flexible, and movable. But what is meant by flexible and movable? Does it consist in my picturing that this wax, being round, is capable of becoming square and of passing from the square into a triangular shape? Certainly not; it is not that, since I conceive it capable of undergoing an infinity of similar changes, and I could not compass this infinity in my imagination. Consequently this conception that I have of the wax is not achieved by the faculty of imagination. . . .

But what is this bit of wax which cannot be comprehended except by the understanding, or by the mind? Certainly it is the same as the one that I see, that I touch, that I imagine; and finally it is the same as I always believed it to be from the beginning. But what is here important to notice is that perception or the action by which we perceive, is not a vision, a touch, nor an imagination, and has never been that, even though it formerly appeared so; but is solely an inspection by the mind, which can be imperfect and confused as it was formerly, or clear and distinct as it is at present, as I attend more or less to the things which are in it and of which it is composed.

From René Descartes, *Meditations on First Philosophy*, translated by Laurence J. LaFleur.

JOHN LOCKE

The Source of Knowledge Is the Senses

John Locke (1632–1704) was a British empiricist and political philosopher.

John Locke rejects rationalism and initiates the school of British empiricism, asserting that experience is the source of knowledge. He asks us to conceive the mind as being empty at birth, like a blank sheet of paper. To carry out the metaphor, experience writes on the mind; that is how it becomes filled. George Berkeley and David Hume, other prominent members of this school, were committed to Locke's starting point that nothing is in the mind which is not first in the senses and developed their own distinctive brands of empiricism.

Let us suppose the mind to be, as we say, white paper, void of all characters, without any ideas; how comes it to be furnished? Whence comes it by that vast store which the busy and boundless fancy of man has painted on it, with an almost endless variety? Whence has it all the materials of reason and knowledge? To this I answer, in one word, from experience; in all that our knowledge is founded, and from that it ultimately derives itself.

From John Locke, *Essay Concerning Human Understanding.*

DAVID HUME

The Source of Knowledge Is the Senses

David Hume (1711–1776) was a Scottish empiricist and skeptic.

David Hume argues for empiricism by classifying the contents of our minds in a way that allows us to trace any of these contents to sensory experience. Hume's classification distinguishes what we are sensing at present from our recollection of it. Obviously, the source of our current sensations, which Hume calls impressions, is the senses. And the ultimate source of what we are not sensing at present—called by Hume ideas—is the senses as well. Many of these ideas are simply faint images of what I had earlier sensed, so their source is the senses. And other ideas are concoctions of what I had initially sensed. My idea of a pink cat wearing a catnip necklace resulted from my combining my actual sensory experiences of cat, pink, catnip, and necklace. In Hume's view I can tell that I am dealing with a fiction if I can find nothing in my actual experience which matches it.

All the perceptions of the human mind resolve themselves into two distinct kinds, which I shall call impressions and ideas. The difference betwixt these consists in the degrees of force and liveliness with which they strike upon the mind, and make their way into our thought or consciousness. Those perceptions, which enter with most force and violence, we may name impressions; and under this name I comprehend all our sensations, passions and emotions, as they make their first appearance in the soul. By ideas I mean the faint images of these in thinking and reasoning; such as, for instance, are all the perceptions excited by the present discourse, excepting only, those which arise from the sight and touch, and excepting the immediate pleasure or uneasiness it may occasion. I believe it will not be very necessary to employ many words in explaining this distinction. Every one of himself will readily perceive the difference betwixt feeling and thinking. The common degrees of these are easily distinguished; tho' it is not impossible but in particular instances they may very nearly approach to each other. Thus in sleep, in a fever, in madness, or in any very violent emotions of soul, our ideas may approach to our impressions: As on the other hand it sometimes happens, that our impressions are so faint and low, that we cannot distinguish them from our ideas. But notwithstanding this near resemblance in a few instances, they are in general so very different that no-one can make a scruple to rank them under distinct heads, and assign to each a peculiar name to mark the difference. . .

There is another division of our perceptions, which it will be convenient to observe, and which extends itself both to our impressions and ideas. This division is into simple and complex. Simple perceptions or impressions and ideas are such as admit of no distinction nor separation. The complex are the contrary to these, and may be distinguished into parts. Tho' a particular colour, taste, and smell are qualities all united together in this apple, 'tis easy to perceive they are not the same, but are at least distinguishable from each other.

From David Hume, *A Treatise of Human Nature.*

Here, therefore, is a proposition which not only seems in itself simple and intelligible, but, if a proper use were made of it, might render every dispute equally intelligible, and banish all that jargon which has so long taken possession of metaphysical reasonings and drawn disgrace upon them. All ideas, especially abstract ones, are naturally faint and obscure. The mind has but a slender hold of them. They are apt to be confounded with other resembling ideas; and when we have often employed any term, though without a distinct meaning, we are apt to imagine it has a determinate idea annexed to it. On the contrary, all impressions, that is, all sensations either outward or inward, are strong and vivid. The limits between them are more exactly determined, nor is it easy to fall into any error or mistake with regard to them. When we entertain, therefore, any suspicion that a philosophical term is employed without any meaning or idea (as is but too frequent), we need but inquire, from what impression is that supposed idea derived? And if it be impossible to assign any, this will serve to confirm our suspicion. By bringing ideas in so clear a light, we may reasonably hope to remove all dispute which may arise concerning their nature and reality.

From David Hume, *An Inquiry Concerning Human Understanding.*

IMMANUEL KANT

The Source of Knowledge Is the Mind and the Senses

Immanuel Kant (1724–1804), born in Prussia, was a philosopher who investigated the scope and nature of reason.

The rationalists and the empiricists were in agreement about one thing: knowledge has a single source. Immanuel Kant challenges this assumption and assigns a role to both the mind and the senses. In the introduction of his major contribution to epistemology, The Critique of Pure Reason, *Kant offers some initial reasons in support of his view. He dismisses the possibility of the mind functioning on its own, since it needs something external to it to awaken it to action. This something would be an object which affects our senses. Further, we cannot account for everything via sensory input, since some things, like space, are not presented to us by the senses. Kant draws this conclusion after performing an ingenious thought experiment where he strips an object in space of all of its sensory qualities. The object disappears before he makes any attempt to remove its feature of being in space. So, it must not have been the senses that told us that the object was in space to begin with; it was an* a priori *contribution of the mind.*

There can be no doubt that all our knowledge begins with experience. For how should our faculty of knowledge be awakened into action did not objects affecting our senses partly of themselves produce representations, partly arouse the activity of our understanding to compare these representations, and, by combining or separating them, work up the raw material of the sensible impressions into that knowledge of objects which is entitled experience? In the order of time, therefore, we have no knowledge antecedent to experience, and with experience all our knowledge begins.

But though all our knowledge begins with experience, it does not follow that it all arises out of experience. For it may well be that even our empirical knowledge is made up of what we receive through impressions and of what our own faculty of knowledge (sensible impressions serving merely as the occasion) supplies from itself. If our faculty of knowledge makes any such addition, it may be that we are not in a position to distinguish it from the raw material, until with long practice of attention we have become skilled in separating it.

This, then, is a question which at least calls for closer examination, and does not allow of any off-hand answer:—whether there is any knowledge that is thus independent of experience and even of all impressions of the senses. Such knowledge is entitled *a priori*, and distinguished from the *empirical*, which has its sources *a posteriori*, that is, in experience. . . .

Such *a priori* origin is manifest in certain concepts, no less than in judgments. If we remove from our empirical concept of a body, one by one, every feature in it which is [merely] empirical, the colour, the hardness or softness, the weight, even the impenetrability, there still remains the space which the body (now entirely vanished) occupied, and this cannot be removed. Again, if we remove from our empirical concept of any object, corporeal or incorporeal, all properties which experience has taught us, we yet cannot take away that property through which the object is thought as substance or as inhering in a substance (although this concept of substance is more determinate than that of an object in general). Owing, therefore, to the necessity with which this concept of substance forces itself upon us, we have no option save to admit that it has its seat in our faculty of *a priori* knowledge.

From Immanuel Kant, *Critique of Pure Reason,* translated by Norman Kemp Smith.

DAVID HUME

Animals Don't Reason But Do Learn from Experience and Custom and Are Guided by Instinct

David Hume (1711–1776) was a Scottish empiricist and skeptic.

David Hume observes that both humans and animals can learn from experience. This type of learning requires the inference of a fact that goes beyond what the senses directly tell us. In the case of humans, the inference can be made by reason, but, in the case of animals, it is only custom that allows for the inference. Animals, in effect, have been trained to respond in certain ways to certain events and in that training consists the "custom." Hume also claims that other aspects of the knowledge of animals can be traced to instincts. Instincts too are something we share with nonhuman animals. In fact, the experimental reasoning of humans is itself but a species of instinct.

All our reasonings concerning matter of fact are founded on a species of *analogy* which leads us to expect from any cause the same events which we have observed to result from similar causes. Where the causes are entirely similar, the analogy is perfect, and the inference drawn from it is regarded as certain and conclusive; nor does any man ever entertain a doubt, where he sees a piece of iron, that it will have weight and cohesion of parts as in all other instances which have ever fallen under his observation. But where the objects have not so exact a similarity, the analogy is less perfect and the inference is less conclusive, though still it has some force, in proportion to the degree of similarity and resemblance. The anatomical observations formed upon one animal are, by this species of reasoning, extended to all animals; and it is certain that, when the circulation of the blood, for instance, is clearly proved to have place in one creature, as a frog or fish, it forms a strong presumption that the same principle has place in all. These analogical observations may be carried further, even to this science of which we are now treating; and any theory by which we explain the operations of the understanding or the origin and connection of the passions in man will acquire additional authority if we find that the same theory is requisite to explain the same phenomena in all other animals. We shall make trial of this with regard to the hypothesis by which we have, in the foregoing discourse, endeavored to account for all experimental reasonings, and it is hoped that this new point of view will serve to confirm all our former observations.

First, it seems evident that animals, as well as men, learn many things from experience and infer that the same events will always follow from the same causes. By this principle they become acquainted with the more obvious properties of external objects and gradually, from their birth, treasure up a knowledge of the nature of fire, water, earth, stones, heights, depths, etc., and of the effects which result from their operation. The ignorance and inexperience of the young are here plainly distinguishable from the cunning and sagacity of the old, who have learned, by long observation, to avoid what hurt them and to pursue what gave ease or pleasure. A horse that has been accustomed to the field becomes acquainted with the proper height which he can leap, and will never attempt what exceeds his force and ability. An old greyhound will trust the more fatiguing part of the chase to the younger and will place himself so as to meet the hare in her doubles; nor are the conjectures which he forms on this occasion founded in anything but his observation and experience.

This is still more evident from the effects of discipline and education on animals, who by the proper application of rewards and punishments may be taught any course of action the most contrary to their natural instincts and propensities. Is it not experience which renders a dog apprehensive of pain when you menace him or lift up the whip to beat him? Is it not even experience which makes him answer to his name and infer, from such an arbitrary sound, that you mean him rather than any of his fellows, and intend to call him when you pronounce it in a certain manner and with a certain tone and accent?

In all these cases we may observe that the animal infers some fact beyond what immediately strikes his senses, and that this inference is altogether founded on past experience, while the creature expects from the present object the same consequences which it has always found in its observation to result from similar objects.

Secondly, it is impossible that this inference of the animal can be founded on any process of argument or reasoning by which he concludes that like events must follow like objects, and that the course of nature will always be regular in its operations. For if there be in reality any arguments of this nature, they surely lie too abstruse for the observation of such imperfect understandings, since it may well employ the utmost care and attention of a philosophic genius to discover and observe them. Animals, therefore, are not guided in these inferences by reasoning; neither are children; neither are the generality of mankind in their ordinary actions and conclusions; neither are philosophers themselves, who, in all the active parts of life, are in the main the same with the vulgar and are governed by the same maxims. Nature must have provided some other principle, of more ready and more general use and application, nor can an operation of such immense consequences in life as that of inferring effects from causes be trusted to the uncertain process of reasoning and argumentation. Were this doubtful with regard to men, it seems to admit of no question with regard to the brute creation; and the conclusion being once firmly established in the one, we have a strong presumption, from all the rules of analogy, that it ought to be universally admitted without any exception or reserve. It is custom alone which engages animals, from every object that strikes their senses, to infer its usual attendant, and carries their imagination from the appearance of the one to conceive the other in that particular manner which we denominate "belief." No other explication can be given of this operation, in all the higher as well as lower classes of sensitive beings which fall under our notice and observation.

But though animals learn many parts of their knowledge from observation, there are also many parts of it which they derive from the original hand of nature, which much exceed the share of capacity they possess on ordinary occasions, and in which they improve little or nothing by the longest practice and experience. These we denominate "instincts," and are so apt to admire as something very extraordinary and inexplicable by all the disquisitions of human understanding.

But our wonder will perhaps cease or diminish when we consider that the experimental reasoning itself, which we possess in common with beasts, and on which the whole conduct of life depends, is nothing but a species of instinct or mechanical power that acts in us unknown to ourselves, and in its chief operations is not directed by any such relations or comparison of ideas as are the proper objects of our intellectual faculties. Though the instinct be different, yet still it is an instinct which teaches a man to avoid the fire, as much as that which teaches a bird, with such exactness, the art of incubation and the whole economy and order of its nursery.

From David Hume, *An Inquiry Concerning Human Understanding.*

Please Help Me. My Brain Is Burning. Painting by Julie Speed, 1994.

ELIZABETH FEE

To Know Is to Be Connected with What Is Known

Elizabeth Fee (1946–), born in Belfast, Northern Ireland, is a philosopher of science and an historian of public health.

Elizabeth Fee presents a feminist critique of how male scientists have gleaned knowledge from nature. They have set themselves apart from nature, dominated nature, and treated nature as a passive, inert entity. Feminists stress our interconnectedness with nature along with our seeing nature as living and active. Taking a broader look at things, Fee observes that many cultures are in agreement with this feminist way of viewing nature. But, in the bigger picture, it is not males who are to blame for disrupting a harmony between people and nature. Sometimes Westerners are blamed; sometimes an exploitative, moneyed class. In general, some group of dominators is to blame. With this analysis, Fee connects knowing about nature with living with nature, and, in so doing, breaks from many traditional analyses which focus only on how and what we can know about nature.

Let us now briefly look at the relationship between feminist epistemologies of science developed within Western capitalist countries and epistemologies of science that are presented as representing African, Indian, Chinese, and working-class perspectives on nature and natural knowledge. All of them appear to embody very similar ideas: conceptions of nature that in one context are denounced as masculine are in another denounced as European, colonial, white, or bourgeois.

Sandra Harding, in a paper on "The Curious Coincidence of African and Feminine World Views," makes part of this case by counterposing sets of quotations from Vernon Dixon's writings on African philosophy with those of feminist writers. Dixon argues that the sense of self in the African world view is intrinsically connected with both community and nature; the individual is defined by his or her relationships within the community, and not, as in the West, by contrast to the collectivity. Just as the individual can exist only in relationship to the community, so too, can he or she exist only in relationship to nature: human culture exists as a part of nature, not in opposition to nature. The epistemological consequences of this perspective are profound. As Harding summarizes the argument

> Because the self is continuous with nature rather than set over and against it, the need to dominate nature as an impersonal object is

replaced by the need to cooperate in nature's own projects. Coming to know is a process which involves concrete interactions, ones which acknowledge the role that emotions, feelings and values play in gaining knowledge and which recognizes the world-to-be-known as having its own values and projects.

Similarly, Russell Means, in his speech "Fighting Words on the Future of the Earth," denounced all forms of "European" thought as devoid of a spiritual appreciation of the natural world and, therefore, as leading merely to different forms of exploitation of the earth and its natural resources. In contrast to what he terms the *European forms of domination*, Means emphasizes American Indian traditions of respect for nature as active and alive rather than passive or dead, and he celebrates ways of knowing that are conceptualized as an interrelationship with natural forces rather than a process of domination and subordination. The argument that only the "Western" or "European" approach has been successful in exploiting the earth's resources is directly challenged: the Indian approaches to nature allowed communities to live in their environments, both using and conserving natural resources, and thus permitting the reproduction of societies for thousands of years. By contrast, the European approach has proved capable of denuding the land or poisoning the waters within remarkably short periods of time; decades or even years of exploitation can do irreversible damage to the land, making it unfit to support human life. From Means' point of view, the description of such an approach as "successful" requires a dangerous perversity of definition and human purpose.

Consider, also, some of Joseph Needham's characterizations of Chinese science. Chinese thought, says Needham, was profoundly non-Cartesian, refusing to make any sharp dichotomy between spirit and matter or between mind and body. Similarly, Chinese traditional medicine integrated spirit, mind, and body, diet and dreams, energy flows and physical sensations and remains highly successful at an empirical level, while resisting all efforts to define it within the categories of physiological reductionism. Chinese physics also remained impervious to mechanical materialism, atomism, and physical reductionism, remaining "perennially faithful to their prototypic wave theory of Yin and Yang. . . . The Yin and Yang, and the Five Elements, never lent themselves to reductionism because they were always inextricably together in the continuum . . . never separated out, isolated or 'purified,' even in theory." Abstract knowledge of the either A or not-A variety was avoided in Chinese science in favor of nonexclusive relationships of forces. In general, "man's" position relative to nature was conceived as one of intimate and harmonious relationship rather than one of domination. . . .

What, then, do we do with all this? Why do the themes presented in the feminist literature sound so similar to those of African, Indian,

Chinese, and working-class or Marxist perspectives on philosophy and science? Clearly, this whole topic deserves more extended exploration but, as a first statement, we can say that it is not sufficient to describe the conception of science being criticized simply as male nor to make the structure of the family and psycho-analytic theory bear the full burden of causal explanation. Indeed, the conception of science defined as male in much of the feminist literature belongs to a specific period of the last 300–400 years and is characteristic of the period of capitalist development; it *is* European and also male, and white, and bourgeois: it is also a historical creation with boundaries in time. At present we have at least three largely separate literatures, all critically addressing the forms of this science. In the literature of black and Indian liberation, it is addressed as white or European science; in the literature of feminism, it is addressed as male science; in at least some of the literature of Marxism, it is addressed as bourgeois science.

Clearly, these different critiques need to be brought together; we need to understand the relationship between them and to explore the question. Is this the same critique, simply expressed in different forms, or are we dealing with three (or more) different sets of problems? It seems to me that any one of these critiques provides a partial, but incomplete, perspective—and each adds important elements otherwise missing in the analysis.

Each of these critiques addresses one set of dominant/dominated power relations articulated and reproduced within scientific knowledge, reflecting the unequal power relations in the social world; the critiques thus undermine the scientific legitimation of those dominant/dominated relations. In this view, scientific knowledge is a synthesis and reflection of dominant/dominated relations in the "natural" (human) world. This is not to say that the sciences do not also provide ways of understanding, using, manipulating, and controlling the natural world; the point is, they do so by means of our human relationships. And these relationships are unequal in terms of power across several boundaries: class and race, as well as of gender. By necessity, all of these power relations are reproduced within scientific knowledge; the scientist, the creator of knowledge, cannot step outside his or her social persona and cannot evade the fact that he or she occupies a particular historical moment. The idea of a pure knowing mind outside history is simply an epistemological conceit. Reflected within science is the particular moment of struggle of social classes, races, and genders found in the real, natural, and human world.

Power, then, cannot simply be discussed in terms of male domination; maleness is articulated within a set of power relations of race, class, and nationality. Similarly, femaleness is not a single thing but is also articulated within a set of power relations—again, class, race, and nation. These forms of domination are not separate, or exterior to each other, but are integrated. Thus, you cannot be a woman without being a woman of a certain class, race, and country; similarly, you cannot be a woman without being a woman in a particular moment in history—and that moment in history will carry its own definition of what it means to be a "woman," what it means to belong to a certain class, race, and so on. All of these terms are continually being redefined in the context of ongoing political and ideological struggles; they are never static.

From Elizabeth Fee, "Critiques of Modern Science: The Relationship of Feminism to Other Radical Epistemologies," in *Feminist Approaches to Science.*

PATRICIA HILL COLLINS

An Afrocentric/Feminist Standpoint Challenges the Tradition of Positivism

Patricia Hill Collins (1948–) is a sociologist who has written extensively on the experiences of African-American women.

Patricia Hill Collins argues that positivist approaches to the acquisition of knowledge—which require that the investigators distance themselves from their subjects and remain as neutral and "objective" as possible—are flawed. As an alternative to the tradition of positivism, she points to the epistemological approaches she believes are used by herself and many other African-American women. Deriving in part from West African traditions, the alternative epistemology values the concrete rather than the abstract, emphasizes the importance of personal experience and testimony, and encourages the pursuit of knowledge through community dialogue.

P ositivist approaches aim to create scientific descriptions of reality by producing objective generalizations. Because researchers have widely differing values, experiences, and emotions, genuine science is thought to be unattainable unless all human characteristics except rationality are eliminated from the research process. By following strict methodological rules, scientists aim to distance themselves from the values, vested interests, and emotions generated by their class, race, sex, or unique situation. By decontextualizing themselves, they allegedly become detached observers and manipulators of nature. Moreover, this researcher decontextualiztion is paralleled by comparable efforts to remove the objects of study from their contexts. The result of this entire process is often the separation of information from meaning.

Several requirements typify positivist methodological approaches. First, research methods generally require a distancing of the researcher from her or his "object" of study by defining the researcher as a "subject" with full human subjectivity and by objectifying the "object" of study. A second requirement is the absence of emotions from the research process. Third, ethics and values are deemed inappropriate in the research process, either as the reason for scientific inquiry or as part of the research process itself. Finally, adversarial debates, whether written or oral, become the preferred method of ascertaining truth: the arguments that can withstand the greatest assault and survive intact become the strongest truths.

Such criteria ask African-American women to objectify ourselves, devalue our emotional life, displace our motivations for furthering knowledge about Black women, and confront in an adversarial relationship those with more social, economic, and professional power. It therefore seems unlikely that Black women would use a positivist epistemological stance in rearticulating a Black women's standpoint. Black women are more likely to choose an alternative epistemology for assessing knowledge claims, one using different standards that are consistent with Black women's criteria for substantiated knowledge and with our criteria for methodological adequacy. If such an epistemology exists, what are its contours?. . .

Because Black women have access to both the Afrocentric and the feminist standpoints, an alternative epistemology used to rearticulate a Black women's standpoint should reflect elements of both traditions. . . . While an Afrocentric feminist epistemology reflects elements of epistemologies used by African-Americans and women as groups, it also paradoxically demonstrates features that may be unique to Black women. On certain dimensions Black women may most closely resemble Black men; on others, white women; and on still others Black women may stand apart from both groups. Black women's both/and conceptual orientation, the act of being simultaneously a member of a group and yet standing apart from it, forms an integral part of Black women's consciousness. . . .

Rather than emphasizing how a Black women's standpoint and its accompanying epistemology are different from those in Afrocentric and feminist analysis, I use Black women's experiences to examine points of contact between the two. Viewing an Afrocentric feminist epistemology in this way challenges additive analyses of oppression claiming that Black women have a more accurate view of oppression than do other groups. Such approaches suggest that oppression can be quantified and compared and that adding layers of oppression produces a potentially clearer standpoint. One implication of standpoint approaches is that the more subordinated the group, the purer the vision of the oppressed group. This is an outcome of the origins of standpoint approaches in Marxist social theory, itself an analysis of social structure rooted in Western either/or dichotomous thinking. Ironically, by quantifying and ranking human oppressions, standpoint theorists invoke criteria for methodological adequacy characteristic of positivism. Although it is tempting to claim that Black women are more oppressed than everyone else and therefore have the best standpoint from which to understand the mechanisms, processes, and effects of oppression, this simply may not be the case. . . .

For most African-American women those individuals who have lived through the experiences about which they claim to be experts are more believable and credible than those who have merely read or thought about such experiences. Thus concrete experience as a criterion for credibility frequently is invoked by Black women when making knowledge claims. For instance, Hannah Nelson describes the importance personal experience has for her: "Our speech is most directly personal, and every black person assumes that every other black person has a right to a personal opinion. In speaking of grave matters, your personal experience is considered very good evidence. With us, distant statistics are certainly not as important as the actual experience of a sober person." Similarly, Ruth Shays uses her concrete experiences to challenge the idea that formal education is the only route to knowledge: "I am the kind of person who doesn't have a lot of education, but both my mother and my father had good common sense. Now, I think that's all you need. I might not know how to use thirty-four words where three would do, but that does not mean that I don't know what I'm talking about. . . . I know what I'm talking about because I'm talking about myself. I'm talking about what I've lived through." Implicit in Ms. Shays's self-assessment is a critique of the type of knowlege that obscures the truth, the "thirty-four words" that cover up a truth that can be expressed in three.

Even after substantial mastery of white masculinist epistemologies, many Black women scholars invoke our own concrete experiences and those of other African-American women in selecting topics for investigation and methodologies used. . . .

Experience as a criterion of meaning with practical images as its symbolic vehicle is a fundamental epistemological tenet in African-American thought systems. . . In valuing the concrete, African-American women invoke not only an Afrocentric tradition but a women's tradition as well. . . .

"Dialogue implies talk between two subjects, not the speech of subject and object. It is a humanizing speech, one that challenges and resists domination," asserts Bell Hooks. For Black women new knowledge claims are rarely worked out in isolation from other individuals and are usually developed through dialogues with other members of a community. A primary epistemological assumption underlying the use of dialogue in assessing knowledge claims is that connectedness rather than separation is an essential component of the knowledge validation process. . . . Not to be confused with adversarial debate, the use of dialogue has deep roots in an African-based oral tradition and in African-American culture.

From Patricia Hill Collins, *Black Feminist Thought.*

RALPH WALDO EMERSON
The Mind Structures Sensory Input

Ralph Waldo Emerson (1803–1882) was a Boston philosopher, poet, and Unitarian minister.

Ralph Waldo Emerson is known for his transcendentalism. This philosophy places emphasis on the individual and the individual's experiences, particularly faith and intuition. Emerson traces the origin of this philosophy's name to Kant. Kant challenged Locke's notion that the mind is empty at birth with his view that transcendental forms of the mind structure our sensory input.

The Transcendentalist adopts the whole connexion of spiritual doctrine. He believes in miracle, in the perpetual openness of the human mind to new influx of light and power; he believes in inspiration, and in ecstasy. He wishes that the spiritual principle should be suffered to demonstrate itself to the end, in all possible applications to the state of man, without the admission of anything unspiritual; that is, anything positive, dogmatic, personal. Thus, the spiritual measure of inspiration is the depth of the thought, and never, who said it? And so he resists all attempts to palm other rules and measures on the spirit than its own. . . .

[I]f there is anything grand and daring in human thought or virtue, any reliance on the vast, the unknown; any presentiment; any extravagance of faith, the spiritualist adopts it as most in nature. The oriental mind has always tended to this largeness. Buddhism is an expression of it. The Buddhist who thanks no man, who says, "do not flatter your benefactors," but who in his conviction that every good deed can by no possibility escape its reward, will not deceive the benefactor by pretending that he has done more than he should, is a Transcendentalist.

You will see by this sketch that there is no such thing as a Transcendental *party;* that there is no pure Transcendentalist; that we know of none but the prophets and heralds of such a philosophy; that all who by strong bias of nature have leaned to the spiritual side in doctrine, have stopped short of their goal. We have had many harbingers and forerunners; but of a purely spiritual life, history has yet afforded no example. I mean, we have yet no man who has leaned entirely on his character, and eaten angels' food; who, trusting to his sentiments, found life made of miracles; who, working for universal aims, found himself fed, he knew not how; clothed, sheltered, and weaponed, he knew not how, and yet it was done by his own hands. Only in the instinct of the lower animals we find the suggestion of the methods of it, and something higher than our understanding. The squirrel hoards nuts, and the bee gathers honey, without knowing what they do, and they are thus provided for without selfishness or disgrace.

Shall we say, then, that Transcendentalism is the Saturnalia, or excess of Faith; the presentiment of a faith proper to man in his integrity, excessive only when his imperfect obedience hinders the satisfaction of his wish. Nature is transcendental, exists primarily, necessarily, ever works and advances, yet takes no thought for the morrow. A man owns the dignity of the life which throbs around him in chemistry, and tree, and animal, and in the involuntary functions of his own body; yet he is baulked when he tries to fling himself into this enchanted circle, where all is done without degradation. Yet genius and virtue predict in man the same absence of private ends, and of condescension to circumstances, united with every trait and talent of beauty and power.

This way of thinking, falling on Roman times, made Stoic philosophers; falling on despotic times, made patriot Catos and Brutuses; falling on superstitious times, made prophets and apostles; on popish times, made Protestants and ascetic monks, preachers of Faith against the preachers of Works; on prelatical times, made Puritans and Quakers; and falling on Unitarian and commercial times, makes the peculiar shades of Idealism which we know.

It is well known to most of my audience, that the Idealism of the present day acquired the name of Transcendental, from the use of that term by Immanuel Kant, of Konigsberg, who replied to the skeptical philosophy of Locke, which insisted that there was nothing in the intellect which was not previously in the experience of the senses, by showing that there was a very important class of ideas, or imperative forms, which did not come by experience, but through which experience was acquired; that these were intuitions of the mind itself; and he denominated them *Transcendental* forms. The extraordinary profoundness and precision of that man's thinking have given vogue to his nomenclature, in Europe and America, to that extent, that whatever belongs to the class of intuitive thought, is popularly called at the present day *Transcendental*.

Although, as we have said, there is no pure transcendentalist, yet the tendency to respect the intuitions, and to give them, at least in our creed, all authority over our experience, has deeply colored the conversation and poetry of the present day; and the history of genius and of religion in these times, though impure, and as yet not incarnated in any powerful individual, will be the history of this tendency.

From Ralph Waldo Emerson, "The Transcendentalist."

WILLARD VAN ORMAN QUINE

Knowledge Involves Justified True Belief with Some Qualifications

Willard Van Orman Quine (1908–) is an American logician and empiricist.

Willard Van Orman Quine considers knowledge as justified true belief. Plato identi-fied these elements of knowledge but didn't think they captured exactly what knowl-edge is. Quine brings out that one might have reasons (a justification) for a true belief but they can turn out to be the wrong reasons. He points to difficulties with thinking that knowledge entails certainty and ultimately suggests that we might do well to give up the notion of knowledge. Instead we should talk only of the various elements like true beliefs and beliefs that are more or less certain. Quine tells us that issues of this sort fall within the scope of epistemology *or the* theory of knowledge.

What counts as knowing something? First, one must believe it. Second, it must be true. Knowledge is true belief. However, as is often pointed out, not all true belief is knowledge. If something is be-lieved for the wrong reason but just happens to be true, it does not qualify as knowledge. Knowledge has accordingly been described more specifically as *justified* true belief.

But this definition is still not narrow enough, as Edmund Gettier pointed out. The justification underlying a belief can be as reasonable and conclusive as you please and yet be contravened by some circum-stance that nobody could reasonably have suspected. If this happens, and if by coincidence the belief is nevertheless true for other and inde-pendent reasons, then it is a justified true belief but still is undeserving of the name of knowledge. It is believed for the wrong reason.

An example is afforded by tabloids that appeared in the streets on November 7, 1918, mistakenly announcing an armistice. Two sports-men set sail from Boston in their little sloop that day, with the news-paper on board and certainly no radio. They landed in Bermuda four days later in the well-founded belief that the war was over. They were right, too; it had just ended. But their belief was not knowledge, for its grounds, though reasonable, were wrong.

The notion of knowledge is beset also by a less subtle difficulty: a vagueness of boundary. Knowledge connotes certainty; what shall we count as certain? Even if one holds that some things are absolutely cer-tain, and is prepared to specify a boundary between absolute certainty and the next best thing, still one would hesitate to limit knowledge to the absolutely certain. That would do violence to both the usage and the utility of the word.

We do better to accept the word "know" on a par with "big," as a matter of degree. It applies only to true beliefs, and only to pretty firm ones, but just how firm or certain they have to be is a question, like how big something has to be to qualify as big.

There is no place in science for bigness, because of this lack of boundary; but there is a place for the relation of biggerness. Here we see the familiar and widely applicable rectification of vagueness: disclaim the vague positive and cleave to the precise comparative. But it is inapplicable to the verb "know," even grammatically. Verbs have no comparative and superlative inflections, *sequitissimur* to the contrary notwithstanding (see *predicate logic*). I think that for scientific or philosophical purposes the best we can do is give up the notion of knowledge as a bad job and make do rather with its separate ingredients. We can still speak of a belief as true, and of one belief as firmer or more certain, to the believer's mind, than another. There is also the element of justification, but we saw its limitations.

These reflections perhaps belong in their rudimentary way to the branch of philosophy known as epistemology, or the theory of knowledge. Rejection of the very concept of knowledge is thus oddly ironical.

It is not skepticism. Skeptics accept the concept of knowledge and deny its applications. What we are concluding rather is that the term does not meet scientific and philosophical standards of coherence and precision. The term retains its rough utility in the vernacular, like "big," and, contrary to what the skeptic claims, there is plenty to which it then most emphatically applies.

The limitations of the concept have had insidious effects, however, even apart from philosophical contexts. Creationists challenge the evolutionists, who, being scientists, scruple to claim absolute certainty. The creationists then respond that the theory of evolution is therefore not known to be true, and hence that creationism should get equal time. Religious apologists and occultists on other fronts take heart in similar fashion. Sometimes also an unscrupulous criminal lawyer sees his way to exploiting the scientist's honest avowal of fallibility: it is not utterly and unequivocally known that the accused was in full possession of his faculties at the time of the atrocity. Beyond a reasonable doubt, perhaps? That, if justice is to prevail, is where the contest is resumed.

In closing I should acknowledge that there are two kinds of knowing: *knowing how*, as in swimming and bicycling, and *knowing that*. It is only the latter that has been exercising us here. *Knowing how* is a matter rather of what, thanks to one's training or insight, one can do. So in French; *on peut faire* is interchangeable, half the time, with *on sait faire*. Indeed our own *know* and *can* are ultimately the same word; compare the *kn* of *know* and the *cn* of *can*. In German, more obviously, we have *kennen* and *können*. The Greek and Latin *gno* of *gnostic* and *ignorant* is the same thing again.

This last recalls a witty coinage by the biochemist Albert Szent-Györgyi, told to me by the biochemist John Edsall. The substance concerned was not yet wholly identified, but had to be in the sugar family along with sucrose, glucose, dextrose, levulose. He called it *ignose*, after considering and rejecting *godnose*. Our admiring chuckle is followed by wonder at the triple play: i*gno*rant, *knows*, and the sugary *-ose*. But the first pair, we now see, is no accident.

From W. V. D. Quine, "Knowledge," in *Quiddities*.

ADRIENNE RICH

Students Must Claim an Education

Adrienne Rich (1929–) is a Pulitzer-prize winning American poet and essayist.

Adrienne Rich argues that students must not position themselves as passive recipients of knowledge. One gains knowledge—and finds one's own voice—only by actively engaging in and taking responsibility for learning.

The first thing I want to say to you who are students, is that you cannot afford to think of being here to *receive* an education; you will do much better to think of yourselves as being here to *claim* one. One of the dictionary definitions of the verb "to claim" is: *to take as the rightful owner; to assert in the face of possible contradiction.* "To receive" is *to come into possession of, to act as receptacle or container for; to accept as authoritative or true.* The difference is that between acting and being acted-upon. . . .

Responsibility to yourself means refusing to let others do your thinking, talking, and naming for you; it means learning to respect and use your own brains and instincts; hence, grappling with hard work. . . It means insisting that those to whom you give your friendship and love are able to respect your mind. . . .

Responsibility to yourself means that you don't fall for shallow and easy solutions—predigested books and ideas, weekend encounters guaranteed to change your life, taking "gut" courses instead of the ones you know will challenge you, bluffing at school and life instead of doing solid work. . . . It means we insist on a life of meaningful work, insist that work be as meaningful as love and friendship in our lives. It means, therefore, the courage to be "different"; not to be continuously available to others when we need time for ourselves and our work; to be able to demand of others—parents, friends, roommates, teachers, lovers, husbands, children—that they respect our sense of purpose and our integrity as persons. . . .

I have said that the contract on the student's part involves that you demand to be taken seriously so that you can also go on taking yourself seriously. This means seeking out criticism, recognizing that the most affirming thing anyone can do for you is demand that you push yourself further, show you the range of what you *can* do. . . .

From Adrienne Rich, "Claiming an Education."

GEORGE SANTAYANA

"Public Opinion"

George Santayana (1863–1952), born in Spain and educated in America, was a metaphysician and aesthetician at Harvard.

In "Public Opinion" George Santayana offers a profile of public opinion, referring to it at one point as parrot talk. He brings out how sometimes it is established by mere repetition of a phrase while, at other times, eloquence is what establishes it. It always begins, however, as someone's private opinion on a controversial matter in society; there is no such creature as a public which can have an opinion. So public opinion has none of the features we associate with knowledge nor does it serve any function in society. As a matter of fact, the proliferation of ideologies through public opinion is the sign of an unhealthy society.

Public opinion is like the wind; it becomes at times a formidable force, something a man finds himself borne along by or fighting against; yet in itself it is invisible, rises suddenly in gusts and squalls, and mysteriously disappears. If we ask ourselves what it is, we may perceive that the phrase, "public opinion," is characteristically fabulous, after the manner of literary philosophy: for the public is not a living organism, with senses and an intellect that can form opinions about ulterior matters. What is meant is some once private opinion that has turned into a form of words now prevalent among the public. Yet more than that is implied. For there are a thousand verbal opinions habitually prevalent in society, for instance about the weather or about money, that are not classed under public opinion, because each man feels them to spring up spontaneously in himself, by the suasion of his senses or most secret impulses: and the fact that other people feel as he does seems to him not a matter of public opinion but a consequence of human uniformity, like having two legs.

Thus "public opinion" does not signify merely private opinions prevalent amongst the public, but such opinions when they touch matters in public dispute or are due to contagion, having not been formed spontaneously among the people but imposed on them by eloquence or iteration. They are parrot opinions. Yet it is by contagion that mankind is most easily, radically, and perfectly educated. By contagion we learn our mother tongue and develop our deepest sentiments. This contagion of example is the greatest of blessings when that example is good: that is to say, when in following it we develop our powers without subjecting ourselves to any alien domination.

Public opinion may therefore be prevalent and even intolerant without being tyrannical, if it merely anticipates, as in rational precepts and true information, that which each individual would have at last discovered painfully for himself. In sparing him that labour and saving him from following false scents, this education liberates his energies, if he has them, to advance independently beyond public opinion, along the same chosen paths; and if he lacks energy, this same education at least domesticates him happily in his proper spiritual home. How far unanimity in a given community may be natural and how far artificial is a biological question to be answered in each case separately, according to the circumstances; but we may safely say that unanimity can never be absolute. The universal shout represents a thousand different sentiments, and outrages many a silent heart; and even when the wave of passion buries all private differences, as it often does for a moment, when the wave subsides the differences come again to the surface, and that unanimity begins to seem, in retrospect, an ignominious drunken unanimity. The leaders, to whom the sentiment then dominant may have been natural and ineradicable, will then be driven to propaganda, or to perpetual preaching in special circles; while the indifferent crowd goes about its private affairs with a smile or a sneer, or a conventional affectation of deference. Then, even if the expression of public opinion seems to be unanimous, in religion, morals, or politics, it will not be unanimous really. It may even not exist at all, if the current expression of it signifies nothing but a cynical or prudent conformity to custom, for the sake of convenience or of ulterior interests. In a complex society, in which various traditions have been superposed and subsist together, there is sometimes a curious coexistence of two contrary public opinions on the same subject, as there used to be about duelling. Everybody as a Christian condemned the practice and everybody as a man of honour approved of it and conformed to it. I think much the same thing happens in regard to immortality. All modern religions—and almost everybody accepts some form of religion—assert it: yet everybody in his secular life and in making his will ignores it, and would be surprised and annoyed to hear it spoken of, out of church, as if it were a fact.

I think, however, that variability is less useful and amiable in public opinion than in the private mind. The private mind begins without experience, quite properly asks every sort of question, and is capable when mature of original ideas and discoveries. But public opinion moves without memory or possible method on a background of antideluvian prejudices: its immediate organs are custom, hearsay, and eloquence, three things not conducive to progress. Yet custom, though conservative and in itself irrational, normally has some *raison d'être*: at least it cannot be so absurd as to have proved suicidal. And many customs rest on primary instincts and social necessities, as language and conscience do; so that the public opinion that insists on them is right in being conservative. It is far more likely to be wise than is any reversal of it. Eloquence, also, though it intoxicates, draws its power from radical impulses and latent aspirations in human nature which it stirs up and brings suddenly to the surface. It may inspire the maddest action, yet it does *inspire*: and this awakening of the soul, however inopportune, opens up a vista towards some real good that wisdom should take account of. It is only the domination of hearsay, vulgar irresponsible hearsay, without piety or eloquence, that renders public opinion helpless and dangerous, inconstant without originality, and destructive without understanding what it destroys. The merciless oblivion that falls then upon things foreign or past removes all possibility of wisdom in political action.

The ballast of wisdom that public opinion draws in a primitive society from custom and eloquence, it draws in a highly organised society from institutions. Institutions are incorporated customs, customs sanctioned by express enactment, or prescribed and perpetuated by special classes of men, like priests, magistrates, or physicians. To keep lunar feasts and divide the month into quarters or weeks, giving each day of the week the name of some planet, was an ancient custom with some peoples; but the Hebrew Sabbath was an institution. So to sing occasionally is a habit, perhaps older than articulate speech; but it becomes an institution when choirs are trained to sing particular hymns on particular days. Spontaneous virtue here turns before our eyes into traditional domination. Institutions define and impose certain customs, which seem to lose the plasticity of nature; on the other hand, they accumulate experience, and supply an enduring basis for elaboration and refinements in the chosen art. At every stage an institution, since it builds on the achievements of its past, carries on a greater body of experience; and it thereby really increases the number of points from which further variations may start. Yet such happy development in the arts cannot be long continued, because human nature retains potentialities neglected by the original choice of a method and a particular direction of growth; and the inspired man cannot be content to go on forever refining the old method and expanding the old theme. He prefers to break away altogether, and begin again at the beginning in a new direction.

Public opinion, too, starts perpetually at the beginning, because all the potentialities of human nature stir unrecognised somewhere in the midst of a crowd; and almost any suggestion will find a response somewhere, at least for a moment. But almost all such awakenings die down at once, like a fire in straw. There is nothing at hand to feed or support them, and the mind lets them drop a little sadly, but resignedly, taking refuge in its old commonplaces and its old vices. Sometimes, however, the new suggestion proves opportune, the spark becomes a bonfire, and there is an attempt at a real revolution, or a seeming success in it. I say a seeming success, because it would be a miracle if a popular cry, founded on no knowledge and representing no broad or constant force in human society, should really initiate a fresh set of institutions. It may at best establish a new nomenclature (as the French and Russian revolutions did for a time) and put in office a new set of men, who will repeat the biography of all governments, if they succeed in retaining power after they have ceased to destroy and begin to construct.

The real change, the radical revolution, will not have been the work of public opinion or of human intention at all. Revolutions do not succeed, they are not even attempted, in healthy commonwealths. Your successful revolutionaries are like malicious doctors at a death bed, who should boast of having killed the patient. They may have wished to do it, and he may have died. They may even have made a fatal injection at the moment when he was about to expire. But he would have died without their help; for if he had been curable they never would have been called to his bedside, nor nursed those hostile intentions. The reformers are themselves symptoms of the public disease.

Health is not conscious of itself, but frees the mind for the perception of other things; and even the joy of health, when it comes to the surface, comes rather in the form of some generous enthusiasm for nature, for sport, or for loveable people. So the health of society does not express itself in public opinion but in public affections, in a general enhanced vitality in all the arts, without controversial theories about them. But when society is deeply troubled, when men do not know what to do, what to think, what to enjoy, or how to avoid hateful compulsions, then every complaint and every panacea gathers adherents, parties arise, and ideologies fill the atmosphere with their quarrels. The misfortunes that meantime overtake the public are attributed to the party lately in power, but they continue unabated; so that the alternation of parties is rapid, yet less disastrous than a naive observer might have suspected. For beneath the follies that each successive party may advocate or even carry out, the vital constitution of society, with its traditional customs and pleasures, continues undisturbed; strangely undisturbed on the whole even amid the most cruel wars. Therefore each party can "point with pride" at the degree of prosperity or at the public works that graced its administration; for all these ideologies are too superficial and these men too commonplace to make much difference in the natural course of events, upward or downward, as the circumstances of the age may determine. For there are real revolutions in things, migrations, and confusion of peoples, decay and invention in the arts, intensification or disappearance of commerce: and on such real mutations the ideas and the shouts of the public play a thin and inconstant treble.

George Santayana, "Public Opinion."

Woodcut illustration of Adam and Eve (*Genesis 3*) from the *Coverdale Bible*.

MORALITY

INTRODUCTION

As thinking, imagining beings, we have the capacity to envision different possible courses of action open to us at a given time. We are creatures who can and must make choices, and some of these choices are really quite difficult. Suppose your best friend comes to you and asks you to lie so that your friend might avoid disciplinary action and possible expulsion from the university. What should you do? You know that there is a general disapprobation against lying in our culture, but at the same time a high value is placed on loyalty to one's friends. You want to be a good friend, and yet you certainly don't want to jeopardize your own college career. You want to "do the right thing," but what should your choice be and upon what considerations should it be based?

Moral philosophers, working in the field of *ethics*, grapple with the thorny questions surrounding the concept of morality. They investigate whether there is a correct moral standard to which we all should subscribe and, if such a standard exists, what its content might be. Suppose, as you try to make a decision, you decide to seek advice from others including your friends, your family, and an authority figure you especially trust, perhaps, for example, a religious leader. You might soon find that there is considerable disagreement in the advice you are given. The divergent opinions about morality—and the variability of moral practices over time and between different cultures and societies—have led a number of moral theorists to argue that there is no one universal moral code that applies to all persons at all times. Some of these theorists, called *ethical relativists*, suggest that, while there is no overarching moral theory that applies to all of us, nonetheless there are "local" moral standards that do tell us what is right or wrong. *Societal ethical relativists* believe that each society has its own moral standards and practices which are correct for and should be followed by the members of the society. If you are a good societal ethical relativist, then you are a good person if you abide by the moral practices of the society at large. The fact that there can be vehement differences among the members of a society about moral issues has led some philosophers to adopt a more extreme form of relativism, called *individual ethical relativism* or *subjectivism*. The individual ethical relativist says that each of us is responsible for creating his or her own morality: there are no moral authorities outside myself and there are no external moral principles which I need to follow. I am a good person, on this view, as long as I follow a moral code of my choosing. *Ethical nihilists*, like the relativists, reject the notion of an overarching universal morality, but, unlike the relativists, they reject the idea that there are any moral standards. The ethical nihilist argues that there is no morality; no actions are morally better than any other. There is no moral good, and there is no moral evil. Our sacred texts are mistaken, our social values have no greater substance than the rules of etiquette, and our own consciences are nothing but delusive inner voices.

While acknowledging the cacophony of voices that comprises ethical discussion, many philosophers, called *ethical universalists*, disagree with both the relativists and the nihilists and argue for—and attempt to delineate the content of—an objective, universal moral standard. Three versions of universalism have been especially prevalent in Western philosophy, and each focuses on and develops a familiar strand of moral reasoning. When thinking about how to respond to your friend's request, you will likely think of the possible consequences of the action. Will lying really help your friend? Who might be hurt by the lie? What about your own well being? You might also wonder whether the consequences matter at all: isn't lying simply wrong? Doesn't any lie dishonor those to whom the lie is told? *Ethical egoism* and *utilitarianism* are two versions of universalism which would have you look at the possible consequences of your action when deciding what to do. The ethical egoist advises you that the "right thing to do" in all cases is to choose the action that maximizes your personal well being over the long run. The utilitarian tells you to take not just yourself, but all individuals affected by your action, into account: the good action is the one that maximizes overall well being rather than your own personal well being. *Kantians* reject the relevance of consequences in moral decision making: to "do the right thing" is to respect others as rational beings. Since lying, stealing, and cheating invariably involve disrespecting others, they are actions which ought never to be performed.

All universalist theories offer rules for action, and, if universalism is correct, then to be a good person is simply (!!) to discover the correct set of rules and apply them to one's life. But, are the principles of morality to be followed without fail in every case? Or, as some pragmatists have argued, should we look upon the rules as guides for action that themselves are open to revision in the light of experience and technological change?

Some recent feminist philosophers who advocate an *ethics of care* have speculated that conceiving of morality as essentially a rule-governed enterprise fails to do justice to the complexity of moral decision-making. They argue that, if we are to be truly responsible for our moral lives and decisions, we must be the authors of those decisions. Rather than reading off our moral decisions from a set of rules, we create the right thing to do through an act of decision—a decision that is not capricious or arbitrary, but is guided by our emotional and affectional ties to ourselves and others, by our caring for those around us.

Thinking about the concept of morality itself—like thinking about the moral decisions we must make—is difficult and often frustrating. The issues are complex, and our own judgements, both intuitive and reflective, often conflict with each other: "What's right for me might be wrong for you" is a relativist catchphrase that has considerable intuitive appeal (and one that conveniently allows us to sweep away criticisms from others of our behavior); but it is a catchphrase that is in tension with another commonplace moral sentiment that there are certain human rights (perhaps, for example, the right not to be tortured) that all societies ought to recognize. However difficult thinking about morality may be, it is a task that critical inquirers should embrace; for in defining the sphere of morality and the moral community around us (do we have obligations only to ourselves? our friends and families? all humans? non-human animals? the biotic system?), we define and shape ourselves.

CHARLES SANDERS PEIRCE
Look to Science for Advice on Moral Development

We saw in Chapter 1 how Charles Sanders Peirce drew on the experimental model of science for rethinking philosophy and developing pragmatism. His commitment to science likewise shapes his thinking about ethics. He finds that science demands certain character traits—sincerity, love of truth, honesty, and fair-mindedness. So the person who goes down the path of science goes down the path of goodness. As long as moral development can proceed hand in hand with scientific development, Peirce has no complaints with morality. But morality has an essentially conservative component to it, since it is basically a set of shared beliefs with a long history that is not to be questioned. In this sense morality will always stand at odds with science which embraces free inquiry as a necessary component. In another passage, Peirce returns to extolling what we might learn about ethics from science. He first brings out how various ethical systems are deficient because of what they identify as desirable to attain. Science, however, strives for reasonableness which Peirce identified as "the only ethically sound motive."

The important thing is to make ourselves thoroughly acquainted, as far as possible from the inside, with a variety of human motives ranging over the whole field of ethics.

I will not go further into ethics than simply to remark that all motives that are directed toward pleasure or self-satisfaction, of however high a type, will be pronounced by every experienced person to be inevitably destined to miss the satisfaction at which they aim. This is true even of the highest of such motives, that which Josiah Royce develops in his *World and Individual*. On the other hand, every motive involving dependence on some other leads us to ask for some ulterior reason. The only desirable object which is quite satisfactory in itself without any ulterior reason for desiring it, is the reasonable itself. I do not mean to put this forward as a demonstration; because, like all demonstrations about such matters, it would be a mere quibble, a sheaf of fallacies. I maintain simply that it is an experiential truth.

The only ethically sound motive is the most general one; and the motive that actually inspires the man of science, if not quite that, is very near to it—nearer, I venture to believe, than that of any other equally common type of humanity.

From C. S. Peirce, "The Scientific Attitude and Fallibilism."

Ascientific man must be single-minded and sincere with himself. Otherwise, his love of truth will melt away, at once. He can, therefore, hardly be otherwise than an honest, fair-minded man. True, a few naturalists have been accused of purloining specimens; and some men have been far from judicial in advocating their theories. Both of these faults must be exceedingly deleterious to their scientific ability. But on the whole, scientific men have been the best of men. It is quite natural, therefore, that a young man who might develop into a scientific man should be a well-conducted person.

Yet in more ways than one an exaggerated regard for morality is unfavourable to scientific progress. I shall present only one of those ways. It will no doubt shock some persons that I should speak of morality as involving an element which can become bad. To them good conduct and moral conduct are one and the same—and they will accuse me of hostility to morality. I regard morality as highly necessary; but it is a means to good life, not necessarily coextensive with good conduct. Morality consists in the folklore of right conduct. A man is brought up to think he ought to behave in certain ways. If he behaves otherwise, he is uncomfortable. His conscience pricks him. That system of morals is the traditional wisdom of ages of experience. If a man cuts loose from it, he will become the victim of his passions. It is not safe for him even to reason about it, except in a purely speculative way. Hence, morality is essentially conservative. Good morals and good manners are identical, except that tradition attaches less importance to the latter. The gentleman is imbued with conservatism. This conservatism is a habit, and it is the law of habit that it tends to spread and extend itself over more and more of the life. In this way, conservatism about morals leads to conservatism about manners and finally conservatism about opinions of a speculative kind. Besides, to distinguish between speculative and practical opinions is the mark of the most cultivated intellects. Go down below this level and you come across reformers and rationalists at every turn—people who propose to remodel the ten commandments on modern science. Hence it is that morality leads to a conservatism which any new view, or even any free inquiry, no matter how purely speculative, shocks.

From C. S. Peirce, "Two Notes."

WILLIAM JAMES

Take a Scientific Approach to Ethics to Maximize Human Satisfaction

Peirce fell short of applying to ethics the pragmatic, experimental method which he borrowed from science. Instead he held the goal of science itself, reasonableness, along with the character traits of the freely inquiring scientist, to be significant for overcoming the problems which he associated with morality and ethical theory. William James asks that we be pragmatic in our ethics and explicitly rejects any final truths in ethics. As we approach ethics in a scientific fashion, we are experimenting to find how we can meet as many human demands as possible with a minimal creation of dissatisfaction.

The main purpose of this paper is to show that there is no such thing possible as an ethical philosophy dogmatically made up in advance. We all help to determine the content of ethical philosophy so far as we contribute to the race's moral life. In other words, there can be no final truth in ethics any more than in physics, until the last man has had his experience and said his say. In the one case as in the other, however, the hypotheses which we now make while waiting, and the acts to which they prompt us, are among the indispensable conditions which determine what that 'say' shall be. . . .

Since everything which is demanded is by that fact a good, must not the guiding principle for ethical philosophy (since all demands conjointly cannot be satisfied in this poor world) be simply to satisfy at all times *as many demands as we can?* That act must be the best act, accordingly, which makes for the *best whole,* in the sense of awakening the least sum of dissatisfactions. In the casuistic scale, therefore, those ideals must be written highest which *prevail at the least cost,* or by whose realization the least possible number of other ideals are destroyed. Since victory and defeat there must be, the victory to be philosophically prayed for is that of the more inclusive side—of the side which even in the hour of triumph will to some degree do justice to the ideals in which the vanquished party's interests lay. The course of history is nothing but the story of men's struggles from generation to generation to find the more and more inclusive order. *Invent some manner* of realizing your own ideals which will also satisfy the alien demands—that and that only is the path of peace. Following this path, society has shaken itself into one sort of relative equilibrium after another by a series of social discoveries quite analogous to those of science. Polyandry and polygamy and slavery, private warfare and liberty to kill, judicial torture and arbitrary royal power have slowly succumbed to actually aroused complaints; and though someone's ideals are unquestionably the worse off for each improvement, yet a vastly greater total number of them find shelter in our civilized society than in the older [societies]. . . .

All this amounts to saying that, so far as the casuistic question goes, ethical science is just like physical science, and instead of being deducible all at once from abstract principles, must simply bide its time, and be ready to revise its conclusions from day to day. . . .

On the whole, then, we must conclude that no philosophy of ethics is possible in the old-fashioned absolute sense of the term. Everywhere the ethical philosopher must wait on facts. . . .

In point of fact, there are no absolute evils, and there are no nonmoral goods; and the *highest* ethical life—however few may be called to bear its burdens—consists at all times in the breaking of rules which have grown too narrow for the actual case. There is but one unconditional commandment, which is that we should seek incessantly, with fear and trembling, so to vote and to act as to bring about the very largest total universe of good which we can see. Abstract rules indeed can help; but they help the less in proportion as our intuitions are more piercing, and our vocation is the stronger for the moral life. For every real dilemma is in literal strictness a unique situation; and the exact combination of ideals realized and ideals disappointed which each decision creates is always a universe without a precedent, and for which no adequate previous rule exists.

From William James, "The Moral Philosopher and the Moral Life."

John Dewey

Abandon Dogmatic Theories of Morality

Like James, John Dewey recommends that we approach morality with the experimental approach we use in science. We must free ourselves from dogmatic theories of morality. These theories require us to apply fixed and unalterable principles to our experience and reject the possibility that experience can guide us in improving our moral principles. While the experimental approach provides for the continued development of moral principles, it does not require us to disregard well-tested moral guidelines. The experimental approach simply insures that our principles and experiences are each relevant for the other. Dewey articulates these ideas well in a work co-authored with James Tufts.

To assume the existence of final and unquestionable knowledge upon which we can fall back in order to settle automatically every moral problem involves commitment to a dogmatic theory of morals. The alternative method may be called experimental. It implies that reflective morality demands observation of particular situations, rather than fixed adherence to a priori principles; that free inquiry and freedom of publication and discussion must be encouraged and not merely grudgingly tolerated; that opportunity at different times and places must be given for trying different measures so that their effects may be capable of observation and of comparison with one another. It is, in short, the method of democracy, of a positive toleration which amounts to sympathetic regard for the intelligence and personality of others, even if they hold views opposed to ours, and of scientific inquiry into facts and testing of ideas.

The opposed method, even when we free it from the extreme traits of forcible suppression, censorship, and intolerant persecution which have often historically accompanied it, is the method of appeal to authority and to precedent. The will of divine beings, supernaturally revealed; of divinely ordained rulers; of so-called natural law, philosophically interpreted; of private conscience; of the commands of the state, or the constitution; of common consent; of a majority; of received conventions; of traditions coming from a hoary past; of the wisdom of ancestors; of precedents set up in the past, have at different times been the authority appealed to. The common feature of the appeal is that there is some voice so authoritative as to preclude the need of inquiry. The logic of the various positions is that while an open mind may be desirable in respect to physical truths a completely settled and closed mind is needed in moral matters.

Adoption of the experimental method does not signify that there is no place for authority and precedent. On the contrary, precedent is a valuable *instrumentality*. But precedents are to be *used* rather than to be implicitly followed; they are to be used as tools of analysis of present situations, suggesting points to be looked into and hypotheses to be tried. They are of much the same worth as are personal memories in individual crises; a storehouse to be drawn upon for suggestion. There is also a place for the use of authorities. Even in free scientific inquiry, present investigators rely upon the findings of investigators of the past. They employ theories and principles which are identified with scientific inquirers of the past. They do so, however, only as long as *no evidence is presented calling for a reexamination of their findings and theories*. They never assume that these findings are so final that under no circumstances can they be questioned and modified. Because of partisanship, love of certainty, and devotion to routine, accepted points of view gain a momentum which for long periods even in science may restrict observation and reflection. But this limitation is recognized to be a weakness of human nature and not a desirable use of the principle of authority.

In moral matters there is also a presumption in favor of principles that have had a long career in the past and that have been endorsed by men of insight; the presumption is especially strong when all that opposes them is the will of some individual seeking exemption because of an impulse or passion which is temporarily urgent. Such principles are no more to be lightly discarded than are scientific principles worked out in the past. But in one as in the other, newly discovered facts or newly instituted conditions may give rise to doubts and indicate the inapplicability of accepted doctrines. In questions of social morality, more fundamental than any particular principle held or decision reached is the attitude of *willingness to reexamine and if necessary to revise current convictions, even if that course entails the effort to change by concerted effort existing institutions, and to direct existing tendencies to new ends.*

It is a caricature to suppose that emphasis upon the social character of morality leads to glorification of contemporary conditions just as they are. The position does insist that morals, to have vitality, must be related to these conditions or be up in the air. But there is nothing in the bare position which indicates whether the relation is to be one of favor or of opposition: A man walking in a bog must pay even more heed to his surroundings than a man walking on smooth pavement but this fact does not mean that he is to surrender to these surroundings. The alternative is not between abdication and acquiescence on one side, and neglect and ignoring on the other; it is between a morals which is effective because related to what is, and a morality which is futile and empty because framed in disregard of actual conditions. Against the social consequences generated by existing conditions there always stands the idea of other and better social consequences which a change would bring into being.

From John Dewey and James H. Tufts, *Ethics*.

Jane Addams

The Moral Equation Is Action Plus Its Social Significance

What counts in our moral lives is neither our motives nor personal integrity. Our motives together with mere speculation about what is right leave our actions out of the picture, and it is these actions which are essential to a correct depiction of moral experience. We gain moral knowledge only as we test our ideas about what is right by acting on them. Also essential is the social significance of these actions. Herein lies Jane Addams's dissatisfaction with the person whose only goal is the cultivation of personal integrity. Such a person fails to connect their efforts with those of the many. Those people who are able to act for all as they act as individuals typify what morality and democracy are all about and get a special satisfaction from acting in this way.

Perhaps the last and greatest difficulty in the paths of those who are attempting to define and attain a social morality, is that which arises from the fact that they cannot adequately test the value of their efforts, cannot indeed be sure of their motives until their efforts are reduced to action and are presented in some workable form of social conduct or control. For action is indeed the sole medium of expression for ethics. We continually forget that the sphere of morals is the sphere of action, that speculation in regard to morality is but observation and must remain in the sphere of intellectual comment, that a situation does not really become moral until we are confronted with the question of what shall be done in a concrete case, and are obliged to act upon our theory. A stirring appeal has lately been made by a recognized ethical lecturer who has declared that "It is insanity to expect to receive the data of wisdom by looking on. We arrive at moral knowledge only by tentative and observant practice. We learn how to apply the new insight by having attempted to apply the old and having found it to fail."

This necessity of reducing the experiment to action throws out of the undertaking all timid and irresolute persons, more than that, all those who shrink before the need of striving forward shoulder to shoulder with the cruder men, whose sole virtue may be social effort, and even that not untainted by self-seeking, who are indeed pushing forward social morality, but who are doing it irrationally and emotionally, and often at the expense of the well-settled standards of morality.

The power to distinguish between the genuine effort and the adventitious mistakes is perhaps the most difficult test which comes to our fallible intelligence. In the range of individual morals, we have learned to distrust him who would reach spirituality by simply renouncing the world, or by merely speculating upon its evils. The result, as well as the process of virtues attained by repression, has become distasteful to us. When the entire moral energy of an individual goes into the cultivation of personal integrity, we all know how unlovely the result may become; the character is upright, of course, but too coated over with the result of its own endeavor to be attractive. In this effort toward a higher morality in our social relations, we must demand that the individual shall be willing to lose the sense of personal achievement, and shall be content to realize his activity only in connection with the activity of the many. . . .

As the acceptance of democracy brings a certain life-giving power, so it has its own sanctions and comforts. Perhaps the most obvious one is the curious sense which comes to us from time to time, that we belong to the whole, that a certain basic well being can never be taken away from us whatever the turn of fortune. Tolstoy has portrayed the experience in "Master and Man." The former saves his servant from freezing, by protecting him with the heat of his body, and his dying hours are filled with an ineffable sense of healing and well-being. Such experiences, of which we have all had glimpses, anticipate in our relation to the living that peace of mind which envelopes us when we meditate upon the great multitude of the dead. It is akin to the assurance that the dead understand, because they have entered into the Great Experience, and therefore must comprehend all lesser ones; that all the misunderstandings we have in life are due to partial experience, and all life's fretting comes of our limited intelligence; when the last and Great Experience comes, it is, perforce, attended by mercy and forgiveness. Consciously to accept Democracy and its manifold experiences is to anticipate that peace and freedom.

From Jane Addams, *Democracy and Social Ethics.*

AYN RAND

Act to Further Self Interest

Ayn Rand (1905–1982), a Russian-born emigre to the United States, was a novelist, essayist, and philosopher.

The basic insight of the ethical egoist is that one acts with ethical correctness when one acts to further one's own good, well being, or interest. Some ethical egoists ground this advice in a theory of human nature known as psychological egoism which depicts us as creatures naturally motivated by self interest. Now, when ethical egoists tell us that we ought *to pursue self interest, they want to insure that we are not blindly propelled by self interest and that we think seriously about furthering self interest. Ayn Rand captures this notion in her theory of objectivism when she stresses the importance of maximizing* rational *self-interest. In her novel,* The Fountainhead, *Rand, speaking through the voice of the protagonist, depicts the sort of person who will be best situated to promote rational self-interest, and this person is not, as might initially be thought, one who gains happiness by exploiting or using others but rather is one who faces nature alone and is therefore a self-sustaining, independent source of personal happiness.*

When one speaks of man's right to exist for his own sake, for his own rational self-interest, most people assume automatically that this means his right to sacrifice others. Such an assumption is a confession of their own belief that to injure, enslave, rob or murder others is in man's self-interest—which he must selflessly renounce. The idea that man's self-interest can be served only by a non-sacrificial relationship with others has never occurred to those humanitarian apostles of unselfishness, who proclaim their desire to achieve the brotherhood of men. And it will not occur to them, or to anyone, so long as the concept "rational" is omitted from the context of "values," "desires," "self-interest" and *ethics.*

The Objectivist ethics proudly advocates and upholds *rational selfishness*—which means: the values required for man's survival *qua* man—which means: the values required for human survival—not the values produced by the desires, the emotions, the "aspirations," the feelings, the whims or the needs of irrational brutes, who have never outgrown the primordial practice of human sacrifices, have never discovered an industrial society and can conceive of no self-interest but that of grabbing the loot of the moment.

The Objectivist ethics holds that human good does not require human sacrifices and cannot be achieved by the sacrifice of anyone to anyone. It holds that the rational interests of men do not clash—that there is no conflict of interests among men who do not desire the unearned, who do not make sacrifices nor accept them, who deal with one another as *traders*, giving value for value.

The principle of *trade* is the only rational ethical principle for all human relationships, personal and social, private and public, spiritual and material. It is the principle of *justice*.

A trader is a man who earns what he gets and does not give or take the undeserved. He does not treat men as masters or slaves, but as independent equals. He deals with men by means of a free, voluntary, unforced, uncoerced exchange—an exchange which benefits both parties by their own independent judgment. A trader does not expect to be paid for his defaults, only for his achievements. He does not switch to others the burden of his failures, and he does not mortgage his life into bondage to the failures of others.

In spiritual issues (by "spiritual" I mean: "pertaining to man's consciousness") the currency or medium of exchange is different, but the principle is the same. Love, friendship, respect, admiration are the emotional response of one man to the virtues of another, the spiritual payment given in exchange for the personal, selfish pleasure which one man derives from the virtues of another man's character. Only a brute or an altruist would claim that the appreciation of another person's virtues is an act of selflessness, that as far as one's own selfish interest and pleasure are concerned, it makes no difference whether one deals with a genius or a fool, whether one meets a hero or a thug, whether one marries an ideal woman or a slut. In spiritual issues, a trader is a man who does not seek to be loved for his weaknesses or flaws, only for his virtues, and who does not grant his love to the weaknesses or the flaws of others, only to their virtues.

To love is to value. Only a rationally selfish man, a man of *self-esteem*, is capable of love—because he is the only man capable of holding firm, consistent, uncompromising, unbetrayed values. The man who does not value himself, cannot value anything or anyone.

It is only on the basis of rational selfishness—on the basis of justice—that men can be fit to live together in a free, peaceful, prosperous, benevolent, *rational* society.

From Ayn Rand, *The Virtue of Selfishness: A New Concept of Egoism.*

The man who attempts to live for others is a dependent. He is a parasite in motive and makes parasites of those he serves. The relationship produces nothing but mutual corruption. It is impossible in concept. The nearest approach to it in reality—the man who lives to serve others—is the slave. If physical slavery is repulsive, how much more repulsive is the concept of servility of the spirit? . . .

Men have been taught that their first concern is to relieve the suffering of others. But suffering is a disease. Should one come upon it, one tries to give relief and assistance. To make that the highest test of virtue is to make suffering the most important part of life. Then man must wish to see others suffer—in order that he may be virtuous. Such is the nature of altruism. . . .

As poles of good and evil, he was offered two conceptions: egoism and altruism. Egoism was held to mean the sacrifice of others to self. Altruism—the sacrifice of self to others. This tied man irrevocably to other men and left him nothing but a choice of pain. . . . Man was forced to accept masochism as his ideal—under the threat that sadism was his only alternative. This was the greatest fraud ever perpetrated on mankind. . . .

The choice is not self-sacrifice or domination. The choice is independence or dependence. . . . The egoist in the absolute sense is not the man who sacrifices others. He is the man who stands above the need of using others in any manner. He does not function through them. He is not concerned with them in any primary matter. . . . He does not exist for any other man—and asks no other man to exist for him. . . . Independence is the only gauge of human virtue and value. What a man does and makes of himself; not what he has or hasn't done for others. There is no substitute for personal dignity.

From Ayn Rand, *The Fountainhead.*

Hazel Barnes

We Are Free to Create Our Own Values

Hazel Barnes (1915–) is an American existentialist philosopher.

Hazel Barnes likens her existentialist ethics to Rand's objectivism: both underscore the importance of liberating the individual from views, whether they be social, religious, or psychological, which impose restraints on individual growth. But Rand's objectivism itself imposes the constraint of rationality on an individual's free acts of creating self and values. In setting out the essential features of an existential humanism, Barnes develops the notion of the human being as a value creator.

There are three concepts absolutely fundamental to humanistic existentialism which many persons, without further examination, accept as self-evident proof that any existentialist ethics is impossible. First, there is the idea that values are "created" by the individual who chooses them; they are not discovered. At most we may say that they are revealed and chosen in the way that the sculptor decides to bring into being *these* potentialities in a piece of marble rather than any others. Values are in no sense a priori. They do not fall into any objectively established hierarchy. Second, there is no ultimate independent and impersonal reference point by which to judge human conduct. There is neither a God nor Absolute Mind nor pre-established Human Nature. Third, the Sartrean view of human relations excludes the possibility of communion between persons which would dissolve the subject-object relationship. Subjects never become each other or directly experience each other's inner life, no matter how great the sympathy or how nearly perfect the communication between them. . . . [T]he existentialist man is an isolated individual who is not compelled to acknowledge his involvement with others unless he cares to do so. His one certainty is his own freedom. He has no source or origin in any divine Being or rational plan, and no pre-established goals. Without a sure pattern, he makes himself be.

I accept this view of what man is. I deny that it leaves no room for an ethics.

It would not be a distortion to say that both Objectivism and existentialism call for the assertion of the free individual against those theologies and those oppressively conformist societies which seek to make him deny his unique self in the interests of ready-made social molds and values. Both oppose a psychology which would reduce man to the animal level or to a mechanistic pattern of stimulus and response. They are equally opposed to the soul-body dichotomy of traditional theology. Objectivists and existentialists argue that every person is responsible for what he has made of his life. Each man is ultimately a free choice. In so far as they claim that man himself is his own end and purpose, both may properly be called humanistic. This is an impressive list of parallels. One might easily suppose that with the sympathetic sharing of such fundamental premises, the general similarity in their over-all positions would outweigh any differences in detail.

Only what emerges is not a common point of view. . . . [Objectivists believe that a] man is what he is. His essence is Reason. His values are rational. In short, every man, insofar as he fulfills his potential essence as Reason, *knows* what is right and what is wrong—absolutely. On this basis, Rand's fictional spokesman, John Galt, finds no difficulty in proclaiming to his audience, "Accept, as your moral ideal, the task of becoming a man."

If we were to prepare a comparable formulation for existentialism, it might run something like this: Man is a being who is what he is not and is not what he is. In him existence precedes his essence. Or better, man's essence is freedom itself, the choice of making his essence what he will. For himself he decides what is right and what is wrong, from his own point of view. His task is to make himself and to help prepare the definition of what man will have been.

"Existence is identity." "Existence precedes essence." *There* is the heart of the difference. Rand's view of man retains the old acorn theory. Man's potentialities may be hidden, but they resemble the embryo oak tree. The question is simply whether the individual will be, as it were, a bigger, stronger oak or a more feeble one. Everyone knows what a good oak tree ought to be and how to judge it. Oak tree nature and human nature are equally limiting. Sartre has pointed out that it is precisely this ideal pattern which is in question. Being a man means deciding what man will be. Reason, instead of being essence and self-evident guiding principle, is but one part of man. . . ."

From Hazel Barnes, *An Existentialist Ethics*.

ANNE BRADSTREET
Good Christians Don't Have Much Self-Love

Anne Bradstreet (1612–1672) was a British-born poet who was among the colonists in New England.

Anne Bradstreet implicitly criticizes both ethical egoism and existentialist ethics when she outlines the tenets of Christian ethics in the aphorisms which she wrote for her son. Prominent themes include doing good for others, sharing, having a good heart, and minimizing self-love and vanity.

FOR MY DEAR SON, SIMON BRADSTREET

Parents perpetuate their lives in their posterity and their manners; in their imitation children do naturally rather follow the failings than the virtues of their predecessors, but I am persuaded better things of you. You once desired me to leave something for you in writing that you might look upon, when you should see me no more; I could think of nothing more fit for you nor of more ease to myself than these short meditations following. Such as they are, I bequeath to you; small legacies are accepted by true friends, much more by dutiful children. I have avoided encroaching upon others' conceptions because I would leave you nothing but mine own, though in value they fall short of all in this kind; yet I presume they will be better prized by you for the author's sake. The Lord bless you with grace here and crown you with glory hereafter, that I may meet you with rejoicing at that great day of appearing, which is the continual prayer of your affectionate mother,

A. B.
March 20, 1664

1

There is no object that we see, no action that we do, no good that we enjoy, no evil that we feel or fear, but we may make some spiritual advantage of all; and he that makes such improvement is wise as well as pious.

2

Many can speak well, but few can do well. We are better scholars in the theory than the practice part, but he is a true Christian that is a proficient in both.

3

Youth is the time of getting, middle age of improving and old age of spending; a negligent youth is usually attended by an ignorant middle age, and both by an empty old age. He that hath nothing to feed on but vanity and lies must needs lie down in the bed of sorrow.

4

A ship that bears much sail and little or no ballast is easily overset, and that man whose head hath great abilities and his heart little or no grace is in danger of foundering.

5

It is reported of the peacock that, priding himself in his gay feathers, he ruffles them up, but spying his black feet, he soon lets fall his plumes; so he that glories in his gifts and adornings should look upon his corruptions, and that will damp his high thoughts.

6

The finest bread hath the least bran, the purest honey the least wax, and the sincerest Christian the least self-love. . . .

55

We read of ten lepers that were cleansed but of one that returned thanks; we are more ready to receive mercies than we are to acknowledge them. Men can use great importunity when they are in distresses and show great ingratitude after their successes, but he that ordereth his conversation aright will glorify him that hear him in the day of his trouble. . . .

62

As a man is called the little world, so his heart may be called the little commonwealth; his more fixed and resolved thoughts are like to inhabitants, his slight and flitting thoughts are like passengers that travel to and fro continually; here is also the great court of justice erected, which is always kept by conscience, who is both accuser, excuser, witness, and judge, whom no bribes can pervert nor flattery cause to favour, but as he finds the evidence, so he absolves or condemns; yea, so absolute is this court of judicature that there is no appeal from it, no not to the court of heaven itself, for if our conscience condemn us, He also who is greater than our conscience will do it much more, but he that would have boldness to go to the throne of grace to be accepted there must be sure to carry a certificate from the court of conscience that he stands right there.

77

God hath by his providence so ordered that no one country hath all commodities within itself, but what it wants another shall supply that so there may be a mutual commerce through the world. As it is with countries, so it is with men; there was never yet any one man that had all excellences, let his parts natural and acquired, spiritual and moral, be never so large, yet he stands in need of something which another man hath (perhaps meaner than himself) which shows us perfection is not below, as also that God will have us beholden one to another.

From Anne Bradstreet, "Meditations Divine and Moral."

JEREMY BENTHAM

Create the Greatest Good for the Greatest Number

Jeremy Bentham (1748–1832) was a British utilitarian and political philosopher.

Utilitarians believe that we should follow the principle of utility: act so as to produce the greatest good for the greatest number. Prominent advocates of this view are Jeremy Bentham and John Stuart Mill. Both of these philosophers identified good with pleasure (and bad with pain), so their principle ultimately amounted to acting to produce as much pleasure with the least pain, taking all affected individuals into account. With this goal, the principle is sometimes dubbed the greatest happiness principle. We are able to follow the principle of utility, Bentham argues, because we are pleasure seekers by nature.

I. Nature has placed mankind under the governance of two sovereign masters, *pain* and *pleasure*. It is for them alone to point out what we ought to do, as well as to determine what we shall do. On the one hand the standard of right and wrong, on the other the chain of causes and effects, are fastened to their throne. They govern us in all we do, in all we say, in all we think: every effort we can make to throw off our subjection, will serve but to demonstrate and confirm it. In words a man may pretend to abjure their empire: but in reality he will remain subject to it all the while. The *principle of utility* recognises this subjection, and assumes it for the foundation of that system, the object of which is to rear the fabric of felicity by the hands of reason and of law. Systems which attempt to question it, deal in sounds instead of sense, in caprice instead of reason, in darkness instead of light.

But enough of metaphor and declamation: it is not by such means that moral science is to be improved.

II. The principle of utility is the foundation of the present work: it will be proper therefore at the outset to give an explicit and determinate account of what is meant by it. By the principle of utility is meant that principle which approves or disapproves of every action whatsoever, according to the tendency which it appears to have to augment or diminish the happiness of the party whose interest is in question: or, what is the same thing in other words, to promote or to oppose that happiness. I say of every action whatsoever; and therefore not only of every action of a private individual, but of every measure of government.

III. By utility is meant that property in any object, whereby it tends to produce benefit, advantage, pleasure, good, or happiness (all this in the present case comes to the same thing), or (what comes again to the same thing) to prevent the happening of mischief, pain, evil, or unhappiness to the party whose interest is considered: if that party be the community in general, then the happiness of the community: if a particular individual, then the happiness of that individual.

IV. The interest of the community is one of the most general expressions that can occur in the phraseology of morals: no wonder that the meaning of it is often lost. When it has a meaning, it is this. The community is a fictitious *body*, composed of the individual persons who are considered as constituting as it were its *members*. The interest of the community then is, what?—the sum of the interests of the several members who compose it.

V. It is in vain to talk of the interest of the community without understanding what is the interest of the individual.

From Jeremy Bentham, *An Introduction to the Principles of Morals and Legislation.*

JOHN STUART MILL
Happiness Is the Ultimate End of Human Conduct

John Stuart Mill (1806–1873) was a British economist, utilitarian, and social philosopher.

John Stuart Mill, in his profoundly influential work, Utilitarianism, *anticipates and attempts to answer a variety of objections to utilitarianism. To those who question whether the pursuit of happiness should be the ultimate end of human conduct, Mill responds by calling upon us to attend to the quality as well as the quantity of happiness when we seek to maximize overall happiness, and he attempts to show that happiness is the basis for all things that we call good in our lives. To those, like the egoist, who question the emphasis on overall rather than personal happiness, Mill responds by emphasizing the "powerful natural sentiments" which connect the sense of our own well being to that of others.*

The creed which accepts as the foundation of morals "utility" or the "greatest happiness principle" holds that actions are right in proportion as they tend to promote happiness, wrong as they tend to produce the reverse of happiness. By happiness is intended pleasure, and the absence of pain; by unhappiness, pain, and the privation of pleasure. . . . [P]leasure, and freedom from pain, are the only things desirable as ends; . . . all desirable things are desirable either for the pleasure inherent in themselves, or as means to the promotion of pleasure and the prevention of pain.

Now such a theory of life excites in many minds, and among them in some of the most estimable in feeling and purpose, inveterate dislike. To suppose that life has (as they express it) no higher end than pleasure—no better and nobler object of desire and pursuit—they designate as utterly mean and groveling, as a doctrine worthy only of swine. . . .

It is quite compatible with the principle of utility to recognize the fact that some kinds of pleasure are more desirable and more valuable than others. It would be absurd that, while in estimating all other things quality is considered as well as quantity, the estimation of pleasure should be supposed to depend on quantity alone. . . . Of two pleasures, if there be one to which all or almost all who have experience of both give a decided preference, irrespective of any feeling of moral obligation to prefer it, that is the more desirable pleasure. . . .

[T]he utilitarian standard is not the agent's own greatest happiness, but the greatest amount of happiness altogether. . . .

The question is often asked, and properly so, in regard to any supposed moral standard—What is its sanction? What are the motives to obey? Or, more specifically, what is the source of its obligation?. . .We may answer, the same as of all other moral standards—the conscientious feelings of mankind. . . . [T]here *is* this basis of powerful natural sentiment; and this it is which, when once the general happiness is recognized as the ethical standard, will constitute the strength of the utilitarian morality. This firm foundation is that of the social feelings of mankind—the desire to be in unity with our fellow creatures, which is already a powerful principle in human nature, and happily one of those which tend to become stronger, even without express inculcation, from the influences of advancing civilization. . . .

Though it is only in a very imperfect state of the world's arrangements that anyone can best serve the happiness of others by the absolute sacrifice of his own, yet so long as the world is in that imperfect state, I fully acknowledge that the readiness to make such a sacrifice is the highest virtue which can be found in man. I will add that in this condition of the world, paradoxical as the assertion may be, the conscious ability to do without happiness gives the best prospect of realizing such happiness as is attainable. For nothing except that consciousness can raise a person above the chances of life, by making him feel that, let fate and fortune do their worst, they have not power to subdue him. . . .

The utilitarian morality does recognize in human beings the power of sacrificing their own greatest good for the good of others. It only refuses to admit that the sacrifice is itself a good. A sacrifice which does not increase, or tend to increase, the sum total of happiness, it considers as wasted. . . .

Questions about ends are questions about what things are desirable. The utilitarian doctrine is, that happiness is desirable, and the only thing desirable, as an end; all other things being only desirable as means to that end. What ought to be required of this doctrine—what conditions is it requisite that the doctrine should fulfil—to make good its claim to be believed?

The only proof capable of being given that an object is visible, is that people actually see it. The only proof that a sound is audible, is that people hear it: and so of the other sources of our experience. In like manner, I apprehend, the sole evidence it is possible to produce that anything is desirable, is that people do actually desire it. If the end which the utilitarian doctrine proposes to itself were not, in theory and in practice, acknowledged to be an end, nothing could ever convince any person that it was so. No reason can be given why the general happiness is desirable, except that each person, so far as he believes it to be attainable, desires his own happiness. This, however, being a fact, we have not only all the proof which the case admits of, but all which it is possible to require, that happiness is a good: that each person's happiness is a good to that person, and the general happiness, therefore, a good to the aggregate of all persons.

It results from the preceding considerations that there is in reality nothing desired except happiness. Whatever is desired otherwise than as a means to some end beyond itself, and ultimately to happiness, is desired as itself a part of happiness, and is not desired for itself until it has become so. Those who desire virtue for its own sake desire it either because the consciousness of it is a pleasure, or because the consciousness of being without it is a pain, or for both reasons united; as in truth the pleasure and pain seldom exist separately, but almost always together—the same person feeling pleasure in the degree of virtue attained, and pain in not having attained more. If one of these gave him no pleasure, and the other no pain, he would not love or desire virtue, or would desire it only for the other benefits which it might produce to himself or to persons whom he cared for.

We have now, then, an answer to the question, of what sort of proof the principle of utility is susceptible. If the opinion which I have now stated is psychologically true—if human nature is so constituted as to desire nothing which is not either a part of happiness or a means of happiness—we can have no other proof, and we require no other, that these are the only things desirable. If so, happiness is the sole end of human action, and the promotion of it the test by which to judge of all human conduct; from whence it necessarily follows that it must be the criterion of morality, since a part is included in the whole. . . .

From John Stuart Mill, *Utilitarianism.*

IMMANUEL KANT

Honor Rationality by Following Universalizable Rules

Immanuel Kant (1724–1804), born in Prussia, was a philosopher who
investigated the scope and nature of reason.

*Immanuel Kant carves out a very different ethical position from moral theories like
egoism or utilitarianism which determine the moral worth of actions by reference to
their consequences. Kant emphasizes the* movtive *we have when acting and maintains that the only morally good actions are those done* exclusively *out of a sense of
duty, following* only *principles which the agent is willing for everyone else to follow.
For Kant, morality is tied to our nature as rational beings and persons capable of envisioning ends. Kant's fundamental principle of morality—the* categorical imperative—*calls upon free agents to honor the decision-making capacity in themselves and
other rational beings.*

Everyone must admit that if a law is to be morally valid, i.e., is to be
valid as a ground of obligation, then it must carry with it absolute
necessity. He must admit that the command, "Thou shalt not lie," does
not hold only for men, as if other rational beings had no need to abide
by it, and so with all other moral laws properly so called. And he must
concede that the ground of obligation here must therefore be sought
not in the nature of man nor in the circumstances of the world in
which man is placed, but must be sought *a priori* solely in the concepts
of pure reason. . . .

There is no possibility of thinking of anything at all in the world,
or even out of it, which can be regarded as good without qualification,
except a *good will*. Intelligence, wit, judgment, and whatever talents of
the mind one might want to name are doubtless in many respects good
and desirable, as are such qualities of temperament as courage, resolution, perseverence. But they can also become extremely bad and harmful if the will, which is to make use of these gifts of nature and which
in its special constitution is called character, is not good. The same
holds with gifts or fortune; power, riches, honor, even health, and that
complete well-being and contentment with one's condition which is
called happiness make for pride and often hereby even arrogance,

unless there is a good will to correct their influence on the mind and herewith also to rectify the whole principle of action and make it universally conformable to its end. It need hardly be mentioned that the sight of a being adorned with no feature of a pure and good will, yet enjoying uninterrupted prosperity, can never give pleasure to a rational impartial observer. Thus the good will seems to constitute the indispensable condition even of worthiness to be happy. . . .

A good will is not good because of what it effects or accomplishes, nor because of its fitness to attain some proposed end; it is good only through its willing, i.e., it is good in itself. . . .

But what sort of law can that be the thought of which must determine the will without reference to any expected effect, so that the will can be called absolutely good without qualification? Since I have deprived the will of every impulse that might arise for it from obeying any particular law, there is nothing left to serve the will as principle except the universal conformity of its actions to law as such, i.e., I should never act except in such a way that I can also will that my maxim should become a universal law. Here mere conformity to law as such (without having as its basis any law determining particular actions) serves the will as principle and must so serve it if duty is not to be a vain delusion and a chimerical concept. . . .

[T]here is only one categorical imperative and it is this: Act only according to that maxim whereby you can at the same time will that it should become a universal law. . . .

We shall now enumerate some duties, following the usual division of them into duties to ourselves and to others and into perfect and imperfect duties.

1. A man reduced to despair by a series of misfortunes feels sick of life but is still so far in possession of his reason that he can ask himself whether taking his own life would not be contrary to his duty to himself. Now he asks whether the maxim of his action could become a universal law of nature. But his maxim is this: from self-love I make as my principle to shorten my life when its continued duration threatens more evil that it promises satisfaction. There only remains the question as to whether this principle of self-love can become a universal law of nature. One sees at once a contradiction in a system of nature whose law would destroy life by means of the very same feeling that acts so as to stimulate the furtherance of life, and hence there could be no existence as a system of nature. Therefore, such a maxim cannot possibly hold as a universal law of nature and is, consequently, wholly opposed to the supreme principle of all duty.

2. Another man in need finds himself forced to borrow money. He knows well that he won't be able to repay it, but he sees also that he will not get any loan unless he firmly promises to repay it within a fixed time. He wants to make such a promise, but he still has conscience enough to ask himself whether it is not permissible and is contrary to duty to get out of difficulty in this way. Suppose, however, that he decides to do so. The maxim of his action would then be expressed as follows: when I believe myself to be in need of money, I will borrow money and promise to pay it back, although I know that I can never do so. Now this principle of self-love or personal advantage may perhaps be quite compatible with one's entire future welfare, but the question is now whether it is right. I then transform the requirement of self-love into a universal law and put the question thus: how would things stand if my maxim were to become a universal law? He then sees at once that such a maxim could never hold as a universal law of nature and be consistent with itself, but must necessarily be self-contradictory. For the universality of a law which says that anyone believing himself to be in difficulty could promise whatever he pleases with the intention of not keeping it would make promising itself and the end to be attained thereby quite impossible, inasmuch as no one would believe what was promised him but would merely laugh at all such utterances as being vain pretenses.

3. A third finds in himself a talent whose cultivation could make him a man useful in many respects. But he finds himself in comfortable circumstances and prefers to indulge in pleasure rather than to bother himself about broadening and improving his fortunate natural aptitudes. But he asks himself further whether his maxim of neglecting his natural gifts, besides agreeing of itself with his propensity to indulgence, might agree also with what is called duty. He then sees that a system of nature could indeed always subsist according to such a universal law, even though every man (like South Sea Islanders) should let his talents rust and resolve to devote his life entirely to idleness, indulgence, propagation, and, in a word, to enjoyment. But he cannot possibly will that this should become a universal law of nature or be implanted in us as such a law by a natural instinct. For as a rational being he necessarily wills that all his faculties should be developed, inasmuch as they are given him for all sorts of possible purposes.

4. A fourth man finds things going well for himself but sees others (whom he could help) struggling with great hardships; and he thinks: what does it matter to me? Let everybody be as happy as Heaven wills or as he can make himself; I shall take nothing from him nor even envy him; but I have no desire to contribute anything to his well-being or to his assistance when in need. If such a way of thinking were to become a universal law of nature, the human race admittedly could very well subsist and doubtless could subsist even better than when everyone prates about sympathy and benevolence and even on occasion exerts himself to practice them but, on the other hand, also cheats when he can, betrays the rights of man, or otherwise violates them. But even though it is possible that a universal law of nature could subsist in accordance with that maxim, still it is impossible to will that such a principle should hold everywhere as a law of nature.

For a will which resolved in this way would contradict itself, inasmuch as cases might often arise in which one would have need of the love and sympathy of others and in which he would deprive himself, by such a law of nature springing from his own will, of all hope of the aid he wants for himself. . . .

[R]ational beings are called persons inasmuch as their nature already marks them out as ends in themselves, i.e., as something which is not to be used merely as means and hence there is imposed thereby a limit on all arbitrary use of such beings, which are thus objects of respect. . . . If then there is to be a supreme practical principle and, as far as the human will is concerned, a categorical imperative, then it must be such that from the conception of what is necessarily an end for everyone. . . . The ground of such a principle is this: rational nature exists as an end in itself. . . . The practical imperative will therefore be the following: Act in such a way that you treat humanity, whether in your own person or in the person of another, always at the same time as an end and never simply as a means. We now want to see whether this can be carried out in practice.

Let us keep to our previous examples.

First, as regards the concept of necessary duty to oneself, the man who contemplates suicide will ask himself whether his action can be consistent with the idea of humanity as an end in itself. If he destroys himself in order to escape from a difficult situation, then he is making use of his person merely as a means so as to maintain a tolerable condition till the end of his life. Man, however, is not a thing and hence is not something to be used merely as a means, he must in all his actions always be regarded as an end in himself. Therefore, I cannot dispose of man in my own person by mutilating, damaging, or killing him. (A more exact determination of this principle so as to avoid all misunderstanding, e.g., regarding the amputation of limbs in order to save oneself, or the exposure of one's life to danger in order to save it, and so on, must here be omitted; such questions belong to morals proper.)

Second, as concerns necessary or strict duty to others, the man who intends to make a false promise will immediately see that he intends to make use of another man merely as a means to an end which the latter does not likewise hold. For the man whom I want to use for my own purposes by such a promise cannot possibly concur with my way of acting toward him and hence cannot himself hold the end of this action. This conflict with the principle of duty to others becomes even clearer when instances of attacks on the freedom and property of others are considered. For then it becomes clear that a transgressor of the rights of men intends to make use of the persons of others merely as a means, without taking into consideration that, as rational beings, they should always be esteemed at the same time as ends, i.e., be esteemed only as beings who must themselves be able to hold the very same action as an end.

Third, with regard to contingent (meritorious) duty to oneself, it is not enough that the action does not conflict with humanity in our own person as an end in itself; the action must also harmonize with this end. Now there are in humanity capacities for greater perfection which belong to the end that nature has in view as regards humanity in our own person. To neglect these capacities might perhaps be consistent with the maintenance of humanity as an end in itself, but would not be consistent with the advancement of this end.

Fourth, concerning meritorious duty to others, the natural end that all men have is their own happiness. Now humanity might indeed subsist if nobody contributed anything to the happiness of others, provided he did not intentionally impair their happiness. But this, after all, would harmonize only negatively and not positively with humanity as an end in itself, if everyone does not also strive, as much as he can, to further the ends of others. For the ends of any subject who is an end in himself must as far as possible be my ends also, if that conception of an end in itself is to have its full effect in me.

From Immanuel Kant, *Grounding for the Metaphysics of Morals*. Translated by James W. Ellington.

ROBERT KANE

Begin a Search for Absolute Values with Kantian Openness and Tolerance

Robert Kane (1938–) is an American philosopher who specializes in metaphysics and ethics.

Robert Kane is concerned with the implications which a world with competing values has for ethical theory, namely that there is nothing universally or absolutely right. His strategy is to begin with an attitude that one view is as good as another, a starting point of openness, and see how the views fare. Is one really as good as another? Will some of these views prove themselves to be wrong? This openness, he says, can be captured with Kant's ends principle of respecting other people which Kane likens to the Golden Rule. According to Kane, we soon find that some views are not worthy of acceptance because they threaten to undermine this world of toleration. With this start, Kane is well on his way to establishing some absolute values.

STEP 1: AN IDEAL OF ACTION

The first step in this search procedure is taken when, in the face of pluralism and uncertainty, we assume an attitude of openness or tolerance to other points of view, governed by the idea that "no point of view (including one's own) should be presumed by its adherents to be right for others who disagree with it or imposed on others who disagree with it against their wills." We are to take up this attitude as an ideal of action, trying to sustain it to the degree possible, and see what happens.

Let us recall the reason for starting this way. It is to lift from ourselves the burden of proving our view right and others wrong and to let others prove themselves right or wrong by their actions. This is why we let them act in accordance with their own views, and do not allow our view or any other view to be imposed on them against their wills. The whole idea is to "get beyond" our limited point of view and let others be heard in the interests of finding out what is good or valuable in general, not just from our point of view.

The second step in the search occurs when we try to act upon this initial attitude of openness and find it cannot be consistently followed. It turns out that you cannot open your mind to all other points of view, a result that has important implications for ethics. But it will take a few sections to show why this is so and I need to clarify a few things first.

To begin with, something must be said about the much-used expression "points of view." We defined pluralism by noting that there are many competing points of view and have talked about being open to other points of view. But how should we understand these points of view? As a first try, let us say that the "points of view" of persons are defined by their beliefs, desires, intentions, hopes, preferences, and other psychological attitudes, which together tell us what they believe about the world and what their "values" are. By the values of persons, we mean what they care about and what is important to them. In other words, such things as what they desire, like friends, social approval, or meaningful work; what they enjoy, such as sports or music or trips to the seashore; their goals or purposes (for a career, for example, or in a marriage); their images of happiness or success; the excellences of achievement they admire and their highest ideals (justice, democracy, and so on).

Understanding "points of view" and "values" in this way, we can better understand what the initial attitude of openness amounts to. It requires a certain *respect* for the points of view of others governed by the principle that "no point of view (including one's own) should be presumed by its adherents to be right for others who disagree with it or can be imposed on others who disagree with it against their wills." And this means respecting the *values* of others in the above sense, that is, allowing them to pursue their purposes, desires, and images of happiness without interference, rather than imposing one's own purposes or desires upon them against their wills.

This looks very much like an ethical principle of sorts, which indeed it is; and anyone familiar with the history of ethics can think of several notable principles to which it bears a resemblance. Some versions of the Golden Rule come to mind ("Do unto others as you would have them do unto you"). Those who know more of the history of ethics will also be reminded of the second formulation of Immanuel Kant's Categorical Imperative, which tells us to treat all persons as "ends in themselves" and not as "mere means to our own ends." But we should not identify the attitude of openness at this stage with any historical ethical principles. First, the fit is not exact. Second, the attitude of openness is not meant to be a "final" ethical principle, but only a first step in a dialectical argument leading to such a principle. We are going to see that it fails as a candidate for a universal principle.

Nonetheless, the resemblance of the attitude of openness to traditional ethical ideas is significant; and Kant's language of "ends" and "means" can be used to express the starting point. The attitude of openness can be translated into the language of "ends" and "means," if we say that to treat persons as ends (in themselves) is to respect their points of view, and hence their values (as the attitude of openness requires), thus allowing them to pursue their purposes, desires, and images of happiness without interference. And to treat them as means to our ends would be to impose our purposes or desires upon them, forcing them to do what we want against their wills. The attitude of openness could then be expressed by saying that persons should act in accordance with a principle similar to Kant's, which I am going to call the

> *Ends Principle*: Treat every person in every situation as an end and never as a means (to your or someone else's ends).

This formulation creates a principle of action from the original idea of openness—that "no point of view (including one's own) should be presumed by its adherents to be right for others who disagree with it or imposed on others who disagree with it against their wills." Despite its similarity to Kant's famous imperative, this principle is not meant to be the same as his or any other traditional ethical principle. It is designed for a different purpose: to capture the attitude of openness which is only an initial attitude taken in a search for truth, not the final answer.

STEP 2: THE BREAKDOWN OF THIS IDEAL

We are now ready to take the second step, which is to show why this attitude of openness cannot be consistently followed as an ideal of action. There are situations in life (many of them, in fact) in which it is impossible to treat all persons as ends—that is, with respect for their points of view and values—as the Ends Principle and the attitude of openness require. These situations are typically ones in which some person or group is already treating some other person or group as a means by coercing, harming, or manipulating them. If you are walking down the street and witness a man attempting to rape a woman and there is something you can do to stop it (by physically intervening or seeking help), then you have entered a situation of this kind. If you do something to prevent the rape, you are not allowing the rapist to live in accordance with his point of view without interference; you are not treating him as an end. But if you just "walk on by" and do nothing, you are not allowing the rape victim to live in accordance with her point of view without interference; you are not treating her as an end, or with respect. Openness or tolerance to all points of view is simply not possible in this case. . . .

THE MORAL SPHERE

To see what ought to be done in such conflict situations, we need a general way of talking about them. Let us define a moral *sphere* of life as a situation in which everyone *can* treat everyone else as an end; in other words, the moral sphere defines a space in which the Ends Principle can be followed by everyone. This is an ideal sphere of action, which clearly may not always obtain in the real world. In the situations we have described, the moral sphere has "broken down," and it is no longer possible to treat everyone as an end. One must choose, but on what basis?

To answer this question, we must return to the starting point. The original attitude of openness was assumed as a search procedure. We were to see what could be learned about how to act toward others by trying to sustain this attitude *to the degree possible* in every situation. (In other words, be open as much as possible if you wish to find whatever truth about these matters is to be found.) Now when the moral sphere breaks down, we cannot be completely open. We cannot respect every point of view. The task, then, is to determine which choice (between not respecting the rapist by thwarting him or the victim by walking on by) comes closest to sustaining the ideal of respect for all in these imperfect conditions. Neither choice does it to the letter because someone's point of view will not be respected. But by choosing not to respect the rapist's point of view—by trying to stop him—we are doing something to sustain the ideal of respect for all that we would not be doing if we just walked by. First, we are attempting to restore the moral sphere by thwarting the one whose actions broke it, which means we are trying to restore conditions in which the ideal of respect for all can be followed once again (for that is what the moral sphere is). Second, by thwarting the rapist we also sustain the ideal by trying to do something to deter others who might break the moral sphere in the future, thereby preserving conditions in which the ideal can be followed by others. . . .

Readers may have suspected from the first statement of the Ends Principle that it has something to do with the so-called Golden Rule ("Do unto others as you would have them do unto you"). Indeed, it does. But we have to be careful. There are at least two historical interpretations of the Golden Rule, one of which is very close to the Ends Principle as we have finally stated it, the other far from the Ends Principle indeed.

Yet the connection between the Ends Principle and the Golden Rule is significant, for the Golden Rule has been endorsed in one form or another by many of the major spiritual traditions of mankind. Here are a few examples.

Christianity: "All things whatsoever ye would that men should do to you, do you even so to them: for this is the Law and the Prophets." (Matthew 7:12)

Judaism: "What is hateful to you, do not to your fellow men. This is the entire law: all the rest is commentary." (Talmud, Shabbat 31a)

Hinduism: "This is the sum of duty: Do naught unto others which would cause you pain if done to you." *(Mahabharata 5:1517)*

Buddhism: "Hurt not others in ways that you yourself would find hurtful." (Udana-Varga, 5:18)

Islam: *"No* one of you is a believer until he desires for his brother that which he desires for himself." (Sunnah)

Confucianism: "Surely it is a maxim of loving kindness: Do not unto others that you would not have them do unto you." *(Analects, 15:23)*

Taoism: "Regard your neighbor's gain as your own gain and your neighbor's loss as your own loss." *(T'ai Shang Kan Ying P'ien)*

Zoroastrianism: "That nature alone is good which refrains from doing unto another whatsoever is not good for itself." (Dadistan-idinik, 94:5)

The negative formulations of Confucius's *Analects* and several of the others ("Do not unto others . . . " "Hurt not others . . .") are sometimes said to express the "Silver Rule," but the general thrust is very much the same as the traditional Golden Rule ("Do unto others . . ."). We do not go wrong if we take them as expressing the same principle.

The astonishing thing about these historical formulations of the Golden Rule is the number of them which add that this rule is "[the sum of] the Law and the Prophets," or "the entire Law: all the rest is commentary," or "this is the sum of duty." If this were true, and the revised Ends Principle did in fact express the Golden Rule, it would encapsulate the Law of many traditions, or the sum of duty. We have already seen how the revised Ends Principle can cover traditional commandments of the Mosaic law not to kill, steal, lie, and so on, as well as their exceptions, and this is suggestive.

From Robert Kane, *Through the Moral Maze.*

LAWRENCE KOHLBERG

Kantianism Is the Highest Stage of Moral Development

Lawrence Kohlberg (1927–) is an American developmental psychologist.

Lawrence Kohlberg seeks to identify the stages that individuals move through as they mature and progress in their ability to think about moral issues. Kohlberg theorizes six stages of moral development: egoistic behavior occupies the lowest rungs of the ladder while utilitarian behavior is seen as a later, higher stage of thinking. The highest stage for Kohlberg exemplifies the abstract respect for personhood found in Kantianism.

U sing hypothetical moral situations, we have interviewed children and adults about right and wrong in the United States, Britain, Turkey, Taiwan, and Yucatan. In all cultures we find the same forms of moral thinking. There are six forms of thinking and they constitute an invariant sequence of stages in each culture. These stages are summarized in the following table.

Levels	Basis of Moral Judgement	Stages of Development
I.	Moral value resides in external, quasi-physical happenings, in bad acts, or in quasi-physical needs rather than in persons and standards	*Stage 1:* Obedience and punishment orientation. Egocentric deference to superior power or prestige, or a trouble-avoiding set. Objective responsibility. *Stage 2:* Naively egoistic orientation. Right action is that instrumentally satisfying the self's needs and occasionally others'. Awareness of relativism of value to each actor's needs and perspective. Naive egalitarianism and orientation to exchange and reciprocity.
II.	Moral value resides in performing good or right roles, in maintaining the conventional order and the expectancies of others	*Stage 3:* Good-boy orientation. Orientation to approval and to pleasing and helping others. Conformity to stereotypical images of majority or natural role behavior, and judgment by intentions. *Stage 4:* Authority and social order maintaining orientation. Orientation to "doing duty" and to showing respect for authority and maintaining the given social order for its own sake. Regard for earned expectations of others.

Levels	Basis of Moral Judgement	Stages of Development
III.	Moral value resides in conformity by the self to shared or shareable standards, rights, or duties	*Stage 5:* Contractual legalistic orientation. Recognition of an arbitrary element or starting point in rules or expectations for the sake of agreement. Duty defined in terms of contract, general avoidance of violation of the will or rights of others, and majority will and welfare. *Stage 6:* Conscience or principle orientation. Orientation not only to actually ordained social rules but to principles of choice involving appeal to logical universality and consistency. Orientation to conscience as a directing agent and to mutual respect and trust.

From Lawrence Kohlberg, "Education for Justice."

CAROL GILLIGAN

Women Approach Morality with an Eye to Caring for Others

Carol Gilligan (1936–) is an American educational psychologist who studied with Lawrence Kohlberg.

Women approach morality in a way different from men, according to Carol Gilligan, and an adequate theory of moral experience will take this difference into account. Men, and traditional moral theories which men have developed, are primarily concerned with articulating objective principles of right and wrong and with determining people's rights and duties. Women, says Gilligan, are concerned with hurt and exploitation, with caring for specific others, and with developing a sense of interconnectedness with others.

In order to go beyond the question, "How much like men women think, how capable are they of engaging in the abstract and hypothetical construction of reality?" it is necessary to identify and define developmental criteria that encompass the categories of women's thought. Haan points out the necessity to derive such criteria from the resolution of the "more frequently occurring, real-life moral dilemmas of interpersonal, empathic, fellow-feeling concerns" which have long been the center of women's moral concern. But to derive developmental criteria from the language of women's moral discourse, it is necessary first to see whether women's construction of the moral domain relies on a language different from that of men and one that deserves equal credence in the definition of development. This in turn requires finding places where women have the power to choose and thus are willing to speak in their own voice.

When birth control and abortion provide women with effective means for controlling their fertility, the dilemma of choice enters a central arena of women's lives. . . .

But just as the conventions that shape women's moral judgment differ from those that apply to men, so also women's definition of the moral domain diverges from that derived from studies of men. Women's construction of the moral problem as a problem of care and responsibility in relationships rather than as one of rights and rules ties the development of their moral thinking to changes in their under-standing of responsibility and relationships just as the conception of morality as justice ties development to the logic of equality and reci-procity. Thus the logic underlying an ethic of care is a psychological logic of relationships, which contrasts with the formal logic of fairness that informs the justice approach.

Women's constructions of the abortion dilemma in particular re-veal the existence of a distinct moral language whose evolution traces a sequence of development. This is the language of selfishness and re-sponsibility, which defines the moral problem as one of obligation to exercise care and avoid hurt. The inflicting of hurt is considered self-ish and immoral in its reflection of unconcern, while the expression of care is seen as the fulfillment of moral responsibility. The reiterative use by the women of the words *selfish* and *responsible* in talking about moral conflict and choice, given the underlying moral orientation that this language reflects, sets the women apart from the men whom Kohlberg studied and points toward a different understanding of moral development. . . .

The third perspective focuses on the dynamics of relationships and dissipates the tension between selfishness and responsibility through a new understanding of the interconnection between other and self. Care becomes the self-chosen principle of a judgment that remains psycho-logical in its concern with relationships and response but becomes uni-versal in its condemnation of exploitation and hurt. Thus a progressively more adequate understanding of the psychology of human relationships—an increasing differentiation of self and other and a growing comprehension of the dynamics of social interaction—informs the development of an ethic of care. This ethic, which reflects a cumulative knowledge of human relationships, evolves around a cen-tral insight, that self and other are interdependent.

The moral imperative that emerges repeatedly in interviews with women is an injunction to care, a responsibility to discern and allevi-ate the "real and recognizable trouble" of this world. For men, the moral imperative appears rather as an injunction to respect the rights of others and thus to protect from interference the rights to life and self-fulfillment. Women's insistence on care is at first self-critical rather than self-protective, while men initially conceive obligation to others negatively in terms of noninterference. Development for both sexes would therefore seem to entail an integration of rights and responsi-bilities through the discovery of the complementarity of these dis-parate views. For women, the integration of rights and responsibilities takes place through an understanding of the psychological logic of re-lationships. This understanding tempers the self-destructive potential of a self-critical morality by asserting the need of all persons to care. For men, recognition through experience of the need for more active responsibility in taking care corrects the potential indifference of a morality of noninterference and turns attention from the logic to the consequences of choice. In the development of a postconventional ethical understanding, women come to see the violence inherent in inequality, while men come to see the limitations of a conception of justice blinded to the differences in human life.

From Carol Gilligan, *In a Different Voice.*

ADRIENNE RICH

Lying Is Self-Destructive and Interferes with Loving Relationships

Adrienne Rich (1929–) is a Pulitzer Prize-winning American poet and essayist.

Adrienne Rich depicts liars as people concerned only with their own feelings and as lonely people. They simplify matters at times with their lies, for truth is complicated. But with their simplification comes a denial of their own lives as well as of other people. Loving, honorable relationships require honesty on the part of the participants: they must together to create and grasp the complexity of truth.

To discover that one has been lied to in a personal relationship, however, leads one to feel a little crazy. . . .

Lying is done with words, and also with silence.

The woman who tells lies in her personal relationships may or may not plan or invent her lying. She may not even think of what she is doing in a calculated way.

A subject is raised which the liar wishes buried. She has to go downstairs, her parking meter will have run out. Or, there is a telephone call she ought to have made an hour ago.

She is asked, point-blank, a question which may lead into painful talk: "How do you feel about what is happening between us?" Instead of trying to describe her feelings in their ambiguity and confusion, she asks, "How do *you* feel?". . . Thus the liar learns more than she tells.

And she may also tell herself a lie: that she is concerned with the other's feelings, not with her own.

But the liar is concerned with her own feelings.

The liar lives in fear of losing control. She cannot even desire a relationship without manipulation, since to be vulnerable to another person means for her the loss of control.

The liar has many friends, and leads an existence of great loneliness. . . .

In speaking of lies, we come inevitably to the subject of truth. There is nothing simple or easy about this idea. There is no "the truth," "a truth"—truth is not one thing, or even a system. It is an increasing complexity. The pattem on the carpet is a surface. When we look closely, or when we become weavers, we learn of the tiny multiple threads unseen in the overall pattern, the knots on the underside of the carpet.

This is why the effort to speak honestly is so important. Lies are usually attempts to make everything simpler—for the liar—than it really is, or ought to be.

In lying to others we end up lying to ourselves. We deny the importance of an event, or a person, and thus deprive ourselves of a part of our lives. Or we use one piece of the past or present to screen out another. Thus we lose faith even with our own lives. . . .

An honorable human relationship—that is, one in which two people have the right to use the word "love"—is a process, delicate, violent, often terrifying to both persons involved, a process of refining the truths they can tell each other.

It is important to do this because it breaks down human self-delusion and isolation.

It is important to do this because we do justice to our own complexity.

It is important to do this because we can count on so few people to go that hard way with us. . . .

The liar leads an existence of unutterable loneliness.

The liar is afraid.

But we are all afraid: without fear we become manic, hubristic, self-destructive. What is this particular fear that possesses the liar?

She is afraid that her own truths are not good enough. . . .

The liar fears the void. . . .

Why do we feel slightly crazy when we realize we have been lied to in a relationship? . . . .

The liar may resist confrontation, denying that she lied. Or she may use other language: forgetfulness, privacy, the protection of someone else. Or, she may bravely declare herself a coward. This allows her to go on lying, since that is what cowards do. She does not say, *I was afraid*, since this would open the question of the other ways of handling her fear. It would open the question of what is actually feared.

She may say, *I didn't want to cause pain*. What she really did not want is to have to deal with the other's pain. . . .

Truthfulness, honor, is not something which springs ablaze of itself; it has to be created between people.

From Adrienne Rich, *On Lies, Secrets, and Silence.*

RUTH BENEDICT

Ethical Correctness Is a Function of One's Culture

Ruth Benedict (1887–1948) was a cultural anthropologist especially interested in the connection between culture and personality.

Ethical or cultural relativism in effect asserts that moral right and wrong is relative to the rules of a particular society or culture at a particular time. In Ruth Benedict's analysis, we have concluded too quickly if we think that the customs of modern civilization are nearly uniform and better than ever. There is great variability in the ways people can and have developed their cultures. What may be normal in one culture is considered aberrant in another. Each society has its own morality, according to Benedict, and that is to say nothing more than each society confers approval on its own unique set of habits.

Modern social anthropology has become more and more a study of the varieties and common elements of cultural environment and the consequences of these in human behavior. For such a study of diverse social orders primitive peoples fortunately provide a laboratory not yet entirely vitiated by the spread of a standardized worldwide civilization. Dyaks and Hopis, Fijians and Yakuts are significant for psychological, and sociological study because only among these simpler peoples has there been sufficient isolation to give opportunity for the development of localized social forms. In the higher cultures the standardization of custom and belief over a couple of continents has given a false sense of the inevitability of the particular forms that have gained currency, and we need to turn to a wider survey in order to check the conclusions we hastily base upon this near-universality of familiar customs. Most of the simpler cultures did not gain the wide currency of the one which, out of our experience, we identify with human nature, but this was for various historical reasons, and certainly not for any that gives us as its carriers a monopoly of social good or of social sanity. Modern civilization, from this point of view, becomes not a necessary pinnacle of human achievement but one entry in a long series of possible adjustments.

These adjustments, whether they are in mannerisms like the ways of showing anger, or joy, or grief in any society, or in major human drives like those of sex, prove to be far more variable than experience in any one culture would suggest. In certain fields, such as that of religion or of formal marriage arrangements, these wide limits of variability are well known and can be fairly described. In others it is not yet possible to give a generalized account, but that does not absolve us of the task of indicating the significance of the work that has been done and of the problems that have arisen.

No one civilization can possibly utilize in its mores the whole potential range of human behavior. Just as there are great numbers of possible phonetic articulations, and the possibility of language depends on a selection and standardization of a few of these in order that speech communication may be possible at all, so the possibility of organized behavior of every sort, from the fashions of local dress and houses to the dicta of a people's ethics and religion, depends upon a similar selection among the possible behavior traits. In the field of recognized economic obligations or sex tabus this selection is as nonrational and subconscious a process as it is in the field of phonetics. It is a process which goes on in the group for long periods of time and is historically conditioned by incidents of isolation or of contact of peoples. In any comprehensive study of Psychology, the selection that different cultures have made in the course of history within the great circumference of potential behavior is of great significance.

Every society, beginning with some slight inclination in one direction or another, carries its preference farther and farther, integrating itself more and more completely upon its chosen basis, and discarding those types of behavior that are uncongenial. Most of those organizations of personality that seem to us most incontrovertibly abnormal have been used by different civilizations in the very foundations of their institutional life. Conversely the most valued traits of our normal individuals have been looked on in differently organized cultures as aberrant. Normality, in short, within a very wide range, is culturally defined. It is primarily a term for the socially elaborated segment of human behavior in any culture; and abnormality, a term for the segment that that particular civilization does not use. The very eyes with which we see the problem are conditioned by the long traditional habits of our own society.

It is a point that has been made more often in relation to ethics than in relation to psychiatry. We do not any longer make the mistake of deriving the morality of our own locality and decade directly from the inevitable constitution of human nature. We do not elevate it to the dignity of a first principle. We recognize that morality differs in every society, and is a convenient term for socially approved habits. Mankind has always preferred to say, "It is morally good," rather than "It is habitual," and the fact of this preference is matter enough for a critical science of ethics. But historically the two phrases are synonymous.

The concept of the normal is properly a variant of the concept of the good. It is that which society has approved. A normal action is one which falls well within the limits of expected behavior for a particular society. Its variability among different peoples is essentially a function of the variability of the behavior patterns that different societies have created for themselves, and can never be wholly divorced from a consideration of culturally institutionalized types of behavior.

Each culture is a more or less elaborate working-out of the potentialities of the segment it has chosen. In so far as a civilization is well integrated and consistent within itself, it will tend to carry farther and farther, according to its nature, its initial impulse toward a particular type of action, and from the point of view of any other culture those elaborations will include more and more extreme and aberrant traits.

Each of these traits, in proportion as it reinforces the chosen behavior patterns of that culture, is for that culture normal. Those individuals to whom it is congenial either congenitally, or as the result of childhood sets, are accorded prestige in that culture, and are not visited with the social contempt or disapproval which their traits would call down upon them in a society that was differently organized. On the other hand, those individuals whose characteristics are not congenial to the selected type of human behavior in that community are the deviants, no matter how valued their personality traits may be in a contrasted civilization. . . .

All our local conventions of moral behavior and of immoral are without absolute validity, and yet it is quite possible that a modicum of what is considered right and what wrong could be disentangled, that is, shared by the whole human race.

From Ruth Fulton Benedict, "Anthropology and the Abnormal."

DAVID HUME

Ethical Correctness Is a Function of One's Feelings

David Hume (1711–1776) was a Scottish empiricist and skeptic.

David Hume is famous for his articulation of ethical skepticism and his assertion that "moral matters are more properly felt than judged of." Our feelings or sentiments are what guide our moral lives. Once we are in the realm of feeling and out of the realm of reason, we can recognize that we are likewise out of the realm of rational knowledge. In other words, while there is a moral right and wrong, it is a function of how we feel about matters and not what we can rationally determine about the way the world is.

Upon the whole, 'tis impossible, that the distinction betwixt moral good and evil, can be made by reason; since that distinction has an influence on our actions, of which reason alone is incapable. . . . But can there be any difficulty in proving, that vice and virtue are not matters of fact, whose existence we can infer by reason? Take any action allow'd to be vicious: Wilful murder, for instance. Examine it in all lights, and see if you can find that matter of fact, or real existence, which you call *vice*. In which-ever way you take it, you will find only certain passions, motives, volitions and thoughts. There is no other matter of fact in the case. The vice entirely escapes you, as long as you consider the object. You never can find it, till you turn your reflexion into your own breast, and find a sentiment of disapprobation, which arises in you, towards this action. Here is a matter of fact; but 'tis the object of feeling, not of reason. It lies in yourself, not in the object. So that when you pronounce any action or character to be vicious, you mean nothing, but that from the constitution of your nature you have a feeling or sentiment of blame from the contemplation of it. Vice and virtue, therefore, may be compar'd to sounds, colours, heat and cold, which, according to modern philosophy, are not qualities in objects, but perceptions in the mind. . . . Nothing can be more real, or concern us more, than our own sentiments of pleasure and uneasiness; and if these be favourable to virtue, and unfavourable to vice, no more can be requisite to the regulation of our conduct and behaviour.

From David Hume, *A Treatise on Human Nature.*

IVAN TURGENEV
There Are No Moral Truths

Ivan Turgenev (1836–1883) was a Russian poet, playwright and novelist.

Nihil is the Latin word for nothing which is precisely what claims to moral right and wrong amount to for the nihilist. While the cultural relativists dismiss the possibility of moral absolutes, they preserve the notions of moral right and wrong so long as we connect them to particular societies. While the skeptics dismiss the possibility of having knowledge of right and wrong, they preserve the notions of moral right and wrong, so long as we connect them with our feelings. But when the nihilists dismiss the notions of moral right and wrong, they preserve nothing in ethics: the moral domain is non-existent. Bazarov, a college student in the novel, Fathers and Sons, *is an advocate of this position.*

"Yes, yes, to be sure. So that surgeon was his father. Hm!" Pavel Petrovitch pulled his moustaches. "Well, and what is Mr. Bazarov himself?" he asked, deliberately.

"What is Bazarov?" Arkady smiled. "Would you like me, uncle, to tell you what he really is?"

"If you will be so good, nephew."

"He's a nihilist."

"Eh?" inquired Nikolai Petrovitch, while Pavel Petrovitch lifted a knife in the air with a small piece of butter on its tip, and remained motionless.

"He's a nihilist," repeated Arkady.

"A nihilist," said Nikolai Petrovitch. "That's from the Latin, *nihil*, *nothing*, as far as I can judge; the word must mean a man who . . . who accepts nothing?"

"Say, 'who respects nothing,'" put in Pavel Petrovitch, and he set to work on the butter again.

"Who regards everything from the critical point of view," observed Arkady.

"Isn't that just the same thing?" inquired Pavel Petrovitch.

"No, it's not the same thing. A nihilist is a man who does not bow down before any authority, who does not take any principle on faith, whatever reverence that principle may be enshrined in."

"Well, and is that good?" interrupted Pavel Petrovitch.

"That depends, uncle. Some people it will do good to, but some people will suffer for it."

"Indeed. Well, I see it's not in our line. We are old-fashioned people; we imagine that without principles, taken as you say on faith, there's no taking a step, no breathing. *Vous avez change tout cela.* God give you good health and the rank of a general, while we will be content to look on and admire. . . ."

Bazarov smiled. "In the first place, experience of life does that; and in the second, I assure you, studying separate individuals is not worth the trouble. All people are like one another, in soul as in body; each of us has brain, spleen, heart, and lungs made alike; and the so-called moral qualities are the same in all; the slight variations are of no importance. A single human specimen is sufficient to judge of all by. People are like trees in a forest; no botanist would think of studying each individual birch-tree."

Katya, who was arranging the flowers, one at a time in a leisurely fashion, lifted her eyes to Bazarov with a puzzled look, and meeting his rapid and careless glance, she crimsoned up to her ears. Anna Sergyevna shook her head.

"The trees in a forest," she repeated. "Then according to you there is no difference between the stupid and the clever person, between the good-natured and ill-natured?"

"No, there is a difference, just as between the sick and the healthy. The lungs of a consumptive patient are not in the same condition as yours and mine, though they are made on the same plan. We know approximately what physical diseases come from; moral diseases come from bad education, from all the nonsense people's heads are stuffed with from childhood up, from the defective state of society; in short, reform society, and there will be no diseases."

From Ivan S. Turgenev, *Fathers and Sons*, translated by Constance Garnett.

ALDO LEOPOLD

The Moral Community Includes
the Land and Natural Processes

Aldo Leopold (1887–1949) was an American wildlife management expert and an ecologist.

Aldo Leopold wrote The Sand County Almanac, *considered the seminal text of the contemporary environmental movement. Articulating the idea of an environmental ethics, Leopold calls upon us to see land not simply as existing for human use. The land and the natural biotic community of which land is a part have intrinsic value and deserve our respect and care–for their own sakes as well as for our own.*

This extension of ethics, so far studied only by philosophers, is actually a process in ecological evolution. Its sequences may be described in ecological as well as in philosophical terms. An ethic, ecologically, is a limitation on freedom of action in the struggle for existence. An ethic, philosophically, is a differentiation of social from anti-social conduct. These are two definitions of one thing. The thing has its origin in the tendency of interdependent individuals or groups to evolve modes of cooperation. The ecologist calls these symbioses. Politics and economics are advanced symbioses in which the original free-for-all competition has been replaced, in part, by cooperative mechanisms within an ethical content.

The complexity of cooperative mechanisms has increased with population density, and with the efficiency of tools. It was simpler, for example, to define the anti-social uses of sticks and stones in the days of the mastodons than of bullets and billboards in the age of motors.

The first ethics dealt with the relation between individuals; the Mosaic Decalogue is an example. Later accretions dealt with the relation between the individual and society. The Golden Rule tries to integrate the individual to society; democracy to integrate social organization to the individual.

There is as yet no ethic dealing with man's relation to land and to the animals and plants which grow upon it. Land, like Odysseus' slave girls, is still property. The land-relation is still strictly economic, entailing privileges but not obligations.

The extension of ethics to this third element in the human environment is, if I read the evidence correctly, an evolutionary possibility and an ecological necessity. It is the third step in a sequence. The first two have already been taken. Individuals since the days of Ezekiel and Isaiah have asserted that the despoliation of land is not only inexpedient but wrong. Society, however, has not yet affirmed their belief. I regard the present conservation movement as the embryo of such an affirmation.

An ethic may be regarded as a mode of guidance for meeting ecological situations so new or intricate, or involving such deferred reactions, that the path of social expediency is not discernible to the average individual. Animal instincts are modes of guidance for the individual in meeting such situations. Ethics are possibly a kind of community instinct in-the-making. . . .

The land ethic simply enlarges the boundaries of the community to include soils, waters, plants, and animals, or collectively: the land. . . .

In short, a land ethic changes the role of *Homo sapiens* from conqueror of the land-community to plain member and citizen of it. It implies respect for his fellow-members, and also respect for the community as such. . . . [A] system of conservation based solely on economic self-interest is hopelessly lopsided. It tends to ignore, and thus eventually to eliminate, many elements in the land community that lack commercial value that the economic parts of the biotic clock will function without the uneconomic parts. It tends to relegate to government many functions eventually too large, too complex, or too widely dispersed to be performed by government.

An ethical obligation on the part of the private owner is the only visible remedy for these situations. . . .

In each field one group (A) regards the land as soil, and its function as commodity-production; another group (B) regards the land as biota, and its function as something broader. . . . In all these cleavages, we see repeated the same basic paradoxes: man the conqueror *versus* man the biotic citizen; science the sharpener of his sword *versus* science the searchlight on his universe; land the slave and servant *versus* land the collective organism. . . .

It is inconceivable to me that an ethical relation to the land can exist without love, respect, and admiration for land, and a high regard for its value. By value, I of course mean something far broader than mere economic value; I mean value in the philosophical sense. . . . Examine each question in terms of what is ethically and aesthetically right, as well as what is economically expedient. A thing is right when it tends to preserve the integrity, stability, and beauty of the biotic community. It is wrong when it tends otherwise.

From Aldo Leopold, *A Sand County Almanac: And Essays on Conservation from Round River.*

ED MCGAA (EAGLE MAN)

Native American Values Promote Living in Harmony with Nature

Ed McGaa (1936–), born in Pine Ridge Reservation, South Dakota, is a writer.

Ed McGaa explains what he identifies as the American Indian view of the world. The Great Spirit created nature and Mother Earth and commanded us to respect the Great Spirit, Mother Earth, our fellow men and women, and individual freedom. McGaa argues that this value system, together with the Native American virtues of generosity and sharing, are ideal for people's living in harmony with nature and themselves. White people have endangered nature with greedy and materialistic pursuits, but they can improve their condition by affirming Native American values which emphasize a spiritual connectedness of people with the entirety of nature.

The plight of the non-Indian world is that it has lost respect for Mother Earth, from whom and where we all come.

We all start out in this world as tiny seeds—no different from our animal brothers and sisters, the deer, the bear, the buffalo, or the trees, the flowers, the winged people. Every particle of our bodies comes from the good things Mother Earth has put forth. Mother Earth is our real mother, because every bit of us truly comes from her, and daily she takes care of us.

The tiny seed takes on the minerals and the waters of Mother Earth. It is fueled by *Wiyo* the sun, and given a spirit by *Wakan Tanka*.

This morning at breakfast we took from Mother Earth to live, as we have done every day of our lives. But did we thank her for giving us the means to live? The old Indian did. When he drove his horse in close to a buffalo running at full speed across the prairie, he drew his bow back and said as he did so, "Forgive me, brother, but my people must live." After he butchered the buffalo, he took the skull and faced it toward the setting sun as a thanksgiving and an acknowledgment that all things come from Mother Earth. He brought the meat back to camp and gave it first to the old, the widowed, and the weak. For thousands of years great herds thrived across the continent because the Indian never took more than he needed. Today, the buffalo is gone.

You say *ecology*. We think the words *Mother Earth* have a deeper meaning. If we wish to survive, we must respect her. It is very late, but there is still time to revive and discover the old American Indian value of respect for Mother Earth. She is very beautiful, and already she is showing us signs that she may punish us for not respecting her. Also, we must remember she has been placed in this universe by the one who is the All Powerful, the Great Spirit Above, or *Wakan Tanka*—God. But a few years ago, there lived on the North American continent people, the American Indians, who knew a respect and value system that enabled them to live on their native grounds without having to migrate, in contrast to the white brothers and sisters who migrated by the thousands from their homelands because they had developed a value system different from that of the American Indian. There is no place now to which we can migrate, which means we can no longer ignore the red man's value system.

Carbon-dating techniques say that the American Indian has lived on the North American continent for thousands upon thousands of years. If we did migrate, it was because of a natural phenomenon—a glacier. We did not migrate because of a social system, value system, and spiritual system that neglected its responsibility to the land and all living things. We Indian people say we were always here.

We, the American Indian, had a way of living that enabled us to live within the great, complete beauty that only the natural environment can provide. The Indian tribes had a common value system and a commonality of religion, without religious animosity, that preserved that great beauty that the two-leggeds definitely need. Our four commandments from the Great Spirit are: (1) respect for Mother Earth, (2) respect for the Great Spirit, (3) respect for our fellow man and woman, and (4) respect for individual freedom (provided that individual freedom does not threaten the tribe or the people or Mother Earth).

We who respect the great vision of Black Elk see the four sacred colors as red, yellow, black, and white. They stand for the four directions–red for the east, yellow for the south, black for the west, and white for the north.

From the east comes the rising sun and new knowledge from a new day.

From the south will come the warming south winds that will cause our Mother to bring forth the good foods and grasses so that we may live.

To the west where the sun goes down, the day will end, and we will sleep; and we will hold our spirit ceremonies at night, from where we will communicate with the spirit world beyond. The sacred color of the west is black; it stands for the deep intellect that we will receive from the spirit ceremonies. From the west come the life-giving rains.

From the north will come the white winter snow that will cleanse Mother Earth and put her to sleep, so that she may rest and store up energy to provide the beauty and bounty of springtime. We will prepare for aging by learning to create, through our arts and crafts, during the long winter season. Truth, honesty, strength, endurance, and courage also are represented by the white of the north. Truth and honesty in our relationships bring forth harmony.

All good things come from these sacred directions. These sacred directions, or four sacred colors, also stand for the four races of humanity: red, yellow, black, and white. We cannot be a prejudiced people, because all men and women are brothers and sisters and because we all have the same mother—Mother Earth. One who is prejudiced, who hates another because of that person's color, hates what the Great Spirit has put here. Such a one hates that which is holy and will be punished, even during this lifetime, as humanity will be punished for violating Mother Earth. Worse, one's conscience will follow into the spirit world, where it will be discovered that all beings are equal. This is what we Indian people believe.

We, the Indian people, also believe that the Great Spirit placed many people throughout this planet: red, yellow, black, and white. What about the brown people? The brown people evolved from the sacred colors coming together. Look at our Mother Earth. She, too, is brown because the four directions have come together. After the Great Spirit, *Wakan Tanka*, placed them in their respective areas, the *Wakan Tanka* appeared to each people in a different manner and taught them ways so that they might live in harmony and true beauty. Some men, some tribes, some nations have still retained the teachings of the Great Spirit. Others have not. Unfortunately, many good and peaceful religions have been assailed by narrow-minded zealots. Our religious beliefs and our traditional Indian people have suffered the stereotype that we are pagans, savages or heathens; but we do not believe that only one religion controls the way to the spirit world that lies beyond. We believe that *Wakan Tanka* loves all of its children equally, although the Great Spirit must be disturbed at time with those children who have destroyed proven value systems that practiced sharing and generosity and kept Mother Earth viable down through time. We kept Mother Earth viable because we did not sell her or our spirituality!

Brothers and sisters, we must go back to some of the old ways if we are going to truly save our Mother Earth and bring back the natural beauty that every person seriously needs, especially in this day of vanishing species, vanishing rain forests, overpopulation, poisoned waters, acid rain, a thinning ozone layer, drought, rising temperatures, and weapons of complete annihilation. . . .

Chief Sitting Bull advised us to take the best of the white man's ways and to take the best of the old Indian ways. He also said, "When you find something that is bad, or turns out bad, drop it and leave it alone.". . . .

My friends, I will never cease to be an Indian. I will never cease respecting the old Indian values, especially our four cardinal commandments and our values of generosity and sharing. It is true that many who came to our shores brought a great amount of good to this world.

Modern medicine, transportation, communications, and food production are but a few of the great achievements that we should all appreciate. But it is also true that too many of those who migrated to North
America became so greedy and excessively materialistic that great harm
has been caused. We have seen good ways and bad ways. The good way
of the non-Indian I am going to keep. The very fact that we can hold
peace-seeking communication and that world leaders meet and communicate for peace shows the wisdom of the brothers and sisters of this
time. By all means, good technology should not be curtailed, but care
must be taken lest our water, air, and earth become irreparably harmed.
The good ways I will always respect and support. But, my brothers and
sisters, I say we must give up this obsession with excess consumption
and materialism, especially when it causes the harming of the sides surrounding our Mother and the pollution of the waters upon her. *She is
beginning to warn us!*

Keep those material goods that you need to exist, but be a more
sharing and generous person. You will find that you can do with less.
Replace this empty lifestyle of hollow impressing of the shallow ones
with active participation for your Mother Earth. At least, then, when
you depart into the spirit world, you can look back with pride and fulfillment. Other spirit beings will gather around you, other spirits of
your own higher consciousness will gather around you and share your
satisfaction with you. The eternal satisfaction of knowing you did not
overuse your Mother Earth and that you were here to protect her will
be a powerful satisfaction when you reach the spirit world.

Indian people do not like to say that the Great Mystery is exactly
this or exactly that, but we do know there is a spirit world that lies beyond. We are allowed to know that through our ceremonies. We know
that we will go into a much higher plane beyond. We know nothing of
hellfire and eternal damnation from some kind of unloving power that
placed us here as little children. None of that has ever been shown to
us in our powerful ceremonies, conducted by kind, considerate, proven,
and very nonmaterialistic leaders. We do know that everything the
Great Mystery makes is in the form of a circle. Our Mother Earth is a
very large, powerful circle.

Therefore, we conclude that our life does not end. A part of it is
within that great eternal circle. If there is a hell, then our concept of
hell would be an eternal knowing that one violated or took and robbed
from Mother Earth and caused this suffering that is being bestowed
upon the generations unborn. This then, if it were to be imprinted
upon one's eternal conscience, this would surely be a terrible, spiritual,
mental hell. Worse, to have harmed and hurt one's innocent fellow beings, and be unable to alter (or conceal) the harmful actions would also
be a great hell. Truth in the spirit world will not be concealed, nor will
it be for sale. Lastly, we must realize that the generations unborn will

also come into the spirit world. Let us be the ones that they wish to thank and congratulate, rather than eternally scorn.

While we are shedding our overabundant possessions, and linking up with those of like minds, and advancing spiritual and environmental appreciations, we should develop a respect for the aged and for family-centered traditions, even those who are single warriors, fighting for the revitalization of our Mother on a lone, solitary, but vital front. We should have more respect for an extended family, which extends beyond a son or daughter, goes beyond to grandparents and aunts and uncles, goes beyond to brothers, sisters, aunts, and uncles that we have adopted or made as relatives—and further beyond, to the animal or plant world as our brothers and sisters, to Mother Earth and Father Sky and then above to *Wakan Tanka*, the *Unci/tankashilah*, the Grandparent of us all. When we pray directly to the Great Spirit, we say *Unci* (Grandmother) or *tankashilah* (Grandfather) because we are so family-minded that we think of the Great Power above as a grandparent, and we are the grandchildren. Of course, this is so because every particle of our being is from Mother Earth, and our energy and life force are fueled by Father Sky. This is a vital part of the great, deep feeling and spiritual psychology that we have as Indian people. It is why we preserved and respected our ecological environment for such a long period. *Mitakuye eyasin!* We are all related!

In conclusion, our survival is dependent on the realization that Mother Earth is a truly holy being, that all things in this world are holy and must not be violated, and that we must share and be generous with one another. You may call this thought by whatever fancy words you wish—psychology, theology, sociology, or philosophy—but you must think of Mother Earth as a living being. Think of your fellow men and women as holy people who were put here by the Great Spirit. Think of being related to all things! With this philosophy in mind as we go on with our environmental ecology efforts, our search for spirituality, and our quest for peace, we will be far more successful when we truly understand the Indians' respect for Mother Earth.

From Ed McGaa, *Mother Earth Spirituality: Native American Paths to Healing Ourselves and Our World.*

The Two-tailed Monkey. Painting by Julie Speed, 1997.

FRANS DE WAAL

Animals Behave in Moral Ways

Frans de Waal (1948–) is an ethologist and primatologist at the Yerkes Regional Primate Research Center.

Frans de Waal is critical of comparative studies of humans and non-human primates which emphasize the vast differences between them. We can recognize that apes are not able to articulate and debate fundamental moral conceptions and principles, but we should consider at the same time the similarities in the behavior of non-human primates and humans. Chimpanzees, for example, exhibit empathy, a central element of human moral experience. De Waal is not prepared to say that non-human primates have a morality in the way humans do but encourages us to think that they "occupy a number of floors of the tower of morality."

Members of some species may reach tacit consensus about what kind of behavior to tolerate or inhibit in their midst, but without language the principles behind such decisions cannot be conceptualized, let alone debated. To communicate intentions and feelings is one thing; to clarify what is right, and why, and what is wrong, and why, is quite something else. Animals are no moral philosophers.

But then, how many *people* are? We have a tendency to compare animal behavior with the most dizzying accomplishments of our race, and to be smugly satisfied when a thousand monkeys with a thousand typewriters do not come close to William Shakespeare. . . .

A chimpanzee stroking and patting a victim of attack or sharing her food with a hungry companion shows attitudes that are hard to distinguish from those of a person picking up a crying child, or doing volunteer work in a soup kitchen. To classify the chimpanzee's behavior as based on instinct and the person's behavior as proof of moral decency is misleading, and probably incorrect. First of all, it is uneconomic in that it assumes different processes for similar behavior in two closely related species. Second, it ignores the growing body of evidence for mental complexity in the chimpanzee, including the possibility of empathy. I hesitate to call the members of any species other than our own "moral beings," yet I also believe that many of the sentiments and cognitive abilities underlying human morality antedate the appearance of our species on this planet.

The question of whether animals have morality is a bit like the question of whether they have culture, politics, or language. If we take the full-blown human phenomenon as a yardstick, they most definitely do not. On the other hand, if we break the relevant human abilities into their component parts, some are recognizable in other animals.

Culture: Field primatologists have noticed differences in tool use and communication among populations of the same species. Thus, in one chimpanzee community all adults may crack nuts with stones, whereas another community totally lacks this technology. Group-specific signals and habits have been documented in bonobos as well as chimpanzees. Increasingly, primatologists explain these differences as learned traditions handed down from one generation to the next.

Language: For decades apes have been taught vocabularies of hand signals (such as American Sign Language) and computerized symbols. Koko, Kanzi, Washoe, and several other anthropoids have learned to effectively communicate their needs and desires through this medium.

Politics: Tendencies basic to human political systems have been observed in other primates, such as alliances that challenge the status quo, and tit-for-tat deals between a leader and his supporters. As a result, status struggles are as much popularity contests as physical battles.

In each of these domains, nonhuman primates show impressive intelligence yet do not integrate information quite the way we do. The utterances of language-trained apes, for example, show little if any evidence of grammar. The transmission of knowledge from one generation to the next is rarely, if ever, achieved through active teaching. And it is still ambiguous how much planning and foresight, if any, go into the social careers of monkeys and apes.

Despite these limitations, I see no reason to avoid labels such as "primate culture," "ape language," or "chimpanzee politics" as long as it is understood that this terminology points out fundamental similarities without in any way claiming *identity* between ape and human. . . . To focus attention on those aspects in which we differ—a favorite tactic of the detractors of the evolutionary perspective—overlooks the critical importance of what we have in common. Inasmuch as shared characteristics most likely derive from the common ancestor, they probably laid the groundwork for much that followed, including whatever we claim as uniquely ours. To disparage this common ground is a bit like arriving at the top of a tower only to declare that the rest of the building is irrelevant, that the precious concept of "tower" ought to be reserved for the summit.

While making for good academic fights, semantics are mostly a waste of time. Are animals moral? Let us simply conclude that they occupy a number of floors of the tower of morality.

From Frans de Waal, *Good-Natured: the Origins of Right and Wrong in Humans and Other Animals*.

GEORGE HERBERT MEAD
"Fragments on Ethics"

George Herbert Mead (1863–1931) was an American pragmatist philosopher.

George Herbert Mead sees his project in ethics as similar to Kant's and the utilitarian's. In each case there is a search for some universal end. For Kant it is a society of people acting rationally. For the utilitarian it is the happiness of the whole community. Mead finds a shortcoming in these approaches in that neither of them state the universal end in terms of "the object of desire of the individual." Mead believes his view overcomes this deficiency with his insight that people are social beings that want to interact and share experiences with other people.

Students often report that participation in discussion groups after a lecture is the most rewarding part of the overall experience. Thus, they find themselves looking forward to the next opportunity to assemble in this way. Mead says that even when we do something alone, like read a book, we want to tell other people about it and see that sharing as making the experience better. When we do interact with other people in this way, we may find that it leads to their recommending a movie that the book reminded them of. We go to the movie, enjoy it, and want to report back. We see how social interaction builds on prior, satisfying experiences with other people and see how it makes sense to say that it is an object of desire.

Mead tells us that the more we become interested in other people, the greater is our interest in life and the happier we become. Good ends are the ones that allow us to actualize ourselves as social beings. When we pursue such ends, we go after something we desire. We find that, when we attain that object, we are glad we did so and want to expand social interactions of that sort. As we do so, the self becomes larger, we develop our social nature, we identify our good with the common good, and we attain moral happiness.

1. It is possible to build up an ethical theory on a social basis, in terms of our social theory of the origin, development, nature, and structure of the self. . . .

4. Both Kant and the Utilitarians wish to universalize, to make universal that in which morality lies. The Utilitarian says it must be the greatest good of the greatest number; Kant says that the attitude of the act must be one which takes on the form of a universal law. I want to point out this common attitude of these two schools which are so opposed to each other in other ways: they both feel that an act which is moral must have in some way a universal character. If you state morality in terms of the result of the act, then you state the results in terms of the

whole community; if in the attitude of the act, it must be in the respect for law, and the attitude must take on the form of a universal law, a universal rule. Both recognize that morality involves universality, that the moral act is not simply a private affair. A thing that is good from a moral standpoint must be a good for everyone under the same conditions. This demand for universality is found in both the Utilitarian and Kantian doctrines.

This picture of a kingdom of ends is hardly to be distinguished from Mill's doctrine, since both set up society as an end. Each of them has to get to some sort of an end that can be universal. The Utilitarian reaches that in the general good, the general happiness of the whole community; Kant finds it in an organization of rational human beings, who apply rationality to the form of their acts. Neither of them is able to state the end in terms of the object of desire of the individual.

Actually, what you have to universalize is the object toward which desire is directed, that upon which your attention must be centered if you are going to succeed. . . .

If you are going to be successful, you have to be interested in an end in terms of the steps which are necessary to carry it out. In that sense the result is present in the act. A person who is taking all the steps to bring about a result sees the result in the steps. It is that which makes one moral or immoral, and distinguishes between a man who really means to do what he says he is going to do, and one who merely "means well.". . .

7. All of our impulses are possible sources of happiness; and in so far as they get their natural expression they lead up to happiness. In the moral act there will be pleasure in our satisfactions; but the end is in the objects, and the motives are in the impulses which are directed toward these objects. When a person, for example, becomes extremely interested in some undertaking, then he has impulses that are directed toward certain ends, and such impulses become the motives of his conduct. We distinguish such impulses from the motive that the Utilitarian recognizes. He recognizes only one motive: the feeling of pleasure that will arise when the desire is satisfied. In place of that we put the impulse which is directed toward the end itself and maintain that such impulses are the motives of moral conduct.

The question then becomes the determination of the sort of ends toward which our action should be directed. What sort of a standard can we set up? Our ends should, first of all, be ends which are desirable in themselves, that is, which do lead to the expression and satisfaction of the impulses. Now there are some impulses which lead simply to disintegration, which are not desirable in themselves. There are certain of our impulses which find their expression, for example, in cruelty. Taken by themselves they are not desirable because the results which they bring are narrowing, depressing, and deprive us of social relations. They also lead, so far as others are concerned, to injury to other individuals.

In Dewey's terms, the moral impulses should be those "which re-inforce and expand not only the motives from which they directly spring but also the other tendencies and attitudes which are sources of happiness." If a person becomes interested in other persons, he finds the interest which he has does lead to reinforcing that motive and to expanding other motives. The more we become interested in persons the more we become interested in general in life. The whole situation within which the individual finds himself takes on new interest. Simi-larly, to get an intellectual motive is one of the greatest boons which one may have, because it expands interest so widely. We recognize such ends as particularly important.

So, looking at happiness from the point of view of impulses them-selves, we can set up a standard in this fashion: the end should be one which reinforces the motive, one which will reinforce the impulse and expand other impulses or motives. That would be the standard pro-posed.

8. All the things worth while are shared experiences. Even when a person is by himself, he knows that the experience he has in nature, in the enjoyment of a book, experiences which we might think of as purely individual, would be greatly accentuated if they could be shared with others. Even when a person seems to retire into himself to live among his own ideas, he is living really with the others who have thought what he is thinking. He is reading books, recalling the experi-ences which he has had, projecting conditions under which he might live. The content is always of a social character. Or it may pass into those mystical experiences in religious life—communion with God. The conception of the religious life is itself a social conception; it gathers about the idea of the community.

It is only in so far as you can identify your own motive and the ac-tual end you are pursuing with the common good that you reach the moral end and so get moral happiness. As human nature is essentially social in character, moral ends must be also social in their nature.

9. If we look at the individual from the point of view of his im-pulses, we can see that those desires which reinforce themselves, or continue on in their expression, and which awaken other impulses, will be good; whereas those which do not reinforce themselves lead to un-desirable results, and those which weaken the other motives are in themselves evil. If we look now toward the end of the action rather than toward the impulse itself, we find that those ends are good which lead to the realization of the self as a social being. Our morality gathers about our social conduct. It is as social beings that we are moral beings. On the one side stands the society which makes the self possible, and on the other side stands the self that makes a highly organized society possible. The two answer to each other in moral conduct.

In our reflective conduct we are always reconstructing the immedi-ate society to which we belong. We are taking certain definite attitudes which involve relationship with others. In so far as those relationships are changed, the society itself is changed. We are continually reconstructing. When it comes to the problem of reconstruction there is one essential demand—that all of the interests that are involved should be taken into account. One should act with reference to all of the interests that are involved: that is what we could call a "categorical imperative."

We are definitely identified with our own interests. One is constituted out of his own interests; and when those interests are frustrated, what is called for then is in some sense a sacrifice of this narrow self. This should lead to the development of a larger self which can be identified with the interests of others. I think all of us feel that one must be ready to recognize the interests of others even when they run counter to our own, but that the person who does that does not really sacrifice himself, but becomes a larger self. . . .

12. The only rule that an ethics can present is that an individual should rationally deal with all the values that are found in a specific problem. That does not mean that one has to spread before him all the social values when he approaches a problem. The problem itself defines the values. It is a specific problem and there are certain interests that are definitely involved; the individual should take into account all of those interests and then make out a plan of action which will rationally deal with those interests. That is the only method that ethics can bring to the individual. It is of the greatest importance that one should define what those interests are in the particular situation. The great need is that one should be able to regard them impartially. We feel that persons are apt to take what we call a selfish attitude with reference to them. I have pointed out that the matter of selfishness is the setting-up of a narrow self over against a larger self. Our society is built up out of our social interests. Our social relations go to constitute the self. But when the immediate interests come in conflict with others we had not recognized, we tend to ignore the others and take into account only those which are immediate. The difficulty is to make ourselves recognize the other and wider interests, and then to bring them into some sort of rational relationship with the more immediate ones. There is room for mistakes, but mistakes are not sins. . . .

13. A man has to keep his self-respect, and it may be that he has to fly in the face of the whole community in preserving this self-respect. But he does it from the point of view of what he considers a higher and better society than that which exists. Both of these are essential to moral conduct: that there should be a social organization and that the individual should maintain himself. The method for taking into account all of those interests which make up society on the one hand and the individual on the other is the method of morality.

From George H. Mead, "Fragments on Ethics."

RELIGION

INTRODUCTION

The belief in a "higher power" or supreme being is a powerful force in the lives of many people and can provide sustenance and comfort in what otherwise seems a harsh and chaotic universe. To believe in the existence of God is to accept a rich framework of beliefs that crucially shape one's experience of the world. The person who accepts a belief in God will look to God as the source of moral authority and may see prayer as a means to know the will of God. For the person who rejects the belief in God, there is no divine being who issues moral commands, and prayer is but a misguided appeal to a fictitious force outside the self.

Throughout the history of Western thought philosophers have been much concerned with both the content and the foundation of religious belief. One central issue concerns the nature of the divine being. What are the attributes of God? Is God a wholly transcendent being forever outside the immediate grasp of human experience? Is God a being with whom humans can have a personal and direct relationship? What should our relationship to the Divine be? Should we envision the Supreme Being as a wise guide, a loving parent, a stern moral authority, or as an implacable being fundamentally unconcerned with the human realm? Is it best to view the Divine as

Witches Apprehended, Examined and Executed, for notable villanies by them committed both by Land and Water.

With a strange and most true triall how to know whether a woman be a Witch or not.

Printed at London for *Edward Marchant*, and are to be sold at his shop ouer against the Crosse in Pauls Church-yard. 1613.

Witches Apprehended, Examined and Executed. London, 1613. The seventeenth-century practice in England of "swimming" women suspected of being witches was used in Connecticut and Virginia as well. If the suspect, with a weight tied to her, sank and drowned, she was not a witch. If she floated, she was a witch and was burned.

that which is revealed to us when we are in close communion and harmony with nature and natural forces?

Some philosophers have argued that once one correctly understands the nature of God, then one will be convinced of the existence of God. Anselm, Descartes, and others sought to construct a rational proof for the existence of God, that is, an argument whose premises can be objectively recognized as true and whose conclusion, guaranteed true by the premises, certifies the existence of God; and they believed that all one needed to construct such a proof was a correct understanding of the concept of God and a grasp of the fundamental laws of logic.

Other philosophers believed with Anselm and Descartes that a rational proof for God's existence could be given, but they opted to base their proofs on observed facts about the world rather than on an intellectual understanding of the concept of God. Many of these proofs seek to establish that there is some fact about the world which can only be fully explained if a Divine Being, God, exists. The argument from miracles, represented in our readings by C. S. Lewis, points to the occurrence of events which seem to conflict with or cannot be explained by our natural laws of physics: how is it that a person with inoperable, terminal cancer is completely cured after making a pilgrimage to a holy place? Surely, the argument runs, miracles are best explained as acts of God, and, so, the existence of miracles establishes the existence of God. Another argument, called the argument from design and illustrated by the selection from William Paley, points to the marvelous complexities and organization in the organisms which make up the universe and the universe itself: for example, the eyes of the rabbit are perfectly situated and suited for sighting the rabbit's predators. Surely, such a high level of organization and functional fittedness demands the existence of a "designer of the universe," namely, God. Yet a third argument, offered by St. Thomas Aquinas, is called the cosmological argument: proponents of the cosmological argument suggest that we cannot adequately explain the existence of the universe at all unless we accept that God exists as the first cause of the universe and all its constituents. An argument that has considerable contemporary currency, with advocates like Elizabeth Kübler-Ross and Raymond Moody, concerns the phenomenon of "near death experiences": what are we to make of people who, when they are near death, have profoundly moving experiences of floating free of the body and of moving toward a bright, welcoming light that suffuses them with joy and well-being? Some philosophers would argue that such experiences can only be fully explained if we understand them as occasions on which persons really do enter the non-physical, spiritual realm and come into communion with the Divine.

Philosophers who are critical of the empirical proofs for the existence of God often try to subvert the proofs by showing that the phenomena in question can be explained without appealing to the existence of God. For example, critics of the argument from "near death" experiences have argued that all of the features of such experiences can be explained in purely neuro-physiological and psychological terms: perhaps endorphins generate intense feelings of well-being that enable elaborate hallucinations. And critics of Aquinas's cosmological argument would argue that the origin of the universe can be explained simply by appeal to something like the "Big Bang" theory, put forward in the selection from Stephen Hawking. You will encounter replies to the argument from miracles and the argument from design in the selections from Hume and Darrow, respectively: look to see how they try to explain, in purely naturalistic terms, the phenomena under investigation. Do you agree with their explanations?

Theorists like Sigmund Freud argue that the phenomenon of religious belief itself can be explained within the scientific framework; for Freud, the belief in God can be explained as a psychological mechanism which arises as people attempt to deal with and make some sense of a hostile and chaotic world. But if science can explain why people believe in a supreme being, then isn't the truth of the belief called into question? Is religious belief nothing but an illusion? A familiar reply to this line of reasoning is that, whatever motives humans have for adopting religious beliefs, the beliefs may nonetheless be true. Psychological explanations of religion do not disprove religious beliefs.

Some philosophers have attempted to construct decisive disproofs of the existence of God and have appealed in particular to the existence of evil—human wrong-doing and suffering—to make their case: how could an all-good and all-powerful God allow humans to suffer? Why doesn't God prevent famines, and air crashes, and human cruelty? A selection from Mark Twain provides a lively version of the "argument from evil," and the selection that follows it by Josiah Royce outlines the position of the theodicist, who believes that the occurrence of evil is not incompatible with the existence of a loving, all-powerful God.

Arguments both for and against the existence of God presuppose the appropriateness of the search for rational grounds on which to base a belief in God, but there are theorists like Immanuel Kant, who sharply demarcate the realm of faith from the realm of reason and who argue that the belief in God properly arises from faith not from reason. On this view scientific explanations of natural phenomena do not preclude a belief in God precisely because no evidence—empirical or otherwise—is needed to justify the commitment to the existence of God. As Søren Kierkegaard tells us, to believe in God is not to accept the conclusion of an argument but to make a "leap of faith." William James takes a similar line when he argues that we are not "made" to believe in the existence of God by the force of logic, but rather we legitimately allow the hope that our religious beliefs are true to lead us to accept their truth.

CHARLES SANDERS PEIRCE

Love and Instinct Rather than Argument Guide Us in Deciding Whether God Exists

Charles Sanders Peirce likens people's experiences with God to experiences with any great person whom they know well and who influence their conduct. In all such cases we can recognize a mind that is doing the influencing. And as to whether God really exists, the guides of love and instinct, not argument, will lead us to an answer.

If a pragmaticist is asked what he means by the word "God," he can only say that just as long acquaintance with a man of great character may deeply influence one's whole manner of conduct, so that a glance at his portrait may make a difference, just as almost living with Dr. Johnson enabled poor Boswell to write an immortal book and a really sublime book, just as long study of the works of Aristotle may make him an acquaintance, so if contemplation and study of the physico-psychical universe can imbue a man with principles of conduct analogous to the influence of a great man's works or conversation, then that analogue of a mind—for it is impossible to say that *any* human attribute is *literally* applicable—is what he means by "God." Of course, various great theologians explain that one cannot attribute *reason* to God, nor perception (which always involves an element of surprise and of learning what one did not know), and, in short, that his "mind" is necessarily so unlike ours, that some—though wrongly—high in the church say that it is only negatively, as being entirely different from every thing else, that we can attach any meaning to the Name. This is not so; because the discoveries of science, their enabling us to predict what will be the course of nature, is proof conclusive that, though we cannot think any thought of God's, we can catch a fragment of His thought, as it were.

Now such being the pragmaticist's answer to the question what he means by the word "God," the question whether there really is such a being is the question whether all physical science is merely the figment—the arbitrary figment—of the students of nature, and further whether the *one* lesson of Gautama Boodha, Confucius, Socrates, and all who from any point of view have had their ways of conduct determined by meditation upon the physico-psychical universe, be only their arbitrary notion or be the Truth behind the appearances which the frivolous man does not think of; and whether the superhuman courage which such contemplation has conferred upon priests who go to pass their lives with lepers and refuse all offers of rescue is mere silly fanaticism, the passion of a baby, or whether it is strength derived from the power of the truth. Now the only guide to the answer to this question lies in the power of the passion of love which more or less overmasters every agnostic scientist and everybody who seriously and deeply considers the universe. But whatever there may be of *argument* in all this is as nothing, the merest nothing, in comparison to its force as an appeal to one's own instinct, which is to argument what substance is to shadow, what bed-rock is to the built foundations of a cathedral.

From "The Concept of God."

WILLIAM JAMES

It Is Not Irrational to Believe Religious Teachings which are Unproved

In his essay, "The Will to Believe," William James takes on the skeptics of religious belief and argues for our right to take a believing attitude in religious matters. Skeptics might charge that believers are being unscientific in their adoption of religious belief without adequate evidence. But these skeptics are simply suggesting that it is better to give in to our fear of being in error about religious belief than our hope for the truth of these beliefs. And why should fear of error triumph over hope for truth when yielding to this fear keeps us from recognizing truths which may exist?

I have brought with me to-night something like a sermon on justification by faith to read to you, I mean an essay in justification of faith, a defence of our right to adopt a believing attitude in religious matters, in spite of the fact that our merely logical intellect may not have been coerced. 'The Will to Believe,' accordingly, is the title of my paper.

I have long defended to my own students the lawfulness of voluntarily adopted faith; but as soon as they have got well imbued with the logical spirit, they have as a rule refused to admit my contention to be lawful philosophically, even though in point of fact they were personally all the time chock-full of some faith or other themselves. I am all the while, however, so profoundly convinced that my own position is correct, that your invitation has seemed to me a good occasion to make my statements more clear. Perhaps your minds will be more open than those with which I have hitherto had to deal. . . .

Moral questions immediately present themselves as questions whose solution cannot wait for sensible proof. A moral question is a question not of what sensibly exists, but of what is good, or would be good if it did exist. Science can tell us what exists; but to compare the *worths*, both of what exists and of what does not exist, we must consult not science, but what Pascal calls our heart. Science herself consults her heart when she lays it down that the infinite ascertainment of fact and correction of false belief are the supreme good for man. Challenge the statement, and science can only repeat it oracularly, or else prove it by showing that such ascertainment and correction bring man all sorts of other goods which man's heart in turn declares. The question of having moral beliefs at all or not having them is decided by our will. . . .

Turn now from these wide questions of good to a certain class of questions of fact, questions concerning personal relations, states of mind between one man and another. *Do you like me or not?*—for example. Whether you do or not depends, in countless instances, on whether I meet you half-way, am willing to assume that you must like me, and show you trust and expectation. The previous faith on my part in your liking's existence is in such cases what makes your liking come. But if I stand aloof, and refuse to budge an inch until I have objective evidence, until you shall have done something apt, as the absolutists say, *ad extorquendum assensum meum*, ten to one your liking never comes. How many women's hearts are vanquished by the mere sanguine insistence of some man that they *must* love him! He will not consent to the hypothesis that they cannot. The desire for a certain kind of truth here brings about that special truth's existence; and so it is in innumerable cases of other sorts. Who gains promotions, boons, appointments, but the man in whose life they are seen to play the part of live hypotheses, who discounts them, sacrifices other things for their sake before they have come, and takes risks for them in advance? His faith acts on the powers above him as a claim, and creates its own verification.

A social organism of any sort whatever, large or small, is what it is because each member proceeds to his own duty with a trust that the other members will simultaneously do theirs. Wherever a desired result is achieved by the co-operation of many independent persons, its existence as a fact is a pure consequence of the precursive faith in one another of those immediately concerned. A government, an army, a commercial system, a ship, a college, an athletic team, all exist on this condition, without which not only is nothing achieved, but nothing is even attempted. A whole train of passengers (individually brave enough) will be looted by a few highwaymen, simply because the latter can count on one another, while each passenger fears that if he makes a movement of resistance, he will be shot before any one else backs him up. If we believed the whole car-full would rise at once with us, we should each severally rise, and train-robbing would never even be attempted. There are, then, cases where a fact cannot come at all unless a preliminary faith exists in its coming. *And where faith in a fact can help create the fact*, that would be an insane logic which should say that faith running ahead of scientific evidence is the 'lowest kind of immorality' into which a thinking being can fall. Yet such is the logic by which our scientific absolutists pretend to regulate our lives!. . .

In truths dependent on our personal action, then, faith based on desire is certainly a lawful and possibly an indispensable thing.

But now, it will be said, these are all childish human cases, and have nothing to do with great cosmical matters, like the question of religious faith. Let us then pass on to that. Religions differ so much in their accidents that in discussing the religious question we must make it very generic and broad. What then do we now mean by the religious hypothesis? Science says things are; morality says some things are better than other things; and religion says essentially two things.

First, she says that the best things are the more eternal things, the overlapping things, the things in the universe that throw the last stone, so to speak, and say the final word. "Perfection is eternal,"—this phrase of Charles Secretan seems a good way of putting this first affirmation of religion, an affirmation which obviously cannot yet be verified scientifically at all.

The second affirmation of religion is that we are better off even now if we believe her first affirmation to be true.

Now, let us consider what the logical elements of this situation are *in case the religious hypothesis in both its branches be really true.* (Of course, we must admit that possibility at the outset. If we are to discuss the question at all, it must involve a living option. If for any of you religion be a hypothesis that cannot, by any living possibility be true, then you need go no farther. I speak to the 'saving remnant' alone.) So proceeding, we see, first that religion offers itself as a *momentous* option. We are supposed to gain, even now, by our belief, and to lose by our non-belief, a certain vital good. Secondly, religion is a *forced* option, so far as that good goes. We cannot escape the issue by remaining sceptical and waiting for more light, because, although we do avoid error in that way *if religion be untrue,* we lose the good, *if it be true,* just as certainly as if we positively chose to disbelieve. It is as if a man should hesitate indefinitely to ask a certain woman to marry him because he was not perfectly sure that she would prove an angel after he brought her home. Would he not cut himself off from that particular angel-possibility as decisively as if he went and married some one else? Scepticism, then, is not avoidance of option; it is option of a certain particular kind of risk. *Better risk loss of truth than chance of error*—that is your faith-vetoer's exact position. He is actively playing his stake as much as the believer is; he is backing the field against the religious hypothesis, just as the believer is backing the religious hypothesis against the field. . . .

I, therefore, for one, cannot see my way to accepting the agnostic rules for truth-seeking, or wilfully agree to keep my willing nature out of the game. I cannot do so for this plain reason, that *a rule of thinking which would absolutely prevent me from acknowledging certain kinds of truth if those kinds of truth were really there, would be an irrational rule.* That for me is the long and short of the formal logic of the situation, no matter what the kinds of truth might materially be. . . .

Indeed we *may* wait if we will—I hope you do not think I am denying you that—but if we do so, we do so at our peril as much as if we believed. In either case we *act,* taking our life in our hands. No one of us ought to issue vetoes to the other, nor should we bandy words of abuse. We ought, on the contrary, delicately and profoundly to respect one another's mental freedom: then only shall we bring about the intellectual republic; then only shall we have that spirit of inner tolerance without which all our outer tolerance is soulless, and which is empiricism's glory; then only shall we live and let live, in speculative as well as in practical things.

From William James, "The Will to Believe."

JOHN DEWEY

Redefining God as a Union of the Ideal and the Actual Helps to Secure Useful Values

John Dewey charges religion with channeling people's energy and emotion to some ideal realm which is remote from the actual, the world of human experience. He proposes that we conceive God as the union of the ideal and the actual. In so doing, we direct our emotions and energies to securing values which make a difference in human affairs rather than holding them to be of value in a realm independent of experience.

It is this active relation between ideal and actual to which I would give the name "God." I would not insist that the name must be given. There are those who hold that the associations of the term with the supernatural are so numerous and close that any use of the word "God" is sure to give rise to misconception and be taken as a concession to traditional ideas.

They may be correct in this view. But the facts to which I have referred are there, and they need to be brought out with all possible clearness and force. There exist concretely and experimentally goods—the values of art in all its forms, of knowledge, of effort and of rest after striving, of education and fellowship, of friendship and love, of growth in mind and body. These goods are there and yet they are relatively embryonic. Many persons are shut out from generous participation in them; there are forces at work that threaten and sap existent goods as well as prevent their expansion. A clear and intense conception of a union of ideal ends with actual conditions is capable of arousing steady emotion. It may be fed by every experience, no matter what its material.

In a distracted age, the need for such an idea is urgent. It can unify interests and energies now dispersed; it can direct action and generate the heat of emotion and the light of intelligence. Whether one gives the name "God" to this union, operative in thought and action, is a matter for individual decision. But the function of such a working union of the ideal and actual seems to me to be identical with the force that has in fact been attached to the conception of God in all the religions that have a spiritual content; and a clear idea of that function seems to me urgently needed at the present time. . . .

What would be the consequences upon the values of human association if intrinsic and immanent satisfactions and opportunities were clearly held to and cultivated with the ardor and the devotion that have at times marked historic religions? The contention of an increasing number of persons is that depreciation of natural social values has resulted, both in principle and in actual fact, from reference of their origin and significance to supernatural sources. Natural relations, of husband and wife, of parent and child, friend and friend, neighbor and neighbor, of fellow workers in industry, science and art, are neglected, passed over, not developed for all that is in them. They are, moreover, highly depreciated. They have been regarded as dangerous rivals of higher values; as offering temptations to be resisted; as usurpations by flesh of the authority of the spirit; as revolts of the human against the divine. . . .

The idea of a double and parallel manifestation of the divine, in which the latter has superior status and authority, brings about a condition of unstable equilibrium. It operates to distract energy, through dividing the objects to which it is directed. It also imperatively raises the question as to why having gone far in recognition of religious values in normal community life, we should not go further. The values of natural human intercourse and mutual dependence are open and public, capable of verification by the methods through which all natural facts are established. By means of the same experimental method, they are capable of expansion. Why not concentrate upon nurturing and extending them? Unless we take this step, the idea of two realms of spiritual values is only a softened version of the old dualism between the secular and the spiritual, the profane and the religious.

From John Dewey, *A Common Faith.*

JANE ADDAMS

Religious Teachings Should Serve as Guides for Human Betterment

Validity comes to religious teachings, Jane Addams argues, when people use them as guides for activity which betters humanity. She registers her concern with educators who fail to make their teachings relevant for such reform and is especially troubled with the effect of this failure on young people. In youth is an instinct for justice, "a divine fire," that needs to be fed.

The Christian youth may have been taught that man's heartbreaking adventure to find justice in the order of the universe moved the God of Heaven himself to send a Mediator in order that the justice man craves and the mercy by which alone he can endure his weakness might be reconciled, but he will not make the doctrine his own until he reduces it to action and tries to translate the spirit of his Master into social terms.

The youth who calls himself an "Evolutionist"—it is rather hard to find a name for this youth, but there are thousands of him and a fine fellow he often is—has read of that struggle beginning with the earliest tribal effort to establish just relations between man and man, but he still needs to be told that after all justice can only be worked out upon this earth by those who will not tolerate a wrong to the feeblest member of the community, and that it will become a social force only in proportion as men steadfastly strive to establish it.

If these young people who are subjected to varied religious instruction are also stirred to action, or rather, if the instruction is given validity because it is attached to conduct, then it may be comparatively easy to bring about certain social reforms so sorely needed in our industrial cities. We are at times obliged to admit, however, that both the school and the church have failed to perform this office, and are indicted by the young people themselves. Thousands of young people in every great city are either frankly hedonistic, or are vainly attempting to work out for themselves a satisfactory code of morals. They cast about in all directions for the clue which shall connect their loftiest hopes with their actual living.

Several years ago a committee of lads came to see me in order to complain of a certain high school principal because "He never talks to us about life. " When urged to make a clearer statement, they added,

"He never asks us what we are going to be; we can't get a word out of him, excepting lessons and keeping quiet in the halls."

Of the dozens of young women who have begged me to make a connection for them between their dreams of social usefulness and their actual living, I recall one of the many whom I had sent back to her clergyman, returning with this remark: "His only suggestion was that I should be responsible every Sunday for fresh flowers upon the altar. I did that when I was fifteen and liked it then, but when you have come back from college and are twenty-two years old, it doesn't quite fit in with the vigorous efforts you have been told are necessary in order to make our social relations more Christian."

All of us forget how very early we are in the experiment of founding self-government in this trying climate of America, and that we are making the experiment in the most materialistic period of all history, having as our court of last appeal against that materialism only the wonderful and inexplicable instinct for justice which resides in the hearts of men—which is never so irresistible as when the heart is young. We may cultivate this most precious possession—or we may disregard it. We may listen to the young voices rising, clear above the roar of industrialism and the prudent councils of *commerce*, or we may become hypnotized by the sudden new emphasis placed upon wealth and power, and forget the supremacy of spiritual forces in men's affairs. It is as if we ignored a wistful, over-confident creature who walked through our city streets calling out, "I am the spirit of Youth! With me, all things are possible!" We fail to understand what he wants or even to see his doings, although his acts are pregnant with meaning, and we may either translate them into a sordid chronicle of petty vice or turn them into a solemn school for civic righteousness.

We may either smother the divine fire of youth or we may feed it. We may either stand, stupidly staring as it sinks into a murky fire of crime and flares into the intermittent blaze of folly or we may tend it into a lambent flame with power to make clean and bright our dingy city streets.

From Jane Addams, *The Spirit of Youth and the City Streets*.

WILLIAM PALEY

We Can Infer God's Existence from Evidence of Design in Nature

William Paley (1743-1805) was a British theologian, moral philosopher and utilitarian.

William Paley likens God to a watchmaker in an analogical argument for God's existence. Upon inspecting a watch, we see that it displays evidence of being designed for a purpose; the parts were assembled for the purpose of telling time. With this evidence, we infer the existence of a watchmaker. Now we find in objects of nature such evidence. We find that the human eye displays evidence of being designed for a purpose, here one of seeing. So on like reasoning, we infer the existence of an intelligent Creator, and we must make this inference, says Paley, since there is no other way of accounting for this design. Further, when we consider all of the many objects in nature like the eye which display similar design, we find that the argument takes on a cumulative nature and that there is ample evidence for the existence of this Creator.

In crossing a heath, suppose I pitched my foot against a *stone* and were asked how the stone came to be there, I might possibly answer that for anything I knew to the contrary it had lain there forever; nor would it, perhaps, be very easy to show the absurdity of this answer. But suppose I had found a *watch* upon the ground, and it should be inquired how the watch happened to be in that place, I should hardly think of the answer which I had before given, that for anything I knew the watch might have always been there. Yet why should not this answer serve for the watch as well as for the stone; why is it not as admissible in the second case as in the first? For this reason, and for no other, namely, that when we come to inspect the watch, we perceive—what we could not discover in the stone—that its several parts are framed and put together for a purpose, e.g., that they are so formed and adjusted as to produce motion, and that motion so regulated as to point out the hour of the day; that if the different parts had been differently shaped from what they are, or placed after any other manner or in any other order than that in which they are placed, either no motion at all would have been carried on in the machine, or none which would have answered the use that is now served by it. To reckon up a few of the plainest of these parts and of their offices, all tending to one result: we see a cylindrical box containing a coiled elastic spring, which, by its endeavor to relax itself, turns round the box. We next observe a flexible chain—artificially wrought for the sake of flexure—communicating the action of the spring from the box to the fusee. We then find a series of wheels, the teeth of which catch in and apply to each other, conducting the motion from the fusee to the balance and from the balance to the pointer, and at the same time, by the size and shape of those wheels, so regulating that motion as to terminate in causing an index, by an equable and measured progression, to pass over a given space in a given time. We take notice that the wheels are made of brass, in order to keep them from rust; the springs of steel, no other metal being so elastic; that over the face of the watch there is placed a glass, a material employed in no other part of the work, but in the room of which, if there had been any other than a transparent substance, the hour could not be seen without opening the case. This mechanism being observed—it requires indeed an examination of the instrument, and perhaps some previous knowledge of the subject, to perceive and understand it; but being once, as we have said, observed and understood—the inference we think is inevitable, that the watch must have had a maker—that there must have existed, at some time and at some place or other, an artificer or artificers who formed it for the purpose which we find it actually to answer, who completely comprehended its construction and designed its use. . . .

Were there no example in the world of contrivance except that of the eye, it would be alone sufficient to support the conclusion which we draw from it, as to the necessity of an intelligent Creator. It could never be got rid of, because it could not be accounted for by any other supposition which did not contradict all the principles we possess of knowledge—the principles according to which things do, as often as they can be brought to the test of experience, turn out to be true or false. Its coats and humors, constructed as the lenses of a telescope are constructed, for the refraction of rays of light to a point, which forms the proper action of the organ; the provision in its muscular tendons for turning its pupil to the object, similar to that which is given to the telescope by screws, and upon which power of direction in the eye the exercise of its office as an optical instrument depends; the further provision for its defense, for its constant lubricity and moisture, which we see in its socket and its lids, in its glands for the secretion of the matter of tears, its outlet or communication with the nose for carrying off the liquid after the eye is washed with it; these provisions compose altogether an apparatus, a system of parts, a preparation of means, so manifest in their design, so exquisite in their contrivance, so successful in their issue, so precious, and so infinitely beneficial in their use, as, in my opinion, to bear down all doubt that can be raised upon the subject. And what I wish, under the title of the present chapter, to observe is that, if other parts of nature were inaccessible to our inquiries, or even if other parts of nature presented nothing to our examination but disorder and confusion, the validity of this example would remain the same. If there were but one watch in the world, it would not be less certain that it had a maker. If we had never in our lives seen any but one single kind of hydraulic machine, yet if of that one kind we understood the mechanism and use, we should be as perfectly assured that it proceeded from the hand and thought and skill of a workman, as if we visited a Museum of the arts and saw collected there twenty different kinds of machines for drawing water, or a thousand different kinds for other purposes. Of this point each machine is a proof independently of all the rest. So it is with the evidences of a divine agency. The proof is not a conclusion which lies at the end of a chain of reasoning, of which chain each instance of contrivance is only a link, and of which, if one link fail, the whole fails; but it is an argument separately supplied by every separate example. An error in stating an example affects only that example. The argument is cumulative in the fullest sense of that term. The eye proves it without the ear; the ear without the eye. The proof in each example is complete; for when the design of the part and the conduciveness of its structure to that design is shown, the mind may set itself at rest; no future consideration can detract anything from the force of the example.

From William Paley, *Natural Theology*.

CHARLES DARWIN

The Human Eye Is the Result of Natural Evolution

Charles Darwin (1809–1882) was the British biologist who proposed the theory of evolution.

Charles Darwin admits that at first blush the notion that the eye is a product of the evolutionary process seems absurd. But upon analysis, we can dispel this blind spot and see how the forces of natural selection have been operative in producing the complex human eye.

To suppose that the eye with all its inimitable contrivances for adjusting the focus to different distances, for admitting different amounts of light, and for the correction of spherical and chromatic aberration, could have been formed by natural selection seems, I freely confess, absurd in the highest degree. When it was first said that the sun stood still and the world turned round, the common sense of mankind declared the doctrine false; but the old saying of *Vox populi Dei*, as every philosopher knows, cannot be trusted in science. Reason tells me, that if numerous gradations from a simple and imperfect eye to one complex and perfect can be shown to exist, each grade being useful to its possessor, as is certainly the case; if further, the eye ever varies and the variations be inherited, as is likewise certainly the case; and if such variations should be useful to any animal under changing conditions of life, then the difficulty of believing that a perfect and complex eye could be formed by natural selection, though insuperable by our imagination, should not be considered as subversive of the theory. . . .

The simplest organ which can be called an eye consists of an optic nerve, surrounded by pigment-cells and covered by translucent skin, but without any lens or other refractive body. We may, however, according to M. Jourdain, descend even a step lower and find aggregates of pigment-cells, apparently serving as organs of vision, without any nerves, and resting merely on sarcodic tissue. Eyes of the above simple nature are not capable of distinct vision, and serve only to distinguish light from darkness. In certain star-fishes, small depressions in the layer of pigment which surrounds the nerves are filled, as described by the author just quoted, with transparent gelatinous matter, projecting with a convex surface, like the cornea in the higher animals. He suggests that this serves not to form an image, but only to concentrate the luminous rays and render their perception more easy. In this concentration of the rays we gain the first and by far the most important step towards the formation of a true, picture-forming eye; for we have only to place the naked extremity of the optic nerve, which in some of the lower animals lies deeply buried in the body, and in some near the surface, at the right distance from the concentrating apparatus, and an image will be formed on it. . . .

When we reflect on these facts, here given much too briefly, with respect to the wide, diversified, and graduated range of structure in the eyes of the lower animals; and when we bear in mind how small the number of all living forms must be in comparison with those which have become extinct, the difficulty ceases to be very great in believing that natural selection may have converted the simple apparatus of an optic nerve, coated with pigment and invested by transparent membrane, into an optical instrument as perfect as is possessed by any member of the Articulate Class. . . .

Within the highest division of the animal kingdom, namely, the Vertebrata, we can start from an eye so simple, that it consists, as in the lancelet, of a little sack of transparent skin, furnished with a nerve and lined with pigment, but destitute of any other apparatus. In fishes and reptiles, as Owen has remarked, "the range of gradations of dioptric structures is very great." It is a significant fact that even in man, according to the high authority of Virchow, the beautiful crystalline lens is formed in the embryo by an accumulation of epidermic cells, lying in a sack-like fold of the skin; and the vitreous body is formed from embryonic subcutaneous tissue. To arrive, however, at a just conclusion regarding the formation of the eye, with all its marvelous yet not absolutely perfect characters, it is indispensable that the reason should conquer the imagination; but I have felt the difficulty far too keenly to be surprised at others hesitating to extend the principle of natural selection to so startling a length.

It is scarcely possible to avoid comparing the eye with a telescope. We know that this instrument has been perfected by the long-continued efforts of the highest human intellects; and we naturally infer that the eye has been formed by a somewhat analogous process. But may not this inference be presumptuous? Have we any right to assume that the Creator works by intellectual powers like those of man?

From Charles Darwin, *The Origin of Species*.

CLARENCE DARROW

Arguments that Attempt to Prove God's Existence from Design and Purpose are Flawed

Clarence Darrow (1857–1938), a distinguished American lawyer, is famed for his participation in the "Scopes monkey trial."

Clarence Darrow takes Paley on, along with other thinkers who claim to have found proof for God's existence in evidence of design and purpose in the universe. In each case, the design or purpose which is alleged to be there really is not. And so we can not base an argument for the existence of God on the claim that there is design and purpose in the universe.

Nature brings hordes of insects that settle over the land and destroy the farmers' crops. Who are the objects of the glorious design: the farmers who so patiently and laboriously raise the crops or the grasshoppers that devour them? It must be the insects, because the farmers hold prayer meetings and implore their God to kill the bugs, but the pests go on with their deadly work unmolested. Man prates glibly about design, but Nature furnishes not a single example or fact as proof. Perhaps the microbe who bores a hole into the vitals of man and brings him down to his death may believe in a Providence and a design. How else could he live so royally on the vitals of one of the lords of creation?

All that we know is that we were born on this little grain of sand we call the earth. We know that it is one of the smallest bits of matter that floats in the great shoreless sea of space, and we have every reason to believe that it is as inconsequential in every other respect. On board the same craft, sailing the same seas, are all sorts of living things, fighting each other, and us, that each may survive. Most of these specimens are living on the carcasses of the dead. The strongest instinct of most of our crew is to stay here and live. The strongest in intellect and prowess live the longest. Nature, in all her manifestations, is at war with life, and sooner or later will doubtless have her way. No one can give a reason for any or all of the manifestations which we call life. We are like a body of shipwrecked sailors clutching to a raft and desperately engaged in holding on.

Men have built faith from hopes. They have struggled and fought in despair. They have frantically clung to life because of the will to live. The best that we can do is to be kindly and helpful toward our friends and fellow passengers who are clinging to the same speck of dirt while we are drifting side by side to our common doom.

From Clarence Darrow, *The Story of My Life*.

Saint Thomas Aquinas

There Is a First Cause of the Universe: God

St. Thomas Aquinas (1224–1274) was an Italian Catholic priest and scholar.

St. Thomas Aquinas offers the Cosmological Argument for the Existence of God which is a cluster of five similar arguments. Each one draws on the interrelatedness of phenomena in the cosmos, like changes and causes, for proof of God's existence. In the following passage, Aquinas focuses on causation, and this statement of the argument is sometimes called the causal version of the cosmological argument or the First Cause Argument. Philosophers and theologians have formulated this argument in a variety of ways, but the basic structure of their reasoning is the same. It begins by considering why an event occurs. We say that it had a cause, and that cause had a cause, and so on. Eventually we have to choose between two possibilities: either this causal series goes on to infinity or it has a first cause or beginning. We must rule the infinite series out, since that possibility prevents us from offering an adequate account of why any event occurs. How could something occur without a beginning? So, there has to be a first cause. Aquinas says this first cause is God.

We find that there is among material things a regular order of causes. But we do not find, nor indeed is it possible, that anything is the cause of itself, for in that case it would be prior to itself, which is impossible. Now it is not possible to proceed to infinity in causes. For if we arrange in order all causes, the first is the cause of the intermediate, and the intermediate the cause of the last, whether the intermediate be many or only one. But if we remove a cause, the effect is removed; therefore, if there is no *first* among causes, neither will there be a last or an intermediate. But if we proceed to infinity in causes there will be no first cause, and thus there will be no ultimate effect, nor any intermediate cause, which is clearly false. Therefore it is necessary to suppose the existence of some first cause, and this men call God.

From Thomas Aquinas, *Summa Theologica*, translated by Laurence Shapcote.

STEPHEN W. HAWKING

The Universe Began with a Big Bang

Stephen W. Hawking (1942–) is a British quantum physicist and natural philosopher.

Everyone has heard of the big bang theory of how the universe began. The following selection by the renowned physicist, Stephen Hawking, presents the essential elements of this theory.

In order to explain the ideas that I and other people have had about how quantum mechanics may affect the origin and fate of the universe, it is necessary first to understand the generally accepted history of the universe, according to what is known as the "hot big bang model." . . .

At the big bang itself, the universe is thought to have had zero size, and so to have been infinitely hot. But as the universe expanded, the temperature of the radiation decreased. One second after the big bang, it would have fallen to about ten thousand million degrees. This is about a thousand times the temperature at the center of the sun, but temperatures as high as this are reached in H-bomb explosions. At this time the universe would have contained mostly photons, electrons, and neutrinos (extremely light particles that are affected only by the weak force and gravity) and their antiparticles, together with some protons and neutrons. As the universe continued to expand and the temperature to drop, the rate at which electron/antielectron pairs were being produced in collisions would have fallen below the rate at which they were being destroyed by annihilation. So most of the electrons and antielectrons would have annihilated with each other to produce more photons, leaving only a few electrons left over. The neutrinos and antineutrinos, however, would not have annihilated with each other, because these particles interact with themselves and with other particles only very weakly. So they should still be around today. If we could observe them, it would provide a good test of this picture of a very hot early stage of the universe. Unfortunately, their energies nowadays would be too low for us to observe them directly. However, if neutrinos are not massless, but have a small mass of their own, as suggested by an unconfirmed Russian experiment performed in 1981, we might be able to detect them indirectly: they could be a form of "dark matter," like that mentioned earlier, with sufficient gravitational attraction to stop the expansion of the universe and cause it to collapse again.

About one hundred seconds after the big bang, the temperature would have fallen to one thousand million degrees, the temperature inside the hottest stars. At this temperature protons and neutrons would no longer have sufficient energy to escape the attraction of the strong nuclear force, and would have started to combine together to produce the nuclei of atoms of deuterium (heavy hydrogen), which contain one proton and one neutron. The deuterium nuclei then would have combined with more protons and neutrons to make helium nuclei, which contain two protons and two neutrons, and also small amounts of a couple of heavier elements, lithium and beryllium. One can calculate that in the hot big bang model about a quarter of the protons and neutrons would have been converted into helium nuclei, along with a small amount of heavy hydrogen and other elements. The remaining neutrons would have decayed into protons, which are the nuclei of ordinary hydrogen atoms. . . .

Within only a few hours of the big bang, the production of helium and other elements would have stopped. And after that, for the next million years or so, the universe would have just continued expanding, without anything much happening. Eventually, once the temperature had dropped to a few thousand degrees, and electrons and nuclei no longer had enough energy to overcome the electromagnetic attraction between them, they would have started combining to form atoms. The universe as a whole would have continued expanding and cooling, but in regions that were slightly denser than average, the expansion would have been slowed down by the extra gravitational attraction. This would eventually stop expansion in some regions and cause them to start to recollapse. As they were collapsing, the gravitational pull of matter outside these regions might start them rotating slightly. As the collapsing region got smaller, it would spin faster—just as skaters spinning on ice spin faster as they draw in their arms. Eventually, when the region got small enough, it would be spinning fast enough to balance the attraction of gravity, and in this way disklike rotating galaxies were born. Other regions, which did not happen to pick up a rotation, would become oval-shaped objects called elliptical galaxies. In these, the region would stop collapsing because individual parts of the galaxy would be orbiting stably round its center, but the galaxy would have no overall rotation. . . .

The earth was initially very hot and without an atmosphere. In the course of time it cooled and acquired an atmosphere from the emission of gases from the rocks. This early atmosphere was not one in which we could have survived. It contained no oxygen, but a lot of other gases that are poisonous to us, such as hydrogen sulfide (the gas that gives rotten eggs their smell). There are, however, other primitive forms of life that can flourish under such conditions. It is thought that they developed in the oceans, possibly as a result of chance combinations of atoms into large structures, called macromolecules, which were capable of assembling other atoms in the ocean into similar structures. They would thus have reproduced themselves and multiplied. In some cases there would be errors in the reproduction. Mostly these errors would have been such that the new macromolecule could not reproduce itself and eventually would have been destroyed. However, a few of the errors would have produced new macromolecules that were even better at reproducing themselves. They would have therefore had an advantage and would have tended to replace the original macromolecules. In this way a process of evolution was started that led to the development of more and more complicated, self-reproducing organisms. The first primitive forms of life consumed various materials, including hydrogen sulfide, and released oxygen. This gradually changed the atmosphere to the composition that it has today and allowed the development of higher forms of life such as fish, reptiles, mammals, and ultimately the human race.

This picture of a universe that started off very hot and cooled as it expanded is in agreement with all the observational evidence that we have today.

From Stephen W. Hawking, *A Brief History of Time.*

A	In *Adam's* Fall We Sinned all.
B	Thy Life to Mend This *Book* Attend.
C	The *Cat* doth play And after flay.
D	A *Dog* will bite A Thief at night.
E	An *Eagles* flight Is out of fight.
F	The Idle *Fool* Is whipt at School.

Page from *The New England Primer* of the late seventeenth century that merged the study of the alphabet with Puritan thinking and beliefs.

JONATHAN EDWARDS
The World Is Coming to an End

Jonathan Edwards (1703–1758) was an American Puritan theologian and philosopher.

In the following passage, Jonathan Edwards turns his attention not to the beginning of the world but to its end. His reasoning brings him to the conclusion that it will have an end.

As it is with the body of man—its meat and its clothing perishes and is continually renewed, and at last the body itself perishes; the food that is taken down quickly perishes and is cast forth to the dunghill, and there is a constant succession of new food; and its garments are worn out and new garments are put on, one after another; at last the body itself, that is thus fed and clothed, wears out—so there is all reason to think it will be with the world, it that needs nourishment. The face of the earth continually needs a new supply of rain, and also of nitrous parts by the snow and frost or by other means gradually drawn in from the atmosphere that it is encompassed with, and of nourishment by falling leaves or rotting plants or otherwise to feed it. The sea is constantly fed by rain and rivers to maintain it. The earth, in all parts, has constant new supplies of water to maintain its fountains and streams that are, as it were, its arteries and veins. The sun itself, that nourishes the whole planetary system, is nourished by comets, by new supplies from time to time communicated from them. And so the world is continually changing its garments, as it were. The face of the earth is annually clothed, as it were with new garments, and is stripped naked in the winter. The successive generations of inhabitants and successive kingdoms and empires and new states of things in the world are, as it were, new garments; and as these wear out, one after another, so there is reason to think the world itself, whose meat and clothing thus perishes, will itself perish at last. The body of man often lies down and sleeps and rises up again, but at last will lie down and rise no more. So the world every year, as it were, perishes in the winter or sinks into an image of death, as sleep is in the body of man, but it is renewed again in the spring. But at last it will perish and rise no more.

From *The Philosophy of Jonathan Edwards From His Private Notebooks.*

C. S. LEWIS

Miracles Do Occur and Are Evidence of God's Existence

C. S. Lewis (1898–1963) was a British novelist and religious thinker.

A popular argument for God's existence is the Argument from Miracles. In effect, the occurrence of the miracle is used as evidence of God's existence. The argument commonly conceives a miracle as an event which goes against, or cannot be explained in terms of, the laws of nature. It continues by asserting that miracles do occur. There are partings of waters which defy the laws of nature; there is water turning to blood as there is wine becoming blood and a walking stick becoming a snake all of which nature tells us is impossible. Since these events do not have a natural cause, their cause is of a supernatural origin, and that supernatural cause is God. Critics of this argument are quick to point to the many events of the past, like a solar eclipse, which people dubbed miraculous but later became perfectly intelligible in natural terms. So, now, if we find some event which appears to be a miracle because it seems to contravene what we know about the natural world, we might better admit that we simply do not know what the naturalistic explanation is rather than commit ourselves to its being a miracle. C. S. Lewis is aware of this difficulty which the Argument from Miracles faces and has us rethink what a miracle is. He argues that an event can be a miracle without going against the laws of nature and that we should expect an explanation in natural terms of events which God causes.

It is therefore inaccurate to define a miracle as something that breaks the laws of Nature. It doesn't. If I knock out my pipe I alter the position of a great many atoms: in the long run, and to an infinitesimal degree, of all the atoms there are. Nature digests or assimilates this event with perfect ease and harmonises it in a twinkling with all other events. It is one more bit of raw material for the laws to apply to, and they apply. I have simply thrown one event into the general cataract of events and it finds itself at home there and conforms to all other events. If God annihilates or creates or deflects a unit of matter He has created a new situation at that point. Immediately all Nature domiciles this new situation, makes it at home in her realm, adapts all other events to it. It finds itself conforming to all the laws. If God creates a miraculous spermatozoon in the body of a virgin, it does not proceed to break any laws. The laws at once take it over. Nature is ready. Pregnancy follows, according to all the normal laws, and nine months later a child is born. We see every day that physical nature is not the least incommoded by the daily inrush of events from biological nature or from psychological nature. If events ever come from beyond Nature altogether, she will be no more incommoded by them. Be sure she will rush to the point where she is invaded, as the defensive forces rush to a cut in our finger, and there hasten to accommodate the newcomer. The moment it enters her realm it obeys all her laws. Miraculous wine will intoxicate, miraculous conception will lead to pregnancy, inspired books will suffer all the ordinary processes of textual corruption, miraculous bread will be digested. The divine art of miracle is not an art of suspending the pattern to which events conform but of feeding new events into that pattern. It does not violate the law's proviso, "If A, then B": it says, "But this time instead of A, A2," and Nature, speaking through all her laws, replies, "Then B2" and naturalises the immigrant, as she well knows how. She is an accomplished hostess.

From C.S. Lewis, *Miracles: a Preliminary Study*.

DAVID HUME

There Are No Reliable Reports of Miracles

David Hume (1711–1776) was a Scottish empiricist and skeptic.

David Hume rejects the notion that miracles have occurred and rests this rejection on evidentiary grounds. There simply is no reliable evidence of miracles having occurred. Hume offers a test for whether we should accept the report of a miracle. Factors like the number of people who perceived the event, the reputation of these people, and the circumstances under which people witnessed the event are elements of Hume's test. When Hume applies his criterion to the reports of miracles which he knows of, he finds that no report passes his test.

In the foregoing reasoning we have supposed that the testimony upon which a miracle is founded may possibly amount to entire proof, and that the falsehood of that testimony would be a real prodigy. But it is easy to show that we have been a great deal too liberal in our concession, and that there never was a miraculous event established on so full an evidence.

For, *first*, there is not to be found, in all history, any miracle attested by a sufficient number of men of such unquestioned good sense, education, and learning as to secure us against all delusion in themselves; of such undoubted integrity as to place them beyond all suspicion of any design to deceive others; of such credit and reputation in the eyes of mankind as to have a great deal to lose in case of their being detected in any falsehood, and at the same time attesting facts performed in such a public manner and in so celebrated a part of the world as to render the detection unavoidable—all which circumstances are requisite to give us a full assurance in the testimony of men.

From David Hume, *An Inquiry Concerning Human Understanding.*

MARK TWAIN

We Cannot Square the Usual Idea of God with All of the Evil in the World

Mark Twain (1835–1910) was an American writer, humorist and social critic.

The Argument from Evil against the existence of God draws our attention to the evil in the world along with our expectation that we should have a world with no evil. After all, if God is omniscient (all-knowing), omnipotent (all-powerful), and omnibenevolent (all-good), would God not have created a world with no evil? God had the power to do so, God knew how to do it, and God wills good to the highest degree. So, if we affirm the existence of unnecessary evil, and indeed we must, we must reject the existence of God so conceived. Mark Twain gets this point across in some letters which Satan sends to his friends. After getting kicked out of heaven, Satan pays a visit to humanity. He finds it absurd that they can hold to such an idealistic notion of God in the face of the evil which surrounds them. Satan shares these thoughts with his friends.

Satan had been making admiring remarks about certain of the Creator's sparkling industries—remarks which, being read between the lines, were sarcasms. He had made them confidentially to his safe friends the other archangels, but they had been overheard by some ordinary angels and reported at Headquarters.

He was ordered into banishment for a day—the celestial day. It was a punishment he was used to, on account of his too flexible tongue. Formerly he had been deported into Space, there being nowhither else to send him, and had flapped tediously around there in the eternal night and the Arctic chill; but now it occurred to him to push on and hunt up the earth and see how the Human-Race experiment was coming along.

By and by he wrote home—very privately—to St. Michael and St. Gabriel about it.

SATAN'S LETTER

This is a strange place, an extraordinary place, and interesting. There is nothing resembling it at home. The people are all insane, the other animals are insane, the earth is insane. Nature itself is insane. Man is a marvelous curiosity. When he is at his very best he is a sort of low grade nickel-plated angel; at his worst he is unspeakable, unimaginable; and first and last and all the time he is a sarcasm. Yet he blandly and in all sincerity calls himself the "noblest work of God." This is the truth I am telling you. And this is not a new idea with him, he has talked it through all the ages, and believed it. Believed it, and found nobody among all his race to laugh at it.

Moreover—if I may put another strain upon you—he thinks he is the Creator's pet. He believes the Creator is proud of him; he even believes the Creator loves him; has a passion for him; sits up nights to admire him; yes, and watch over him and keep him out of trouble. He prays to Him, and thinks He listens. Isn't it a quaint idea? Fills his prayers with crude and bald and florid flatteries of Him, and thinks He sits and purrs over these extravagancies and enjoys them. He prays for help, and favor, and protection, every day; and does it with hopefulness and confidence, too, although no prayer of his has ever been answered. The daily affront, the daily defeat, do not discourage him, he goes on praying just the same. There is something almost fine about this perseverance. I must put one more strain upon you: he thinks he is going to heaven!

He has salaried teachers who tell him that. They also tell him there is a hell, of everlasting fire, and that he will go to it if he doesn't keep the Commandments. What are the Commandments? They are a curiosity. I will tell you about them by and by. . . .

The best minds will tell you that when a man has begotten a child he is morally bound to tenderly care to it, protect it from hurt, shield it from disease, clothe it, feed it, bear with its waywardness, lay no hand upon it save in kindness and for its own good, and never in any case inflict upon it a wanton cruelty. God's treatment of his earthly children, every day and every night, is the exact opposite of all that, yet those best minds warmly justify these crimes, condone them, excuse them, and indignantly refuse to regard them as crimes at all, when *he* commits them. Your country and mine is an interesting one, but there is nothing there that is half so interesting as the human mind.

Very well, God banished Adam and Eve from the Garden, and eventually assassinated them. All for disobeying a command which he had no right to utter. But he did not stop there, as you will see. He has one code of morals for himself, and quite another for his children. He requires his children to deal justly—and gently—with offenders, and forgive them seventy-and-seven times; whereas he deals neither justly nor gently with anyone, and he did not forgive the ignorant and thoughtless first pair of juveniles even their first small offense and say, "You may go free this time, I will give you another chance."

On the contrary! He elected to punish *their* children, all through the ages to the end of time, for a trifling offense committed by others before they were born. He is punishing them yet. In mild ways? No, in atrocious ones.

You would not suppose that this kind of a Being gets many compliments. Undeceive yourself: the world calls him the All-Just, the All-Righteous, the All-Good, the All-Merciful, the All-Truthful, the All-Loving, the Source of All Morality. These sarcasms are uttered daily, all over the world. But not as conscious sarcasms. No, they are meant seriously: they are uttered without a smile. . . .

From Mark Twain, *Letters from the Earth.*

JOSIAH ROYCE
The Evil of Suffering Is Necessary

Josiah Royce (1855–1916) was an American idealist philosopher.

Josiah Royce recounts how the problem of evil arises in Job. The evil is Job's suffering and the problem is reconciling it with the traditional notion of God. Royce identifies some of the major responses to the problem of evil including claims that evil is of the natural world and not God's doing, that it serves an instructional function, and that it is a necessary ingredient of a plan to test the faith of beings with free wills. He then makes his own contribution of philosophical idealism which holds that our souls are one with God and that any suffering which we experience is also God's. And God's suffering is necessary for him to be the perfect being that he is. He would fall short of perfection were he to have no experience with suffering.

Job's world, as he sees it, is organized in a fashion extremely familiar to us all. The main ideas of this cosmology are easy to be reviewed. The very simplicity of the scheme of the universe here involved serves to bring into clearer view the mystery and horror of the problem that besets Job himself. The world, for Job, is the work of a being who, in the very nature of the case, ought to be intelligible (since he is wise), and friendly to the righteous, since, according to tradition, and by virtue of his divine wisdom itself, this God must know the value of a righteous man. But—here is the mystery—this God, as his works get known through our human experiences of evil, appears to us not friendly, but hopelessly foreign and hostile in his plans and his doings. The more, too, we study his ways with man, the less intelligible seems his nature. Tradition has dwelt upon his righteousness, has called him merciful, has magnified his love towards his servants, has described his justice in bringing to naught the wicked. One has learned to trust all these things, to conceive God in these terms, and to expect all this righteous government from him. Moreover, tradition joins with the pious observation of nature in assuring us of the omnipotence of God. Job himself pathetically insists that he never doubts, for an instant, God's power to do whatever in heaven or earth he may please to do. Nothing hinders God. No blind faith thwarts him. Sheol is naked before him. The abyss has no covering. The earth hangs over chaos because he orders it to do so. His power shatters the monsters and pierces the dragons. He can, then, do with evil precisely what he does with Rahab or with the shades, with the clouds or with the light or with the sea, namely, exactly what he chooses. Moreover, since he knows everything, and since the actual value of a righteous man is, for Job, an unquestionable and objective fact, God cannot fail to know this real worth of righteousness in his servants, as well as the real hatefulness and mischief of the wicked. God knows worth, and cannot be blind to it, since it is as real a fact as heaven and earth themselves. . . .

The question at issue between maker and creature is therefore one that demands a direct statement and a clear decision. "Why, since you can do precisely as you choose, and since you know, as all-knower, the value of a righteous servant, do you choose, as enemy, to persecute the righteous with this fury and persistence of hate?" Here is the problem.

The human interest of the issue thus so clearly stated by Job lies, of course, in the universality of just such experiences of undeserved ill here upon earth. . . .

But what is to-day as fresh and real to us as it was to our poet is the fact that all about us, say in every child born with an unearned heredity of misery, or in every pang of the oppressed, or in every arbitrary coming of ill-fortune, some form of innocence is beset with an evil that the sufferer has not deserved. Job wins dramatic sympathy as an extreme, but for the purpose all the more typical, case of this universal experience of unearned ill-fortune. In every such case we therefore still have the interest that Job had in demanding the solution of this central problem of evil. Herein, I need not say, lies the permanent significance of the problem of Job—a problem that wholly outlasts any ancient Jewish controversy as to the question whether the divine justice always does or does not act as Job's friends, in their devotion to tradition, declare that it acts. . . .

In the second place, one may deal with our problem by attempting any one, or a number, of those familiar and popular compromises between the belief in a world of natural law and the belief in a teleological order, which are all, as compromises, reducible to the assertion that the presence of evil in the creation is a relatively insignificant, and an inevitable, incident of a plan that produces sentient creatures subject to law. Writers who expound such compromises have to point out that, since a burnt child dreads the fire, pain is, on the whole, useful as a warning. Evil is a transient discipline, whereby finite creatures learn their place in the system of things. Again, a sentient world cannot get on without some experience of suffering, since sentience means tenderness. Take away pain (so one still again often insists), take away pain, and we should not learn our share of natural truth. Pain is the pedagogue to teach us natural science. The contagious diseases, for instance, are useful in so far as they lead us in the end to study Bacteriology, and thus to get an insight into the life of certain beautiful creatures of God whose presence in the world we should otherwise blindly overlook! . . .

A third method of dealing with our problem is in essence identical with the course which, in a very antiquated form, the friends of Job adopt. This method takes its best known expression in the doctrine that the presence of evil in the world is explained by the fact that the value of free will in moral agents logically involves, and so explains and justifies, the divine permission of the evil deeds of those finite beings who freely choose to sin, as well as the inevitable fruits of the sins. God creates agents with free will. He does so because the existence of such agents has of itself an infinite worth. Were there no free agents, the highest good could not be. But such agents, because they are free, can offend. The divine justice of necessity pursues such offenses with attendant evils. These evils, the result of sin, must, logically speaking, be permitted to exist, if God once creates the agents who have free will, and himself remains, as he must logically do, a just God. How much ill thus results depends upon the choice of the free agents, not upon God, who wills to have only good chosen, but of necessity must leave his free creature to their own devices, so far as concerns their power to sin.

There remains a fourth doctrine as to our problem. This doctrine is in essence the thesis of philosophical idealism. . . .

The answer to Job is: God is not in ultimate essence another being than yourself. He is the Absolute Being. You truly are one with God, part of his life. He is the very soul of your soul. And so, here is the first truth: When you suffer, *your sufferings are God's sufferings*, not his external work, not his external penalty, not the fruit of his neglect, but identically his own personal woe. In you god himself suffers, precisely as you do, and has all your concern in overcoming this grief.

The true question then is: Why does God thus suffer? The sole possible, necessary, and sufficient answer is, Because without suffering, without ill, without woe, evil, tragedy, God's life could not be perfected. This grief is not a physical means to an external end. It is a logically necessary and eternal constituent of the divine life. It is logically necesary that the Captain of your salvation should be perfect through suffering. No outer nature compels him. He chooses this because he chooses his own perfect selfhood. He is perfect. His world is the best possible world. Yet all its finite regions know not only of joy but of defeat and sorrow, for thus alone, in the completeness of his eternity, can God in his wholeness be triumphantly perfect.

From Josiah Royce, "The Problem of Job."

LUCRETIUS
Religion Has Caused People to Do Great Evil

Lucretius (c. 99–55 B.C.E.) was a Roman metaphysical poet.

Lucretius believes that religion embraces superstitions which lead people to perform wicked deeds. He offers the needless sacrifice of the young girl, Iphigeneia, whose father slaughtered her at the altar on her wedding day to create favorable conditions for his ships to sail. "Such are the heights of wickedness to which men are driven by superstition." Lucretius lambasts the preachers for conjuring up fears in people.

Remember how at Aulis the altar of the Virgin Goddess was foully stained with the blood of Iphigeneia by the leaders of the Greeks, the patterns of chivalry. The headband was bound about her virgin tresses and hung down evenly over both her cheeks. Suddenly she caught sight of her father standing sadly in front of the altar, the attendants beside him hiding the knife and her people bursting into tears when they saw her. Struck dumb with terror, she sank on her knees to the ground. Poor girl, at such a moment it did not help her that she had been first to give the name of father to a king. Raised by the hands of men, she was led trembling to the altar. Not for her the sacrament of marriage and the loud chant of Hymen. It was her fate in the very hour of marriage to fall a sinless victim to a sinful rite, slaughtered to her greater grief by a father's hand, so that a fleet might sail under happy auspices. Such are the heights of wickedness to which men are driven by superstition.

You yourself, if you surrender your judgement at any time to the blood-curdling declamations of the prophets, will want to desert our ranks. Only think what phantoms they can conjure up to overturn the tenor of your life and wreck your happiness with fear. And not without cause. For, if men saw that a term was set to their troubles, they would find strength in some way to withstand the hocus-pocus and intimidations of the prophets. As it is, they have no power of resistance, because they are haunted by the fear of eternal punishment after death.

From Lucretius, *On the Nature of the Universe*, translated and introduced by R.E. Latham.

SIGMUND FREUD

Religion Is Humanity's Neurosis

Sigmund Freud (1856–1939), a neurologist and psychologist, was born in Morovia and was the founder of psychoanalysis.

Sigmund Freud thinks that people turn to religion to make themselves feel better in a troubling world where life may otherwise seem lonely and meaningless. Religions provide people with beliefs which accord with their childish wishes for a secure world in which a strong and loving father rules and watches over them. The scientific perspective has shown the shortcomings of the religious worldview or Weltanschauung. And psychoanalysis makes the special contribution of showing how, with religious belief, people distort reality to accord with their wishes. Freud ultimately likens the place of religion in human evolution to a neurosis which people must overcome as they mature.

Ladies and gentlemen—At our last meeting we were occupied with little everyday concerns—putting our own modest house in order, as it were. I propose that we should now take a bold leap and venture upon answering a question which is constantly being asked in other quarters: does psycho-analysis lead to a particular *Weltanschauung* and, if so, to which?

"*Weltanschauung*" is, I am afraid, a specifically German concept, the translation of which into foreign languages might well raise difficulties. If I try to give you a definition of it, it is bound to seem clumsy to you. In my opinion, then, a *Weltanschauung* is an intellectual construction which solves all the problems of our existence uniformly on the basis of one overriding hypothesis, which, accordingly, leaves no question unanswered and in which everything that interests us finds its fixed place. It will easily be understood that the possession of a *Weltanschauung* of this kind is among the ideal wishes of human beings. Believing in it one can feel secure in life, one can know what to strive for, and how one can deal most expediently with one's emotions and interests.

If that is the nature *of* a *Weltanschauung*, the answer as regards psycho-analysis is made easy. As a specialist science, a branch of psychology—a depth-psychology or psychology *of* the unconscious—it is quite unfit to construct a *Weltanschauung* of its own: it must accept the scientific one. . . .

For the same person to whom the child owes his existence, the father (or more correctly, no doubt, the parental agency compounded of

the father and mother), also protected and watched over him in his feeble and helpless state, exposed as he was to all the dangers lying in wait
in the external world; under his father's protection he felt safe. When
a human being has himself grown up, he knows, to be sure, that he is
in possession of greater strength, but his insight into the perils of life
has also grown greater, and he rightly concludes that fundamentally he
still remains just as helpless and unprotected as he was in his childhood, that faced by the world he is still a child. Even now, therefore, he
cannot do without the protection which he enjoyed as a child. But he
has long since recognized, too, that his father is a being of narrowly restricted power, and not equipped with every excellence. He therefore
harks back to the mnemic image of the father whom in his childhood
he so greatly overvalued. He exalts the image into a deity and makes it
into something contemporary and real. The effective strength of this
mnemic image and the persistence of his need for protection jointly
sustain his belief in God. . . .

I feel sure that while you have been listening to me you have been
bothered by a number of questions which you would be glad to hear
answered. I cannot undertake to do so here and now, but I feel confident that none of these detailed enquiries would upset our thesis that
the religious *Weltanschauung* is determined by the situation of our
childhood. . . .

The scientific spirit, strengthened by the observation of natural
processes, has begun, in the course of time, to treat religion as a human
affair and to submit it to a critical examination. Religion was not able
to stand up to this. What first gave rise to suspicion and scepticism
were its tales of miracles, for they contradicted everything that had
been taught by sober observation and betrayed too clearly the influence
of the activity of the human imagination. After this its doctrines explaining the origin of the universe met with rejection, for they gave evidence of an ignorance which bore the stamp of ancient times and to
which, thanks to their increased familiarity with the laws of nature,
people knew they were superior. . . .

The last contribution to the criticism of the religious *Weltanschauung* was effected by psycho-analysis, by showing how religion
originated from the helplessness of children and by tracing its contents
to the survival into maturity of the wishes and needs of childhood. This
did not precisely mean a contradiction of religion, but it was nevertheless a necessary rounding-off of our knowledge about it, and in one respect at least it was a contradiction, for religion itself lays claim to a
divine origin. And, to be sure, it is not wrong in this, provided that our
interpretation of God is accepted.

In summary, therefore, the judgement of science on the religious
Weltanschauung is this. While the different religions wrangle with one
another as to which of them is in possession of the truth, our view is
that the question of the truth of religious beliefs may be left altogether

on one side. Religion is an attempt to master the sensory world in which we are situated by means of the wishful world which we have developed within us as a result of biological and psychological necessities. But religion cannot achieve this. Its doctrines bear the imprint of the times in which they arose, the ignorant times of the childhood of humanity. Its consolations deserve no trust. Experience teaches us that the world is no nursery. The ethical demands on which religion seeks to lay stress need, rather, to be given another basis; for they are indispensable to human society and it is dangerous to link obedience to them with religious faith. If we attempt to assign the place of religion in the evolution of mankind, it appears not as a permanent acquisition but as a counterpart to the neurosis which individual civilized men have through in their passage from childhood to maturity.

From Sigmund Freud, *New Introductory Lectures on Psycho-analysis*. Translated and edited by James Strachey.

TERTULLIAN

Faith Is One Thing and Reason Another

Tertullian (c. 160–230) was an African Christian theologian and stoic.

Tertullian offers one of the earliest formulations of the notion that we cannot expect the teachings of a religion to make rational sense. The domain of faith is a territory which is separate from the province of reason. As Tertullian put it, Jerusalem is one thing, Athens another. Jerusalem represents the Christian faith, and Athens, the philosophy of Socrates and Plato. Tertullian is also well known for his flamboyant claim which so clearly puts faith at odds with reason, "credo quia absurdam," "I believe because it is absurd."

From philosophy come those fables and endless genealogies and fruitless questionings, those "words that creep like as doth a canker" [2 Tim. 2:17]. To hold us back from such things, the Apostle testifies expressly in his letter to the Colossians that we should beware of philosophy. "Take heed lest any man circumvent you through philosophy or vain deceit, after the tradition of men" [Col. 2:8], against the providence of the Holy Ghost. He had been at Athens where he had come to grips with the human wisdom which attacks and perverts truth, being itself divided up into its own swarm of heresies by the variety of its mutually antagonistic sects. What has Jerusalem to do with Athens, the Church with the Academy, the Christian with the heretic? Our principles come from the Porch of Solomon, who had himself taught that the Lord is to be sought in simplicity of heart [cf. Wis. 1:1]. I have no use for a Stoic or a dialectic Christianity. After Jesus Christ we have no need of speculation, after the Gospel no need of research. When we come to believe, we have no desire to believe anything else; for we begin by believing that there is nothing else which we have to believe. . . .

The Rule of Faith—to state here and now what we maintain—is of course that by which we believe that there is but one God, who is none other than the Creator of the world, who produced everything from nothing through his Word, sent forth before all things; that this Word is called his Son, and in the Name of God was seen in divers ways by the patriarchs, was ever heard in the prophets and finally was brought down by the Spirit and Power of God the Father into the Virgin Mary, was made flesh in her womb, was born of her and lived as Jesus Christ; who thereafter proclaimed a new law and a new promise of the kingdom of heaven, worked miracles, was crucified, on the third day rose again, was caught up into heaven and sat down at the right hand of the Father; that he sent in his place the power of the Holy Spirit to guide believers; that he will come with glory to take the saints up into the fruition of the life eternal and the heavenly promises and to judge the wicked to everlasting fire, after the resurrection of both good and evil with the restoration of their flesh.

This Rule, taught (as will be proved) by Christ, allows of no questions among us, except those which heresies introduce and which make heretics.

Provided the essence of the Rule is not disturbed, you may seek and discuss as much as you like. You may give full rein to your itching curiosity where any point seems unsettled and ambiguous or dark and obscure. There must surely be some brother endowed with the gift of knowledge who can teach you, someone who moves among the learned who will share your curiosity and your inquiry. In the last resort, however, it is better for you to remain ignorant, for fear that you come to know what you should not know. For you do know what you should know. "Thy faith hath saved thee," it says [Luke 18:42]; not thy biblical learning. Faith is established in the Rule. There it has its law, and it wins salvation by keeping the law. Learning derives from curiosity and wins glory only from its zealous pursuit of scholarship. Let curiosity give place to faith, and glory to salvation. Let them at least be no hindrance, or let them keep quiet. To know nothing against the Rule is to know everything. . . .

From *Early Latin Theology*.

SØREN KIERKEGAARD

Faith Makes Certain what Reason Finds Uncertain or Absurd

Søren Kierkegaard (1813–1855) was a Danish existentialist philosopher and religious thinker.

Søren Kierkegaard offers a modern statement of the rift between faith and reason which Tertullian articulated. Kierkegaard refers to Christian teachings, like God's becoming man, as "the absurd." Looked at from an objective standpoint, we are always uncertain about the truth of such a claim. From that standpoint, we are emphasizing the "what" of the belief and are seeking to verify this claim in a rational, scientific fashion. But when we turn inward and enter the subjective realm, when we go against the declaration of uncertainty which reason has issued, we embrace these truths with certainty. Here, we are emphasizing the "how" of the belief, the relationship not between it and the way the world is but between the belief and ourselves. We draw it inwardly, we "appropriate" it for ourselves, and we embrace it passionately. When we do so, we have achieved through faith what reason was unable to provide, a certainty. Kierkegaard captures these ideas in his famous definition of truth: "An objective uncertainty held fast in an appropriation process of the most passionate inwardness is the truth, the highest attainable for an existing individual."

*W*hen the question of truth is raised in an objective manner, reflection is directed objectively to the truth, as an object to which the knower is related. Reflection is not focused upon the relationship, however, but upon the question of whether it is the truth to which the knower is related. If only the object to which he is related is the truth, the subject is accounted to be in the truth. When the question of the truth is raised subjectively, reflection is directed subjectively to the nature of the individual's relationship: if only the mode of this relationship is in the truth, the individual is in the truth, even if he should happen to be thus related to what is not true. Let us take as an example the knowledge of God. Objectively, reflection is directed to the problem of whether this object is the true God; subjectively, reflection is directed to the question whether the individual is related to a something *in such a manner* that his relationship is in truth a God-relationship. . . .

   Here is such a definition of truth: *An objective uncertainty held fast in an appropriation-process of the most passionate inwardness is the truth,* the highest truth attainable for an *existing individual. . . .*

But the above definition of truth is an equivalent expression for faith. Without risk there is no faith. Faith is precisely the contradiction between the infinite passion of the individual's inwardness and the objective uncertainty. If I am capable of grasping God objectively, I do not believe, but precisely because I cannot do this I must believe. If I wish to preserve myself in faith I must constantly be intent upon holding fast the objective uncertainty, so that in the objective uncertainty I am out "upon the seventy thousand fathoms of water," and yet believe. . . .

In relation to the absurd, the objective approximation-process is like the comedy, *Misunderstanding upon Misunderstanding,* which is generally played by *Privatdocents* and speculative philosophers. The absurd is precisely by its objective repulsion the measure of the intensity of faith in inwardness. Suppose a man who wishes to acquire faith; let the comedy begin. He wishes to have faith, but he wishes also to safeguard himself by means of an objective inquiry and its approximation-process. What happens? With the help of the approximation-process the absurd becomes increasingly probable, it becomes extremely and emphatically probable. Now he is ready to believe it, and he ventures to claim for himself that he does not believe as shoemakers and tailors and simple folk believe, but only after long deliberation. Now he is ready to believe it; and lo, now it has become precisely impossible to believe it. Anything that is almost probable, or probable, or extremely and emphatically probable, is something he can almost know, or as good as know, or extremely and emphatically almost *know*—but it is impossible to *believe.* For the absurd is the object of faith, and the only object that can be believed.

Or suppose a man who says that he has faith, but desires to make his faith clear to himself, so as to understand himself in his faith. Now the comedy begins again. The object of faith becomes almost probably, as good as probable, extremely and emphatically probable. He has completed his investigations, and he ventures to claim for himself that he does not believe as shoemakers and tailors and other simple folk believe, but that he has understood himself in his believing. Strange understanding! On the contrary, he has in fact learned something else about faith than when he believed; and he has learned that he no longer believes, since he almost knows, or as good as knows, or extremely and emphatically almost knows.

From Søren Kierkegaard, *Concluding Unscientific Postscript to the "Philosophical Fragments."* Translated by David F. Swenson, Lillian Marvin Swenson, and Walter Lowrie.

IMMANUEL KANT

I Deny Knowledge (Not Reason) to Make Room for Faith

Immanuel Kant (1724–1804), born in Prussia, was a philosopher who investigated the scope and nature of reason.

Immanuel Kant's study of the human mind led him to conclude that it is within our abilities to gain knowledge of the natural or immanent realm. But beyond that reason could glean no knowledge of the transcendent realm. It is beyond the capabilities of the human mind to know whether in that realm beyond sensory experience such things as God or absolute freedom exist. Reason cannot give us knowledge of such things. So, Kant thinks that he can offer a model for being a person of faith without our having to go against reason as Tertullian and Kierkegaard believed. Kant claims to deny knowledge to make room for faith. The title of one of his books is revealing: Religion within the Limits of Reason Alone.

This discussion as to the positive advantage of critical principles of pure reason can be similarly developed in regard to the concept of *God* and of the *simple nature* of our *soul*; but for the sake of brevity such further discussion may be omitted. [From what has already been said, it is evident that] even the *assumption*—as made on behalf of the necessary practical employment of my reason—of *God, freedom,* and *immortality* is not permissible unless at the same time speculative reason be deprived of its pretensions to transcendent insight. For in order to arrive at such insight it might make use of principles which, in fact, extend only to objects of possible experience, and which, if also applied to what cannot be an object of experience, always really change this into an appearance, thus rendering all *practical extension* of pure reason impossible. I have therefore found it necessary to deny *knowledge*, in order to make room for *faith*. . . .

If the empirical philosopher had no other purpose in propounding his antithesis than to subdue the rashness and presumption of those who so far misconstrue the true vocation of reason as to boast of insight and knowledge just where true insight and knowledge cease, and to represent as furthering speculative interests that which is valid only in relation to practical interests (in order, as may suit their convenience, to break the thread of physical enquiries, and then under the pretence of extending knowledge to fasten it to transcendental ideas, through which we really know only that we know nothing); if, I say, the empiricist were satisfied with this, his principle would be a maxim urging moderation in our pretensions, modesty in our assertions, and yet at the same time the greatest possible extension of our understanding, through the teacher fittingly assigned to us, namely, through experience. If such were our procedure, we should not be cut off from employing intellectual *presuppositions* and faith on behalf of our practical interest; only they could never be permitted to assume the title and dignity of science and rational insight. Knowledge, which as such is speculative, can have no other object than that supplied by experience; if we transcend the limits thus imposed, the synthesis which seeks, independently of experience, new species of knowledge, lacks that substratum of intuition upon which alone it can be exercised.

But when empiricism itself, as frequently happens, becomes dogmatic in its attitude towards ideas, and confidently denies whatever lies beyond the sphere of its intuitive knowledge, it betrays the same lack of modesty; and this is all the more reprehensible owing to the irreparable injury which is thereby caused to the practical interests of reason.

From Immanuel Kant, *The Critique of Pure Reason*, translated by Norman Kemp Smith.

BLAISE PASCAL
Wager!

Blaise Pascal (1623–1662) was a French mathematician, philosopher, physicist and theologian.

Blaise Pascal finds himself at an impasse similar to that which thinkers like Tertullian, Kierkegaard, and Kant had reached: reason either has not or cannot tell us anything definitive about God's existence. Further, much is at stake—the possibility of eternal happiness—in deciding whether to believe in God. So we do not want to leave matters as simply unresolved but rather want to make the best bet under the circumstances. After analyzing the matter, Pascal advises that we bet on the existence of God.

Let us then examine this point, and say, "God is, or He is not." But to which side shall we incline? Reason can decide nothing here. There is an infinite chaos which separated us. A game is being played at the extremity of this infinite distance where heads or tails will turn up. What will you wager? According to reason, you can do neither the one thing nor the other; according to reason, you can defend neither of the propositions. . . .

Yes; but you must wager. It is not optional. You are embarked. Which will you choose then? Let us see. Since you must choose, let us see which interests you least. You have two things to lose, the true and the good; and two things to stake, your reason and your will, your knowledge and your happiness; and your nature has two things to shun, error and misery. Your reason is no more shocked in choosing one rather than the other, since you must of necessity choose. This is one point settled. But your happiness? Let us weigh the gain and the loss in wagering that God is. Let us estimate these two chances. If you gain, you gain all; if you lose, you lose nothing. Wager, then, without hesitation that He is. . . .

From Blaise Pascal, *Pensées*, translated by W. F. Trotter.

ALBERT EINSTEIN

Be Truly Religious by Abandoning Belief in a Personal God and Appreciating the Rational Order of the Universe

Albert Einstein (1879–1955) was the German-born physicist who devised the theory of relativity.

Renowned physicist Albert Einstein reports how incongruous he finds the teachings of a personal God with the rational order which we discover in the world. Religion should not concern itself with making us fearful about some things and hopeful about others, he argues. We should see a reverence for "reason incarnate in existence" as the pinnacle of religiosity. So for Einstein, unlike Tertullian, Kierkegaard, Kant, and Pascal, being religious does not entail believing in things about which reason does not or cannot inform us. Rather, being religious entails a respect for reason and its grandeur in the world.

The main source of the present-day conflicts between the spheres of religion and of science lies in this concept of a personal God. . . . The more a man is imbued with the ordered regularity of all events the firmer becomes his conviction that there is no room left by the side of this ordered regularity for causes of a different nature. For him neither the rule of human nor the rule of divine will exists as an independent cause of natural events. To be sure, the doctrine of a personal God interfering with natural events could never be *refuted,* in the real sense, by science, for this doctrine can always take refuge in those domains in which scientific knowledge has not yet been able to set foot.

But I am persuaded that such behavior on the part of the representatives of religion would not only be unworthy but also fatal. For a doctrine which is able to maintain itself not in clear light but only in the dark, will of necessity lose its effect on mankind, with incalculable harm to human progress. In their struggle for the ethical good, teachers of religion must have the stature to give up the doctrine of a personal God, that is, give up that source of fear and hope which in the past placed such vast power in the hands of priests. In their labors they will have to avail themselves of those forces which are capable of cultivating the Good, the True, and the Beautiful in humanity itself. This is, to be sure, a more difficult but an incomparably more worthy task.

After religious teachers accomplish the refining process indicated they will surely recognize with joy that true religion has been ennobled and made more profound by scientific knowledge.

If it is one of the goals of religion to liberate mankind as far as possible from the bondage of egocentric cravings, desires, and fears, scientific reasoning can aid religion in yet another sense. Although it is true that it is the goal of science to discover rules which permit the association and foretelling of facts, this is not its only aim. It also seeks to reduce the connections discovered to the smallest possible number of mutually independent conceptual elements. It is in this striving after the rational unification of the manifold that it encounters its greatest successes, even though it is precisely this attempt which causes it to run the greatest risk of falling a prey to illusions. But whoever has undergone the intense experience of successful advances made in this domain, is moved by profound reverence for the rationality made manifest in existence. By way of the understanding he achieves a far-reaching emancipation from the shackles of personal hopes and desires, and thereby attains that humble attitude of mind towards the grandeur of reason incarnate in existence, and which, in its profoundest depths, is inaccessible to man. This attitude, however, appears to me to be religious, in the highest sense of the word. And so it seems to me that science not only purifies the religious impulse of the dross of its anthropomorphism but also contributes to a religious spiritualization of our understanding of life.

The further the spiritual evolution of mankind advances, the more certain it seems to me that the path to genuine religiosity does not lie through the fear of life, and the fear of death, and blind faith, but through striving after rational knowledge. In this sense I believe that the priest must become a teacher if he wishes to do justice to his lofty educational mission.

From Albert Einstein, *Out of my Later Years.*

CHARLES HARTSHORNE
God Is Social; God Is Personal

Charles Hartshorne (1897–) is an American process theologian and philosopher of religion.

Charles Hartshorne insists that God is a personal being and agrees with Hume that any other conception is indistinguishable from atheism. Hartshorne's starting point is with God as a social being whose nature is shaped by interacting with other persons. From this starting point we can then ask about how a social being can be absolute or perfect. In structuring our thinking in this way, Hartshorne inverts the usual approach of beginning with the conception of God as a perfect and absolute being and then asking whether, so understood, the Divine can also be said to be a personal or social being.

We have also to remember that if there is religious value in the absoluteness of God, as requisite for his reliability, there is equally manifest religious value in another trait which seems unequivocally to imply relativity rather than absoluteness. This is the social or personal nature of God. What is a person if not a being qualified and conditioned by social relations, relations to other persons? And what is God if not the supreme case of personality? Those who deny this have yet to succeed in distinguishing their position from atheism, as Hume pointedly noted. Either God really does love all beings, that is, is related to them by a sympathetic union surpassing any human sympathy, or religion seems a vast fraud. The common query "Can the Absolute or Perfect Being be personal or social?" should really run "In what sense, if any, can a social being be absolute or perfect?" For God is conceived socially before he is conceived absolutely or as perfect. God is the highest ruler, judge, benefactor; he knows, loves, and assists man; he has made the world with the design of sharing his bliss with lesser beings. . . .

The question "Can a supreme being be social?" is important not merely because men generally have meant by God a supreme social being. There are grounds for thinking that the popular religious emphasis is philosophically sound, that a supreme being must, for rational reasons, be conceived socially. Human nature is the supreme instance of nature in general, as known to us (apart from the "nature" of God himself), and moreover, it is the instance which in some respects at least is much more certainly and intimately known to us than any other. Human nature is social through and through. All our thought is some sort of conversation or dialogue or social transaction; when we have no one else to converse with, we converse, silently or even aloud, with ourselves. We love and hate and sympathize, not only in relation to others but in relation to our own past, future, or potential selves. Not only human beings stimulate such response, but animals, plants, mountains, ships, the moon, colors, sounds (think of groaning brakes, growling thunder, merry sunshine). One may say simply, all classes of concrete objects at least can be social objects for man. What would poetry be without personification, overt or implicit; what would art be without empathy, which is social response of a kind?

Now, further, not simply man, but all life whatsoever, has social structure. All organisms on the multicellular level are associations of cells. There is scarcely a line between societies and individuals formed by societies which reach a sufficient grade of integration. Cells themselves are associations of similar molecules and atoms. It becomes a question of how broadly one wishes to use terms where one says that the social begins, if indeed it ever begins, in the ascending scale of emergence. And the higher one goes in the scale the more obviously do the social aspects assume a primary role. Does this point to the conclusion that the supreme being is not social at all?

From Charles Hartshorne, *The Divine Relativity.*

JEFFREY MASSON
AND
SUSAN MCCARTHY

Non-Human Animals Perhaps Perform Rituals
for their Dead and Worship

Jeffrey Masson (1941–   ) is an American psychoanalyst and author.

Jeffrey Masson and Susan McCarthy's book, When Elephants Weep: The Emotional Lives of Animals, *supports the view that non-human animals experience and express a broad range of emotions. Religion, they claim, has an emotional dimension to rituals and worship. There is evidence that elephants perform a ceremony of sorts when one of them is dying. In one interpretation of the activity of lemurs, they are worshiping the sun. The authors suggest that further studies of the behavior of non-human animals should assist us with better understanding our own practices.*

An observer once came across a band of African elephants surrounding a dying matriarch as she swayed and fell. The other elephants clustered around her and tried mightily to get her up. A young male tried to raise her with his tusks, put food into her mouth, and even tried sexually mounting her, all in vain. The other elephants stroked her with their trunks; one calf knelt and tried to suckle. At last the group moved off, but one female and her calf stayed behind. The female stood with her back to the dead matriarch, now and then reaching back to touch her with one foot. The other elephants called to her. Finally, she walked slowly away.

Cynthia Moss describes the behavior of an elephant herd circling a dead companion "disconsolately several times, and if it is still motionless they come to an uncertain halt. They then face outward, their trunks hanging limply down to the ground. After a while they may prod and circle again, and then again stand, facing outward." Finally—perhaps when it is clear the elephant is dead—"they may tear out branches and grass clumps from the surrounding vegetation and drop these on and around the carcass." The standing outward suggests that the elephants may find the sight painful; maybe they want to stay close but find it intrusive to watch such suffering; perhaps it has a ritual meaning we do not yet comprehend.

It was once thought that elephants went to special elephant grave-yards to die. While this has been disproved, Moss speculates that ele-phants do have a concept of death. They are strongly interested in elephant bones, not at all in the bones of other species. Their reaction to elephant bones is so predictable that cinematographers have no dif-ficulty filming elephants examining bones. Smelling them, turning them over, running their trunks over the bones, the elephants pick them up, feel them, and sometimes carry them off for a distance before dropping them. They show the greatest interest in skulls and tusks. Moss speculates that they are trying to recognize the individual.

Once Moss brought the jawbone of a dead elephant—an adult fe-male—into her camp to determine its exact age. A few weeks after this elephant's death, her family happened to pass through the camp area. They made a detour to be with and examine the jaw. Long after the others had moved on, the elephant's seven-year-old calf stayed behind, touching the jaw and turning it over with his feet and trunk. One can only agree with Moss's conclusion that the calf was somehow reminded of his mother—perhaps remembering the contours of her face. He felt her there. It seems certain that the calf's memory is at work here. Whether he experienced a feeling of melancholic nostalgia, sorrow, per-haps joy in remembering his mother, or was moved by some emotional experience we might not be able to identify, it would be difficult to deny that feelings were involved. . . .

RELIGION AND THE SOUL

People have immortal souls and animals do not, according to much of Western religion. Animal lovers resist this, citing animals' virtues and affirming that they must have souls; heaven would be a paltry place if there were no dogs in it. The question of who has a soul and who does-n't is far more problematic than the parallel question of emotions. Sci-ence is of no help. Yet the theological view may point to a difference between the emotional lives of humans and those of other animals. An-imals do not seem to need to believe in higher powers. Animals have not been observed to have religious practices, while people do.

Some traditional tribes in Madagascar say that when sifaka lemurs lie on high branches in the morning, facing the sun, with their eyes closed, they are worshiping the sun. Some say that the sifakas are in-carnations of their own sun-worshiping ancestors. Primatologist Alison Jolly commented, "It is difficult to watch a sunning lemur without being anthropomorphic, but to Western eyes it seems less like religious fervor than like our indolent cult of Sunday at the beach." There is no reason to suppose that sifakas themselves are lemuromorphic, that they invest the sun with creature qualities (though we cannot prove that they do not) and worship those qualities. The explanation that they enjoy the warmth seems sufficient to explain their behavior, but the traditional explanation of the Malagasy people has the advantage of poetry.

Like art, religion is not an emotionless affair of pure intellect. Awe, faith, righteousness, abasement, worship, seeking salvation—all have emotional components. Some theorists describe awe as a form of shame. Are the religious emotions ones that animals simply do not feel? Or are they emotions that exist in other parts of life that in humans may be focused on the religious impulse? Animal emotions may shed some light. Elizabeth Marshall Thomas compares the behavior of a person humbly kneeling to pray and a dog showing its belly—demonstrating submission—to a person. Her husband's dog, she notes, ritually shows his belly first thing in the morning, like a morning devotion. In the end, Thomas concludes that the parallel is not exact, that dogs probably do not think of humans as gods, yet, "as we need God more than he needs us, dogs need us more than we need them, and they know it." Further study of such dynamics could shed considerable comparative light on human religious rites.

From Jeffrey M. Masson and Susan McCarthy, *When Elephants Weep: The Emotional Lives of Animals*.

N. Scott Momaday

The Native American Has a Personal Relationship with Nature

N. Scott Momaday (1934–) is a Native American folklorist and author.

N. Scott Momaday explains elements of the personal relationship with nature he believes is characteristic of traditional Native American cultures. It involves a type of give and take where people take from nature but through imagination give nature a primary place in their experience. And knowledge of a long history of conceiving self and nature in this way is part of the experience. This reverence for nature suggests guidelines for conduct with one factor being what seems appropriate in this relationship. Momaday tells of a hunter's unwillingness to kill an animal for food for his expecting wife and hungry family; he thought it was inappropriate to be taking life when childbirth was near.

The first thing to say about the native American perspective on environmental ethics is that there is a great deal to be said. I don't think that anyone has clearly understood yet how the Indian conceives of himself in relation to the landscape. We have formulated certain generalities about that relationship, and the generalities have served a purpose, but they have been rather too general. For example, take the idea that the Indian reveres the earth, thinks of it as the place of his origin and thinks of the sky also in a personal way. These statements are true. But they can also be misleading because they don't indicate anything about the nature of the relationship which is, I think, an intricate thing in itself. I have done much thinking about the "Indian worldview," as it is sometimes called. And I have had some personal experience of Indian religion and Indian societies within the framework of a worldview. Sometime ago I wrote an essay entitled "An American Land Ethic" in which I tried to talk in certain ways about this idea of a native American attitude toward the landscape. And in that essay I made certain observations. I tried to express the notion first that the native American ethic with respect to the physical world is a matter of reciprocal appropriation: appropriations in which man invests himself in the landscape, and at the same time incorporates the landscape into his own most fundamental experience. That suggests a dichotomy, or a paradox, and I think it is a paradox. It is difficult to understand a relationship which is defined in these terms, and yet I don't know how better to define it.

Secondly, this appropriation is primarily a matter of the imagination. The appropriation is realized through an act of the imagination which is moral and kind. I mean to say that we are all, I suppose, at the most fundamental level what we imagine ourselves to be. And this is certainly true of the American Indian. If you want a definition, you would not go, I hope, to the stereotype which has burdened the American Indian for many years. He is not that befeathered spectacle who is always chasing John Wayne across the silver screen. Rather, he is someone who thinks of himself in a particular way and his idea comprehends his relationship to the physical world, among other things. He imagines himself in terms of that relationship and others. And it is that act of the imagination, that moral act of the imagination, which I think constitutes his understanding of the physical world.

Thirdly, this imagining, this understanding of the relationship between man and the landscape, or man and the physical world, man and nature, proceeds from a racial or cultural experience. I think his attitude toward the landscape has been formulated over a long period of time, and the length of time itself suggests an evolutionary process perhaps instead of a purely rational and decisive experience. Now I am not sure that you can understand me on this point, perhaps I should elaborate. I mean that the Indian has determined himself in his imagination over a period of untold generations. His racial memory is an essential part of his understanding. He understands himself more clearly than perhaps other people, given his situation in time and space. His heritage has always been rather closely focused, centered upon the landscape as a particular reality. Beyond this, the native American has a particular investment in vision and in the idea of vision. You are familiar with the term "vision quest" for example. This is another essential idea to the Indian worldview, particularly that view as it is expressed among the cultures of the Plains Indians. This is significant. I think we should not lose the force of the idea of seeing something or envisioning something in a particular way. I happen to think that there are two visions in particular with reference to man and his relationship to the natural world. One is physical and the other is imaginative. And we all deal in one way or another with these visions simultaneously. If I can try to find an analogy, it's rather like looking through the viewfinder of a camera, the viewfinder which is based upon the principle of the split image. And it is a matter of trying to align the two planes of that particular view. This can be used as an example of how we look at the world around us. We see it with the physical eye. We see it as it appears to us, in one dimension of reality. But we also see it with the eye of the mind. It seems to me that the Indian has achieved a particularly effective alignment of those two planes of vision. He perceives the landscape in both ways. He realizes a whole image from the possibilities within his reach. The moral implications of this are very far-reaching. Here is where we get into the consideration of religion and religious ideas and ideals.

There is another way in which I think one can very profitably and accurately think of the Indian in relation to the landscape and in terms of his idea of that relationship. This is to center on such a word as *appropriate*. The idea of "appropriateness" is central to the Indian experience of the natural world. It is a fundamental idea within his philosophy. I recall the story told to me some years ago by a friend, who is not himself a Navajo, but was married for a time to a Navajo girl and lived with her family in Southern Utah. And he said that he had been told this story and was passing it on to me. There was a man living in a remote place on the Navajo reservation who had lost his job and was having a difficult time making ends meet. He had a wife and several children. As a matter of fact, his wife was expecting another child. One day a friend came to visit him and perceived that his situation was bad. The friend said to him "Look, I see that you're in tight straits, I see you have many mouths to feed, that you have no wood and that there is very little food in your larder. But one thing puzzles me. I know you're a hunter, and I know, too, there are deer in the mountains very close at hand. Tell me, why don't you kill a deer so that you and your family might have fresh meat to eat?" And after a time the man replied, "No, it is inappropriate that I should take life just now when I am expecting the gift of life."

The implications of that idea, and the way in which the concept of appropriateness lies at the center of that little parable is a central consideration within the Indian world. You cannot understand how the Indian thinks of himself in relation to the world around him unless you understand his conception of what is appropriate; particularly what is morally appropriate within the context of that relationship.

From N. Scott Momaday, "Native American Attitudes to the Environment."

CHAUNCEY WRIGHT
"Letter to Mr. F.E. Abbot"

Chauncey Wright (1830–1875) was an American pragmatist philosopher.

Chauncey Wright was a member of the Metaphysical Club which is usually credited with giving birth to pragmatism. James, Peirce, and Holmes were among the luminaries who attended the meetings of the Club in Cambridge, Massachusetts. In comparison to these men, Wright wrote and published very little. His letters contain some of his philosophical thinking. In a letter to Mr. Abbot, Wright sets out his views on belief in God and an afterlife.

Toward the end of the letter we learn that Abbot had left the ministry, his profession, apparently because of doubts about his faith. Wright suggests this is a healthy state of mind in that the existence of God and an afterlife have not been proven. Wright recommends that we suspend judgment on these matters given, for one thing, the state of the evidence. Further, he urges that we keep our feelings out of matters of religion much as we do with matters of science.

These views do not keep Wright from thinking that preachers and instructors of religion perform the valuable task of teaching people how to live in accord with life's ideals. In fact he suggests that Abbot consider becoming a religious instructor even though he has left the ministry.

To Mr. F. E. Abbot

Cambridge, Oct. 28, 1867.

You ask to be admitted to my confidence by learning from me my speculative beliefs concerning the existence of a God and the immortality of the soul, and promise not to be shocked by any revelations I may make. The verdict of "not proven" is the kind of judgment I have formed on these matters; but not on that account am I warranted in taking up a position against the general opinion of my fellow citizens, for this would be to become as illogical as the most confident among them. Atheism is speculatively as unfounded as theism, and practically can only spring from bad motives. I mean, of course, dogmatic atheism. A bigoted atheist seems to me the meanest and narrowest of men. In fact, practical considerations determine that a state of suspended judgment on these themes is the state of stable equilibrium. I have no desire to wake into a strange, unknown future life, and I can discover no valid reasons for any confidence in such a waking. As purely speculative or scientific doctrines, these demand assent no more cogently than a theory that some distant planet is inhabited, or, better still, that the planet is largely composed of granite or some other stated substance—for we might have a sentimental bias in favor of an inhabited planet.

Practical grounds are really the basis of belief in the doctrines of theology. The higher moral sentiments have attached themselves so strongly to these traditions that doubts of them seem to the believers like contempt for all that is noble or worthy in human character. This paralogism even goes so far as to declare man's life utterly worthless, unless it is to be prolonged to infinity; that is, I suppose, the worth of any part—say a year's life—is infinitesimal, even if filled with the purest enjoyments, the noblest sympathies, and the most beneficent activities. In whichever conclusion respecting a future life I might seek at last to cease from questioning and to willfully resolve my doubts, I should never cease to repudiate such a view of the value of the present human life.

You perceive that on practical grounds I openly dissent from orthodoxy, but I may appear to you to evade the speculative questions. I do not think that I do; for though I may not consistently hold on all occasions the even balance of judgment and the open mind which I think as proper in such matters as in all others, it is at any rate my design to do so. Whichever way we yield assent, we feel ourselves carried, not by evidence, but by the prejudices of feeling. We fall into one or another form of superstitious belief. Suspension of judgment appears to me to be demanded, therefore, not merely by the evidence, but as a discipline of character—that faith and moral effort may not waste themselves on idle dreams but work among the realities of life. Practical theism, if it means, as it ordinarily does, the exclusion from the mind of all evidence not favorable to received religious doctrines seems to me to put religious sentiment in a false position—one incompatible, not only with intellectual freedom, but with the soundest development of religious character—with that unreserved devotion to the best *we know*, which tries all things, and holds fast to that which is good.

Very few men could confess a belief in a God or a disbelief in one without expressing more than their speculative convictions. So far from being like their opinions on the law of gravitation, it would almost necessarily be with feelings of exultation, enthusiasm, and hope, or with bitterness, contempt, or despair—so strong are the associations of feeling attached to this word. Nevertheless, it is a doctrine of positivism that the real interests of moral and religious culture, no less than those of scientific knowledge, are quite independent in fact (and might be made so in education) of these doctrines and associations. And this is also my belief.

I sincerely regret to learn from you that your views have brought you into such difficulties as to render it necessary to give up your profession [ministry]. Would teaching private pupils, fitting boys for college, be an employment you would like? It is one of the most remunerative to those who are in the way to get it; and, although I am not in that way, I think it would not be difficult to find such employment. I should be happy to use all my influence to this end. I am told that there is a good opportunity at present to start a school for young ladies in Boston; for, though there are several excellent schools kept by ladies, there are none equal to Professor Torrey's, which he gave up when he came to Cambridge.

But I hope that I have misunderstood you, and that you will be able to continue, as a religious instructor, to exemplify how irrelevant metaphysics really are to the clergyman's true influence—quite as much so, I think, as to that of the scientific teacher. The pursuit of philosophy ought to be a side study. Nothing so much justifies that shameful assumption by ecclesiastical bodies of control over speculative opinions as the inconsiderate preaching of such opinions, in place of the warnings, encouragements, sympathies, and persuasions of the true religious instructor. The lessons which he has to deliver are really very easy to understand but hard to live up to. To help to live up to the true ideals of life seems to me the noblest, if not the only, duty of the preacher.

From Chauncey Wright, "Letter to Mr. F.E. Abbot."

ART

INTRODUCTION

Philosophy of art, like all of the "philosophy ofs"—philosophy of law, philosophy of history, philosophy of science—includes as a major part of its study the nature of what is being philosophized about. What is history? What is law? And so on. When we come to philosophy of art, or aesthetics, we find the question of what it is no less pressing. Is the urinal of Marcel Duchamp art? Can drawings of chimpanzees be considered art?

We turn to theories of what art is to answer in part questions like these. The Russian novelist, Leo Tolstoy, for example, offers that art is a vehicle for communicating feeling; art causes us to feel just as the artist did when the artist created the work. Other thinkers emphasize not the realm of feeling for understanding the nature of art but that of reason; Nelson Goodman, argues, for example, that art serves to structure our experience and thereby allows us to gain understanding and knowledge.

The question whether art is aligned more with the cognitive or more with the emotive in human experience has its origin in a debate between Plato and Aristotle. Plato's investigation led him to conclude not only that artists do not give us knowledge but also that they actually sidetrack us from an attempt to understand reality. Further, art has a disruptive effect on our

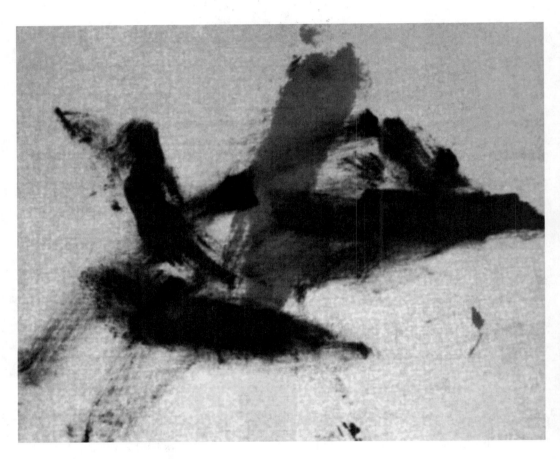

Bird. Painting by Koko, a gorilla.

psychological well-being when it appeals to the baser elements of our souls and undermines reason. This analysis enjoys a contemporary expression in the work of Allan Bloom who targets how rock music with its appeal to primitive emotions and drives frustrates the learning enterprise. When Plato's student, Aristotle, took up the questions of his mentor, he came to just the opposite conclusions. Aristotle held that art does give us knowledge, and, although art may rouse turbulent emotions, it provides, in the end, a release for them.

Investigations into the nature of art evidently reveal something about its function and purpose. If art does indeed purge us of bad impulses as Aristotle claimed, it can be seen as a useful vehicle for accomplishing this purpose. Other claims about art seem to hover on the border of these considerations of its nature and purpose. William James brings out how well artists present us with accounts of experiences which make life worth living, and George Santayana highlights how they assist us with breaking free from traditional ways of thinking about our lives. Jane Addams points to how art can give us lively ideas to focus on when we are engaged in boring tasks. We wonder whether art serves any purpose at all when Andy Warhol urges that art is junk, but we hesitate to be too quick to discard it when we find Whitman claiming that America itself is a poem.

Peirce introduces gender to the dialogue on art with his observation that some art appears to be the product of a masculine mind and other art of a feminine mind. Lucy Lippard calls on women to put more of themselves into their art. Dewey's call for reform is of a more general nature in that he wants to reconnect art with purposeful human activity.

The chapter concludes with an essay by the American thinker W.E.B. Du Bois, "The Art and Art Galleries of Western Europe."

CHARLES SANDERS PEIRCE

Raphael Has a Feminine Mind and Michelangelo a Masculine Mind

Charles Sanders Peirce compares the French artist, Raphael, and the Italian artist, Michelangelo. Raphael, he says, has a feminine mind while that of Michelangelo is masculine. Peirce rejects the common notion that essential to the masculine mind is intellectual understanding and essential to the feminine mind is the heart. He claims that men have no less heart than women but identifies a third faculty, the sensibilities, which distinguishes men from women. Peirce speaks of Raphael approaching beauty in a sensitive way while Michelangelo does so in an intellectual way.

Raphael and Michael Angelo seem to have been made to be compared. . . .

By their very greatness, these men have much in common; but I must remember that my object, in a comparison, is to exhibit their relations to each other and this can only be done by showing their differences not their similarities. Their great difference, then, is this—Michael Angelo's was a masculine, Raphaello's a feminine mind; nor is this a difference of intellect, alone; it extends to their taste, as exhibited in their productions and to their morals. This is a common observation. May I venture, now, to question the usual statement of the difference between the male and female nature?

The common notion, I believe, is that

The Understanding: Man = The Heart: Woman

. . . The *heart is* that which loves; which flies toward a fellow being, as such. The sensibilities do not do this, neither do they conceive; hence they are a distinct element of the soul. In my opinion

1. The Intellect &c. or that which says I,

2. The Heart &c. or that which says THOU,

3. The Sense &c. or that which says IT,

compose the inward nature. Why I think these include everything, I will not detail here, thus much I have been obliged to say as a key to what follows. Now I cannot think that the element marked 2. which includes that charity which is the foundation of christianity has been given to one class of persons, naturally, more than to another. At any rate, I think, that as a fact, it is the element marked 3. which is the real characteristic of women; men have as much *love* though not so much *affection* as they. . . .

The exact difference then between Michael Angelo and Raphael, I should state to be this: Michael Angelo was intellectual, Raphael sensitive, so I should expect that one to talk of his *ideas* of beauty, justice, truth, etc., this of his *sense* of beauty, justice, &c. I should expect that one to excel in understanding this in making use of his understanding. As to largeness of view, Michael Angelo had more grandeur, Raphael more variety; as we say, the one represented the Sublime, the other the Beautiful. Raphael was inferior to Michael Angelo in power on account of their difference in kind. Self was a centre for the latter; his intellectual faculties were *self*-directed, *self*-poised, *self*-ordered. In the former there is a conglomeration of the finest qualities—sympathies and sensibilities without a centre.

From C.S. Peirce, *Writings of Charles S. Peirce: A Chronological Edition.*

WILLIAM JAMES
Artists Capture Experiences which Give Life Meaning

William James never developed an aesthetics and indicates that it is with regret that he did not do so. In his work, Psychology: Briefer Course, *a shortened version of* The Principles of Psychology, *he says, "I regret that I have not been able to supply chapters on pleasure and pain, aesthetics, and the moral sense. Possibly the defect may be made up in a later edition, if such a thing should ever be demanded" (Cambridge: Harvard University Press, 1984, p. 1). He does make several observations about art in these works. In* The Principles, *he observes that one of the things that underlies our aesthetic principles is habit; we say that certain notes sound good with other notes because we are accustomed to hearing them together. In* Briefer Course, *he brings out that the task of the artist is essentially one of elimination in that artists must decide which tones, colors, or shapes to reject to create a unified and harmonious work.*

In his discussion of the meaningfulness of human life, James indirectly comments on an important function which the artist serves. James believes that what makes life meaningful is a certain vigor which we bring to our experiences, a robustness that converts the otherwise dull and monotonous happenings of the world into an exciting reality. As he develops this point in Talk to Students, *he moves from one artist to another, with each one expressing the zeal which that artist brings to experience and transforms it into something meaningful and magical. The implication is that artists are especially gifted both in having these feelings and in helping us to recognize their significance for leading meaningful lives.*

Wherever a process of life communicates an eagerness to him who lives it, there the life becomes genuinely significant. Sometimes the eagerness is more knit up with the motor activities, sometimes with the perceptions, sometimes with the imagination, sometimes with reflective thought. But, wherever it is found, there is the zest, the tingle, the excitement of reality; and there *is* 'importance' in the only real and positive sense in which importance ever anywhere can be. . . .

This higher vision of an inner significance in what, until then, we had realized only in the dead external way, often comes over a person suddenly; and, when it does so, makes an epoch in his history. As Emerson says, there is a depth in those moments that constrains us to ascribe more reality to them than to all other experiences. The passion of love will shake one like an explosion, or some act will awaken a remorseful compunction that hangs like a cloud over all one's later day. . . .

Walt Whitman, for instance, is accounted by many of us a contemporary prophet. He abolishes the usual human distinctions, brings all conventionalisms into solution, and loves and celebrates hardly any human attributes save those elementary ones common to all members of the race. For this he becomes a sort of ideal tramp, a rider on omnibus-tops and ferry-boats, and, considered either practically or academically, a worthless, unproductive being. His verses are but ejaculations—things mostly without subject or verb, a succession of interjections on an immense scale. He felt the human crowd as rapturously as Wordsworth felt the mountains, felt it as an overpoweringly significant presence, simply to absorb one's mind in which should be business sufficient and worthy to fill the days of a serious man. As he crosses Brooklyn ferry, this is what he feels:

Flood-tide below me! I watch you, face to face;

Clouds of the west! sun there half an hour high! I see you also face to face.

Crowds of men and women attired in the usual costumes! how curious you are to me!

On the ferry-boats, the hundreds and hundreds that cross, returning home, are more curious to me than you suppose;

And you that shall cross from shore to shore years hence, are more to me, and more in my meditations, than you might suppose.

From William James, *Talks to Teachers on Psychology: And to Students on Some of Life's Ideals.*

JOHN DEWEY
Art Should Connect to Human Experience

John Dewey laments how we have come to the point of severing art from its connection with human experience. We tuck it away in museums and forget its original and essential ties with the emotions, needs, activities, and aspirations of human life. He uses the Parthenon as an example of a work of art which played an important role in the civic and religious lives of the ancient Athenians and how we could not begin to appreciate it as art without perceiving it in this context.

By one of the ironic perversities that often attend the course of affairs, the existence of the works of art upon which formation of an esthetic theory depends has become an obstruction to theory about them. For one reason, these works are products that exist externally and physically. In common conception, the work of art is often identified with the building, book, painting, or statue in its existence apart from human experience. Since the actual work of art is what the product does with and in experience, the result is not favorable to understanding. In addition, the very perfection of some of these products, the prestige they possess because of a long history of unquestioned admiration, creates conventions that get in the way of fresh insight. When an art product once attains classic status, it somehow becomes isolated from the human conditions under which it was brought into being and from the human consequences it engenders in actual life experience.

When artistic objects are separated from both conditions of origin and operation in experience, a wall is built around them that renders almost opaque their general significance, with which esthetic theory deals. Art is remitted to a separate realm, where it is cut off from that association with the materials and aims of every other form of human effort, undergoing, and achievement. A primary task is thus imposed upon one who undertakes to write upon the philosophy of the fine arts. This task is to restore continuity between the refined and intensified forms of experience that are works of art and the everyday events, doings, and sufferings that are universally recognized to constitute experience. Mountain peaks do not float unsupported; they do not even just rest upon the earth. They *are* the earth in one of its manifest operations. It is the business of those who are concerned with the theory of the earth, geographers and geologists, to make this fact evident in its various implications. The theorist who would deal philosophically with fine art has a like task to accomplish.

If one is willing to grant this position, even if only by way of temporary experiment, he will see that there follows a conclusion at first sight surprising. In order to understand the meaning of artistic products, we have to forget them for a time, to turn aside from them and have recourse to the ordinary forces and conditions of experience that we do not usually regard as esthetic. We must arrive at the theory of art by means of a detour. For theory is concerned with understanding, insight, not without exclamations of admiration, and stimulation of that emotional outburst often called appreciation. It is quite possible to enjoy flowers in their colored form and delicate fragrance without knowing anything about plants theoretically. But if one sets out to *understand* the flowering of plants, he is committed to finding out something about the interactions of soil, air, water and sunlight that condition the growth of plants.

By common consent, the Parthenon is a great work of art. Yet it has esthetic standing only as the work becomes an experience for a human being. And, if one is to go beyond personal enjoyment into the formation of a theory about that large republic of art of which the building is one member, one has to be willing at some point in his reflections to turn from it to the bustling, arguing, acutely sensitive Athenian citizens, with civic sense identified with a civic religion, of whose experience the temple was an expression, and who built it not as a work of art but as a civic commemoration. The turning to them is as human beings who had needs that were a demand for the building and that were carried to fulfillment in it; it is not an examination such as might be carried on by a sociologist in search for material relevant to his purpose. The one who sets out to theorize about the esthetic experience embodied in the Parthenon must realize in thought what the people into whose lives it entered had in common, as creators and as those who were satisfied with it, with people in our own homes and on our own streets.

From John Dewey, *Art as Experience*.

Jane Addams
Art Enlivens Our Thinking

Jane Addams finds in art a way for people to escape their humdrum existence. Art can give a rich content to the otherwise empty thoughts of people. Addams tells about a factory worker who attended the Shakespeare Club at Hull-House and who reported how characters of the plays occupied her thinking while she was at work in the factory.

The residents of Hull-House place increasing emphasis upon the great inspirations and solaces of literature and are unwilling that it should ever languish as a subject for class instruction or for reading parties. The Shakespeare club has lived a continuous existence at Hull-House for sixteen years during which time its members have heard the leading interpreters of Shakespeare, both among scholars and players. I recall that one of its earliest members said that her mind was peopled with Shakespeare characters during her long hours of sewing in a shop, that she couldn't remember what she thought about before she joined the club, and concluded that she hadn't thought about anything at all. To feed the mind of the worker, to lift it above the monotony of his task, and to connect it with the larger world, outside of his immediate surroundings, has always been the object of art, perhaps never more nobly fulfilled than by the great English bard. Miss Starr has held classes in Dante and Browning for many years and the great lines are conned with never failing enthusiasm. I recall Miss Lathrop's Plato club and an audience who listened to a series of lectures by Dr. John Dewey on "Social Psychology," as genuine intellectual groups consisting largely of people from the immediate neighborhood, who were willing to make "that effort from which we all shrink, the effort of thought."

From Jane Addams, *Twenty Years at Hull-House.*

PLATO

Keep Artists Out of Society, Since they Lead us Away from Reality and Upset the Psychic Harmony of the Soul

Plato (c. 430–350 B.C.E.), the Greek philosopher who was a student of Socrates and teacher of Aristotle, is one of the most influential thinkers in the Western tradition.

Plato takes an extreme stand on art as he develops his case for excluding artists from the well-formed republic. For one thing, he argues, painters produce works which are twice removed from reality. They imitate objects which are already imitations of the real essence. The divinely created form or real essence of say, a couch, is the higher reality which we should concern ourselves with. Carpenters are already imitating this entity when they build couches in our world of objects. So when artists imitate these couches which the carpenters made, artists give us imitations of imitations! Furthermore, when dramatists choose personalities for their works, they turn to people whose reasoning is dislodged and whose souls are guided by the baser elements of desire and will. These characters serve as bad examples for us and undermine the very thing which we should be striving to strengthen—our reasoning.

Shall we, then, start the inquiry at this point by our customary procedure? We are in the habit, I take it, of positing a single idea or form in the case of the various multiplicities to which we give the same name. Do you not understand?

I do.

In the present case, then, let us take any multiplicity you please; for example, there are many couches and tables.

Of course.

But these utensils imply, I suppose, only two ideas or forms, one of a couch and one of a table.

Yes.

And are we not also in the habit of saying that the craftsman who produces either of them fixes his eyes on the idea or form, and so makes in the one case the couches and in the other the tables that we use, and similarly of other things? For surely no craftsman makes the idea itself. How could he?

By no means.

But now consider what name you would give to this craftsman. What one?

Him who makes all the things that all handicraftsmen severally produce. . . .

I take it that the painter too belongs to this class of producers, does he not?

Of course.

But you will say, I suppose, that his creations are not real and true. And yet, after a fashion, the painter too makes a couch, does he not?

Yes, he said, the appearance of one, he too.

What of the cabinetmaker? Were you not just now saying that he does not make the idea or form which we say is the real couch, the couch in itself, but only some particular couch?

Yes, I was.

Then if he does not make that which really is, he could not be said to make real being but something that resembles real being but is not that. . . .

We get, then, these three couches, one, that in nature, which, I take it, we would say that God produces, or who else?

No one, I think.

And then there was one which the carpenter made.

Yes, he said.

And one which the painter. Is not that so?

So be it.

The painter, then, the cabinetmaker, and God, there are these three presiding over three kinds of couches.

Yes, three.

Now God, whether because he so willed or because some compulsion was laid upon him not to make more than one couch in nature, so wrought and created one only, the couch which really and in itself is. . . .

Shall we also say that the painter is the creator and maker of that sort of thing?

By no means.

What will you say he is in relation to the couch?

This, said he, seems to me the most reasonable designation for him, that he is the imitator of the thing which those others produce.

Very good, said I. The producer of the product three removes from nature you call the imitator?. . . This, then, was what I wished to have agreed upon when I said that poetry, and in general the mimetic art, produces a product that is far removed from truth in the accomplishment of its task, and associates with the part in us that is remote from intelligence, and is its companion and friend for no sound and true purpose.

By all means, said he.

Mimetic art, then, is an inferior thing cohabiting with an inferior and engendering inferior offspring.

It seems so.

Does that, said I, hold only for vision or does it apply also to hearing and to what we call poetry?

Presumably he said, to that also.

Let us not, then, trust solely to the plausible analogy from painting, but let us approach in turn that part of the mind to which mimetic poetry appeals and see whether it is the inferior or the nobly serious part. . . .

Then, we say, the best part of us is willing to conform to these precepts of reason.

Obviously.

And shall we not say that the part of us that leads us to dwell in memory on our suffering and impels us to lamentation, and cannot get enough of that sort of thing, is the irrational and idle part of us, the associate of cowardice?

Yes, we will say that.

And does not the fretful part of us present many and varied occasions for imitation, while the intelligent and temperate disposition, always remaining approximately the same, is neither easy to imitate nor to be understood when imitated, especially by a nondescript mob assembled in the theater? For the representation imitates a type that is alien to them.

By all means.

And is it not obvious that the nature of the mimetic poet is not related to this better part of the soul and his cunning is not framed to please it, if he is to win favor with the multitude, but is devoted to the fretful and complicated type of character because it is easy to imitate?

It is obvious.

This consideration, then, makes it right for us to proceed to lay hold of him and set him down as the counterpart of the painter, for he resembles him in that his creations are inferior in respect of reality, and the fact that his appeal is to the inferior part of the soul and not to the best part is another point of resemblance. And so we may at last say that we should be justified in not admitting him into a well-ordered state, because he stimulates and fosters this element in the soul, and by strengthening it tends to destroy the rational part, just as when in a state one puts bad men in power and turns the city over to them and ruins the better sort.

From Plato, *The Republic*, translated by Paul Shorey.

ALLAN BLOOM

Plato Helps Us to Understand How Rock Music Interferes with Liberal Education

Allan Bloom (1930–) is an American philosopher who specializes in ancient Greek thought.

Allan Bloom marshalls Plato's insight about the disruptive effect of art on the soul to make his case against rock music. His main complaint is that this music interferes with the listener's attaining a liberal education by deadening the imagination and appealing to passions which are inconsistent with the mindset which liberal education encourages.

Though students do not have books, they most emphatically do have music. Nothing is more singular about this generation than its addiction to music. This is the age of music and the states of soul that accompany it. To find a rival to this enthusiasm, one would have to go back at least a century to Germany and the passion for Wagner's operas. They had the religious sense that Wagner was creating the meaning of life and that they were not merely listening to his works but experiencing that meaning. Today, a very large proportion of young people between the ages of ten and twenty live for music. It is their passion; nothing else excites them as it does; they cannot take seriously anything alien to music. When they are in school and with their families, they are longing to plug themselves back into their music. Nothing surrounding them—school, family, church—has anything to do with their musical world. At best that ordinary life is neutral, but mostly it is an impediment, drained of vital content, even a thing to be rebelled against. Of course, the enthusiasm for Wagner was limited to a small class, could be indulged only rarely and only in a few places, and had to wait on the composer's slow output. The music of the new votaries, on the other hand, knows neither class nor nation. It is available twenty-four hours a day everywhere. There is the stereo in the home, in the car, there are concerts; there are music videos, with special channels exclusively devoted to them, on the air nonstop; there are the Walkmans so that no place—not public transportation, not the library—prevents students from communing with the Muse, even while studying. And, above all, the musical soil has become tropically rich. No need to wait for one unpredictable genius. Now there are many geniuses, producing all the time, two new ones rising to take the place of every fallen hero. There is no dearth of the new and the startling. . . .

It is Plato's teaching that music, by its nature, encompasses all that is today most resistant to philosophy. So it may well be that through the thicket of our greatest corruption runs the path to awareness of the oldest truths.

Plato's teaching about music is, put simply, that rhythm and melody, accompanied by dance, are the barbarous expression of the soul. Barbarous, not animal. Music is the medium of the *human* soul in its most ecstatic condition of wonder and terror. Nietzsche, who in large measure agrees with Plato's analysis, says in *The Birth of Tragedy* (not to be forgotten is the rest of the title, *Out of the Spirit of Music*) that a mixture of cruelty and coarse sensuality characterized this state, which of course was religious, in the service of gods. Music is the soul's primitive and primary speech and it is alogon, without articulate speech or reason. It is not only not reasonable, it is hostile to reason. Even when articulate speech is added, it is utterly subordinate to and determined by the music and the passions it expresses.

Civilization or, to say the same thing, education is the taming or domestication of the soul's raw passion—not suppressing or excising them, which would deprive the soul of its energy—but forming and in-forming them as art. . . .

But rock music has one appeal only, a barbaric appeal, to sexual desire—not love, not eros, but sexual desire undeveloped and untu-tored. It acknowledges the first emanations of children's emerging sen-suality and addresses them seriously, eliciting them and legitimating them, not as little sprouts that must be carefully tended in order to grow into gorgeous flowers, but as the real thing. Rock gives children, on a silver platter, with all the public authority of the entertainment in-dustry, everything their parents always used to tell them they had to wait for until they grew up and would understand later. . . .

My concern here is not with the moral effects of this music—whether it leads to sex, violence or drugs. The issue here is its effect on education, and I believe it ruins the imagination of young people and makes it very difficult for them to have a passionate relationship to the art and thought that are the substance of liberal education. The first sensuous experiences are decisive in determining the taste for the whole of life, and they are the link between the animal and spiritual in us. The period of nascent sensuality has always been used for sublima-tion, in the sense of making sublime, for attaching youthful inclina-tions and longings to music, pictures and stories that provide the transition to the fulfillment of the human duties and the enjoyment of the human pleasures. Lessing, speaking of Greek sculpture, said "beau-tiful men made beautiful statues, and the city had beautiful statues in part to thank for beautiful citizens." This formula encapsulates the fun-damental principle of the esthetic education of man. Young men and women were attracted by the beauty of heroes whose very bodies expressed their nobility. The deeper understanding of the meaning of nobility comes later, but is prepared for by the sensuous experience and is actually contained in it. What the senses long for as well as what reason later sees as good are thereby not at tension with one another. Education is not sermonizing to children against their instincts and pleasures, but providing a natural continuity between what they feel and what they can and should be.

But this is a lost art. Now we have come to exactly the opposite point. Rock music encourages passions and provides models that have no relation to any life the young people who go to universities can possibly lead, or to the kinds of admiration encouraged by liberal studies. Without the cooperation of the sentiments, anything other than technical education is a dead letter.

Rock music provides premature ecstacy and, in this respect, is like the drugs with which it is allied. It artificially induces the exaltation naturally attached to the completion of the greatest endeavors—victory in a just war, consummated love, artistic creation, religious devotion and discovery of the truth. Without effort, without talent, without virtue, without exercise of the faculties, anyone and everyone is accorded the equal right to the enjoyment of their fruits. In my experience, students who have had a serious fling with drugs—and gotten over it—find it difficult to have enthusiasms or great expectations. It is as though the color has been drained out of their lives and they see everything in black and white. The pleasure they experienced in the beginning was so intense that they no longer look for it at the end, or as the end. They may function perfectly well, but dryly, routinely. Their energy has been sapped, and they do not expect their life's activity to produce anything but a living, whereas liberal education is supposed to encourage the belief that the good life is the pleasant life and that the best life is the most pleasant life. I suspect that the rock addiction, particularly in the absence of strong counterattractions, has an effect similar to that of drugs. The students will get over this music, or at least the exclusive passion for it. But they will do so in the same way Freud says that men accept the reality principle—as something harsh, grim and essentially unattractive, a mere necessity. These students will assiduously study economics or the professions and the Michael Jackson costume will slip off to reveal a Brooks Brothers suit beneath. They will want to get ahead and live comfortably. But this life is as empty and false as the one they left behind. The choice is not between quick fixes and dull calculation. This is what liberal education is meant to show them. But as long as they have the Walkman on, they cannot bear what the great tradition has to say. And, after its prolonged use, when they take it off, they find they are deaf.

From Allan Bloom, *The Closing of the American Mind.*

ARISTOTLE

Plato Is Wrong—Art Gives Us Knowledge and Provides a Valuable Outlet for Our Emotions

Aristotle (348–322 B.C.E.) was a Greek philosopher of ethics, metaphysics, logic, and aesthetics.

Aristotle takes issue with his mentor, Plato, and argues that we do learn from the artist's imitations and this learning is the source of delight for us. Further, in his analysis of the nature of tragedy, Aristotle thinks that dramatic incidents serve to purge us of emotions like pity and fear. So, far from adopting the qualities of the characters in the drama, as Plato thought, we ultimately are cleansed of certain emotions.

Our subject being Poetry, I propose to speak not only of the art in general but also of its species and their respective capacities; of the structure of plot required for a good poem; of the number and nature of the constituent parts of a poem; and likewise of any other matters in the same line of inquiry. Let us follow the natural order and begin with the primary facts.

Epic poetry and Tragedy, as also Comedy, Dithyrambic poetry, and most flute-playing and lyre-playing, are all, viewed as a whole, modes of imitation. But at the same time they differ from one another in three ways, either by a difference of kind in their means, or by differences in the objects, or in the manner of their imitations. . . .

It is clear that the general origin of poetry was due to two causes, each of them part of human nature. Imitation is natural to man from childhood, one of his advantages over the lower animals being this, that he is the most imitative creature in the world, and learns at first by imitation. And it is also natural for all to delight in works of imitation. The truth of this second point is shown by experience: though the objects themselves may be painful to see, we delight to view the most realistic representations of them in art, the forms for example of the lowest animals and of dead bodies. The explanation is to be found in a further fact: to be learning something is the greatest of pleasures not only to the philosopher but also to the rest of mankind, however small their capacity for it; the reason of the delight in seeing the picture is that one is at the same time learning—gathering the meaning of things, e. g. that the man there is so-and-so; for if one has not seen the thing before, one's pleasure will not be in the picture as an imitation of it, but will be due to the execution or colouring or some similar cause. Imitation, then, being natural to us—as also the sense of harmony and rhythm, the metres being obviously species of rhythms—it was through their original aptitude, and by a series of improvements for the most part gradual on their first efforts, that they created poetry out of their improvisations.

Let us proceed now to the discussion of Tragedy; before doing so, however, we must gather up the definition resulting from what has been said. A tragedy, then, is the imitation of an action that is serious and also, as having magnitude, complete in itself; in language with pleasurable accessories, each kind brought in separately in the parts of the work; in a dramatic, not in a narrative form; with incidents arousing pity and fear, wherewith to accomplish its catharsis of such emotions. Here by 'language with pleasurable accessories' I mean that with rhythm and harmony or song superadded; and by 'the kinds separately' I mean that some portions are worked out with verse only, and others in turn with song.

From Aristotle, *De Poetica*, translated by Ingram Bywater.

GEORGE SANTAYANA
Art Is Liberating

George Santayana (1863–1952), who was born in Spain and studied and taught in America, was a metaphysician and aesthetician.

George Santayana was deeply concerned with the ways in which society, custom, and habit inhibit our freedom and our experimenting in a playful fashion with different and viable ways of living. He turns to art as a vehicle for liberating us and for creating happiness for us. Besides identifying the utility of art, Santayana says its essence is to reveal nature truly in a manner that speaks to all people.

The value of art lies in making people happy, first in practising the art and then in possessing its product. This observation might seem needless, and ought to be so; but if we compare it with what is commonly said on these subjects, we must confess that it may often be denied and more often, perhaps, may not be understood. Happiness is something men ought to pursue, although they seldom do so; they are drawn away from it at first by foolish impulses and afterwards by perverse customs. To secure happiness conduct would have to remain spontaneous while it learned not to be criminal; but the fanatical attachment of men, now to a fierce liberty, now to a false regimen, keeps them barbarous and wretched. A rational pursuit of happiness—which is one thing with progress or with the Life of Reason—would embody that natural piety which leaves to the episodes of life their inherent values, mourning death, celebrating love, sanctifying civic traditions, enjoying and correcting nature's ways. To discriminate happiness is therefore the very soul of art, which expresses experience without distorting it, as those political or metaphysical tyrannies distort it which sanctify unhappiness. A free mind, like a creative imagination, rejoices at the harmonies it can find or make between man and nature; and, where it finds none, it solves the conflict so far as it may and then notes and endures it with a shudder.

A morality organized about the human heart in an ingenuous and sincere fashion would involve every fine art and would render the world pervasively beautiful—beautiful in its artificial products and beautiful in its underlying natural terrors. The closer we keep to elementary human needs and to the natural agencies that may satisfy them, the closer we are to beauty. . . .

Art, in its nobler acceptation, is an achievement, not an indulgence. It prepares the world in some sense to receive the soul, and the soul to master the world; it disentangles those threads in each that can be woven into the other. That the artist should be eccentric, homeless, dreamful may almost seem a natural law, but it is none the less a scandal. An artist's business is not really to cut fantastical capers or be licensed to play the fool. His business is simply that of every keen soul to build well when it builds, and to speak well when it speaks, giving the treatment everywhere the greatest possible affinity to the theme and the most delicate adjustment to every faculty it affects. The wonder of an artist's performance grows with the range of his penetration, with the instinctive sympathy that makes him, in his mortal isolation, considerate of other men's fate and a great diviner of their secret, so that his work speaks to them kindly, with a deeper assurance than they could have spoken with to themselves. And the joy of his great sanity, the power of his adequate vision, is not the less intense because he can lend it to others and has borrowed it from a faithful study of the world.

From George Santayana, *The Life of Reason.*

LUCY LIPPARD

Women Should Express their Bodily and Intellectual Experiences to Create a Women's Art

Lucy Lippard (1937–) is an art historian and critic.

Lucy Lippard explores in a lively dialogue what sense we can make of there being a women's art. The case for a women's art rests on women's experiences, bodily and intellectual, being different from men's. If they are true to themselves, women will reveal these experiences in their art. Women may have reasons for concealing what they uniquely perceive; they may, for example, feel inferior from being seen as sexual objects and fear that they will just make matters worse if they call attention to their bodies in their art. Nonetheless, women should not shy from divulging their experiences with their art, as they thereby affirm their respect for themselves and contribute to a world where they are accorded respect.

Is there a women's art?

What do you mean—an art by women?

A lot of women do art, but is there an art made only by women?

All women?

No, just an art, no matter how little of it—not a style and not a technique, but something broader—that's done only by women.

I don't know. Is there?

Well, there should be. Women's experience—social and biological—in this and every other society, is different from men's.

And every *person's* experience is different from every other person's. Art is individual.

It's still possible to generalize about it. Black experience is different from white. Poor is different from rich. Child's art is different from adult's. And women's is different from men's.

But art is a mixture. Art is androgynous.

Sure, artists are probably more androgynous than "normal" people. Like male artists, no matter how macho they are (or because of it), have more of the woman in them than some other men in other professions. God knows women artists have traditionally had to have some "male" in them to get the hell up and create something on the primary level—or rather to have it seen as such. It takes imagination to transcend your sex. But it's dangerous, like building a house on sand. If you don't know your own identity, the real meaning of your own experience, you can't just jump up and "transcend." Eva Hesse once described the female part of her art as its sensitivity and the male part as its strength. Hopefully a year later she would have realized it could all be unified, that strength is female too.

Why will so few women admit to using their own bodies or biological experience even as *unconscious* subject matter?

Because it has been common knowledge that "women are inferior" and women artists trying to transcend that in their work sensibly don't want to identify with inferiority. So why not aspire to "maleness"?

But now that everybody knows women aren't inferior?

Ha! Everybody hasn't gotten the message yet. Anyway, it still holds in our generations, through conditioning. It's in the back of our minds, as fear or as rage, even when the rhetoric's on our lips.

Not in the back of mine, it isn't.

You're lucky, then. Another reason women don't like their art to be seen through their bodies is that women have been sex objects all along and to let your art be seen that way is just falling right back into the same old rut.

Not once attitudes are changed. Not once you can be proud of being a woman.

Nobody whose consciousness has been raised wants to be seen as just a vagina, an interior space, a cunt. You're hardly doing women a favor by laying that kind of restriction on them.

It's not a restriction. It's a basic element to our own identities we have to come to terms with. Did you hear yourself say *"just* a vagina"? Anyway, I didn't say that sexual or biological identity was the only factor in women's art. But to make art that is together, unified with the maker, that too has to be acknowledged instead of apologized for. And it's *there*. I looked at the New York Women's Art Registry—something like twenty-five hundred slides of women's work; I saw them with a man and he kept saying, "a man couldn't have made this work." It wasn't necessarily a compliment, but it was a fact we could both see. A huge amount of the work, especially the more naive or funky (and therefore often more directly inside art, less affected by bandwagon art-world numbers), did have blatant sexual matter, and so did a lot of the work made by women who deny that subject matter even when it's visible, by saying, "oh, I wasn't thinking about that so it isn't there." Sex is bound to be a factor in women's work precisely because women have been sex objects and are much more aware of their bodies than men. Men are aware of their pricks. Women are aware that every movement they make in public is supposed to have sexual content for the opposite sex. *Some* of that *has* to come out in the work. When it's absolutely absent, when it isn't even suggested, I wonder.

But that's like the cliche "Women are irrational and men are rational"; "Women are illogical, men are logical." You're taking women down to the level of mere bodies, while men can repress that and are allowed to make art with their minds.

No. No, not at all. Just that good art by either sex, no matter how "objective" or "nonobjective," has to have both elements or it's dead. But I must say that I think a lot of what we call logic and rationality is a male-focused, male-invented code. So-called logic is often insanely illogical, but it's still called logic because it works within its own system. Like formalist or Minimal art is popularly supposed to be logical because it looks like it should be, while work with a more obviously psychological basis is called illogical. I'd like to see those terms forgotten and have people look at everything according to a new set of criteria, criteria that don't imply value judgments through the use of certain code words or phrases. When I write that something is illogical in art, and I like it, I have to add "marvelously illogical" or it will be seen as a put-down. Not so with logic, which I often think is "merely logical." R. D. Laing pointed out the same thing about subjective and objective; he said it was always "merely subjective." I'm constantly called illogical, and I don't care, because for me it's logical, according to my own system.

Crazy lady.

Maybe, but I know that a certain kind of fragmentation, certain rhythms, are wholly sensible to me even if I can't analyze them. I find that fragmentation more and more often in the art—written and visual—of women who are willing to risk something, willing to let more of themselves out, let more of themselves be subject to ridicule according to the prevailing systems. Part of the energy that emerges from that impetus is sexual. Part is intellectual in a new way. Of course there's still an endless stream of art by women who are copying the old way, who are scared to alter the mathematics or geometry or logic or whatever it is they're interested in toward a new and perhaps more vulnerable model. I'm certainly not saying that any of those things should be tabu for women's art. But I'm convinced that women *feel* them differently and *that* either does come out or should come out in the art. Like the way so many women artists are using geometry or the grid primarily to blur its neat edges, to alter its meaning, to subtly screw up the kind of order that runs the world. The most convincing women's art I see, of any style, is very personal, and by being very personal finds a system of its own.

But you're so vague.

I know. On one hand I don't want to draw any conclusions. I mistrust conclusions because they get taken for granted and stop the flow of things. On the other hand, even if I wanted to, I couldn't draw conclusions on this subject now because I don't know enough. And because society hasn't radically changed yet for women, so what we're seeing is a mixture of what women really want to do and what they think they should do.

From Lucy Lippard, "Six."

WALT WHITMAN
America Is Poetry

Walt Whitman (1819–1892) was an American author, journalist, and poet.

In the preface to the 1855 edition of Leaves of Grass, *Walt Whitman forges some fascinating connections between America and poetry. Americans themselves are poetical by nature and America itself is a poem. As yet it is unrhymed, and all of its features, including its greatest feature of all—its common folk—are awaiting the treatment of the poet. If we think about American society in this way, we would have great difficulty in implementing Plato's advice to keep the poets out of society, since we would be rejecting what makes America and Americans special.*

America does not repel the past or what it has produced under its forms or amid other politics or the idea of castes or the old religions . . . accepts the lesson with calmness . . . is not so impatient as has been supposed that the slough still sticks to opinions and manners and literature while the life which served its requirements has passed into the new life of the new forms . . . perceives that the corpse is slowly borne from the eating and sleeping rooms of the house . . . perceives that it waits a little while in the door . . . that it was fittest for its days . . . that its action has descended to the stalwart and wellshaped heir who approaches . . . and that he shall be fittest for his days.

The Americans of all nations at any time upon the earth have probably the fullest poetical nature. The United States themselves are essentially the greatest poem. In the history of the earth hitherto the largest and most stirring appear tame and orderly to their ampler largeness and stir. Here at last is something in the doings of man that corresponds with the broadcast doings of the day and night. Here is not merely a nation but a teeming nation of nations. Here is action untied from strings necessarily blind to particulars and details magnificently moving in vast masses. Here is the hospitality which forever indicates heroes. . . . Here are the roughs and beards and space and ruggedness and nonchalance that the soul loves. Here the performance disdaining the trivial unapproached in the tremendous audacity of its crowds and groupings and the push of its perspective spreads with crampless and flowing breadth and showers its prolific and splendid extravagance. One sees it must indeed own the riches of the summer and winter, and need never be bankrupt while corn grows from the

Tribute to American Jazz. Collage with artists' construction paper. Alan M. Cano, 1991.

ground or the orchards drop apples or the bays contain fish or men beget children upon women.

Other states indicate themselves in their deputies . . . but the genius of the United States is not best or most in its executives or legislatures, nor in its ambassadors or authors or colleges or churches or parlors, nor even in its newspapers or inventors . . . but always most in the common people. Their manners speech dress friendships—the freshness and candor of their physiognomy—the picturesque looseness of their carriage . . . their deathless attachment to freedom—their aversion to anything indecorous or soft or mean—the practical acknowledgment of the citizens of one state by the citizens of all other states—the fierceness of their roused resentment—their curiosity and welcome of novelty—their self-esteem and wonderful sympathy—their susceptibility to a slight—the air they have of persons who never knew how it felt to stand in the presence of superiors—the fluency of their speech—their delight in music, the sure symptom of manly tenderness and native elegance of soul . . . their good temper and openhandedness—the terrible significance of their elections—the President's taking off his hat to them not they to him—these too are unrhymed poetry. It awaits the gigantic and generous treatment worthy of it.

From Walt Whitman, *Leaves of Grass.*

LESLIE MARMON SILKO
Aesthetics Cannot Be Separated from Metaphysics

Leslie Marmon Silko (1948–), born in the Laguna Pueblo reservation, is of Pueblo, Laguna, Mexican, and White ancestry. She is a novelist and essayist.

Leslie Marmon Silko argues that the aesthetic choices that people make are inflected by their relationship to the world around them. For example, the traditional Pueblo people saw themselves as part of—not separate from—the natural world around them and did not think their representations of nature could improve upon the world in which they participated. They were inclined, then, away from realistic depictions of nature and toward abstract depictions of natural objects that would capture the complex relationships the objects had to the whole of the natural system.

Pueblo potters, the creators of petroglyphs and oral narratives, never conceived of removing themselves from the earth and sky. So long as the human consciousness remains *within* the hills, canyons, cliffs, and the plants, clouds, and sky, the term *landscape*, as it has entered the English language, is misleading. "A portion of territory the eye can comprehend in a single view" does not correctly describe the relationship between the human being and his or her surroundings. This assumes the viewer is somehow *outside* or *separate* from the territory she or he surveys. Viewers are as much a part of the landscape as the boulders they stand on.

There is no high mesa edge or mountain peak where one can stand and not immediately be part of all that surrounds. Human identity is linked with all the elements of creation through the clan you might belong to: the Sun Clan or the Lizard Clan or the Corn Clan or the Clay Clan. Standing deep within the natural world, the ancient Pueblo understood the thing as it was—the squash blossom, grasshopper, or rabbit itself could never be created by the human hand. Ancient Pueblos took the modest view that the thing itself (the landscape) could not be improved upon. The ancients did not presume to tamper with what had already been created. Thus *realism*, as we now recognize it in painting and sculpture, did not catch the imaginations of Pueblo people until recently.

The squash blossom itself is *one thing*: itself. So the ancient Pueblo potter abstracts what she saw to be the key elements of the squash blossom—the four symmetrical petals, with four symmetrical stamens in the center. These key elements, while suggesting the squash flower, also link it with the four cardinal directions. Represented only in its intrinsic form, a squash flower or a cloud or a lightning bolt became intricately connected with a complex system of relationships that the ancient Pueblo people maintained with each other and with the populous natural world they lived within. A bolt of lightning is itself, but at the same time it may mean much more. It may be a messenger of good fortune when summer rains are needed. It may deliver death, perhaps the result of manipulations by the Gunnadeyahs, destructive necromancers. Lightning may strike down an evildoer, or lightning may strike a person of goodwill. If the person survives, lightning endows him or her with heightened power.

Pictographs and petroglyphs of constellations or elk or antelope draw their magic in part from the process wherein the focus of all prayer and concentration is upon the thing itself, which, in its turn, guides the hunter's hand. Connection with the spirit dimensions requires a figure or form that is all-inclusive. A lifelike rendering of an elk is too restrictive. Only the elk *is* itself. A *realistic* rendering of an elk would be only one particular elk anyway. The purpose of the hunt rituals and magic is to make contact with *all* the spirits of the elk.

From Leslie Marmon Silko, "Interior and Exterior Landscapes: The Pueblo Migration Stories."

GLORIA ANZALDÚA

Art and Ritual Cannot Be Separated in Tribal Cultures

Gloria Anzaldúa (1942–) is an essayist, poet, and novelist who explores the complexity of her Chicana/Indian/White heritage.

Gloria Anzaldua contrasts the role of art in traditional tribal cultures with what she identifies as the "aesthetics of vituosity" in modern Western society. In traditional cultures the meaning of an art work could not be understood apart from its role in ritual and in everyday life, but in the "aesthetics of virtuosity" art works are viewed simply as "things in themselves," to be displayed in museums and understood and evaluated apart from any context of use.

In the ethno-poetics and performance of the shaman, my people, the Indians, did not split the artistic from the functional, the sacred from the secular, art from everyday life. The religious, social, and aesthetic purposes of art were all intertwined. Before the Conquest, poets gathered to play music, dance, sing, and read poetry in open-air places around the *Xochicuahuitl, el Arbol Florido,* Tree-in-Flower. (The *Coaxihuitl* or morning glory is called the snake plant and its seeds, known as *ololiuhqui,* are hallucinogenic.) The ability of story (prose and poetry) to transform the storyteller and the listener into something or someone else is shamanistic. The writer, as shape-changer, is a *nahual,* a shaman. . . .

I make my offerings of incense and cracked corn, light my candle. In my head I sometimes will say a prayer—an affirmation and a voicing of intent. Then I run water, wash the dishes or my underthings, take a bath, or mop the kitchen floor. This "induction" period sometimes takes a few minutes, sometimes hours. But always I go against a resistance. Something in me does not want to do this writing. Yet once I'm immersed in it, I can go fifteen to seventeen hours in one sitting and don't want to leave it.

My "stories" are acts encapsulated in time, "enacted" every time they are spoken aloud or read silently. I like to think of them as performances and not as inert and "dead" objects (as the aesthetics of Western culture think of art works). Instead the work has an identity; it is a "who" or a "what" and contains the presences of persons, that is, incarnations of gods or ancestors or natural and cosmic powers. The work manifests the same needs as a person, it needs to be "fed," *la tengo que banar y vestir*.

When invoked in rite, the object/event is "present"; that is, "enacted," it is both a physical thing and the power that infuses it. It is metaphysical in that it "spins its energies between gods and humans" and its task is to move the gods. This type of work dedicates itself to managing the universe and its energies. I'm not sure what it is when it is at rest (not in performance). It may or may not be a "work" then. A mask may only have the power of presence during a ritual dance and the rest of the time it is merely a "thing." Some works exist forever invoked, always in performance. I'm thinking of totem poles, cave paintings. Invoked art is communal and speaks of everyday life. It is dedicated to the validation of humans; that is, it makes people hopeful, happy, secure, and it can have negative effects as well, which propel one towards a search for validation.

The aesthetic of virtuosity, art typical of Western European cultures, attempts to manage the energies of its own internal system such as conflicts, harmonies, resolutions and balances. It bears the presences of qualities and internal meanings. It is dedication to the validation of itself. Its task is to move humans by means of achieving mastery in content, technique, feeling. Western art is always whole and always "in power." It is individual (not communal). It is "psychological" in that it spins its energies between itself and its witness.

Western cultures behave differently toward works of art than do tribal cultures. The "sacrifices" Western cultures make are in housing their art works in the best structures designed by the best architects; and in servicing them with insurance, guards to protect them, conservators to maintain them, specialists to mount and display them, and the educated and upper classes to "view" them. Tribal cultures keep art works in honored and sacred places in the home and elsewhere. They attend them by making sacrifices of blood (goat or chicken), libations of wine. They bathe, feed, and clothe them. The works are treated not just as objects, but also as persons. The "witness" is a participant in the enactment of the work in a ritual, and not a member of the privileged classes.

Ethnocentrism is the tyranny of Western aesthetics. An Indian mask in an American museum is transported into an alien aesthetic system where what is missing is the presence of power invoked through performance ritual. It has become a conquered thing, a dead "thing" separated from nature and, therefore, its power.

Modern Western painters have "borrowed," copied, or otherwise extrapolated the art of tribal cultures and called it cubism, surrealism, symbolism. The music, the beat of the drum, the Blacks' jive talk. All taken over. Whites, along with a good number of our own people, have cut themselves off from their spiritual roots, and they take our spiritual art objects in an unconscious attempt to get them back. If they're going to do it, I'd like them to be aware of what they are doing and to go about doing it in the right way. Let's all stop importing Greek myths and the Western Cartesian split point of view and root ourselves in the mythological soil and soul of this continent.

From Gloria Anzaldúa, *"Tlilli, Tlapalli*: The Path of the Red and Black Ink."

ANDY WARHOL
Art Is Junk

Andy Warhol (1928–1987) was an American *avant garde* artist and filmmaker.

Andy Warhol's claims about art may be as flamboyant and provocative as his art itself. This is the man who is famous for his depictions of a Campbell soup can, of Marilyn Monroe, and of an executioner's electric chair. He says that his art is junk. Our expectation is that we could learn little about art from someone who holds it in so low regard or seems to have mistaken it for something else. Yet, when we see the larger picture within which he makes this claim, we see that indeed he does have views of beauty and art which make it plausible to conceive art, in a sense, as junk. Warhol extols unadorned space, whether in a manmade structure or naturally occurring, as the ideal and as beautiful in itself. Place a beautiful chair in a space and, however beautiful that chair is, it will never be as beautiful as the space itself. We waste space when we adorn it with objects. And to the extent artists create objects that waste space, their creations are junk. But to say that art, in this sense, is junk is not to say that no standards guide the production of good art, for the artist can fill the space well or badly.

What makes a painting beautiful is the way the paint's put on, but I don't understand how women put on makeup, It gets on your lips, and it's so heavy. Lipstick and makeup and powder and shadow creams. And Jewelry. It's all so heavy. . . . I can never get over when you're on the beach how beautiful the sand looks and the water washes it away and straightens it up and the trees and the grass all look great. I think having land and not ruining it is the most beautiful art that anybody could ever want to own. . . .

Space is all one space and thought is all one thought, but my mind divides its spaces into spaces into spaces and thoughts into thoughts into thoughts. Like a large condominium. Occasionally I think about the one Space and the one Thought, but usually I don't. Usually I think about my condominium.

The condominium has hot and cold running water, a few Heinz pickles thrown in, some chocolate-covered cherries, and when the Woolworth's hot fudge sundae switch goes on, then I know I really have something.

(This condominium meditates a lot: it's usually closed for the afternoon, evening, and morning.)

Your mind makes spaces into spaces. It's a lot of hard work. A lot of hard spaces. As you get older you get more spaces, and more compartments. And more things to put in the compartments.

To be really rich, I believe, is to have one space. One big empty space.

I really believe in empty spaces, although, as an artist, I make a lot of junk.

Empty space is never-wasted space.

Wasted space is any space that has art in it.

An artist is somebody who produces things that people don't need to have but that he—for *some reason*—thinks it would be a good idea to give them.

Business Art is a much better thing to be making than Art Art, because Art Art doesn't support the space it takes up, whereas Business Art does, (if Business Art doesn't support its own space it goes out-of-business.)

So on the one hand I really believe in empty spaces, but on the other hand, because I'm still making some art, I'm still making junk for people to put in their spaces that I believe should be empty: i.e., I'm helping people *waste* their space when what I really want to do is help them *empty* their space.

I go even further in not following my own philosophy, because I can't even empty my own spaces. It's not that my philosophy is failing me, it's that I am failing my own philosophy. I breach what I preach more than I practice it.

When I look at things, I always see the space they occupy. I always want the space to reappear, to make a comeback, because it's lost space when there's something in it. If I see a chair in a beautiful space, no matter how beautiful the chair is, it can never be as beautiful to me as the plain space.

My favorite piece of sculpture is a solid wall with a hole in it to frame the space on the other side.

When I paint:

I look at my canvas and I space it out right. I think, "Well, over here in this corner it looks like it sort of belongs," and so I say, "Oh yes, that's where it belongs, all right." So I look at it again and I say, "The space in that corner there needs a little blue," and so I put my blue up there and then, then I look over there and it looks blue over there so I take my brush and I move it over there and I make it blue over there, too. And then it needs to be more spaced, so I take my little blue brush and I blue it over there, and then I take my green brush and I put my green brush on it and I green it there, and then I walk back and I look at it and see if it's spaced right. And then—sometimes it's not spaced right—I take my colors and I put another little green over there and then if it's spaced right I leave it alone.

From Andy Warhol, *The Philosophy of Andy Warhol.*

W.E.B. Du Bois

"The Art and Art Galleries of Modern Europe"

W.E.B. Du Bois (1868–1963) was an American sociologist, philosopher, and founding member of the NAACP.

W.E.B. Du Bois writes of his good fortune of studying at Harvard when such luminaries as James, Santayana, and Royce were there. He singles out James for having special significance for his education. Du Bois is primarily known for his writings and activism directed at revealing and improving the lives of African Americans. The Soul of Black Folk *and* From Dusk to Dawn *are the hallmarks of his intellectual achievement as the NAACP (National Association for the Advancement of Colored People) is of his social activism.*

Du Bois's other writings show him philosophizing about matters like art and immortality without race relations being at the fore of the discussion. In the following essay about art, Du Bois entertains such recurring philosophical themes as the nature of beauty and the effect of art on our lives.

I propose tonight to tell you something of the Art and Art Galleries of Modern Europe, not from the standpoint of the artist or art critic, but from the standpoint of one who loves beautiful things and whose good fortune it has been to give a passing glance at many of the great art collections of the modern world.

We who take interest in the training of men believe steadfastly and conscientiously in the full rounded development of man. We believe that there can be no sturdy moral growth without deep intellectual training; and we believe too that there can be no true lasting moral worth and mental development without healthy physical life; and we believe that all exceptions to these propositions merely prove the rule. But these three factors of life are not coordinate; the physical development of man is not an end in itself but a means to an end; the great underlying life principle which conserves life for the sake of those great ends which make life worth living. Therefore tonight the Athletic Association asks you to listen not to a dissertation on physical culture but rather to a talk on one of the three great ends of living for the attainment of which healthy muscular manhood is the first prerequisite.

Three things in life beckon the human soul: the Good, the True and the Beautiful. We hear of the good every day—hear of it so much in fact that we sometimes become deaf from very hearing and forget that simple goodness is the end of all moral strife; and that it is just as impossible to be a Christian and be bad, as it is to be full and empty at the same time. Again we hear much of the True; the object of our being here in school, the object of all right training, the object of all science is to search out and make known the real Truth about the world we live in. But there is a third something—a third dimension in life without which we cannot truly live: it is the Beautiful. Goodness is a matter of the Will power, Truth, a matter with which the mind deals; but the heart and the emotions deal with the Beautiful.

We immediately see how inexpressibly broad a field we have here, how infinitely varied in aspect and product and with what tact and delicacy it must be cultivated and fertilized. It is always extremely difficult to teach young people to give proper attention to the beautiful things of life, to realize that the object of all life is to make the universal beautiful; so to use the Good, that we may realize the Beautiful in the True. And yet it is a problem how to bring this central fact before the many varieties of character which are represented here.

The first place of such training is of course the home—the picture books of early years, the paintings in the parlor, the decorations of the bedroom, the mother's Sunday clothes—all these are the materials out of which the youth must form his ideals of what is beautiful. How important then are the little decorations of home, and how easily can a hideous combination of colors, or a tawdry picture make a man an aesthetic idiot for life. Unfortunately we as a people are just beginning to build our homes and consequently many of us have missed the vast educational power of beautiful surroundings in childhood. These must train themselves by the study of beautiful things in after life. For this purpose the first great art school is Nature: here at Wilberforce we are surrounded by an art gallery which treasures countless masterpieces, and yet there are dozens of us who will go through this coming Springtide and see nought but dirt and water—unmindful of the glory of the sunsets beyond the western meadows, unmindful of the daily panorama of sun, and clouds and sky.

Thus far I have attempted to bring to your minds the fact that the Beautiful is one of the great ends of life and that we can train ourselves to appreciate the beautiful things in life and even discover beauties hidden to untrained hearts. One gallery of the beautiful I have said is the world about. I now come to the second great reservoir of the Beautiful, which we call Art: Art is beauty created by man; it is something of which a human soul conceives, a human hand executes and all human hearts everywhere acknowledge beautiful. Take for instance a little flower. If I ask you why it is beautiful you could not tell me—it simply is beautiful; it raises pleasing sensations—a sort of mental satisfaction almost indescribable. Again take another work of Art—a great building. I remember sailing along a blue rushing river, once, when suddenly rounding a bend, two dark and mighty towers seemed to shoot into the air, capping a wilderness of graceful fretwork and mighty buttress, standing there in that calm August day like twin giants. It was the Cathedral of Cologne. Why was it beautiful? "If eyes were made for seeing, then beauty is its own excuse for being."' And yet some reasons one may give as to why it was beautiful. Was it not because of the thoughts it raised in me? The awe, the wonder, the feeling of strength, the lust of creative manhood, and yet withal the sweet symmetry of life?

Take a wonderful painting, is it beautiful because it imitates a beautiful thing? Possibly, but if so it is no more than is a photograph, not a work of Art. A real masterpiece of art is beautiful in proportion to what it creates, to the emotions it raises in the hearts of its beholders. Let me illustrate. At the National Galleries in Berlin there hung once a picture. It was a strange weird thing in grey and blue with great long-necked swans sailing down a river. We had all viewed it when the young lady of the house, who was a wee bit strong minded, expressed her opinion and said, "Why that picture is simply absurd—who ever saw swans with necks like that?" But one of those present said: That makes no difference—suppose no such swans ever did exist; so long as the artist succeeds in embodying a great idea, in creating a beautiful thing, is not his object accomplished? Is an artist a mere photographer of chickens' heads? No: Art does nor imitate nature, but nature imitates art. Or to put it better both strive toward one vast Ideal, the infinite beauty of the other world.

If then true art is to be measured by our own emotions, how necessary it is that those feelings be capable of responding to the highest, that the nature of the beholder be so nicely attuned that it responds to the lightest touch and most subtle harmony of the work of Art. Let me illustrate: suppose we have two pictures: a mere chromo, the other is an excellent work. What is the difference? Perhaps some of you would not see any difference—if so it would merely mean that your aesthetic nature—your perception and appreciation of [the] really beautiful—is in sad need of training. Some of you must instinctively feel that these paintings are of different degrees of merit and yet could not give a reason; finally a few of you could immediately say: the masterpiece is cunning in execution—in light and shade, in harmonious colors, in careful painting. The other is inharmonious and blaring; the masterpiece has unity of idea. It is not that it exactly imitates ship and sea—one who had never seen either would get the same idea of strength and beauty. On the other hand, the other picture is overdone—the underlying idea is evident but it is too broadly and crudely brought out—there is none of that nice suiting of means to end which is so important. . . .

This brings me to urge in conclusion that you should early learn to appreciate and surround yourselves with beautiful things: "A thing of beauty is a joy forever." This has deeper meaning than we can imagine because we so misuse the word beautiful; but things of real lasting beauty: bits of china, graceful furniture, pretty wallpaper, neat dress, little pieces of statuary and above all beautiful pictures—these things will add enough to your lives to make even your sorrows curves of grace in a crooked world. Not in evil, not in idleness, not in sensuality, comes the real fulness of life; pedantry is not learning, extravagance is not art and yelling is not religion—but all life is one striving toward the Eternally Beautiful.

Whichever lives and loves

One God, one law, one element,

And one far-off divine event

To which the whole creation moves.

From W.E.B. Du Bois, "The Art and Art Galleries of Modern Europe."

SOCIETY 7

INTRODUCTION

Throughout recorded history human beings have lived together in groups. Clans, tribes, city-states, and countries have connected their members by ties of kinship, religion, tradition, and government. The benefits of community are evident: humans living in groups can protect each other and share resources and talents; they can develop technologies and arts that would not be possible if persons lived in isolation. But communities can also place burdens upon their members: citizens are called to war to defend the commonwealth, taxes are imposed to fund projects deemed in the public interest, individual behaviors are curtailed for the sake of a more harmonious whole. When are the benefits and burdens of living in a society fairly distributed among its members? What principles, if any, are there to guide us in determining how to promote the public interest?

Questions such as these fall into the domain of political philosophy. The task of the *political philosopher* is to step back from specific social arrangements and communities and reflect upon the nature and justification of community itself. Themes that are often addressed by political philosophers include:

Wood Engraving. Johann Froschauer, *c.* 1505. Presumed to be the first European woodcut depicting Native Americans.

(a) The justification of political authority: Why should I obey the law? Why is the state entitled to limit my actions in certain ways? Is the state's authority based upon divine command? secular morality? tradition? the consent of those governed? Under what conditions am I released from my obligation to the state?

(b) The relationship between the individual and the community: Do individuals come together simply to further their private interests, or does genuine community involve ties to others that go beyond self-interest? Is there a "human nature" around which all societies must be developed, or is the very self so much a product of acculturation that it makes little sense to speak of a human identity apart from a particular social context?

(c) The nature of justice: Is there a model society toward which we should strive? what values inform this model? freedom? equality? fairness? unity? Are there certain human rights which every society should honor? How do we avoid ethnocentrism—the privileging of our own social practices—when thinking about justice? Is the search for a universal, objective notion of justice misguided from the outset? Should we rest content with finding what social arrangements seem to work best for our society at this point in time?

(d) The path to justice: What measures may you take if you believe that the present social arrangements do not promote public interest? What steps are appropriate for pointing to and correcting injustice? What if speaking out and negotiating with those in power fail to create change? Under what conditions is it appropriate to violate the laws of the state or to commit acts of violence in an effort to address injustice?

(e) The role of aggression in the quest for peace: How is the state best to protect its citizens and foster peace? Can a society both inculcate the values requisite to maintain a military force and pursue peace? If aggression is part of human nature, is conflict between societies and individuals within societies inevitable? Is war always undesirable?

You will find, as you read the selections in this section, that the themes and questions outlined here intertwine: it is difficult for a theorist to address one topic without tackling issues in another. For example, when Hobbes, Rousseau, Jefferson, and Rawls seek a foundation for the authority of the state, they base their theories on a view of humans as essentially individualistic and self-interested. Their assumptions about human nature and the relationship between the individual and the state are challenged in the writings of Peirce, Marx, Mead, Li, and Wolff, all of whom, in different ways, endorse a more communitarian vision of human nature.

When you read the selections, ask yourself what questions the theorists are addressing, and look for points of connection among the various readings. Mill, for example, defends the importance of laws, while Wolff calls for laws to be abolished; yet a close look at their arguments will show that they both promote the value of individual freedom. And Martin Luther King, Jr. and Malcolm X argue from different religious traditions and endorse different routes to justice, but both are committed to a very similar vision of human rights and universal justice.

As always, use your reading as an occasion to discover and hone your own views. Do you agree with Marx's critique of capitalism? Wolff's anarchism? Mill's defense of individual liberty? Addams' recipe for a peaceful, flourishing society? Burke's appeal to tradition? By identifying the points at which you agree and disagree with the thinkers represented on the following pages, you will be well on your way to uncovering your own assumptions and arguments about human nature, the relation between the individual and society, and the nature of justice.

CHARLES SANDERS PEIRCE

Logic Requires Us to Be Concerned with the Whole Community

Charles Sanders Peirce sees it as a matter of logic that we be concerned with the interests of other people and not simply worry about pursuing self-interest. He has us consider an insurance company which, by its nature, has to take various risks about who and what to insure. If the company loses some money because one risk turns out to be a bad one, the company can still prosper because it has scattered its risks. One thing that would be clearly irrational is for the company to take one risk so large that it could not cover its losses even if all of the other risks paid off. The company always has to consider the whole picture. The same reasoning holds for people. They cannot rationally put all of their eggs in the basket of self-interest. Logic aside, Peirce thinks that as a matter of fact people care about each other's welfare and that theories of human nature which mask this fact are faulty.

Each of us is an insurance company, in short. But, now, suppose an insurance company, among its risks, should take one exceeding in amount the sum of all the others. Plainly, it would then have no security whatever. Now, has not every single man such a risk? What shall it profit a man if he shall gain the whole world and lose his own soul? If a man has a transcendent personal interest infinitely outweighing all others, then, upon the theory of validity of inference just developed, he is devoid of all security, and can make no valid inference whatever. What follows? That logic rigidly requires, before all else, that no determinate fact, nothing which can happen to a self, should be of more consequence to him than everything else. He who would not sacrifice his own soul to save the whole world, is illogical in all his inferences, collectively. So the social principle is rooted intrinsically in logic.

That being the case, it becomes interesting to inquire how it *is* with men as a matter of fact. There is a psychological theory that man cannot act without a view to his own pleasure. This theory is based on a falsely assumed subjectivism. Upon our principles of the object of knowledge, it could not be based, and if they are correct it is reduced to an absurdity. It seems to me that the usual opinion of the selfishness of man is based in large measure upon this false theory. I do not think that the facts bear out the usual opinion. The immense self-sacrifices which the most wilful men often make, show that wilfulness is a very different thing from selfishness. The care that men have for what is to happen after they are dead, cannot be selfish. And finally and chiefly, the constant use of the word "we"—as when we speak of our possessions on the Pacific—our destiny as a republic—in cases in which no personal interests at all are involved, show conclusively that men do not make their personal interests their only ones, and therefore may, at least, subordinate them to the interests of the community.

From C. S. Peirce, *Writings of Charles S. Peirce: A Chronological Edition.*

I t seems to me that we are driven to this, that logicality inexorably requires that our interests shall not be limited. They must not stop at our own fate, but must embrace the whole community. This community, again, must not be limited, but must extend to all races of beings with whom we can come into immediate or mediate intellectual relation. It must reach, however vaguely, beyond this geological epoch, beyond all bounds. He who would not sacrifice his own soul to save the whole world, is, as it seems to me, illogical in all his inferences, collectively. Logic is rooted in the social principle.

To be logical men should not be selfish; and, in point of fact, they are not so selfish as they are thought. The willful prosecution of one's desires is a different thing from selfishness. The miser is not selfish; his money does him no good, and he cares for what shall become of it after his death. We are constantly speaking of *our* possessions on the Pacific, and of *our* destiny as a republic, where no personal interests are involved, in a way which shows that we have wider ones. We discuss with anxiety the possible exhaustion of coal in some hundreds of years, or the cooling-off of the sun in some millions, and show in the most popular of all religious tenets that we can conceive the possibility of a man's descending into hell for the salvation of his fellows.

Now, it is not necessary for logicality that a man should himself be capable of the heroism of self-sacrifice. It is sufficient that he should recognize the possibility of it, should perceive that only that man's inferences who has it are really logical, and should consequently regard his own as being only so far valid as they would be accepted by the hero. So far as he thus refers his inferences to that standard, he becomes identified with such a mind.

From C. S. Peirce, "On the Doctrine of Chances with Later Reflections."

WILLIAM JAMES
End War, Establish Peace, but Preserve the Manly Virtues

William James takes issue with people who think that war is an inevitable condition of the human race. He identifies a peaceful world both as an attainable condition and as his utopia. Important for this peace enduring, however, is the preservation of an element of war—the virtues of the military, virtues like boldness and hatred of easy ways. The way to do this is to create an army against nature where the youth would acquire the important values as they mined coal and iron and built skyscrapers. These activities comprise James's "moral equivalent of war."

Having said this much in preparation, I will now confess my own utopia. I devoutly believe in the reign of peace and in the gradual advent of some sort of a socialistic equilibrium. The fatalistic view of the war-function is to me nonsense, for I know that war-making is due to definite motives and subject to prudential checks and reasonable criticisms, just like any other form of enterprise. And when whole nations are the armies, and the science of destruction vies in intellectual refinement with the sciences of production, I see that war becomes absurd and impossible from its own monstrosity. Extravagant ambitions will have to be replaced by reasonable claims, and nations must make common cause against them. I see no reason why all this should not apply to yellow as well as to white countries, and I look forward to a future when acts of war shall be formally outlawed as between civilized peoples.

All these beliefs of mine put me squarely into the anti-militarist party. But I do not believe that peace either ought to be or will be permanent on this globe, unless the states pacifically organized preserve some of the old elements of army-discipline. A permanently successful peace-economy cannot be a simple pleasure-economy. In the more or less socialistic future towards which mankind seems drifting we must still subject ourselves collectively to those severities which answer to our real position upon this only partly hospitable globe. We must make new energies and hardihoods continue the manliness to which the military mind so faithfully clings. Martial virtues must be the enduring cement; intrepidity, contempt of softness, surrender of private interest, obedience to command, must still remain the rock upon which states are built—unless, indeed, we wish for dangerous reactions against commonwealths fit only for contempt, and liable to invite attack whenever a centre of crystallization for military-minded enterprise gets formed anywhere in their neighborhood.

The war-party is assuredly right in affirming and reaffirming that the martial virtues, although originally gained by the race through war, are absolute and permanent human goods. Patriotic pride and ambition in their military form are, after all, only specifications of a more general competitive passion. They are its first form, but that is no reason for supposing them to be its last form. Men now are proud of belonging to a conquering nation, and without a murmur they lay down their persons and their wealth, if by so doing they may fend off subjection. But who can be sure that *other aspects of one's* country may not, with time and education and suggestion enough, come to be regarded with similarly effective feelings of pride and shame? Why should men not some day feel that it is worth a blood-tax to belong to a collectivity superior in any ideal respect? Why should they not blush with indignant shame if the community that owns them is vile in any way whatsoever? Individuals, daily more numerous, now feel this civic passion. It is only a question of blowing on the spark till the whole population gets incandescent, and on the ruins of the old morals of military honor, a stable system of morals of civic honor builds itself up. What the whole community comes to believe in grasps the individual as in a vise. The war-function has grasped us so far; but constructive interests may some day seem no less imperative, and impose on the individual a hardly lighter burden.

Let me illustrate my idea more concretely. There is nothing to make one indignant in the mere fact that life is hard, that men should toil and suffer pain. The planetary conditions once for all are such, and we can stand it. But that so many men, by mere accidents of birth and opportunity, should have a life of *nothing else* but toil and pain and hardness and inferiority imposed upon them, should have no vacation, while others natively no more deserving never get any taste of this campaigning life at all—*this is,* capable of arousing indignation in reflective minds. It may end by seeming shameful to all of us that some of us have nothing but campaigning, and others nothing but unmanly ease. If now—and this is my idea—there were, instead of military conscription a conscription of the whole youthful population to form for a certain number of years a part of the army enlisted against Nature, the injustice would tend to be evened out, and numerous other goods to the commonwealth would follow. The military ideals of hardihood and discipline would be wrought into the growing fibre of the people; no one would remain blind as the luxurious classes now are blind, to man's relations to the globe he lives on, and to the permanently sour and hard foundations of his higher life. To coal and iron mines, to freight trains, to fishing fleets in December, to dishwashing, clothes-washing, and window-washing, to road-building and tunnel-making, to foundries and stoke-holes, and to the frames of skyscrapers, would our gilded youths be drafted off, according to their choice, to get the child-ishness knocked out of them, and to come back into society with healthier sympathies and soberer ideas. They would have paid their blood-tax, done their own part in the immemorial human warfare against nature; they would tread the earth more proudly, the women would value them more highly, they would be better fathers and teach-ers of the following generation.

Such a conscription, with the state of public opinion that would have required it, and the many moral fruits it would bear, would pre-serve in the midst of a pacific civilization the manly virtues which the military party is so afraid of seeing disappear in peace. We should get toughness without callousness, authority with as little criminal cruelty as possible, and painful work done cheerily because the duty is tempo-rary, and threatens not, as now, to degrade the whole remainder of one's life. I spoke of the "moral equivalent" of war. So far, war has been the only force that can discipline a whole community, and until an equivalent discipline is organized, I believe that war must have its way. But I have no serious doubt that the ordinary prides and shames of so-cial man, once developed to a certain intensity, are capable of organiz-ing such a moral equivalent as I have sketched, or some other just as effective for preserving manliness of type. It is but a question of time, of skillful propagandism, and of opinion-making men seizing historic opportunities.

From William James, "The Moral Equivalent of War."

JOHN DEWEY

Experiment with Forms of Government

John Dewey's The Public and Its Problems *presents a case for our breaking from any notion of there being some one correct theory of the state. Rather, we should take an experimental approach to how officials and agencies can best protect public interest and think of the state as nothing more than how the public at any point is organized for this protection. Publics, their interests, and their officials are no more fixed throughout time than the organization or state best suited to protecting the public's interest. Just what organization best serves some public is a matter to determine through experimentation.*

Only the exigencies of a rigid philosophy can lead us to suppose that there is some one form or idea of The State which these protean historic states have realized in various degrees of perfection. The only statement which can be made is a purely formal one: the state is the organization of the public effected through officials for the protection of the interests shared by its members. But what the public may be, what the officials are, how adequately they perform their function, are things we have to go to history to discover.

Nevertheless, our conception gives a criterion for determining how good a particular state is: namely, the degree of organization of the public which is attained, and the degree in which its officers are so constituted as to perform their function of caring for public interests. But there is no a priori rule which can be laid down and by which when it is followed a good state will be brought into existence. In no two ages or places is there the same public. Conditions make the consequences of associated action and the knowledge of them different even when it is achieved. Or it may proceed more intelligently, because guided by knowledge of the conditions which must be fulfilled. But it is still experimental. And since conditions of action and of inquiry and knowledge are always changing, the experiment must always be retried; the State must always be rediscovered. Except, once more, in formal statement of conditions to be met, we have no idea what history may still bring forth. It is not the business of political philosophy and science to determine what the state in general should or must be. What they may do is to aid in creation of methods such that experimentation may go on less blindly, less at the mercy of accident, more intelligently, so that men may learn from their errors and profit by their successes. The belief in political *fixity*, of the sanctity of some form of state consecrated by the efforts of our fathers and hallowed by tradition, is one of the stumbling-blocks in the way of orderly and directed change; it is an invitation to revolt and revolution.

From John Dewey, *The Public and Its Problems*.

Jane Addams

A Separation of the Haves from the Have-Nots Preserves Social Ills

Jane Addams offers social clubs, like the ones at her Hull-House in Chicago, as a means of creating conditions for people from different sectors of society to interact. Their dialogue serves to make people who are better off aware of the adverse conditions of less fortunate people, an important first step in addressing social problems. Addams had long believed that the absence of discourse like this was a root cause of social injustices continuing. She relates how, twenty years prior to her work with social clubs, she was keenly aware of this problem. At that point, however, she could do little more than define it. The following passage concludes with Addams's portrayal of society when people with advantages keep their distance from the downtrodden.

Thus the value of social clubs broadens out in one's mind to an instrument of companionship through which many may be led from a sense of isolation to one of civic responsibility, even as another type of club provides recreational facilities for those who have had only meaningless excitements, or, as a third type, opens new and interesting vistas of life to those who are ambitious. . . .

The social clubs form a basis of acquaintanceship for many people living in other parts of the City. Through friendly relations with individuals, which is perhaps the sanest method of approach, they are thus brought into contact, many of them for the first time, with the industrial and social problems challenging the moral resources of our contemporary life. During our twenty years hundreds of these non-residents have directed clubs and classes, and have increased the number of Chicago citizens who are conversant with adverse social conditions and conscious that only by the unceasing devotion of each, according to his strength, shall the compulsions and hardships, the stupidities and cruelties of life be overcome. The number of people thus informed is constantly increasing in all our American cities, and they may in time remove the reproach of social neglect and indifference which has so long rested upon the citizens of the new world. . . .

The entire social development of Hull-House is so unlike what I predicted twenty years ago, that I venture to quote from that ancient writing an end to this chapter.

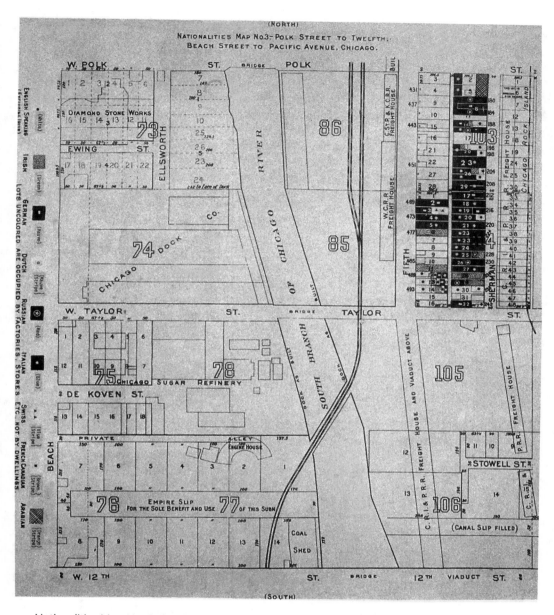

Nationalities Map No. 3 showing the ethnicity of the people in the neighborhood of Hull-House, Jane Addams's settlement house in Chicago.

The social organism has broken down through large districts of our great cities. Many of the people living there are very poor, the majority of them without leisure or energy for anything but the gain of subsistence.

They live for the moment side by side, many of them without knowledge of each other, without fellowship, without local tradition or public spirit, without social organization of any kind. Practically nothing is done to remedy this. The people who might do it, who have the social tact and training, the large houses, and the traditions and customs of hospitality, live in other parts of the city. The club houses, library, galleries and semi-public conveniences for social life are also blocks away. We find workingmen organized into armies of producers because men of executive ability and business sagacity have found it to their interest thus to organize them. But these workingmen are not organized socially; although lodging in crowded houses, they are living without a corresponding social contact. The chaos is as great as it would be were they working in huge factories without foreman or superintendent. Their ideas and resources are cramped, and the desire for higher social pleasure becomes extinct. They have no share in the traditions and energy which make for progress. Too often their only place of meeting is a saloon, their only host a bartender; a local demagogue forms their public opinion. Men of ability and refinement, of social power and university cultivation, stay away from them. Personally, I believe the men who lose most are those who thus stay away. But the paradox is here: when cultivated people do stay away from a certain portion of the population, when all social advantages are persistently withheld, it may be for years, the result itself is pointed to as a reason and is used as an argument, for the continued withholding.

It is constantly said that because the masses have never had social advantages, they do not want them, that they are heavy and dull, and that it will take political or philanthropic machinery to change them. This divides a city into rich and poor; into the favored, who express their sense of the social obligation by gifts of money, and into the unfavored, who express it by clamoring for a "share"—both of them actuated by a vague sense of justice. This division of the city would be more justifiable, however, if the people who thus isolate themselves on certain streets and use their social ability for each other, gained enough thereby and added sufficient to the sum total of the social progress to justify the withholding of the pleasures and results of that progress, from so many people who ought to have them. But they cannot accomplish this for the social spirit discharges itself in many forms, and no one form is adequate to its total expression.

From Jane Addams, *Twenty Years at Hull-House*.

THOMAS HOBBES

We Should Agree to Establish Government to Secure Peace

Thomas Hobbes (1588–1679), author of the influential work *Leviathan*, was an English political philosopher.

Thomas Hobbes sees us as competitive, aggressive, and self-interested by nature. Far from envisioning a Garden of Eden in our past, Hobbes saw our original condition as a state of war with each person out for oneself. We extricate ourselves from this condition by agreeing to submit to a powerful, governmental authority, the supreme sovereign who will compel us to be peaceful. This agreement or the consent of the governed is the cornerstone of the contract theory of government. In this theory there are inducements on each side for participating in the agreement where the state gets our willingness to comply with its dictates in exchange for the benefits which we seek; in this case the primary benefit is peace. Hobbes locates this approach in a natural law of reason, which is a principle for the governance of conduct which all rational people can apprehend.

So that in the nature of man, we find three Principal causes of quarrel. First, competition; second, diffidence; thirdly, glory.

The first, maketh men invade for gain; the second, for safety; and the third, for reputation. The first use violence, to make themselves masters of other men's persons, wives, children, and cattle; the second, to defend them; the third, for trifles, as word, a smile, a different opinion, and any other sign of undervalue, either direct in their persons, or by reflection in their kindred, their friends, their nation, their profession, or their name.

Hereby it is that during the time men live without a common power to keep them all in awe, they are in that condition which is called war; and such a war, as is of every man, against every man. For war, consisteth not in battle only, or the act of fighting; but in a tract of time, wherein the will to contend by battle is sufficiently known: and therefore the notion of *time*, is to be considered to the nature of war; as it is in the nature of weather. For as the nature of foul weather, lieth not in a shower or two of rain; but in an inclination thereto of many days together: so the nature of war, consisteth not in actual fighting; but in the known disposition thereto, during all the time there is no assurance to the contrary. All other time is PEACE.

Whatsoever therefore is consequent to a time of war, where every man is enemy to every man; the same is consequent to the time, wherein men live without other security, than what their own strength, and their own invention shall furnish them withal. In such condition, there is no place for industry; because the fruit thereof is uncertain: and consequently no culture of the earth; no navigation, nor use of the commodities that may be imported by sea; no commodious building; no instruments of moving, and removing, such things as require much force; no knowledge of the face of the earth; no account of time; no arts; no letters; no society; and which is worst of all, continual fear, and danger of violent death; and the life of man, solitary, poor, nasty, brutish, and short. . . .

The RIGHT OF NATURE, which writers commonly call *jus naturale*, is the liberty each man hath, to use his own power, as he will himself, for the preservation of his own nature; that is to say, of his own life; and consequently, of doing anything, which in his own judgment, and reason, he shall conceive to be the aptest means thereunto. . . .

A LAW OF NATURE, *lex naturalis*, is a precept or general rule, found out by reason, by which a man is forbidden to do that, which is destructive of his life, or taketh away the means of preserving the same; and to omit that, by which he thinketh it may be best preserved.

From this fundamental law of nature, by which men are commanded to endeavour peace, is derived this second law; that a man be willing, when others are so too, as far forth, as for peace, and defence of himself he shall think it necessary, to lay down this right to all things; and be contented with so much liberty against other men, as he would allow other men against himself. . . .

The only way to erect such a common power, as may be able to defend them from the invasion of foreigners, and the injuries of one another, and thereby to secure them in such sort, as that by their own industry, and by the fruits of the earth, they may nourish themselves and live contentedly; is, to confer all their power and strength upon one man, or upon one assembly of men, that may reduce all their wills, by plurality of voices, unto one will: which is as much as to say, to appoint one man, or assembly of men, to bear their person; and every one to own, and acknowledge himself to be author of whatsoever he that so beareth their person, shall act, or cause to be acted, in those things which concern the common peace and safety; and therein to submit their wills, every one to his will, and their judgments, to his judgment. This is more than consent, or concord; it is a real unity of them all, in one and the same person, made by covenant of every man with every man, in such manner, as if every man should say to every man, *I authorize and give up my right of governing myself, to this man, or to this assembly of men, on this condition, that thou give up thy right to him, and authorize all his actions in like manner.* This done, the multitude so united in one person, is called a COMMONWEALTH, in Latin CIVITAS. This is the generation of that great LEVIATHAN, or rather, to speak more reverently, of that *mortal god,* to which we owe under the immortal *God,* our peace and defence. For by this authority, given him by every particular man in the commonwealth, he hath the use of so much power and strength conferred on him, that by terror thereof, he is enabled to perform the wills of them all, to peace at home, and mutual aid against their enemies abroad. And in him consisteth the essence of the commonwealth; which, to define it, is *one person, of whose acts a great multitude, by mutual covenants one with another, have made themselves every one the author, to the end he may use the strength and means of them all, as he shall think expedient, for their peace and common defence.*

And he that carrieth this person, is called SOVEREIGN, and said to have *sovereign power*; and every one besides, his SUBJECT.

From Thomas Hobbes, *Leviathan.*

JEAN-JACQUES ROUSSEAU

We Should Agree to Pool Our Individual Wills with the General Will

Jean-Jacques Rousseau (1712–1778) was a French political philosopher and novelist.

Jean-Jacques Rousseau envisioned our natural condition quite differently from Hobbes. In the state of nature before government and society we were free and equal and took from nature's bounty according to our needs. Life was "free, good, happy, and heathy." The introduction of property disrupted this condition, since it provided a means of measuring one person against another and ultimately of introducing inequality and struggle. Rousseau depicts early attempts to still the chaos with government as unsuccessful, since the laws merely made it legal for the powerful people with property to exploit the have-nots. Rousseau finds the solution in our agreeing to create a government, the General Will or Body Politic, which is the composite of all of our wills. Since each of our wills is an indistinguishable part of the Body Politic, we can each say that my will is the General Will. If so, then the government can never force me to do something against my will, since the government is nothing more than the General Will which is my will! Rousseau has thus resolved what he found to be the greatest paradox of his day. As he states it in the first sentence of his work, The Social Contract, "By nature all men are free yet everywhere they are in chains." We regain our freedom through the creation of the General Will. Rousseau finds a representative democracy to be no viable alternative if we wish to remain free and points to how the people of England are back in chains upon their election of a representative.

*N*on in depravatis, sed in his quae bene secundum naturam se habent considerandum est quid sit naturale. [We should consider what is natural not in things which are depraved but in those which are rightly ordered according to nature.] ARISTOTLE, *Politics*, Bk. i, ch. 2.

. . . [S]o many writers have hastily concluded that man is naturally cruel, and requires civil institutions to make him more mild; whereas nothing is more gentle than man in his primitive state, as he is placed by nature at an equal distance from the stupidity of brutes, and the fatal ingenuity of civilized man. Equally confined by instinct and reason to the sole care of guarding himself against the mischiefs which threaten him, he is restrained by natural compassion from doing any injury to others, and is not led to do such a thing even in return for injuries received. For, according to the axiom of the wise Locke, "There can be no injury, where there is no property."

So long as men remained content with their rustic huts, so long as they were satisfied with clothes made of the skins of animals and sewn together with thorns and fish-bones, adorned themselves only with feathers and shells, and continued to paint their bodies different colours, to improve and beautify their bows and arrows, and to make with sharp-edged stones fishing-boats or clumsy musical instruments; in a word, so long as they undertook only what a single person could accomplish, and confined themselves to such arts as did not require the joint labour of several hands, they lived free, healthy, honest, and happy lives, in so far as their nature allowed, and they continued to enjoy the pleasures of mutual and independent intercourse. But from the moment one man began to stand in need of the help of another; from the moment it appeared advantageous to any one man to have enough provisions for two, equality disappeared, property was introduced, work became indispensable, and vast forests became smiling fields, which man had to water with the sweat of his brow, and where slavery and misery were soon seen to germinate and grow up with the crops.

From Jean-Jacques Rousseau, *A Discourse on the Origin of Inequality*.

I suppose men to have reached the point at which the obstacles in the way of their preservation in the state of nature show their power of resistance to be greater than the resources at the disposal of each individual for his maintenance in that state. That primitive condition can then subsist no longer; and the human race would perish unless it changed its manner of existence.

But as men cannot engender new forces, but only unite and direct existing ones, they have no other means of preserving themselves than the formation, by aggregation, of a sum of forces great enough to overcome the resistance. These they have to bring into play by means of a single motive power, and cause to act in concert.

This sum of forces can arise only where several persons come together: but, as the force and liberty of each man are the chief instruments of his self-preservation, how can he pledge them without harming his own interests, and neglecting the care he owes to himself. This difficulty, in its bearing on my present subject, may be stated in the following terms: "The problem is to find a form of association which will defend and protect with the whole common force the person and goods of each associate, and in which each, while uniting himself with all, may still obey himself alone, and remain as free as before."

This is the fundamental problem of which the social contract provides the solution.

The clauses of this contract are so determined by the nature of the act that the slightest modification would make them vain and ineffective; so that, although they have perhaps never been formally set forth, they are everywhere the same and everywhere tacitly admitted and recognized, until, on the violation of the social compact, each regains his original rights and resumes his natural liberty, while losing the conventional liberty in favour of which he renounced it.

These clauses, properly understood, may be reduced to one—the total alienation of each associate, together with all his rights, to the whole community; for, in the first place, as each gives himself absolutely, the conditions are the same for all; and, this being so, no one has any interest in making them burdensome to others. . . .

If then we discard from the social compact what is not of its essence, we shall find that it reduces itself to the following terms:

> Each of us puts his person and all his power in common under the supreme direction of the general will, and, in our corporate capacity, we receive each member as an indivisible part of the whole.

At once, in place of the individual personality of each contracting party, this act of association creates a corporate and collective body, composed of as many members as the assembly contains voters, and receiving from this act its unity, its common identity, its life, and its will. This public person, so formed by the union of all other persons, formerly took the name of *city*, and now takes that of *Republic or body politic*; it is called by its members *State* when passive, *Sovereign* when active, and *Power* when compared with others like itself. Those who are associated in it take collectively the name of *people*, and severally are called *citizens*, as sharing in the sovereign authority, and *subjects*, as being under the laws of the State. But these terms are often confused and taken one for another: it is enough to know how to distinguish them when they are being used with precision.

From Jean-Jacques Rousseau, *The Social Contract*.

DAVID HUME
History Shows the Implausibility of a Social Contract

David Hume (1711–1776) was a Scottish empiricist and skeptic.

David Hume knew well the primary motifs of the contractarian thinkers of his time. The contractarians "deduced" human nature from their examination of how people would behave in the state of nature. They then showed the kind of government humans of this sort would agree to when entering into a social contract. In challenging the contractarian tradition, Hume alleges that the state of nature is a fiction: since we are social beings by nature, we could not have at any point been roaming freely and independently outside of some social unit. And Hume finds the notion of governments seeking the consent of its citizens for the authority to rule an absurdity. He invites contractarians to just look around them and observe how different the world really is. Rulers think in terms of owning their citizens as much as citizens naturally see themselves as their rulers' property.

This *poetical* fiction of the *golden age,* is in some respects, of a piece with the *philosophical* fiction of the *state of nature;* only that the former is represented as the most charming and most peaceable condition, which can possibly be imagined; whereas the latter is painted out as a state of mutual war and violence, attended with the most extreme necessity. On the first origin of mankind, we are told, their ignorance and savage nature were so prevalent, that they could give no mutual trust, but must each depend upon himself and his own force or cunning for protection and security. No law was heard of: No rule of justice known: No distinction of property regarded. Power was the only measure of right; and a perpetual war of all against all was the result of men's untamed selfishness and barbarity.

Whether such a condition of human nature could ever exist, or if it did, could continue so long as to merit the appellation of a *state,* may justly be doubted. Men are necessarily born in a family-society, at least; and are trained up by their parents to some rule of conduct and behaviour.

From David Hume, *An Enquiry Concerning the Principles of Morals.*

But philosophers . . . assert not only that government in its earliest infancy arose from consent, or rather the voluntary acquiescence of the people, but also that, even at present, when it has attained its full maturity, it rests on no other foundation. They affirm that all men are still born equal, and owe allegiance to no prince or government unless bound by the obligation and sanction of a *promise.* And as no man, without some equivalent, would forego the advantages of his native liberty and subject himself to the will of another, this promise is always understood to be conditional, and imposes on him no obligation, unless he meet with justice and protection from his sovereign. These advantages the sovereign promises him in return; and if he fail in the execution, he has broken on his part the articles of engagement, and has thereby freed his subject from all obligations to allegiance. Such, according to these philosophers, is the foundation of authority in every government, and such the right of resistance possessed by every subject.

But would these reasoners look abroad into the world, they would meet with nothing that in the least corresponds to their ideas, or can warrant so refined and philosophical a system. On the contrary, we find everywhere princes who claim their subjects as their property, and assert their independent right of sovereignty from conquest or succession. We find also everywhere subjects who acknowledge this right in their prince, and suppose themselves born under obligations of obedience to a certain sovereign, as much as under the ties of reverence and duty to certain parents, These connexions are always conceived to be equally independent of our consent, in Persia and China, in France and Spain, and even in Holland and England, wherever the doctrines above mentioned have not been carefully inculcated. Obedience or subjection becomes so familiar that most men never make any inquiry about its origin or cause, more than about the principle of gravity, resistance, or the most universal laws of nature. Or if curiosity ever move them, as soon as they learn that they themselves and their ancestors have, for several ages, or from time immemorial, been subject to such a form of government or such a family, they immediately acquiesce and acknowledge their obligation to allegiance. Were you to preach, in most parts of the world, that political connexions are founded altogether on voluntary consent or a mutual promise, the magistrate would soon imprison you as seditious for loosening the ties of obedience, if your friends did not before shut you up as delirious for advancing such absurdities. It is strange that an act of the mind, which every individual is supposed to have formed, and after he came to the use of reason too, otherwise it could have no authority—that this act, I say, should be so much unknown to all of them that over the face of the whole earth there scarcely remain any traces or memory of it.

From David Hume, "Of the Original Contract."

JOHN RAWLS

Consider What Principles People Would Agree to in an Initial Position

John Rawls (1921–) is an American political philosopher and liberal social theorist.

What if people were assembling to create a new government or to revise their current government. Think of them as being in an initial position where each person is equal in bargaining power, rational, and self-interested. Further, everyone is ignorant of their positions in the new society. John Rawls thinks that people would agree to two principles which emphasize liberty and equality in society. By thinking in these terms, Rawls preserves two essential components of classical contract theory. His initial position is a hypothetical state of nature and our agreement to the two principles is a social contract of a hypothetical nature. This contemporary contract theory is immune from Hume's criticisms which hinged on states of nature and social contracts being matters of fact. When Rawls asks "What if . . . ?" he deflates Hume's challenge of "That never happened."

My aim is to present a conception of justice which generalizes and carries to a higher level of abstraction the familiar theory of the social contract . . . . [T]he guiding idea is that the principles of justice for the basic structure of society are the object of the original agreement. They are the principles that free and rational persons concerned to further their own interests would accept in an initial position of equality. . . . [The principles] specify the ends of social cooperation that can be entered into and the forms of government that can be established. . . . [W]e are to imagine that those who engage in social cooperation choose together, in one joint act, the principles which are to assign basic rights and duties and to determine the division of social benefits. . . . Just as each person must decide by rational reflection what constitutes his good . . . so a group of persons must decide once and for all what is to count among them as just and unjust. . . . [The original position] is understood as a purely hypothetical situation characterized so as to lead to a certain conception of justice. Among the essential features of this situation is that no one knows his place in society, his class position or social status, nor does any one know his fortune in the distribution of natural assets and abilities, his intelligence, strength, and the like. I shall even assume that the parties do not know their conceptions of the good. . . . The principles of justice are chosen from behind a veil of ignorance. This ensures that no one is advantaged or disadvantaged in the choice of principles by the outcome of natural chance or the contingency of social circumstances. Since all are similarly situated and no one is able to design principles to favor his particular situation, the principles of justice are the result of a fair agreement or bargain. . . .

I shall now state in a provisional form the two principles of justice that I believe would be chosen in the original position. . . .

First: each person is to have an equal right to the most extensive basic liberty compatible with a similar liberty for others.

Second: social and economic inequalities are to be arranged so that they are both (a) reasonably expected to be to everyone's advantage, and (b) attached to positions and offices open to all. . . . The basic liberties of citizens are, roughly speaking, political liberty (the right to vote and to be eligible for public office) together with freedom of speech and assembly; liberty of conscience and freedom of thought; freedom of the person along with the right to hold (personal) property; and freedom from arbitrary arrest and seizure as defined by the concept of the rule of law. These liberties are all required to be equal by the first principle, since citizens of a just society are to have the same basic rights. The second principle applies, in the first approximation, to the distribution of income and wealth and to the design of organizations that make use of differences in authority and responsibility. . . . While the distribution of wealth and income need not be equal, it must be to everyone's advantage, and at the same time, positions of authority and offices of command must be accessible to all (who are qualified) the first principle (is) prior to the second. . . . The distribution of wealth and income, and the hierarchies of authority, must be consistent with both the liberties of equal citizenship and equality of opportunity.

From John Rawls, *A Theory of Justice.*

THOMAS JEFFERSON

Each Generation Makes Its Own Government

Thomas Jefferson (1743–1826) was an American statesman, president, and political philosopher.

An obvious difficulty plagued classical contract theory. Suppose we do create a government which is based on the consent of the governed. The citizens have entered into a social contract which is the foundation for the government's legitimacy. Now look down the road one generation. No one here participated in striking this bargain, so the government is no longer legitimate. John Locke was aware of the problem and addressed it with his doctrine of tacit consent, the idea that people in subsequent generations in effect give consent by remaining and enjoying the benefits which the government offers. Rawls avoids the problem by locating the essence of the social contract in what people would do. In the following passage, Thomas Jefferson renders the problem moot by insisting that each generation consider what it is that it wants from government to secure its happiness.

Let us . . . not weakly believe that one generation is not as capable as another of taking care of itself, and of ordering its own affairs. Let us avail ourselves of our reason and experience, to correct the crude essays of our first and unexperienced, although wise, virtuous, and well-meaning councils. And lastly, let us provide in our constitution for its revision at stated periods. What these periods should be, nature herself indicates. By the European tables of mortality, of the adults living at any one moment of time, a majority will be dead in about nineteen years. At the end of that period, then, a new majority is come into place; or, in other words, a new generation. Each generation is as independent of the one preceding as that was of all which had gone before. It has, then, like them, a right to choose for itself the form of government it believes most promotive of its own happiness; consequently, to accommodate to the circumstances in which it finds itself, that received from its predecessors; and it is for the peace and good of mankind, that a solemn opportunity of doing this every nineteen or twenty years, should be provided by the constitution; so that it may be handed on, with periodical repairs, from generation to generation, to the end of time, if anything human can so long endure. It is now forty years since the constitution of Virginia was formed. The same tables inform us that, within that period, two-thirds of the adults then living are now dead. Have, then, the remaining third, even if they had the wish, the right to hold in obedience to their will, and to the laws heretofore made by them, the other two-thirds, who, with themselves, compose the present mass of adults? If they have not, who has? The dead? But the dead have no rights. They are nothing and nothing cannot own something. Where there is no substance, there can be no accident. This corporeal globe, and everything upon it, belong to its present corporeal inhabitants, during their generation. They alone have a right to direct what is the concern of themselves alone, and to declare the law of that direction; and this declaration can only be made by their majority.

From Thomas Jefferson: *The Wisdom of Thomas Jefferson.*

EDMUND BURKE

The State Is a Contract of a Very Special Sort

Edmund Burke (1729–1797) was a conservative Irish political author.

Edmund Burke argues for our thinking of the state as a contract while distancing himself from the contractarians. They have us think in base terms of trade and exchange for security that people, the contracting parties, are seeking at any given point in time. We trade liberty for peace as we trade coffee for pepper. Burke injects the conservative's commitment to tradition and aversion to innovation into his elevated notion of the state as contract. In this conception the state is an entity which endures and is all-embracing of human endeavor. We are partners with people of the past and future who have contributed and who will contribute to the continuity and vitality of this spiritual entity which transcends the passing urgings of any particular population.

Government is not made in virtue of natural rights, which may and do exist in total independence of it, and exist in much greater clearness and in a much greater degree of abstract perfection; but their abstract perfection is their practical defect. By having a right to everything they want everything. Government is a contrivance of human wisdom to provide for human *wants*. Men have a right that these wants should be provided for by this wisdom. Among these wants is to be reckoned the want, out of civil society, of a sufficient restraint upon their passions. Society requires not only that the passions of individuals should be subjected, but that even in the mass and body, as well as in the individuals, the inclinations of men should frequently be thwarted, their will controlled, and their passions brought into subjection. This can only be done *by a power out of themselves*, and not, in the exercise of its function, subject to that will and to those passions which it is its office to bridle and subdue. In this sense the restraints on men, as well as their liberties, are to be reckoned among their rights. But as the liberties and the restrictions vary with times and circumstances and admit to infinite modifications, they cannot be settled upon any abstract rule; and nothing is so foolish as to discuss them upon that principle. . . .

The science of government being therefore so practical in itself and intended for such practical purposes—a matter which requires experience, and even more experience than any person can gain in his whole life, however sagacious and observing he may be—it is with infinite caution that any man ought to venture upon pulling down an edifice which has answered in any tolerable degree for ages the common purposes of society, or on building it up again without having models and patterns of approved utility before his eyes. . . . To avoid, therefore, the evils of inconstancy and versatility, ten thousand times worse than those of obstinacy and the blindest prejudice, we have consecrated the state, that no man should approach to look into its defects or corruptions but with due caution, that he should never dream of beginning its reformation by its subversion, that he should approach to the faults of the state as to the wounds of a father, with pious awe and trembling solicitude. By this wise prejudice we are taught to look with horror on those children of their country who are prompt rashly to hack that aged parent in pieces and put him into the kettle of magicians, in hopes that by their poisonous weeds and wild incantations they may regenerate the paternal constitution and renovate their father's life.

SOCIETY is indeed a contract. Subordinate contracts for objects of mere occasional interest may be dissolved at pleasure—but the state ought not to be considered as nothing better than a partnership agreement in a trade of pepper and coffee, calico, or tobacco, or some other such low concern, to be taken up for a little temporary interest, and to be dissolved by the fancy of the parties. It is to be looked on with other reverence, because it is not a partnership in things subservient only to the gross animal existence of a temporary and perishable nature. It is a partnership in all science; a partnership in all art; a partnership in every virtue and in all perfection. As the ends of such a partnership cannot be obtained in many generations, it becomes a partnership not only between those who are living, but between those who are living, those who are dead, and those who are to be born. Each contract of each particular state is but a clause in the great primeval contract of eternal society, linking the lower with the higher natures, connecting the visible and invisible world, according to a fixed compact sanctioned by the inviolable oath which holds all physical and all moral natures, each in their appointed place. This law is not subject to the will of those who by an obligation above them, and infinitely superior, are bound to submit their will to that law. The municipal corporations of that universal kingdom are not morally at liberty at their pleasure, and on their speculations of a contingent improvement, wholly to separate and tear asunder the bands of their subordinate community and to dissolve it into an unsocial, uncivil, unconnected chaos of elementary principles. It is the first and supreme necessity only, a necessity that is not chosen but chooses, a necessity paramount to deliberation, that admits no discussion and demands no evidence, which alone can justify a resort to anarchy. This necessity is no exception to the rule, because this necessity itself is a part, too, of that moral and physical disposition of things to which man must be obedient by consent or force; but if that which is only submission to necessity should be made the object of choice, the law is broken, nature is disobeyed, and the rebellious are outlawed, cast forth, and exiled from this world of reason, and order, and peace, and virtue, and fruitful penitence, into the antagonist world of madness, discord, vice, confusion, and unavailing sorrow.

From Edmund Burke, *Reflections on the Revolution in France.*

JOHN STUART MILL

Government Should Not Interfere with Self-Government Unless there Is Harm to Other People

John Stuart Mill (1806–1873) was a British economist, utilitarian and social philosopher.

John Stuart Mill's thesis of liberalism justifies the restriction of individual liberty to prevent harm to other people. Mill cites a few exceptions like children and "barbarians" whose liberty we can curtail in the name of promoting their own good, but believes that rational adults in general should be free to pursue their own ends even if they risk harm by so doing. As individuals find the activities that best promote their personal happiness, the overall happiness of the society will be maximized.

The object of this essay is to assert one very simple principle, as entitled to govern absolutely the dealings of society with the individual in the way of compulsion and control whether the means used be physical force in the form of legal penalties, or the moral coercion of public opinion. That principle is, that the sole end for which mankind are warranted, individually or collectively, in interfering with the liberty of action of any member of the civilized community, against his will, is to prevent harm to others. His own good, either physical or moral, is not a sufficient warrant. He cannot rightfully be compelled to do or forbear because it would be better for him to do so, because it would make him happier, because, in the opinions of others, to do so would be wise, or even right. These are good reasons for remonstrating with him, or reasoning with him, or persuading him, or entreating him, but not for compelling him, or visiting him with any evil in case he do otherwise. To justify that, the conduct from which it is desired to deter him must be calculated to produce evil to someone else. The only part of the conduct of anyone, for which he is amenable to society, is that which concerns others. In the part which merely concerns himself, his independence is, of right, absolute. Over himself, over his own body and mind, the individual is sovereign.

It is perhaps hardly necessary to say that this doctrine is meant only to apply to human beings in the maturity of their faculties. We are not speaking of children, or of young persons below the age which the law may fix as that of manhood or womanhood. Those who are still in a state to require being taken care of by others, must be protected against their own actions as well as against external injury. For the same reason, we may leave out of consideration those backward states of society in which the race itself may be considered as in its nonage. The early difficulties in the way of spontaneous progress are so great, and there is seldom any choice of means for overcoming them; and a ruler full of the spirit of improvement is warranted in the use of any expedients that will attain an end, perhaps otherwise unattainable. Despotism is a legitimate mode of government in dealing with barbarians, provided the end be their improvement, and the means justified by actually effecting that end. Liberty, as a principle, has no application to any state of things anterior to the time when mankind have become capable of being improved by free and equal discussion. Until then, there is nothing for them but implicit obedience to an Akbar or a Charlemagne, if they are so fortunate as to find one. But as soon as mankind have attained the capacity of being guided to their own improvement by conviction or persuasion (a period long since reached in all nations with whom we need here concern ourselves), compulsion, either in the direct form or in that of pains and penalties for non-compliance, is no longer admissible as a means to their own good and justifiable only for the security of others.

From John Stuart Mill, *On Liberty*.

KARL MARX AND FRIEDRICH ENGELS

Workers of the World Unite!

Karl Marx (1818–1883) was a German-born social theorist whose work provided the foundation for modern socialism.

Friedrich Engels (1820–1895), born in Germany, was a political theorist who worked with Karl Marx to develop the theory of Communism.

Karl Marx calls into question much traditional wisdom about the nature of work: Work, says Marx, is not a punishment for our having fallen from grace, but meaningful work is what gratifies us as socially productive beings. Government is the instrument by which the economically advantaged further their interests; political theory merely offers apologies for these exploitative regimes after they have formed. And we do not move from some state of nature to government to solve our woes; rather government has been the cause of our woes, and we should seek to organize society without government. Marx believes class struggle has defined human history. One group always secures what is important to have in its economic system—property, capital, wampum—and uses government to further its interests and exploit people with meager resources. The underclass eventually revolts, takes control, and class struggle begins anew. Marx offers an alternative to the class struggle which he has diagnosed in the human history: the elimination of private property. Without property, there are no classes. Without classes, there is no class struggle or revolution and the accompanying misery. And without classes, there is no need for government which was merely a tool of the ruling class. Marx presents many of these ideas both in his own writings and in the manifesto which he co-authored with Friedrich Engels.

In political economy this realization of labour appears as a loss of reality for the worker, objectification as a loss of the object or slavery to it, and appropriation as alienation, as externalization. . . . The appropriation of the object appears as alienation to such an extent that the more objects the worker produces, the less he can possess and the more he falls under the domination of his product, capital. All of these consequences follow from the fact that the worker relates to the product of his labour as to an alien object. For it is evident from this presupposition that the more the worker externalizes himself in his work, the more powerful becomes the alien, objective world that he creates opposite himself, the poorer he becomes himself in his inner life and the less he can call his own. . . . We have treated the act of alienation of practical human activity, labour, from two aspects. (1) The relationship of the worker to the product of his labour as an alien object that has power over him. This relationship is the relationship of the worker to his own activity as something that is alien and does not belong to him; it is activity that is passivity, power that is weakness, procreation that is castration, the worker's own physical and intellectual energy, his personal life (for what is life except activity?) as an activity directed against himself, independent of him and not belonging to him. It is self-alienation, as above it was alienation of the object . . . alienated labour . . . alienates from man his own body, nature exterior to him, and his intellectual being, his human essence.

From "Economic and Philosophical Manuscripts."

The history of all hitherto existing society is the history of class struggles. Freeman and slave, patrician and plebeian, lord and serf, guild-master and journeyman, in a word, oppressor and oppressed stood in constant opposition to one another, carried on an uninterrupted now hidden, now open fight, a fight that each time ended, either in a revolutionary reconstitution of society at large, or in the common ruin of the contending classes.

In the earlier epochs of history, we find almost everywhere a complicated arrangement of society into various orders, a manifold gradation of social rank. In ancient Rome we have patricians, knights, plebeians, slaves; in the Middle Ages, feudal lords, vassals, guild-masters, journeymen, apprentices, serfs, in almost all of these classes, again, subordinate gradations.

The modern bourgeois society that has sprouted from the ruins of feudal society has not done away with class antagonisms. It has but established new classes, new conditions of oppression, new forms of struggle in place of the old ones.

Our epoch, the epoch of the bourgeoisie, possesses, however, this distinctive feature: it has simplified the class antagonisms. Society as a whole is more and more splitting up into two great hostile camps, into two great classes directly facing each other: Bourgeoisie and Proletariat. . . .

Owing to the extensive use of machinery and to division of labour, the work of the proletarians has lost all individual character, and consequently, all charm for the workman. He becomes an appendage of the machine, and it is only the most simple, most monotonous, and most easily acquired knack, that is required of him. . . .

The bourgeoisie has stripped of its halo every occupation hitherto honoured and looked up to with reverent awe. It has converted the physician, the lawyer, the priest, the poet, the man of science, into its paid wage-labourers.

The bourgeoisie has torn away from the family its sentimental veil, and has reduced the family relation to a mere money relation. . . .

The distinguishing feature of Communism is not the abolition of property generally, but the abolition of bourgeois property. But modern bourgeois private property is the final and most complete expression of the system of producing and appropriating products, that is based on class antagonisms, on the exploitation of the many by the few.

In this sense, the theory of the Communists may be summed up in the single sentence: Abolition of private property. . . .

In short, the Communists everywhere support every revolutionary movement against the existing social and political order of things. In all these movements they bring to the front, as the leading question in each, the property question no matter what its degree of development at the time. Finally, they labour everywhere for the union and agreement of the democratic parties of all countries. The Communists disdain to conceal their views and aims. They openly declare that their ends can be attained only by the forcible overthrow of all existing social conditions. Let the ruling classes tremble at a *Communistic* revolution, the proletarians have nothing to lose but their chains. They have a world to win.

WORKING MEN OF ALL COUNTRIES, UNITE!

From Karl Marx and Friedrich Engels, *The Communist Manifesto*

EDWARD BELLAMY
Here Is How a Marxist Society Works

Edward Bellamy (1850–1898) was an American writer and social critic.

Edward Bellamy's Looking Backward *was a best-selling novel at the turn of the century and paints a utopia with distinctively Marxist colors. The premise is that a man falls asleep in 1887 in a society which was plagued by greedy, capitalistic entrepreneurs exploiting the working class. He wakes up in 2000 and steps into the utopia. Bellamy dedicated most of the book to showing the newcomer, who represents the reader, the features of this well-run society. The following passage illustrates how this society conceives work.*

Few, ESPECIALLY among the younger readers of this book, will realize that Edward Bellamy's *Looking Backwards* is one of the most remarkable books ever published in America. First of all in terms of its popularity—after *Uncle Tom's Cabin* and *Ben-Hur,* it was the most popular book at the turn of the century, printed in many millions of copies in the United States, translated into over twenty languages. But the fact that it was one of the three greatest bestsellers in itself means little in comparison with the intellectual and emotional influence this book had, following its publication in 1888. It stimulated utopian thinking to such in extent that from 1889 to 1900 forty-six other utopian novels were published in the United States and quite a few others in Europe. Three outstanding personalities, Charles Beard, John Dewey, Edward Weeks, independently making a list of the twenty-five most influential books published since 1885, all put Bellamy's work in the second place, Karl Marx's *Das Kapital* being the first.

> Foreword by Erich Fromm in Edward Bellamy, *Looking Backward.*

The waiter, a fine-looking young fellow, wearing a slightly distinctive uniform, now made his appearance. I observed him closely, as it was the first time I had been able to study particularly the bearing of one of the enlisted members of the industrial army. This young man, I knew from what I had been told, must be highly educated, and the equal, socially and in all respects, of those he served. But it was perfectly evident that to neither side was the stipulation in the slightest degree embarrassing. Doctor Leete addressed the young man in a tone devoid, of course, as any gentleman's would be, of superciliousness, but at the same time not in any way deprecatory, while the manner of the young man was simply that of a person intent on discharging correctly the task he was engaged in, equally without familiarity or obsequiousness. It was, in fact, the manner of a soldier on duty, but without the military stiffness. As the youth left the room, I said, "I cannot get over my wonder at seeing a young man like that serving so contentedly in a menial position."

"What is that word 'menial'? I never heard of it," said Edith.

"It is obsolete now," remarked her father. "If I understand it rightly, it applied to persons who performed particularly disagreeable and unpleasant tasks for others, and carried with it an implication of contempt. Was it not so, Mr. West?"

"That is about it," I said. "Personal service, such as waiting on tables, was considered menial, and held in such contempt, in my day, that persons of culture and refinement would suffer hardship before condescending to it."

"What a strangely artificial idea," exclaimed Mrs. Leete, wonderingly.

"And yet these services had to be rendered," said Edith.

"Of course," I replied. "But we imposed them on the poor, and those who had no alternative but starvation."

"And increased the burden you imposed on them by adding your contempt," remarked Doctor Leete.

"I don't think I clearly understand," said Edith. "Do you mean that you permitted people to do things for you which you despised them for doing, or that you accepted services from them which you would have been unwilling to render them? You can't surely mean that, Mr. West?"

I was obliged to tell her that the fact was just as she had stated. Doctor Leete, however, came to my relief.

"To understand why Edith is surprised," he said, "You must know that nowadays it is an axiom of ethics that to accept a service from another which we would be unwilling, to return in kind, if need were, is like borrowing with the intention of not repaying, while to enforce such a service by taking advantage of the poverty of necessity of a person would be an outrage like forcible robbery. It is the worst thing about any system which divides men, or allows them to be divided, into classes and castes, that it weakens the sense of a common humanity. Unequal distribution of wealth, and, still more effectually, unequal opportunities of education and culture, divided society in your day into classes which in many respects regarded each other as distinct races. There is not, after all, such a difference as might appear between our ways of looking at this question of service. Ladies and gentlemen of the cultured class in your day would no more have permitted persons of their own class to render them services they would scorn to return than we would permit anybody to do so. The poor and the uncultured, however, they looked upon as of another kind from themselves. The equal wealth and equal opportunities of culture which all persons now enjoy have simply made us all members of one class, which corresponds to the most fortunate class with you. Until this equality of condition had come to pass, the idea of the solidarity of humanity, the brotherhood of all men, could never have become the real conviction and practical principle of action it is nowadays. In your day the same phrases were indeed used, but they were phrases merely."

"Do the waiters, also, volunteer?"

"No," replied Doctor Leete. "The waiters are young men in the unclassified grade of the industrial army who are assignable to all sorts of miscellaneous occupations not requiring special skill. Waiting on table is one of these, and every young recruit is given a taste of it. I myself served as a waiter for several months in this very dining house some forty years ago. Once more you must remember that there is recognized no sort of difference between the dignity of the different sorts of work required by the nation. The individual is never regarded, nor regards himself, as the servant of those he serves, nor is he in any way dependent upon them. It is always the nation which he is serving. No difference is recognized between a waiter's functions and those of any other worker. The fact that his is a personal service is indifferent from our point of view. So is a doctor's. I should as soon expect our waiter today to look down on me because I served him as a doctor, as think of looking down on him because he serves me as a waiter."

After dinner my entertainers conducted me about the building, of which the extent, the magnificent architecture and richness of embellishment, astonished me. It seemed that it was not merely a dining hall, but likewise a great pleasure house and social rendezvous of the quarter and no appliance of entertainment of recreation seemed lacking.

"You find illustrated here," said Doctor Leete, when I had expressed my admiration, "what I said to you in our first conversation, when you were looking out over the city, as to the splendor of our public and common life as compared with the simplicity of our private and home life, and the contrast which, in this respect, the twentieth bears to, the nineteenth century. To save ourselves useless burdens, we have as little gear about us at home as is consistent with comfort, but the social side of our life is ornate and luxurious beyond anything the world ever knew before. All the industrial and professional guilds have clubhouses as extensive as this, as well as country, mountain, and seaside houses for sport and rest in vacations."

From Edward Bellamy, *Looking Backward*.

ROBERT PAUL WOLFF

Create a Society with No Government

Robert Paul Wolff (1933–) is an American political philosopher.

Anarchism is the doctrine that calls for the abolition of government and elevates each person to the level of ruler of his or her own affairs. Robert Paul Wolff argues in favor of anarchism by pointing to the incompatibility of self-governance or autonomy with government. He suggests that our moral development is stunted when we submit to the authority of government and likens us to children who do as they are told.

If autonomy and authority are genuinely incompatible, only two courses are open to us. Either we must embrace philosophical anarchism and treat *all* governments as non-legitimate bodies whose commands must be judged and evaluated in each instance before they are obeyed; or else, we must give up as quixotic the pursuit of autonomy in the political realm and submit ourselves (by an implicit promise) to whatever form of government appears most just and beneficent at the moment. (I cannot resist repeating yet again that if we take this course, *there is no universal or* a priori reason for binding ourselves to a democratic government rather than to any other sort. In some situations, it may be wiser to swear allegiance to a benevolent and efficient dictatorship than to a democracy which imposes a tyrannical majority on a defenseless minority. *And in those cases where we have sworn to obey the rule of the majority, no additional binding force will exist beyond what would be present had we promised our allegiance to a king!*)

It is out of the question to give up the commitment to moral autonomy. Men are no better than children if they not only accept the rule of others from force of necessity, but embrace it willingly and forfeit their duty unceasingly to weigh the merits of the actions which they perform. When I place myself in the hands of another, and permit him to determine the principles by which I shall guide my behavior, I repudiate the freedom and reason which give me dignity. I am then guilty of what Kant might have called the sin of willful heteronomy. There would appear to be no alternative but to embrace the doctrine of anarchism and categorically deny *any* claim to legitimate authority by one man over another.

From Robert Paul Wolff, *In Defense of Anarchism.*

SIGMUND FREUD
War Is Not Inevitable

Sigmund Freud (1856–1939), a neurologist and psychologist, was born in Morovia and was the founder of psychoanalysis.

Albert Einstein wrote Sigmund Freud asking what he thought about war and humanity's future. Freud connects war with an aggressive component of our nature but denies that it is inevitable. Culture is the force which can elevate people to a peaceful condition.

Vienna, September, 1932

Dear Professor Einstein,

When I heard that you intended to invite me to an exchange of views on some subject that interested you and that seemed to deserve the interest of others besides yourself, I readily agreed. I expected you to choose a problem on the frontiers of what is knowable to-day, a problem to which each of us, a physicist and a psychologist, might have our own particular angle of approach and where we might come together from different directions upon the same ground. You have taken me by surprise, however, by posing the question of what can be done to protect mankind from the curse of war. . . .

You express astonishment at the fact that it is so easy to make men enthusiastic about a war and add your suspicion that there is something at work in them—an instinct for hatred and destruction—which goes halfway to meet the efforts of the warmongers. Once again, I can only express my entire agreement. We believe in the existence of an instinct of that kind and have in fact been occupied during the last few years in studying its manifestations. Will you allow me to take this opportunity of putting before you a portion of the theory of the instincts which, after much tentative groping and many fluctuations of opinion, has been reached by workers in the field of psychoanalysis?

According to our hypothesis human instincts are of only two kinds: those which seek to preserve and unite—which we call "erotic," exactly in the sense in which Plato uses the word "Eros" in his *Symposium*, or "sexual," with a deliberate extension of the popular conception of "sexuality"—and those which seek to destroy and kill and which we class together as the aggressive or destructive instinct. As you see, this is in fact no more than a theoretical clarification of the universally familiar opposition between Love and Hate which may perhaps have some fundamental relation to the polarity of attraction and repulsion that plays a part in your own field of knowledge. We must not be too hasty in introducing ethical judgements of good and evil. Neither of these instincts is any less essential than the other; the phenomena of life arise from the operation of both together, whether acting in concert or in opposition. It seems as though an instinct of the one sort can scarcely ever operate in isolation; it is always accompanied—or, as we say, alloyed—with an element from the other side, which modifies its aim or is, in some cases, what enables it to achieve that aim. Thus, for instance, the instinct of self-preservation is certainly of an erotic kind, but it must nevertheless have aggressiveness at its disposal if it is to fulfil its purpose. So, too, the instinct of love, when it is directed towards an object, stands in need of some contribution from the instinct of mastery if it is in any way to possess that object. The difficulty of isolating the two classes of instinct in their actual manifestations is indeed what has so long prevented us from recognizing them. . . .

For our immediate purpose then, this much follows from what has been said: there is no use in trying to get rid of men's aggressive inclinations. We are told that in certain happy regions of the earth, where nature provides in abundance everything that man requires, there are races whose life is passed in tranquillity and who know neither compulsion nor aggressiveness. I can scarcely believe it and I should be glad to hear more of these fortunate beings. The Russian Communists, too, hope to be able to cause human aggressiveness to disappear by guaranteeing the satisfaction of all material needs and by establishing equality in other respects among all the members of the community. That, in my opinion, is an illusion. They themselves are armed to-day with the most scrupulous care and not the least important of the methods by which they keep their supporters together is hatred of everyone beyond their frontiers. In any case, as you yourself have remarked, there is no question of getting rid entirely of human aggressive impulses; it is enough to try to divert them to such an extent that they need not find expression in war. . . .

My belief is this. For incalculable ages mankind has been passing through a process of evolution of culture. (Some people, I know, prefer to use the term "civilization.") We owe to that process the best of what we have become, as well as a good part of what we suffer from. Though its causes and beginnings are obscure and its outcome uncertain, some of its characteristics are easy to perceive. It may perhaps be leading to the extinction of the human race, for in more than one way it impairs the sexual function; uncultivated races and backward strata of the population are already multiplying more rapidly than highly cultivated ones. The process is perhaps comparable to the domestication of certain species of animals and it is undoubtedly accompanied by physical alterations; but we are still unfamiliar with the notion that the evolution of culture is an organic process of this kind. The psychical modifications that go along with the cultural process are striking and unambiguous. They consist in a progressive displacement of instinctual aims and a restriction of instinctual impulses. Sensations which were pleasurable to our ancestors have become indifferent or even intolerable to ourselves; there are organic grounds for the changes in our ethical and aesthetic ideals. Of the psychological characteristics of culture two appear to be the most important: a strengthening of the intellect, which is beginning to govern instinctual life, and an internalization of the aggressive impulses, with all its consequent advantages and perils. Now war is in the crassest opposition to the psychical attitude imposed on us by the cultural process, and for that reason we are bound to rebel against it; we simply cannot any longer put up with it. This is not merely an intellectual and emotional repudiation; we pacifists have a constitutional intolerance of war, an idiosyncracy magnified, as it were, to the highest degree. It seems, indeed, as though the lowering of aesthetic standards in war plays a scarcely smaller part in our rebellion than do its cruelties. And how long shall we have to wait before the rest of mankind become pacifists too? There is no telling. But it may not be Utopian to hope that these two factors, the cultural attitude and the justified dread of the consequences of a future war, may result within a measurable time in putting an end to the waging of war. By what paths or by what side-tracks this will come about we cannot guess. But one thing we can say: whatever fosters the growth of culture works at the same time against war.

I trust you will forgive me if what I have said has disappointed you, and I remain, with kindest regards,

Yours sincerely,
SIGM. FREUD

From Sigmund Freud, *Sigmund Freud: Collected Papers*.

BLACK ELK

Smoke the Peace Pipe to Bring Good Among People

Black Elk (18?–19?), second cousin to Crazy Horse, was a Holy Man of the Ogala Sioux.

Black Elk explains what different parts of the peace pipe signify in a world view which highlights the interconnectedness of people and nature. He begins to smoke the pipe to signal the Great Spirit of the ceremony and invites the participants to partake to promote good among them. This ceremony suggests that peaceful relations develop as we collectively reflect on our place in the larger scheme of things.

BLACK ELK SPEAKS
Being the Life Story of a Holy Man of the Oglala Sioux
as told through JOHN G. NEIHARDT *(Flaming Rainbow)*

See, I fill this sacred pipe with the bark of the red willow; but before we smoke it, you must see how it is made and what it means. These four ribbons hanging here on the stem are the four quarters of the universe. The black one is for the west where the thunder beings live to send us rain; the white one for the north, whence comes the great white cleansing wind; the red one for the east, whence springs the light and where the morning star lives to give men wisdom; the yellow for the south, whence come the summer and the power to grow.

But these four spirits are only one Spirit after all, and this eagle feather here is for that One, which is like a father, and also it is for the thoughts of men that should rise high as eagles do. Is not the sky a father and the earth a mother, and are not all living things with feet or wings or roots their children? And this hide upon the mouthpiece here, which should be bison hide, is for the earth, from whence we came and at whose breast we suck as babies all our lives, along with all the animals and birds and trees and grasses. And because it means all this, and more than any man can understand, the pipe is holy.

There is a story about the way the pipe first came to us. A very long time ago, they say, two scouts were out looking for bison; and when they came to the top of a high hill and looked north, they saw something coming a long way off, and when it came closer they cried out, "It is a woman!" and it was. Then one of the scouts, being foolish, had bad thoughts and spoke them; but the other said: "That is a sacred woman; throw all bad thoughts away." When she came still closer, they saw that she wore a fine white buckskin dress, that her hair was very long and that she was young and very beautiful. And she knew their thoughts and said in a voice that was like singing: "You do not know me, but if you want to do as you think, you may come." And the foolish one went; but just as he stood before her, there was a white cloud that came and covered them. And the beautiful young woman came out of the cloud. and when it blew away the foolish man was a skeleton covered with worms. Then the woman spoke to the one who was not foolish: "You shall go home and tell your people that I am coming and that a big tepee shall be built for me in the center of the nation." And the man, who was very much afraid, went quickly and told the people, who did at once as they were told; and there around the big tepee they waited for the sacred woman. And after a while she came, very beautiful and singing, and as she went into the tepee this is what she sang:

> With visible breath I am walking.
> A voice I am sending as I walk.
> In a sacred manner I am walking.
> With visible tracks I am walking.
> In a sacred manner I walk.

And as she sang, there came from her mouth a white cloud that was good to smell. Then she gave something to the chief, and it was a pipe with a bison calf carved on one side to mean the earth that bears and feeds us, and with twelve eagle feathers hanging from the stem to mean the sky and the twelve moons, and these were tied with a grass that never breaks. "Behold!" she said. "With this you shall multiply and be a good nation. Nothing but good shall come from it. Only the hands of the good shall take care of it and the bad shall not even see it." Then she sang again and went out of the tepee; and as the people watched her going, suddenly it was a white bison galloping away and snorting, and soon it was gone.

This they tell, and whether it happened so or not I do not know; but if you think about it, you can see that it is true.

Now I light the pipe, and after I have offered it to the powers that are one Power, and sent forth a voice to them, we shall smoke together. Offering the mouthpiece first of all to the One above—so—send a voice: Hey hey! hey hey! hey hey! hey hey! Grandfather, Great Spirit, you have been always, and before you no one has been. There is no other one to pray to but you. You yourself, everything that you see, everything has been made by you. The star nations all over the universe you have finished. The four quarters of the earth you have finished. The day, and in that day, everything you have finished. Grandfather Great Spirit, lean close to the earth that you may hear the voice I send. You towards where the sun goes down, behold me; Thunder Beings, behold me! You where the White Giant lives in power, behold me! You where the sun shines continually, whence come the day-break star and the day, behold me! You where the summer lives, behold me! You in the depths of the heavens, an eagle of power, behold! And you, Mother Earth, the only Mother, you who have shown mercy to your children! Hear me, four quarters of the world—a relative I am! Give me the strength to walk the soft earth, a relative to all that is! Give me the eyes to see and the strength to understand, that I may be like you. With your power only can I face the winds. Great Spirit, Great Spirit, my Grandfather, all over the earth the faces of living things are all alike. With tenderness have these come up out of the ground. Look upon these faces of children without number and with children in their arms, that they may face the winds and walk the good road to the day of quiet. This is my prayer; hear me! The voice I have sent is weak, yet with earnestness I have sent it. Hear me! It is finished. Hetchetu aloh!

Now, my friend, let us smoke together so that there may be only good between us.

From *Black Elk Speaks*, as told through John G. Niehardt.

ROBERT NOZICK

Some Governmental Constraints on Aggressive Behavior Are Justifiable

Robert Nozick (1938–) is an American philosopher and libertarian social theorist.

In developing his theory of the state, Robert Nozick considers what constraints on people's physical aggression are justifiable. He explores this issue by examining constraints on our treatment of animals.

A nonaggression principle is often held to be an appropriate principle to govern relations among nations. What difference is there supposed to be between sovereign individuals and sovereign nations that makes aggression permissible among individuals? Why may individuals jointly, through their government, do to someone what no nation may do to another? If anything, there is a stronger case for nonaggression among individuals; unlike nations, they do not contain as parts individuals that others legitimately might intervene to protect or defend. . . .

CONSTRAINTS AND ANIMALS

We can illuminate the status and implications of moral side constraints by considering living beings for whom such stringent side constraints (or any at all) usually are not considered appropriate: namely, nonhuman animals. Are there any limits to what we may do to animals? Have animals the moral status of mere *objects*? Do some purposes fail to entitle us to impose great costs on animals? What entitles us to use them at all?

Animals count for something. Some higher animals, at least, ought to be given some weight in people's deliberations about what to do. It is difficult to prove this. (It is also difficult to prove that people count for something!) We first shall adduce particular examples, and then arguments. If you felt like snapping your fingers, perhaps to the beat of some music, and you knew that by some strange causal connection your snapping your fingers would cause 10,000 contented, unowned cows to die after great pain and suffering, or even painlessly and

335

instantaneously, would it be perfectly all right to snap your fingers? Is there some reason why it would be morally wrong to do so?

Some say people should not do so because such acts brutalize them and make them more likely to take the lives *of persons,* solely for pleasure. These acts that are morally unobjectionable in themselves, they say, have an undesirable moral spillover. (Things then would be different if there were no possibility of such spillover, for example, for the person who knows himself to be the last person on earth.) But why *should* there be such a spillover? If it is, in itself, perfectly all right to do anything at all to animals for any reason whatsoever, then provided a person realizes the clear line between animals and persons and keeps it in mind as he acts, why should killing animals tend to brutalize him and make him more likely to harm or kill persons? Do butchers commit more murders? (Than other persons who have knives around?) If I enjoy hitting a baseball squarely with a bat, does this significantly increase the danger of my doing the same to someone's head? Am I not capable of understanding that people differ from baseballs, and doesn't this understanding stop the spillover? Why should things be different in the case of animals? To be sure, it is an empirical question whether spillover does take place or not; but there is a puzzle as to why it should, at least among readers of this essay, sophisticated people who are capable of drawing distinctions and differentially acting upon them. If some animals count for something, which animals count, how much do they count, and how can this be determined? Suppose (as I believe the evidence supports) that *eating* animals is not necessary for *health* and is not less expensive than alternate equally healthy diets available to people in the United States. The gain, then, from the eating of animals is pleasures of the palate, gustatory delights, varied tastes. I would not claim that these are not truly pleasant, delightful, and interesting. The question is: do they, or rather does the marginal addition in them gained by eating animals rather than only nonanimals, *outweigh* the moral weight to be given to animals' lives and pain? Given that animals are to count for *something, is* the *extra* gain obtained by eating them rather than nonanimal products greater than the moral cost? How might these questions be decided? . . .

Such examples and questions might help someone to see what sort of line *he* wishes to draw, what sort of position he wishes to take. . . . It would appear that a person's characteristics, by virtue of which others are constrained in their treatment of him, must themselves be valuable characteristics. . . .

The traditional proposals for the important individuating characteristic connected with moral constraints are the following: sentient and self-conscious; rational (capable of using abstract concepts, not tied to responses to immediate stimuli); possessing free will; being a moral agent capable of guiding its behavior by moral principles and capable of engaging in mutual limitation of conduct; having a soul. . . . But haven't we been unfair in treating rationality, free will, and moral agency individually and separately? In conjunction, don't they add up to something whose significance is clear: a being able to formulate long-term plans for its life, able to consider and decide on the basis of abstract principles or considerations it formulates to itself and hence not merely the plaything of immediate stimuli, a being that limits its own behavior in accordance with some principles or picture it has of what an appropriate life is for itself and others, and so on.

From Robert Nozick, *Anarchy State, and Utopia.*

STEPHEN L. CARTER

The Exercise of Free Choice Is Properly Constrained by Morality

Stephen L. Carter (1954–) is an American legal scholar, author, and social critic.

While he endorses the value of individual freedom, Stephen L. Carter argues that in a genuinely civil society it is appropriate that free choice be constrained by the norms of the community. We should not follow tradition slavishly but we should repudiate tradition and the norms encoded by tradition only when we find those norms to be immoral. If we act as if the norms of the community have no claim on us whatsoever, then we in effect are declaring ourselves not to be members of the community after all.

A society that is free must allow the broadest possible scope for personal choice, but a society that is civil must recognize that the exercise of free choice must always be bounded by morality. This is not to say that immoral choices ought to be illegal. Rather, we as individuals have the responsibility to exercise moral judgment about the choices we make. Otherwise, we are no better than animals. Jean-Jacques Rousseau captured this point in *The Social Contract*: "[T]he mere impulse of appetite is slavery, while obedience to a law which we prescribe to ourselves is liberty." The liberty of self-control Rousseau called "moral liberty"; it was, he argued, part of what we gained when we left the state of nature and entered civil society.

A part of that moral liberty—if society is to survive—must be the discipline to resist the modern urge to ignore the rules whenever we happen to find them inconvenient. When we find the norms of our community immoral, we should have the moral strength to defy them: conformity for its own sake shows no moral judgment. But neither does nonconformity for its own sake. If we lack serious moral arguments against particular norms or traditions, we should try to adhere to them if at all possible; otherwise, the signal that we send is that we fundamentally disbelieve in the virtue of community.

In our evaluation of the fork-norm, for example, we may think the norm is silly or outdated. But I doubt that it is possible to make a serious case that the norm is immoral. . . . [W]e should recognize that the fork-norm is at least descended from a rule carrying an important moral message: human beings are different from animals and can discipline the desires of the body, even the desire to eat. . . .

Norms that develop over time to inform the character and the actions of members of the community are the community's traditions. The historian Jaroslav Pelikan has cautioned that is is important to distinguish *tradition* from *traditionalism*. Tradition, in Pelikan's view, celebrates the "living faith of the dead"; traditionalism, as he defines it, is the "dead faith of the living." A reference for tradition . . . calls upon us to respect and extend the faith of those who preceded us. We need not, however, suspend our own critical faculties. On the contrary, if we wish to avoid the trap of traditionalism, we must not assume that every voice from the past has matters precisely right. . . .

Edmund Burke criticized the French Revolution on the ground that it seemed bent on overturning traditions for no reason but that they were traditions. Since the 1960s, when a number of genuinely immoral traditions were swept away, America has too often behaved as though what was bad about them was the fact that they were traditions—whereas what was bad about them was the fact that they were wicked traditions. . . .

One cannot build a community of any kind by encouraging everybody to invent their own norms as needed, and then to abandon them according to whim. The very idea of democracy rests upon the broad popular acceptance of a set of democratic norms—the best examples are liberty and equality, but there are more—and our national community is built around them. Should we all feel free to discard them as we wish, we would no longer be a democratic community. . . .

[M]ost norms must be self-enforcing. . . . Nevertheless, norms are sometimes violated. When they have the force of law, that violation may entail legal punishment. Most norms, however, are not laws, and they are enforced, if at all, through community pressure. . . . one neighbor may hint to another that the grass is getting a little high. A boss may suggest that an employee wear something more appropriate to the office tomorrow. A pastor may warn a parishioner that a course of conduct runs contrary to the denomination's understanding of God's law. In each case, the pressure, if successful, rests in part on the status anxiety of the pressured—in short, the need to belong to a group.

From Stephen L. Carter, *Civility.*

XIAORONG LI

The Asian Conception of Society Does Not Negate Human Rights

Xiaorong Li (1958–), born in China and now a U.S. citizen, is a political philosopher and public policy theorist.

Xiaorong Li identifies various Asian values which allegedly conflict with universal human rights. Most significant for understanding this tension is the value which Asians attach to community and the value which the West attaches to the individual. Human rights go hand in hand with a value which assigns to the individual a precedence over society. So, in this line of thinking, human rights are incompatible with the Asian view. Li rejects this reasoning by endorsing a view of community where free expression, association, and toleration contribute to the vitality of the community.

This essay makes a preliminary attempt to identify the myths, misconceptions, and fallacies that have gone into creating an "Asian view" of human rights. By sorting out the various threads in the notions of "cultural specificity" and "universality," it shows that the claim to "Asian values" hardly constitutes a serious threat to the universal validity of human rights. . . .

    Claim II. The community takes precedence over individuals. The importance of the community in Asian culture is incompatible with the primacy of the individual, upon which the Western notion of human rights rests. The relationship between individuals and communities constitutes the key difference between Asian and Western cultural "values." An official statement of the Singapore government, *Shared Values (1991),* stated that "[a]n emphasis on the community has been a key survival value for Singapore." Human rights and the rule of law, according to the "Asian view," are individualistic by nature and hence destructive of Asia's social mechanism. Increasing rates of violent crime, family breakdown, homelessness, and drug abuse are cited as evidence that Western individualism (particularly the American variety) has failed. . . .

CULTURE, COMMUNITY, AND THE STATE

The second claim, that Asians value community over individuality, obscures more than it reveals about community, its relations to the state and individuals, and the conditions congenial to its flourishing. The so-called Asian value of "community harmony" is used as an illustration of "cultural" differences between Asian and Western societies, in order to show that the idea of individuals' inalienable rights does not suit Asian societies. This "Asian communitarianism" is a direct challenge to what is perceived as the essence of human rights, i.e., its individual-centered approach, and it suggests that Asia's community-centered approach is superior.

However, the "Asian view" creates confusions by collapsing "community" into the state and the state into the (current) regime. When equations are drawn between community, the state and the regime, any criticisms of the regime become crimes against the nation-state, the community, and the people. The "Asian view" relies on such a conceptual maneuver to dismiss individual rights that conflict with the regime's interest, allowing the condemnation of individual rights as anti-communal, destructive of social harmony, and seditionist against the sovereign state.

At the same time, this view denies the existence of conflicting interests between the state (understood as a political entity) and communities (understood as voluntary, civil associations) in Asian societies. What begins as an endorsement of the value of community and social harmony ends in an assertion of the supreme status of the regime and its leaders. Such a regime is capable of dissolving any non-governmental organizations it dislikes in the name of "community interest," often citing traditional Confucian values of social harmony to defend restrictions on the right to free association and expression, and thus wields ever more pervasive control over unorganized individual workers and dissenters. A Confucian communitarian, however, would find that the bleak, homogeneous society that these governments try to shape through draconian practices—criminal prosecutions for "counterrevolutionary activities," administrative detention, censorship, and military curfew—has little in common with her ideal of social harmony.

Contrary to the "Asian view," individual freedom is not intrinsically opposed to and destructive of community. Free association, free expression, and tolerance are vital to the well-being of communities. Through open public deliberations, marginalized and vulnerable social groups can voice their concerns and expose the discrimination and unfair treatment they encounter. In a liberal democratic society, which is mocked and denounced by some Asian leaders for its individualist excess, a degree of separation between the state and civil society provides a public space for the flourishing of communities.

From Xiaorong Li, "Asian Values and the Universality of Human Rights."

MARTIN LUTHER KING, JR.

Challenge Unjust Laws through Nonviolent Acts of Civil Disobedience

Martin Luther King, Jr. (1929–1968) was an American minister and leader in the civil rights movement.

Martin Luther King, Jr. coupled Christian teachings with Gandhi's thinking on nonviolent resistance. King advocates civil disobedience of discriminatory laws as part of an effort to combat racism and to improve the status of African-Americans. Through their nonviolent actions, they can draw attention to the injustice of the law which they resist, create tension in the community, and force the oppressors to negotiate. But the protesters must be willing to endure such consequences of their disobedience as arrest and punishment.

My dear Fellow Clergymen,

While confined here in the Birmingham City jail, I came across your recent statement calling our present activities "unwise and untimely." Seldom, if ever, do I pause to answer criticism of my work and ideas. If I sought to answer all of the criticisms that cross my desk, my secretaries would be engaged in little else in the course of the day, and I would have no time for constructive work. But since I feel that you are men of genuine goodwill and your criticisms are sincerely set forth, I would like to answer your statement in what I hope will be patient and reasonable terms. . . .

In any nonviolent campaign there are four basic steps: (1) Collection of the facts to determine whether injustices are alive (2) Negotiation (3) Self-purification and (4) Direct Action. We have gone through all of these steps in Birmingham. There can be no gainsaying of the fact that racial injustice engulfs this community.

Birmingham is probably the most thoroughly segregated city in the United States. Its ugly record of police brutality is known in every section of this country. Its unjust treatment of Negroes in the courts is a notorious reality. There have been more unsolved bombings of Negro homes and churches in Birmingham than any city in this nation. These are the hard, brutal and unbelievable facts. On the basis of these conditions Negro leaders sought to negotiate with the city fathers. But the political leaders consistently refused to engage in good faith negotiation.

Then came the opportunity last September to talk with some of the leaders of the economic community. In these negotiating sessions certain promises were made by the merchants—such as the promise to remove the humiliating racial signs from the stores. On the basis of these promises Rev. Shuttlesworth and the leaders of the Alabama Christian Movement for Human Rights agreed to call a moratorium on any type of demonstrations. As the weeks and months unfolded we realized that we were the victims of a broken promise. The signs remained. Like so many experiences of the past we were confronted with blasted hopes, and the dark shadow of a deep disappointment settled upon us. So we had no alternative except that of preparing for direct action, whereby we would present our very bodies as a means of laying our case before the conscience of the local and national community. We were not unmindful of the difficulties involved. So we decided to go through a process of self-purification. We started having workshops on nonviolence and repeatedly asked ourselves the questions, "Are you able to accept blows without retaliating?" "Are you able to endure the ordeals of jail?". . .

You may well ask, "Why direct action? Why sit-ins, marches, etc.? Isn't negotiation a better path?" You are exactly right in your call for negotiation. Indeed, this is the purpose of direct action. Nonviolent direct action seeks to create such a crisis and establish such creative tension that a community that has constantly refused to negotiate is forced to confront the issue. It seeks so to dramatize the issue that it can no longer be ignored. I just referred to the creation of tension as a part of the work of the nonviolent resister. This may sound rather shocking. But I must confess that I am not afraid of the word tension. I have earnestly worked and preached against violent tension, but there is a type of constructive nonviolent tension that is necessary for growth. Just as Socrates felt that it was necessary to create a tension in the mind so that individuals could rise from the bondage of myths and half-truths to the unfettered realm of creative analysis and objective appraisal, we must see the need of having nonviolent gadflies to create the kind of tension in society that will help men to rise from the dark depths of prejudice and racism to the majestic heights of understanding and brotherhood. So the purpose of the direct action is to create a situation so crisis-packed that it will inevitably open the door to negotiation. We, therefore, concur with you in your call for negotiation. Too long has our beloved Southland been bogged down in the tragic attempt to live in monologue rather than dialogue. . . .

One of the basic points in your statement is that our acts are untimely. . . . We know through painful experience that freedom is never voluntarily given by the oppressor; it must be demanded by the oppressed. Frankly, I have never yet engaged in a direct action movement that was "well timed" according to the timetable of those who have not suffered unduly from the disease of segregation. For years now I have heard the words "Wait!" It rings in the ear of every Negro with a piercing familiarity. This "Wait" has almost always meant "Never." It has been a tranquilizing thalidomide, relieving the emotional stress for a moment, only to give birth to an ill-formed infant of frustration. We must come to see with the distinguished jurist of yesterday that "justice too long delayed is justice denied." We have waited for more than three hundred and forty years for our constitutional and God-given rights. The nations of Asia and Africa are moving with jet-like speed toward the goal of political independence, and we still creep at horse and buggy pace toward the gaining of a cup of coffee at a lunch counter. I guess it is easy for those who have never felt the stinging darts of segregation to say, "Wait." But when you have seen vicious mobs lynch your mothers and fathers at will and drown your sisters and brothers at whim; when you have seen hate-filled policemen curse, kick, brutalize and even kill your black brothers and sisters with impunity; when you see the vast majority of your twenty million Negro brothers smothering in an air-tight cage of poverty in the midst of an affluent society; when you suddenly find your tongue twisted and your speech stammering as you seek to explain to your six-year-old daughter why she can't go to the public amusement park that has just been advertised on television, and see tears welling up in her little eyes when she is told that Funtown is closed to colored children, and see the depressing clouds of inferiority begin to form in her little mental sky, and see her begin to distort her little personality by unconsciously developing a bitterness toward white people; when you have to concoct an answer for a five-year-old son asking in agonizing pathos: "Daddy, why do white people treat colored people so mean?"; when you take a cross country drive and find it necessary to sleep night after night in the uncomfortable corners of your automobile because no motel will accept you; when you are humiliated day in and day out by nagging signs reading "white" and "colored"; when your first name becomes "nigger" and your middle name becomes "boy" (however old you are) and your last name becomes "John," and when your wife and mother are never given the respected title "Mrs."; when you are harried by day and haunted at night by the fact that you are a Negro, living constantly at tip-toe stance never quite knowing what to expect next, and plagued with inner fears and outer resentments; when you are forever fighting a degenerating sense of "nobodiness"; then you will understand why we find it difficult to wait. There comes a time when the cup of endurance runs over, and men are no longer willing to be plunged into an abyss of injustice where they experience the blackness of corroding despair. I hope, sirs, you can understand our legitimate and unavoidable impatience.

Martin Luther King, Jr.

From Martin Luther King, Jr., "Letter from Birmingham City Jail."

MALCOLM X

Use Violence in the Fight against Injustice But Only in Self-Defense

Malcolm X (1925–1965) was an African-American political activist, speaker, and essayist.

Malcolm X rejected Christianity because he believed it to be a tool of oppression. He first turned to Black Nationalism as espoused by Elijah Muhammad, but later in his life embraced Islam which he felt was truly a colorblind religion. When he was affiliated with Black Nationalism, Malcolm X urged African-Americans to think of the white man as the devil and argued for black separatism. After his sojourns to Mecca to learn the ways of traditional Muslims, he abandoned separatism and came to see the demand for an end to racial discrimination as part of a call for universal human rights. Malcolm X did advocate that African-Americans turn to violence but only sanctioned the use of violence for self-defense. Besides his interest in assisting his people in affirming their worth in a racist society, Malcolm X developed an agenda for advancing the interests of African-Americans through the power of the vote.

*M*alcolm: You're out of your mind if you don't think that there's a racist element in the State Department. I'm not saying that everybody in the State Department is a racist but I'm saying they've sure got some in there—a whole lot of them in there. They've got them in powerful positions in there. This is the element that became worried about the changing Negro mood and the changing Negro behavior, especially if that mood and that behavior became one of what they call violence. By violence they only mean when a black man protects himself against the attacks of a white man. This is what they mean by violence. They don't mean what you mean. Because they don't even use the word violence until someone gives the impression that you're about to explode. When it comes time for a black man to explode they call it violence. But white people can be exploding against black people all day long, and it's never called violence. I even have some of you come to me and ask me, am I for violence? I'm the victim of violence, and you're the victim of violence. But you've been so victimized by it that you can't recognize it for what it is today.

HARYOU-ACT Forum New York.
December 12, 1964

How to Get Allies

Malcolm X went to England on December 3, 1964, to participate in a debate sponsored by the Oxford Union Society and presented over television by the British Broadcasting Corporation. The question debated was "Extremism in the defense of liberty is no vice, moderation in the pursuit of justice is no virtue," a theme that had aroused heated controversy when it was propounded earlier in 1964 by Senator Barry Goldwater, the conservative Republican candidate for president. There were three speakers on each side, Malcolm being the final speaker for the affirmative. Despite continued efforts, we were unable to get more than a fragment of the transcript. . . .

Malcolm: My reason for believing in extremism, intelligently directed extremism, extremism in defense of liberty, extremism in quest of liberty, is because I firmly believe in my heart that the day that the black man takes an uncompromising step and realizes that he's within his rights, when his own freedom is being jeopardized, to use any means necessary to bring about his freedom or put a halt to that injustice, I don't think he'll be by himself. I live in America where there are only 22 million blacks, against probably 160 million whites. One of the reasons why I'm in no way reluctant or hesitant to do whatever is necessary to see that blacks do something to protect themselves is I honestly believe that the day they do, many whites will have more respect for them, and there will be more whites on their side than are now on their side with these little wishywashy love-thy-enemy approaches that they've been using up to now. And if I'm wrong, then you are racialists.

From Malcolm X, *By Any Means Necessary*, second edition.

Here is what I wrote . . . from my heart:

"Never have I witnessed such sincere hospitality and the spirit of true brotherhood as is practiced by people of all colors and races here in this Ancient Holy Land, the home of Abraham, Muhammad, and all the other prophets of the Holy Scriptures. For the past week, I have been utterly speechless and spellbound by the graciousness I see displayed all around me by people of *all colors*.

"I have been blessed to visit the Holy City of Mecca. I have made my seven circuits around the Ka'ba, led by a young *Mutawaf* named Muhammad. I drank water from the well of Zem Zem. I ran seven times back and forth between the hills of Mt. Al-Safa and Al-Marwah. I have prayed in the ancient city of Mina, and I have prayed on Mt. Arafat.

"There were tens of thousands of pilgrims, from all over the world. They were of all colors, from blue-eyed blonds to black-skinned Africans. But we were all participating in the same ritual, displaying a spirit of unity and brotherhood that my experiences in America had led me to believe never could exist between the white and the non-white.

"America needs to understand Islam because this is the one religion that erases from its society the race problem. Throughout my travels in the Muslim world, I have met, talked to, and even eaten with people who in America would have been considered 'white'—but the 'white' attitude was removed from their minds by the religion of Islam. I have never before seen *sincere* and *true* brotherhood practiced by all colors together, irrespective of their color. . . .

"They called me "the angriest Negro in America." I wouldn't deny that charge. I spoke exactly as I felt. "I *believe* in anger. The Bible says there is a *time* for anger." They called me "a teacher, a fomenter of violence." I would say point blank, "That is a lie. I'm not for wanton violence, I'm for justice. I feel that if white people were attacked by Negroes—if the forces of law prove unable, or inadequate, or reluctant to protect those whites from those Negroes—then those white people should protect and defend themselves from those Negroes, using arms if necessary. And I feel that when the law falls to protect Negroes from whites' attack, then those Negroes should use arms, if necessary, to defend themselves.

"Malcolm X Advocates Armed Negroes!"

What was wrong with that? I'll tell you what was wrong. I was a black man talking about physical defense against the white man. The white man can lynch and burn and bomb and beat Negroes—that's all right: "Have patience" . . . . "The customs are entrenched" "Things are getting better.

Well, I believe it's a crime for anyone who is being brutalized to continue to accept that brutality without doing something to defend himself. If that's how "Christian" philosophy is interpreted, if that's what Gandhian philosophy teaches, well, then, I will call them criminal philosophies.

I tried in every speech I made to clarify my new position regarding white people—"I don't speak against well-meaning, good white people. I have learned that there *are* some. I have learned that not all white people are racists. I am speaking against and my fight is against the white *racists*. I firmly believe that Negroes have the right to fight against these racists, by any means that are necessary."

But the white reporters kept wanting me linked with that word "violence." I doubt if I had one interview without having to deal with that accusation.

I *am* for violence if non-violence means we continue postponing a solution to the American black man's problem—just to *avoid* violence. I don't go for non-violence if it also means a delayed solution. To me a delayed solution is a non-solution. Or I'll say it in another way. If it must take violence to get the black man his human rights in this country, I'm *for* violence exactly as you know the Irish, the Poles, or Jews would be if they were flagrantly discriminated against. I am just as they would be in that case and they would be for violence—no matter what the consequences, no matter who was hurt by the violence. . . .

The cornerstones of this country's operation are economic and political strength and power. The black man doesn't have the economic strength—and it will take time for him to build it. But right now the American black man has the political strength and power to change his destiny overnight.

It was a big order—the organization I was creating in my mind, one which would help to challenge the American black man to gain his human rights, and to cure his mental, spiritual, economic, and political sicknesses. But if you ever intend to do anything worthwhile, you have to start with a worthwhile plan.

Substantially, as I saw it, the organization I hoped to build would differ from the Nation of Islam in that it would embrace all faiths of black men, and it would carry into practice what the Nation of Islam had only preached. . . .

I called a press conference. The microphones stuck up before me. The flashbulbs popped. The reporters, men and women, white and black, representing media that reached around the world, sat looking at me with their pencils and open notebooks.

I made the announcement: "I am going to organize and head a new mosque in New York City known as the Muslim Mosque, Inc. This will give us a religious base, and the spiritual force necessary to rid our people of the vices that destroy the moral fiber of our community.

"Muslim Mosque, Inc. will have its temporary headquarters in the Hotel Theresa in Harlem. It will be the working base for an action program designed to eliminate the political oppression, the economic exploitation, and the social degradation suffered daily by twenty-two million Afro-Americans."

From Malcolm X, *The Autobiography of Malcolm X*, with the assistance of Alex Haley.

AYN RAND

To Change the World, Speak!

Ayn Rand (1905–1982), a Russian-born emigre to the United States, was a novelist, essayist, and philosopher.

In answering the commonly asked question of what one person can do to better the world, Ayn Rand weaves her simple answer of "SPEAK" with her view of the significance of philosophy for change. She makes a case for a struggle to change the world being a philosophical rather than a political problem. As such, as we speak out to change the world, we must be guided by some well thought out ideas.

This question is frequently asked by people who are concerned about the state of today's world and want to correct it. More often than not, it is asked in a form that indicates the cause of their helplessness: "What can *one person* do?"

I was in the process of preparing this article when I received a letter from a reader who presents the problem (and the error) still more eloquently: "How can an individual propagate your philosophy on a scale large enough to effect the immense changes which must be made in every walk of American life in order to create the kind of ideal country which you picture?"

If this is the way the question is posed, the answer is: he can't. No one can change a country single-handed. So the first question to ask is: why do people approach the problem this way?

Suppose you were a doctor in the midst of an epidemic. You would not ask: "How can one doctor treat millions of patients and restore the whole country to perfect health?" You would know, whether you were alone or part of an organized medical campaign, that you have to treat as many people as you can reach, according to the best of your ability, and that nothing else is possible.

It is a remnant of mystic philosophy—specifically, of the mind-body split—that makes people approach intellectual issues in a manner they would not use to deal with physical problems. They would not seek to stop an epidemic overnight, or to build a skyscraper single-handed. Nor would they refrain from renovating their own crumbling house, on the grounds that they are unable to rebuild the entire city. But in the realm of man's consciousness, the realm of ideas, they still tend to regard knowledge as irrelevant, and they expect to perform instantaneous miracles, somehow—or they paralyze themselves by projecting an impossible goal.

(The reader whose letter I quoted was doing the right things, but felt that some wider scale of action was required. Many others merely ask the question, but do nothing.)

If you are seriously interested in fighting for a better world, begin by identifying the nature of the problem. The battle is primarily intellectual *(philosophical)*, not political. Politics is the last consequence, the practical implementation, of the fundamental (metaphysical-epistemological-ethical) ideas that dominate a given nation's culture. You cannot fight or change the consequences without fighting and changing the cause; nor can you attempt any practical implementation without knowing what you want to implement.

In an intellectual battle, you do not need to convert everyone. History is made by minorities—or, more precisely, history is made by intellectual movements, which are created by minorities. Who belongs to these minorities? Anyone who is able and willing actively to concern himself with intellectual issues. Here, it is not quantity, but quality, that counts (the quality—and consistency—of the ideas one is advocating).

An intellectual movement does not start with organized action. Whom would one organize? A philosophical battle is a battle for men's minds, not an attempt to enlist blind followers. Ideas can be propagated only by men who understand them. An organized movement has to be preceded by an *educational* campaign, which requires trained—self-trained teachers (self-trained in the sense that a philosopher can offer you the material of knowledge, but it is your own mind that has to absorb it). Such training is the first requirement for being a doctor during an ideological epidemic—and the precondition of any attempt to "change the world."

"The immense changes which must be made in every walk of American life" cannot be made singly, piecemeal or "retail," so to speak; an army of crusaders would not be enough to do it. But the factor that underlies and determines every aspect of human life is philosophy; teach men the right philosophy—and their own minds will do the rest. Philosophy is the wholesaler in human affairs.

Man cannot exist without some form of philosophy, i.e., some comprehensive view of life. Most men are not intellectual innovators, but they are receptive to ideas, are able to judge them critically and to choose the right course, when and if it is offered. There are also a great many men who are indifferent to ideas and to anything beyond the concrete-bound range of the immediate moment; such men accept subconsciously whatever is offered by the culture of their time, and swing blindly with any chance current. They are merely social ballast—be they day laborers or company presidents—and, by their own choice, irrelevant to the fate of the world.

Today, most people are acutely aware of our cultural ideological vacuum; they are anxious, confused, and groping for answers. Are you able to enlighten them?

Can you answer their questions? Can you offer them a consistent case? Do you know how to correct their errors? Are you immune from the fallout of the constant barrage aimed at the destruction of reason—and can you provide others with antimissile missiles? A political battle is merely a skirmish fought with muskets; a philosophical battle is a nuclear war.

If you want to influence a country's intellectual trend, the first step is to bring order to your own ideas and integrate them into a consistent case, to the best of your knowledge and ability. This does not mean memorizing and reciting slogans and principles, Objectivist or otherwise: knowledge necessarily includes the ability to apply abstract principles to concrete problems, to recognize the principles in specific issues, to demonstrate them, and to advocate a consistent course of action. This does not require omniscience or omnipotence; it is the subconscious expectation of automatic omniscience in oneself and in others that defeats many would-be crusaders (and serves as an excuse for doing nothing). What is required *is honesty*—intellectual honesty, which consists in knowing what one does know, constantly expanding one's knowledge, and *never* evading or failing to correct a contradiction. This means: the development of an *active* mind as a permanent attribute.

When or if your convictions are in your conscious, orderly control, you will be able to communicate them to others. This does not mean that you must make philosophical speeches when unnecessary and inappropriate. You need philosophy to back you up and give you a consistent case when you deal with or discuss specific issues.

If you like condensations (provided you bear in mind their full meaning), I will say: when you ask: "What can one do?"—the answer is "SPEAK" (provided you know what you are saying).

A few suggestions: do not wait for a national audience. Speak on any scale open to you, large or small—to your friends, your associates, your professional organizations, or any legitimate public forum. You can never tell when your words will reach the right mind at the right time. You will see no immediate results—but it is of such activities that public opinion is made.

Do not pass up a chance to express your views on important issues. Write letters to the editors of newspapers and magazines, to TV and radio commentators and, above all, to your Congressmen (who depend on their constituents). If your letters are brief and rational (rather than incoherently emotional), they will have more influence than you suspect.

The opportunities to speak are all around you. I suggest that you make the following experiment: take an ideological "inventory" of one week, i.e., note how many times people utter the wrong political, social and moral notions as if these were self-evident truths, with your silent sanction. Then make it a habit to object to such remarks—no, not to make lengthy speeches, which are seldom appropriate, but merely to say: "I don't agree." (And be prepared to explain why, if the speaker wants to know.) This is one of the best ways to stop the spread of vicious bromides. (If the speaker is innocent, it will help him; if he is not, it will undercut his confidence the next time.) Most particularly, do not keep silent when your own ideas and values are being attacked.

If a dictatorship ever comes to this country, it will be by the default of those who keep silent. We are still free enough to speak. Do we have time? No one can tell. But time is on our side—because we have an indestructible weapon and an invincible ally (if we learn how to use them): reason and reality.

From Ayn Rand, "What Can One Do?"

AUDRE LORDE

Oppressed People Should Seize all Opportunities to Better Themselves

Audre Lorde (1934–1992) was an African-American political activist, poet, and essayist.

Audre Lorde brings out the fact that discrimination against race, sex, and sexuality no less characterizes the eighties than the sixties. But oppressed people should learn from the sixties that they cannot solve these problems instantaneously with a single revolution. Nor should they be fighting among themselves. Speaking as a member of three oppressed groups, Audre Lorde, an African-American lesbian, urges unity among victims of discrimination as they take advantage of all opportunities, however small, to create a world where people respect each other despite their differences.

Malcolm X is a distinct shape in a very pivotal period of life. I stand here now—Black, Lesbian, Feminist—an inheritor of Malcolm and in his tradition, doing my work, and the ghost of his voice though my mouth asks each one of you here tonight: Are you doing yours? . . .

The 60s for me was time of promise and excitement, but the 60s was also a time of isolation and frustration from within. It often felt like I was working and raising my children in a vacuum, and that it was my own fault—if I was only Blacker, things would be fine. It was a time of much wasted energy, and I was often in a lot of pain. Either I denied or chose between various aspects of my identity, or my work and my Blackness would be unacceptable. As a Black lesbian mother in an interracial marriage, there was usually some part of me guaranteed to offend everybody's comfortable prejudices of who I should be. That is how I learned that if I didn't define myself for myself, I would be crunched into other people's fantasies for me and eaten alive. My poetry, my life, my work, my energies for struggle were not acceptable unless I pretended to match somebody else's norm. I learned that not only couldn't I succeed at that game, but the energy needed for that masquerade would be lost to my work. And there were babies to raise, students to teach. The Vietnam War was escalating, our cities were burning, more and more of our school kids were nodding out in the halls, junk was overtaking our streets. We needed articulate power, not conformity. There were other strong Black workers whose visions were racked and silenced upon some imagined grid of narrow Blackness. Nor were Black women immune. At a national meeting of Black women for political action, a young civil rights activist who had been beaten and imprisoned in Mississippi only a few years before, was trashed and silenced as suspect because of her white husband. Some of us made it and some of us were lost to the struggle. It was a time of great hope and great expectation; it was also a time of great waste. That is history. We do not need to repeat these mistakes in the 80s.

The raw energy of Black determination released in the 60s powered changes in Black awareness and self-concepts and expectations. This energy is still being felt in movements for change among women, other peoples of Color, gays, the handicapped—among all the disenfranchised peoples of this society. That is a legacy of the 60s to ourselves and to others. But we must recognize that many of our high expectations of rapid revolutionary change did not in fact occur. And many of the gains that did are even now being dismantled. This is not a reason for despair, nor for rejection of the importance of those years. But we must face with clarity and insight the lessons to be learned from the oversimplification of any struggle for self-awareness and liberation, or we will not rally the force we need to face the multidimensional threats to our survival in the 80s.

There is no such thing as a single-issue struggle because we do not live single-issue lives. Malcolm knew this. Martin Luther King, Jr. knew this. Our struggles are particular, but we are not alone. We are not perfect, but we are stronger and wiser than the sum of our errors. Black people have been here before us and survived. We can read their lives like signposts on the road and find, as Bernice Reagon says so poignantly, that each one of us is here because somebody before us did something to make it possible. To learn from their mistakes is not to lessen our debt to them, nor to the hard work of becoming ourselves, and effective. . . .

Can any one of us here still afford to believe that efforts to reclaim the future can be private or individual? Can any one here still afford to believe that the pursuit of liberation can be the sole and particular province of any one particular race, or sex, or age, or religion, or sexuality, or class?

Revolution is not a one-time event. It is becoming always vigilant for the smallest opportunity to make a genuine change in established, outgrown responses; for instance, it is learning to address each other's difference with respect.

We share a common interest, survival, and it cannot be pursued in isolation from others simply because their differences make us uncomfortable. We know what it is to be tied to. The 60s should teach us how important it is not to lie to ourselves.

Not to believe that revolution is a one-time event, or something that happens around us rather than inside of us. Not to believe that freedom can belong to any one group of us without the others also being free. How important it is not to allow even our leaders to define us to ourselves, or to define our sources of power to us.

You do not have to be me in order for us to fight alongside each other. I do not have to be you to recognize that our wars are the same. What we must do is commit ourselves to some future that can include each other and to work toward that future with the particular strengths of our individual identities. And in order to do this, we must allow each other our differences at the same time as we recognize our sameness.

If our history has taught us anything, it is that action for change directed only against the external conditions of our oppressions is not enough. In order to be whole, we must recognize the despair oppression plants within each of us—that thin persistent voice that says our efforts are useless, it will never change, so why bother, accept it. And we must fight that inserted piece of self-destruction that lives and flourishes like a poison inside of us, unexamined until it makes us turn upon ourselves in each other. But we can put our finger down upon that loathing buried deep within each one of us and see who it encourages us to despise, and we can lessen its potency by the knowledge of our real connectedness, arcing across our differences.

Hopefully, we can learn from the 60s that we cannot afford to do our enemies' work by destroying each other.

From Audre Lorde, *Sister Outsider*.

GEORGE HERBERT MEAD
The Mind and the Self Are Products of Society

George Herbert Mead (1863–1931) was an American pragmatist philosopher.

In George Mead's view, mind and self are products of society, of experience and activity within a social group. This view inverts some common thinking which depicts society developing from individual minds and selves. One reason which Mead offers for rejecting the notion that mind precedes society is that lower animals without minds, like bees, have complex social organizations. To establish that mind is a product of society, Mead points to the need for our interacting with other people to attain self-consciousness. We reach this state by seeing ourselves from the perspective of other people.

Even in the most modern and highly-evolved forms of human civilization the individual, however original and creative he may be in his thinking or behavior, always and necessarily assumes a definite relation to, and reflects in the structure of his self or personality, the general organized pattern of experience and activity exhibited in or characterizing the social life-process in which he is involved, and of which his self or personality is essentially a creative expression or embodiment. No individual has a mind which operates simply in itself, in isolation from the social lifeprocess in which it has arisen or out of which it has emerged, and in which the pattern of organized social behavior has consequently been basically impressed upon it. . . .

Our contention is that mind can never find expression, and could never have come into existence at all, except in terms of a social environment; that an organized set or pattern of social relations and interactions (especially those of communication by means of gestures functioning as significant symbols and thus creating a universe of discourse) is necessarily presupposed by it and involved in its nature. . . . [T]he supposition that the social process presupposes, and is in some sense a product of, mind seems to be contradicted by the existence of the social communities of certain of the lower animals, especially the highly complex social organizations of bees and ants, which apparently operate on a purely instinctive or reflex basis, and do not in the least involve the existence of mind or consciousness in the individual organisms which form or constitute them. . . .

The individual enters as such into his own experience only as an object, not as a subject; and he can enter as an object only on the basis of social relations and interactions, only by means of his experiential transactions with other individuals in an organized social environment. . . . Self-consciousness involves the individual's becoming an object to himself by taking the attitudes of other individuals toward himself within an organized setting of social relationships, and that unless the individual had thus become an object to himself he would not be self-conscious or have a self at all. Apart from his social interactions with other individuals, he would not relate the private or "subjective" contents of his experience to himself, and he could not become aware of himself as such, that is, as an individual, a person, merely by means or in terms of these contents of his experience; for in order to become aware of himself as such he must, to repeat, become an object to himself, or enter his own experience as an object, and only by social means—only by taking the attitudes of others toward himself—is he able to become an object to himself.

It is true, of course, that once mind has arisen in the social process it makes possible the development of that process into much more complex forms of social interaction among the component individuals than was possible before it had arisen. But there is nothing odd about a product of a given process contributing to, or becoming an essential factor in, the further development of that process. The social process, then, does not depend for its origin or initial existence upon the existence and interactions of selves; though it does depend upon the latter for the higher stages of complexity and organization which it reaches after selves have arisen within it.

From George Herbert Mead, *Mind, Self, and Society.*

C.I. LEWIS

Individuals Profit from Society, and Society Profits from Individuals

C.I. Lewis (1883–1964) was an American philosopher who specialized in logic, ethics, and epistemology.

C.I. Lewis underscores the reciprocal contributions which societies and individuals make. On the one hand, it is only the thoughts of particular, individual people that have led to advances in society; society itself has no brain to think with. On the other hand, we must acknowledge how important society is for individual development and how extensive the knowledge is which society is able to pass along to each generation's advantage. Lewis explores this point with a provocative scenario about the demise of civilization and the rebuilding of it. With our legacy of ideas, we could construct it again in a generation's time. Without it, we must make all of the discoveries again since the stone age and repeat all of history.

This in turn is the deepest miracle of the human social order. Man is the animal—the only animal—conscious of his history as a species, and by this self-consciousness affecting his own evolution and capable of directing it to his human values. Other creatures merely are evolved by natural forces they are incapable of comprehending. But man, by some capacity to penetrate the natural process, in measure controls his destiny. It is so that man alone evolves socially, and in a manner vitally affecting every individual human life, in a manner and with a speed which far transcends the limits of his biological evolution as an animal. If men today are biologically superior to men in—say—ancient Athens, that is hardly by natural selections, but mainly because his young have more to eat and are better spared the laming vicissitudes to which infancy in Athens was subject, by reason of comparative ignorance and the lack of control of conditions of life which that relative ignorance implies.

Each generation of other species begins where its parents began, because there is no social memory: nothing learned from the experience of past generations, no perpetuation in memory beyond the individual memory. For that, human language is essential. Man is the animal that remembers as a species and not merely as an individual. And the great instrument of his evolution, as a self-directed progress, is the social inheritance of ideas—the great traditions of agriculture, of technology, of science, of mores, of music and the arts, or religion and culture generally—by reason of which successive generations, with perhaps no heightening of the average I.Q. or other biological capacities, may still so immensely increase their knowledge and so rapidly extend the possible realization of human value and control of the conditions of good living. . . .

Strip the present generation of all their material trappings and reduce them to naked animals in the old environment, but leave them all their historically acquired knowledge and their acquired mores, it is not then implausible that men might come near to recreating our present human world in a generation or two. But strip the present generation of all faintest recollection of what has been learned since the Stone Age, and all their acquired habits of social living, and it is equally plausible that, in that case, the whole historical process would have, painfully, to repeat itself, and take an equal time. . . .

On the one side, every item of what men are aware of as the world around them and the possibilities of their individual doing is something discovered originally to some individual in his individual self-consciousness. The only brains society has to think with and learn with and for perpetuation of itself as a mental and spiritual ongoing force are individual brains. There is no slightest conquest in human history which is due to anything but the thinking of autonomous individual thinkers. By language, what any individual learns may become a common possession of all. But it is by sorting and sifting of the social process that although individually acquired ideas are more frequently false than true, the true is elicited and remembered, the mistaken rejected and forgotten. But to impose the social authority of the traditional and accepted upon the spontaneity of individual human thinking would be, obviously, to stop the clock. It is by individual freedom of thought, and the respect for the individual in his own initiative and self-criticism, that human society has become human instead of an ant colony. Only the self-governing and self-criticizing animal is human and could be moral.

On the other hand, the human individual is human only by participation in a human society. The social historical process has made him what he is, and offers the only opportunity he has of what he may achieve and what he may become. Separate him from the social spiritual process, and he must return to the Old Stone Age, or to the level of ape-living even. He is what he is and may realize any value that he individually cherishes only as he meets the conditions of membership in a social order of individuals, cooperating in the pursuit of values cherished in common.

From C.I. Lewis, "The Individual and the Social Order."

HENRY DAVID THOREAU

We May Have Bigger Houses But Have We Advanced from Our Savage Condition?

Henry David Thoreau (1817–1862) was an American transcendental philosopher and essayist.

Like many of the thinkers of the Enlightenment, Henry David Thoreau asks about our original circumstances which he refers to as our savage state. What he observes is that all families had shelters which served their needs and each shelter was as good as the other. Thoreau looks over the present state of affairs in which many people do not own their own homes, many people have large mortgages on their homes, and all homeowners pay taxes. "Are we better off?" Thoreau asks. Thoreau invites us to join him in asking just what a house is, something which he thinks few people have thought much about.

In the savage state every family owns a shelter as good as the best, and sufficient for its coarser and simpler wants; but I think that I speak within bounds when I say that, though the birds of the air have their nests, and the foxes their holes, and the savages their wigwams, in modern civilized society not more than one half the families own a shelter. In the large towns and cities, where civilization especially prevails, the number of those who own a shelter is a very small fraction of the whole. The rest pay an annual tax for this outside garment of all, become indispensable summer and winter, which would buy a village of Indian wigwams, but now helps to keep them poor as long as they live. I do not mean to insist here on the disadvantage of hiring compared with owning, but it is evident that the savage owns his shelter because it costs so little, while the civilized man hires his commonly because he cannot afford to own it; nor can he, in the long run, any better afford to hire. But answers one, by merely paying this tax the poor civilized man secures an abode which is a palace compared with the savage's. An annual rent of from twenty-five to a hundred dollars (these are the country rates) entitles him to the benefit of the improvements of centuries, spacious apartments, clean paint and paper, Rumford fireplace, back plastering, Venetian blinds, copper pump, spring lock, a commodious cellar, and many other things. But how happens it that he who is said to enjoy these things is so commonly a poor civilized man, while the savage, who has them not, is rich as a savage? If it is asserted that civilization is a real advance in the condition of man—

and I think that it is, though only the wise improve their advantages—it must be shown that it has produced better dwellings without making them more costly; and the cost of a thing is the amount of what I will call life which is required to be exchanged for it, immediately or in the long run. An average house in this neighborhood costs perhaps eight hundred dollars, and to lay up this sum will take from ten to fifteen years of the laborer's life, even if he is not encumbered with a family—estimating the pecuniary value of every man's labor at one dollar a day, for if some receive more, others receive less—so that he must have spent more than half his life commonly before his wigwam will be earned. If we suppose him to pay a rent instead, this is but a doubtful choice of evils. Would the savage have been wise to exchange his wigwam for a palace on these terms? . . .

Granted that the *majority* are able at last either to own or hire the modern house with all its improvements. While civilization has been improving our houses, it has not equally improved the men who are to inhabit them. It has created palaces, but it was not so easy to create noblemen and kings. And *if the civilized man's pursuits are no worthier than the savage's, if he is employed the greater part of his life in obtaining gross necessaries and comforts merely, why should he have a better dwelling than the former?* . . .

Most men appear never to have considered what a house is, and are actually though needlessly poor all their lives because they think that they must have such a one as their neighbors have. . . .

I had three pieces of limestone on my desk, but I was terrified to find that they required to be dusted daily, when the furniture of my mind was all undusted still, and I threw them out the window in disgust. How, then, could I have a furnished house? I would rather sit in the open air, for no dust gathers on the grass, unless where man has broken ground. . . .

I would rather ride on earth in an ox cart, with a free circulation, than go to heaven in the fancy car of an excursion train and breathe a malaria all the way.

The very simplicity and nakedness of man's life in the primitive ages imply this advantage, at least, that they left him still but a sojourner in nature. When he was refreshed with food and sleep, he contemplated his journey again. He dwelt, as it were, in a tent in this world, and was either threading the valleys, or crossing the plains, or climbing the mountain-tops. But lo! men have become the tools of their tools. The man who independently plucked the fruits when he was hungry is become a farmer; and he who stood under a tree for shelter, a housekeeper. We now no longer camp as for a night, but have settled down on earth and forgotten heaven. We have adopted Christianity merely as an improved method of *agri*-culture. We have built for this world a family mansion, and for the next a family tomb.

From Henry David Thoreau, *Walden*.

FREDERICK DOUGLASS
The Right to Vote Belongs to All People

Frederick Douglass (1817–1895), an escaped slave, was an essayist and orator.

Frederick Douglass grounds universal suffrage in human nature. He argues that of all the animals, humans are the only ones that create governments and a right to participate in them is thereby self-evident. Douglass's particular concern is to secure the right for African-Americans. Douglass brings out that, just as we have abolished slavery, we must abandon the view that some people have no rights.

Man is the only government-making animal in the world. His right to a participation in the production and operation of government is an inference from his nature, as direct and self-evident as is his right to acquire property or education. It is no less a crime against the manhood of a man, to declare that he shall not share in the making and directing of the government under which he lives, than to say that he shall not acquire property and education. The fundamental and unanswerable argument in favor of the enfranchisement of the negro is found in the undisputed fact of his manhood. He is a man, and by every fact and argument by which any man can sustain his right to vote, the negro can sustain his right equally. It is plain that, if the right belongs to any, it belongs to all. The doctrine that some men have no rights that others are bound to respect, is a doctrine which we must banish as we have banished slavery, from which it emanated. If black men have no rights in the eyes of white men, of course the whites can have none in the eyes of the blacks.

From Frederick Douglass, "An Appeal to Congress for Impartial Suffrage."

EMMA GOLDMAN
"Woman Suffrage"

Emma Goldman (1869–1940) was a Russian-born anarchist who was active in America and Europe.

Once one knows that Emma Goldman is an anarchist, one can easily predict that she would not attach much value to women getting the right to vote. Why worry about voting when your overall objective is to organize society without government?

Goldman, like most political philosophers, grounds her view about the optimal society in human nature. She likens the problem of understanding human nature when humans are not free to that of learning about animals when they are in cages. Human nature—and human possibility—can only be known when humans are free from external constraint—especially the constraint of laws and governmental dictates.

In "Woman Suffrage" Goldman offers a blueprint for how women in America might better themselves by exercising a will "to be and do" instead of expending effort to secure the right to vote. She applauds efforts like those of the women at the Seneca Falls Convention in New York who demanded such things as equal education and access to the professions. Ultimately, she develops her general vision for an anarchist society by specifying how women can free themselves from subservient roles and what women can contribute.

We boast of the age of advancement, of science, and progress. Is it not strange, then, that we still believe in fetich worship? True, our fetiches have different form and substance, yet in their power over the human mind they are still as disastrous as were those of old.

Our modern fetich is universal suffrage. Those who have not yet achieved that goal fight bloody revolutions to obtain it, and those who have enjoyed its reign bring heavy sacrifice to the altar of this omnipotent deity. Woe to the heretic who dare question that divinity!

Woman, even more than man, is a fetich worshipper, and though her idols may change, she is ever on her knees, ever holding up her hands, ever blind to the fact that her god has feet of clay. Thus woman has been the greatest supporter of all deities from time immemorial. Thus, too, she has had to pay the price that only gods can exact—her freedom, her heart's blood, her very life.

Nietzsche's memorable maxim, "When you go to woman, take the whip along," is considered very brutal, yet Nietzsche expressed in one sentence the attitude of woman towards her gods.

Religion, especially the Christian religion, has condemned woman to the life of an inferior, a slave. It has thwarted her nature and fettered her soul, yet the Christian religion has no greater supporter, none more devout, than woman. Indeed, it is safe to say that religion would have long ceased to be a factor in the lives of the people, if it were not for the support it receives from woman. The most ardent churchworkers, the most tireless missionaries the world over, are women, always sacrificing on the altar of the gods that have chained her spirit and enslaved her body.

The insatiable monster, war, robs woman of all that is dear and precious to her. It exacts her brothers, lovers, sons, and in return gives her a life of loneliness and despair. Yet the greatest supporter, and worshiper of war is woman. She it is who instills the love of conquest and power into her children; she it is who whispers the glories of war into the ears of her little ones, and who rocks her baby to sleep with the tunes of trumpets and the noise of guns. It is woman, too, who crowns the victor on his return from the battlefield. Yes, it is woman who pays the highest price to that insatiable monster, war.

Then there is the home. What a terrible fetich it is! How it saps the very life-energy of woman—this modern prison with golden bars. Its shining aspect blinds woman to the price she would have to pay as wife, mother, and housekeeper. Yet woman clings tenaciously to the home, to the power that holds her in bondage.

It may be said that because woman recognizes the awful toll she is made to pay to the Church, State, and the home, she wants suffrage to set herself free. That may be true of the few; the majority of suffragists repudiate utterly such blasphemy. On the contrary, they insist always that it is woman suffrage which will make her a better Christian and homekeeper, a staunch citizen of the State. Thus suffrage is only a means of strengthening the omnipotence of the very Gods that woman has served from time immemorial.

What wonder, then, that she should be just as devout, just as zealous, just as prostrate before the new idol, woman suffrage. As of old, she endures persecution, imprisonment, torture, and all forms of condemnation, with a smile on her face. As of old, the most enlightened, even, hope for a miracle from the twentieth-century deity—suffrage. Life, happiness, joy, freedom, independence—all that, and more, is to spring from suffrage. In her blind devotion woman does not see what people of intellect perceived fifty years ago: that suffrage is an evil, that it has only helped to enslave people, that it has but closed their eyes that they may not see how craftily they were made to submit.

Woman's demand for equal suffrage is based largely on the contention that woman must have the equal right in all affairs of society. No one could, possibly, refute that, if suffrage were a right. Alas, for the ignorance of the human mind, which can see a right in an imposition. Or is it not the most brutal imposition for one set of people to make laws that another set is coerced by force to obey? Yet woman clamors for that "golden opportunity" that has wrought so much misery in the world, and robbed man of his integrity and self-reliance; an imposition which has thoroughly corrupted the people, and made them absolute prey in the hands of unscrupulous politicians.

The poor, stupid, free American citizen! Free to starve, free to tramp the highways of this great country, he enjoys universal suffrage, and, by that right, he has forged chains about his limbs. The reward that he receives is stringent labor laws prohibiting the right of boycott, of picketing, in fact, of everything, except the right to be robbed of the fruits of his labor. Yet all these disastrous results of the twentieth-century fetich have taught woman nothing. But, then, woman will purify politics, we are assured.

Needless to say, I am not opposed to woman suffrage on the conventional ground that she is not equal to it. I see neither physical, psychological, nor mental reasons why woman should not have the equal right to vote with man. But that can not possibly blind me to the absurd notion that woman will accomplish that wherein man has failed. If she would not make things worse, she certainly could not make them better. To assume, therefore, that she would succeed in purifying something which is not susceptible of purification, is to credit her with supernatural powers. Since woman's greatest misfortune has been that she was looked upon as either angel or devil, her true salvation lies in being placed on earth; namely, in being considered human, and therefore subject to all human follies and mistakes. Are we, then, to believe that two errors will make a right? Are we to assume that the poison already inherent in politics will be decreased, if women were to enter the political arena? The most ardent suffragists would hardly maintain such a folly.

Nothing is so dangerous as the dissection of a fetich. If we have outlived the time when such heresy was punishable by the stake, we have not outlived the narrow spirit of condemnation of those who dare differ with accepted notions. Therefore I shall probably be put down as an opponent of woman. But that can not deter me from looking the question squarely in the face. I repeat what I have said in the beginning: I do not believe that woman will make politics worse; nor can I believe that she could make it better. If, then, she cannot improve on man's mistakes, why perpetrate the latter?

History may be a compilation of lies; nevertheless, it contains a few truths, and they are the only guide we have for the future. The history of the political activities of man proves that they have given him absolutely nothing that he could not have achieved in a more direct, less costly, and more lasting manner. As a matter of fact, every inch of ground he has gained has been through a constant fight, a ceaseless struggle for self-assertion, and not through suffrage. There is no reason whatever to assume that woman, in her climb to emancipation, has been, or will be, helped by the ballot.

In the darkest of all countries, Russia, with her absolute despotism, woman has become man's equal, not through the ballot, but by her will to be and to do. Not only has she conquered for herself every avenue of learning and vocation, but she has won man's esteem, his respect, his comradeship; aye, even more than that: she has gained the admiration, the respect of the whole world. That, too, not through suffrage, but by her wonderful heroism, her fortitude, her ability, willpower, and her endurance in her struggle for liberty. Where are the women in any suffrage country or State that can lay claim to such a victory? When we consider the accomplishments of woman in America, we find also that something deeper and more powerful than suffrage has helped her in the march to emancipation.

It is just sixty-two years ago since a handful of women at the Seneca Falls Convention set forth a few demands for their right to equal education with men, and access to the various professions, trades, etc. What wonderful accomplishments, what wonderful triumphs! Who but the most ignorant dare speak of woman as a mere domestic drudge? Who dare suggest that this or that profession should not be open to her? For over sixty years she has molded a new atmosphere and a new life for herself. She has become a world-power in every domain of human thought and activity. And all that without suffrage, without the right to make laws, without the "privilege" of becoming a judge, a jailer, or an executioner.

Yes, I may be considered an enemy of woman; but if I can help her see the light, I shall not complain.

The misfortune of woman is not that she is unable to do the work of a man, but that she is wasting her life-force to outdo him, with a tradition of centuries which has left her physically incapable of keeping pace with him. Oh, I know some have succeeded, but at what cost, at what terrific cost! The import is not the kind of work woman does, but rather the quality of the work she furnishes. She can give suffrage or the ballot no new quality, nor can she receive anything from it that will enhance her own quality. Her development, her freedom, her independence, must come from and through herself. First, by asserting herself as a personality, and not as a sex commodity. Second, by refusing the right to anyone over her body; by refusing to bear children, unless she wants them; by refusing to be a servant to God, the State, society, the husband, the family, etc.; by making her life simpler, but deeper and richer. That is, by trying to learn the meaning and substance of life in all its complexities, by freeing herself from the fear of public opinion and public condemnation. Only that, and not the ballot, will set woman free, will make her a force hitherto unknown in the world, a force for real love, for peace, for harmony; a force of divine fire, of life-giving; a creator of free men and women.

From Emma Goldman, "Woman Suffrage."